Singin' The Blues

Neil Nixon

Terrace Banter

For 'Alan' Ross
b. James Allan Ross
26 May 1942 - 2 Nov 1999
466 Games for Carlisle United 1963-1978
A hero

Singin' The Blues - My Story Of Carlisle United (Pbk)

© Neil Nixon, 2000

ISBN 0 9535920 1 4

Published by Terrace Banter, Scotland
Printed by Heritage Press, England

Picture credits
Front cover - Thom Nixon in the shirt (photo Scott Brewer)
Back cover - Rod Thomas and Neil Nixon (photo David Reeves)

Terrace Banter
PO Box 12, Lockerbie, Dumfriesshire. DG11 3BW. Scotland
www.terracebanter.com

Thanks!

THIS BOOK IS a personal recollection but I couldn't have done it without the help, co-operation and goodwill of several people. Their efforts deserve recognition and praise.

My psychotherapist wife, Jane, deals with obsession, misery and anger at things which cannot be controlled, irrational behaviour and the stubborn refusal of a client who can't or won't change. After she's dealt with me and my love Carlisle United, she goes off to see her paying clients, who - by and large - are easier to deal with and less afflicted! Thanks is never enough when it comes to acknowledging the love and attention she continues to devote to me. I love you Jane, more than football itself.

Others who have played a part in my life are also mentioned. In those cases where I remain in contact with the people, I owe them a debt of thanks for allowing me to include stories and/or opinions in this book. My sister Lesley and brother-in-law Rich deserve particular thanks in this regard. Special thanks are also due to Kath Harding, who appears in this book as Kate Graham. She shared memories over the phone and allowed me to include stories that play a central part over several years covered by this book.

A special thanks is due to Tim Pocock, first and foremost because he kept the faith with the excellent United fanzine, *So Jack Ashurst Where's My Shirt?* Tim's tireless work provided a pre-internet lifeline for exiled Blues like myself and his willingness to let me pillage my old material to compile the stories that make up chunks of chapters nine to 11 is much appreciated.

My work-mates in the South endure a steady stream of stories about one northern outpost and its football team. They have heard more about Carlisle United than they ever wanted, and still they share lunch-hours, cups of coffee and other private moments with me. It was Michael Ellis who allowed me to talk him into coming to Wembley in 1997, and Roger Blackman who taped a picture of a jubilant Jimmy Glass across my computer screen on the 10th of May, 1999. These people, along with Jenie, Clair, Pauline, Sally and many others past and present do not deserve thanks. They deserve a medal, a massive index-linked income for life and a luxury home, each!

Finally, although this book is a personal recollection, it has drawn on the help of a number of people officially and unofficially linked with the club. For their willingness to share memories and confirm facts I am particularly indebted to David Steele and Jonathan Fuller. For as long as dedication like theirs continues to flourish, the spirit that sustains Carlisle United will live on.

Neil Nixon

Introduction

IT STRUCK ME quite early on in the writing of this book that it is a love story. The more I thought about a life spent following Carlisle United, the more I realised that the team and I had lived around each other, been there for each other, and . . . well, it's a love story. We've both changed in the time covered by this book, but when all is said and done there are times I've needed Carlisle and times they've needed me.

When the need has been greatest, we've never let each other down. As a child I needed heroes. I found Alan Ross, Chris Balderstone, and others who were more than I could have dreamed they'd be. Years later, Carlisle needed anyone with a pulse and spare change. I was equal to the challenge, paying up when I knew that the other side of the turnstiles offered the sight of Mike Graham and Eric Gates heaping shame and disgrace on the once proud blue shirt. If you were there, you'll know the commitment it took to pay good money and watch that team.

This is a love story. It is a few other things too and we'd better get these sorted out from the start. This book is the truth. Or, more accurately, the 'truth'. It is an honest account of my undying devotion. But sometimes the truth takes strange turns. Each chapter is preceded by a Blue Nightmare. These weird ramblings are a wind up, but each one throws up a truth you'll find in the following chapter. So, for example, John Inman signs for Carlisle in the mid-Nineties. In 'truth', the successes of the Knighton era go hand in hand with crowd pleasing stunts and incredible statements, and, sometimes, in my eyes at least, the overall effect has all the reality and substance of decent pantomime.

You'll also find a few strange events in the chapters. They're piss-takes too, but there is a point. You'll know such events when you meet the legless boy in the school cloak room or encounter Paul Bannon brandishing a pistol in the directors' box at Charlton. Such wind ups should be obvious, but there is truth here. Whatever others say about my school, it was a big comprehensive for such a small town, a place in which heads could be kicked in without mercy. Paul Bannon was a genuine enigma and to this day the mystery of Bannon is a talking point amongst the Blue Army. So, if the story takes a few odd turns, there is truth of a sort in the things you read. And, be assured, grim reality will return within a few lines.

Elsewhere, it is as accurate as I can remember. I've checked little more than spellings and dates because this is not a definitive history. It is a history of opinions and the way I saw things happen. It is the story of one fan and his team, and a love that will last as long as both exist. The opinions and memories are mine and mine alone. I've got reasons for my opinions and these are made clear, but sometimes - such as my take on the strange creature that was Paul Bannon - I know I'm out on my own. So, take these descriptions and opinions for what they are. The way I saw things.

If you were there you may have seen it differently. If you are a football fan who follows another team, you might want to check my opinions against others before making up your mind. If you are one of the players singled out for a literary hammering, you'll certainly see it differently. Just remember, these are my opinions. I do not claim them as hard provable facts. I'm trying to be honest as I saw it, not as the cold statistics in those anorak bibles record it. One spectactor sees a miskick as a brave attempt, another sees only the money wasted on Eric Gates' wage packet. Either way, it is a passionate issue. I'm sure you get the idea. I did my best. I never said I was perfect!

I've pulled a few punches, but not many. People who sold or took drugs get mentioned, but not named. You'd probably want your teenage recreational habits left out too. 'Nuff said. I've gone easy where people disappeared from my life and vanished without trace. I've also taken it easy when people disappeared from my life and both of us were glad to see the back of each other. Since I couldn't contact these people, I chose to say nothing about them.

So it's a love story, not exactly a definitive autobiography. There are people I care about, my sister for one, who barely get a look in. I love you Lesley, but you've never been to Brunton Park! And the only time I got your husband along to a game, he complained that it was cold and raining! It was Boxing Day in Carlisle for fuck's sake.

In the way of all great love stories, everything else is secondary to the central characters. I care about my sister, my family, the friends who've stuck with me and the people I've lost over the years. But this book is about one man and his team. And, it is a 'true' story.

Why Carlisle United?

I COULD TAKE you to where I was born, but it wouldn't be wise to stand around. For starters, if we stood on the exact spot where I emerged into this world, we'd be run down by traffic. There used to be a general hospital of sorts in Workington, but now, so I'm told, the old location of the maternity ward is part of the traffic system. Assuming we did get run down looking for the spot that isn't there anymore, the ambulance crew would pour what was left into the back of the wagon and head off to the new hospital at Hensingham near Whitehaven, a little further down the coast and a little closer to Sellafield.

I've heard loads of stories about Workington, most of them told by people who lived in or around Carlisle. One memorable tale involved the baby born in the same hospital as me. Like many babies it came out with a look of naked fear in its eyes and gave all of the onlookers a brief sense that this baby had lived before. Unlike most other babies, it didn't descend into a weeping mass and slowly adjust itself to the new surroundings. Flopping off the delivery table, the little bundle of life crawled to the window as the doctors and its amazed mother watched in awe. Forcing its feeble limbs into action, it hauled itself up to peer through the open top of the window, taking in the incomparable Workington skyline with its grim stonework and grey skies. With a deep breath the baby yelled, 'Fookin' Hell', and made a dive to get back in before mum had time to close her legs. Some story, and oh how we laughed. And the moral of this story is you don't have much when you're born in Workington, but you do have a choice about where you'd like to be.

I had a hell of a lot more than most. Middle class parents with attitudes that were light years ahead of the times. I've even got pictures of my Dad changing my nappy and pushing the pram with his young son on board. If that doesn't sound too exciting you've got to consider that I grew up on the borders of West Cumbria and men just didn't do those kind of things then. Soon after my birth, with my Mum ill and me still helpless in hospital, my Dad did more than push a pram. He took me and my carry cot and marched out of the hospital determined to organise better care than I was getting from the nearest available nurse every time I cried. This wasn't so much a criminal act as full-blooded blasphemy by the standards of the time and the place. But, remember, you've got a choice about where you'd like to be!

Quite a few people have made choices about being in Workington. There's the hospital for starters, which chose to move a few miles down the road. They chose to close the steelworks in 1982, and for decades, people who live within striking distance of Borough Park, home of Workington Reds, have been choosing to head up the A596 to watch Carlisle United play football.

Workington means 'working town'. Which, with the kind of grim northern humour that sees a belly laugh where your average punter sees only the terminal illness, is really pretty funny. Workington, the 'working town' in which I was born, is an unemployment blackspot and has been for most of my life. If you want to meet a guy from Workington with a job, head for Kent, because that's where I live these days.

We're big on grim humour, West Cumbrians. If you want a real laugh, try this one on for size. Workington Reds used to be a Football League team. When the Premiership was the First Division and the Fourth Division was as low as you could go, Workington were stalwarts of the bottom flight. Young people out there might be confused at this stage. After all, those ex-league teams are all in the Conference - Southport, Hereford, Doncaster, they're all there, right? Well, no, not exactly. If you've got a minute or two to spare on a Sunday morning you could try looking for Workington's result. You'll need a decent paper, one that prints hundreds of results. Start where it says Unibond League and work your way down, and down, and down, and . . . a magnifying glass might help. To put this in perspective, if you see a national paper that prints Workington results, there will probably be more results on the page than there were spectators at that Workington game. But that isn't the real grim joke. Hang on for a few minutes, there's a real corker coming.

Workington were, by common agreement, crap, when I was growing up. Like your average kid I took an interest in football, knew my local teams, and gradually learned players names, details of the strip, the name of the ground, and a few other facts that mattered. Soon enough, I was off to games and into an experience that would follow me through every stage of my life.

Workington Reds had their moments. Whilst the rest of the world went mad for colour, drugs and free love in the Sixties, Workington got seriously high with a finish in the play-off positions of the Third Division. The good news is, this is the old Third Division - the one we all know and love as the Second Division today. The bad news is that Workington were in a play-off place over 20 years before anyone invented the play-offs.

By the Seventies, Workington, the town, was dying on its feet and the team were doing their best to stay in step. I was in my apprenticeship as a football supporter then. The period when quoting football facts and figures as you fish the gristle out of the gloop on your school dinner plate is worth something by way of status. Workington had their uses.

SOME OTHER KID - It's right, they used Roker Park as a ground in the World Cup when they had it in England.
NEIL - Isn't big enough, you're making it up.
SOME OTHER KID - Am not, my Dad went.
NEIL - Your Dad's been everywhere.
SOME OTHER KID - He's seen loads of football games. He's taking me to Sunderland.

NEIL - He's never seen Workington.
SOME OTHER KID - Eh?
NEIL - Hardly anybody sees them. I saw in the paper, there was 973 there last Saturday, only game in the whole league with less than a thousand.

I'd like to think that kid was impressed. Then again, I'd like to think my second hand Honda was a Lambourghini. Workington, turning the clock back, liked to think they'd hang on to their league status, but the writing was on the wall when Barrow, then in Lancashire, now in Cumbria, baled out of the League in 1972. Workington and Barrow didn't share a county then, but there were some obvious similarities. Geographically speaking, both towns are on the road to nowhere, which is a pretty good summary of the football they played in the Seventies too. If the 1,000 odd spectators who braved the merciless Solway winds to watch Workington Reds were treated to anything, it was a decent pie at half-time.

The few away supporters who struggled along the single carriageway of the curving A66 to watch a grisly encounter had it slightly better. There was always the prospect of a near certain away win to cheer their long journey home. If Workington Reds had their moments in the mid-Seventies it was when they were at home tucked up in bed with their wives. They were fucking about on the pitch too, but that wasn't anywhere near as much fun.

By 1977, Workington were noted the length and breadth of the country as re-election specialists. This is another historical detail that may need explaining. Before we had automatic promotion and relegation to and from what is now the Conference, we had re-election which meant that any team finishing in the bottom four of the League would have to apply to a meeting of the whole lot for the right to stick around in Division Four for another year.

On the positive side for the League clubs, this meant that everyone who had a few pals could lean on them for a favour and the end result was that, most of the time, all the League clubs stayed as League clubs and the part-timers didn't get a look in. When they finally abandoned this system, Hartlepool United would emerge with the all time record having applied for re-election 14 times. Barrow bit the dust in 1972 when their 11th application was turned down in favour of admitting Hereford United.

The down side of this system was that you didn't need to finish bottom to get booted out. By 1977, and the era of punk when being hopeless, working class and belligerent was seriously credible, Workington's hopeless, working class and occasionally belligerent football was suprisingly doing them no favours. In front of crowds that would have looked thin standing around a bonfire, they were reduced to spiralling long balls, kick and run attacks, and furious last ditch defending. The predictably pathetic finish didn't impress anyone and the club ran out of favours with their seventh attempt at re-election.

Apart from anything else, if it was down to the other clubs to vote on Workington, anyone with experience of the lower flight knew the length of the return trip along that single carriageway road. Anyway, it was obvious. The last refuge of a hopeless team was the long ball game, supplemented with crunching tackles and blatant attempts to break up the opposition's rhythm. It was poor entertainment and a symptom of everything that was wrong with an increasingly cynical game.

I warned you there was a real corker coming. In 1977, the Football League finally decided they had no place for Workington and their cynical long ball game. So they kicked them out and let in Wimbledon! Eleven years later, The Dons took the same tactics to their greatest achievement in the English game when they got to Wembley and turned over the mighty Liverpool to win the FA Cup with a performance built on the long ball game, supplemented with crunching tackles and blatant attempts to break up the opposition's rhythm (although to be fair, Dave Beasant, the Wimbledon goalie, had a superb game, and he was worth his wages for one seriously good penalty save alone).

The dismissal hurt the faithful few, although in truth it was part of a trend. In 1978, Southport were also ejected from the league. Barrow, Workington, and Southport, three small seaside towns in the North West, all dying on their feet, were replaced by Hereford, Wimbledon, and Wigan, all inland and with some upwardly mobile pretensions in the Seventies. If any of the ex-Workington players watched Wimbledon's march to Cup glory in 1988, perhaps they felt a deep envy of those in the leafy London suburbs. Their envy could have been justified. If you're going to play a game which involves hoisting the ball into the air and racing to get on the end of it, then the balmy and still confines of South East London are a more promising location than rain lashed, gale hammered, Workington.

In the mid-Seventies, the generally hated A66 trunk road was widened to make a fast and efficient link to the M6 motorway. The thinking behind this involved better communications and new opportunities for business in Workington. At least, these were the arguments given in response to the complaints about the damage to the scenic beauty of the Lake District that resulted. Within ten years of the widening and upgrading, manufacturing industry and League football had fled down the improved road seemingly never to return to Workington. Maybe if they'd taken the turnstiles out of Borough Park in 1977, and slapped them on the end of the A66, they could have ensured that people got in and nothing else got out of Workington. In the 'working town' where I was born even the footballers are part-timers these days.

As my conversations swing round to football, I'm often asked 'why Carlisle United?' This book is about the reasons, and they're not always simple. But keep one thing in mind. If you wonder why I support Carlisle United, you never saw Workington!

Blue Nightmare #1

CARLISLE UNITED HAS been home to some great players over the years. We've seen international class in the ranks. Some future internationals - Bowles, Beardsley - have played their way up. Some others - notably Eric Gates - have plumbed the depths at the end of once great careers.

For all of this there is one man, and one man only, who can rightfully claim to have earned international caps whilst playing for Carlisle United. That man is Eric Welsh and, naturally enough, he played on the wing for Northern Ireland. His country called him four times in the Sixties whilst he was on the books at Brunton Park, and to this day, whenever men gather in earnest huddles, strangle pints and argue about legendary encounters in that green and pleasant land that lies on Warwick Road, the name of Eric Welsh remains a legend.

Another situation in which intense conversation and ale strangling go hand in hand involves the serious competitions to test football knowledge. Put a Cumbrian in such situations and the other assembled anoraks will accost him in a predictable way. Grappling with massive tomes printed on cheap paper, and delivering no photographs within their 600 pages, they will test the Cumbrian's potential with questions as cutting as flick knives.

'Come on you Northern git give us some answers.'

The answers in question revolve around the information in the book which is, of course, about football.

ANORAK - Nickname?

CUMBRIAN - The Cumbrians.

ANORAK - Ground?

CUMBRIAN - Brunton Park.

ANORAK - Most capped player?

CUMBRIAN - Eric Welsh.

Hell, it's easy. There is no other candidate and history teaches us no-one will ever threaten Welsh. But there is a difference between this and other questions. We've seen the ground, we heard chants of '1-0 to The Cumbrians,' but Welsh is a legend. Virtually no-one around on the terraces these days saw Welsh play. And, with each passing year, his status as 'most capped and the only capped' seems secure. Brunton Park appears cursed for those with international aspirations.

In recent years, Jason Priestley - a goalie and no relation to the Jason Priestly you might be picturing - trained with the England under-21 squad. Within minutes he was in the local papers keeping goal for Carlisle City where a walk to catch a missed shot might find a goalie retrieving a ball from the jaws of a watching dog. In 1994, the Jamaican Christopher Dias was briefly touted as an international addition to the Carlisle squad.

Maybe he put an XR3-i through the front window of Bulloughs, maybe he ran foul of all the newsagents when he asked for some 'erb', but Dias doesn't appear in any history of the club. Fair enough, he never appeared on the pitch, and to this day you'll meet Blues who deny that the man existed, and give reports of Dias sightings the same credence that they give to Michael Knighton's ten year plan to reach the Premiership.

Troubled by the lack of an international and suspecting that pictures of Eric Welsh were simply fakes concocted along with fuzzy alien snaps and the Ben Nevis Yeti portrait that once adorned the *Sunday Sport*, a Cumbrian once went in search of the great man. It was a long and troubled journey broken only by transport cafe fry ups and furtive encounters with hunched figures in doorways. Glancing anywhere but into his eyes, they would engulf the Cumbrian in a hale of bad breath and mutter through broken teeth that Welsh could be found '50 miles to the north in a street that bears no name.'

After several long days of useless directions, the Cumbrian finally came upon the legendary Eric Welsh. The venue was a a smoke filled room. The Cumbrian felt his blood run cold as a nightmare of epic proportions unfolded before him. The 'room' was a local theatre, Welsh was on stage and his 'act' said it all.

He started slowly. A glance, some general patter, a grunt or two and then the killer line.

'I played football for Northern Ireland . . . and I was on the books at Carlisle at the same time!'

Howls of laughter, loud slaps on legs, the audience collapsing onto the floor in tears.

Welsh went for it without mercy.

'Seriously, I played for Carlisle and I played international football in the same week!'

More laughter.

Suddenly it became clear to the Cumbrian. Welsh is the new Frankie Howerd. An act capable of reducing the hardest heart to hysterics with a routine built on nothing. The Cumbrian stood rooted to the spot as the crowd howled through two hours of unrelenting comic genius. The following morning, their sides aching, the crowd would attempt to explain to their work-mates how the man had amused them almost into unconsciousness.

'Tell us a joke he told you,' the work-mates would howl.

'Well, it was about Carlisle and being an international and . . . look, if you'd been there you'd understand.'

The Cumbrian was there, and he did understand. The following night he told what he had learned in a rural Cumbrian pub. 'Eric Welsh is real,' he whispered, 'I saw him, I heard him speak.'

'So what is he doing now?' asked the other Cumbrians.

'He's, ermmm . . . well . . . he's a legend.'

'AWWWWW, for fuck's sake, we knew that already,' roared the Cumbrians.

But Eric Welsh is real, he lives, he breathes, and he once played international football whilst he was signed to Carlisle. Eric Welsh is a legend. And I know this because I was that Cumbrian.

Chapter One - Alan Ross

MENTIONED FOR THE FIRST TIME IN THIS CHAPTER:

Chris Balderstone - Stylish and unflappable midfielder. Once dubbed 'the best player never to appear in the First Division'.

Frank Barton - Free ranging midfielder with notable skills in holding possession, sneaking up on the blind side of opposing players, and laying off accurate balls.

Bob Hatton - Confident and prolific goal scoring centre forward.

George McVitie - Speedy winger, deadly on the break and a crowd favourite, especially with the younger end of the support.

Alan Ross - Tall, skinny and agile Scots goalie. Holder of all time appearance record for Carlisle United with 466 games to his name, including one outfield substitute appearance.

Graham 'Tot' Winstanly - Imposing centre half, central to success of 'classic' Carlisle teams of early Seventies.

I'M SURE THERE is such a thing as love at first sight, but if it's going to work, really work, you've got to put the effort in. That's true for most things in life - marriage, bringing up kids, and the really important stuff, like football. This book is a love story about one football team and a fan. I'm not the most devoted supporter Carlisle United have ever seen - hell I fled South years ago and I'm still there. But I am loyal, and my support for the club has lasted through great days and dark depressing slides to the very brink of existence. Like Elton John, I'm still standing. Well, I don't stand exactly like him, but let's not sink into cheap homophobic gags this early in the proceedings, eh?

Like most schoolboys, I liked football. I was never so good that my talent dazzled the rest of the playground into submission. Then again, I was never so hopeless as to get left to last when the teams were picked. My performance was so well defined in its mixture of inspiration and predictability that the English language contained a word to describe it. Average. I had that cocktail of qualities that defines an average kid in a playground kick around. Lacking in pace, a decent shot, tall enough to make contact in the air, not particularly accurate in bringing the ball down in the right place. On the really positive side, I was surprisingly keen on long stints in goal. And at seven years old in the playground of Allhallows School, Fletchertown, I did have my moments. Mainly hurling myself against the tarmac as my shot stopping capabilities between the two drains on the canteen wall held the other team at bay.

The serious post match analysis occasionally revolved around any pretensions I had to being the best playtime goalie. I'd steer the conversations in this direction because discussions on the best outfield performance never included my name. Once in a while the whole show gravitated to the Rec, the sloping field that doubled as a recreation ground for the village. This was serious and official stuff in which Mr Bell, the headmaster and father of my best mate, Geraint, doubled as ref. You could tell it was serious because we got to wear the football boots we'd cadged, borrowed or inherited.

This venue had its attractions. Mainly the smaller chance that I'd break bones or come up concussed in the event of a mis-timed dive. I was eight or nine at the height of my powers as a serious contender to replace Gordon Banks in the England goal. The footballers whose names I could recite by this point had a record of high profile games, nights of European glory, laps of honour clutching the FA Cup, and eleven of these players could claim that they were part of the best team on the planet. Well, they could claim this until the quarter final of the 1970 World Cup Finals when the reigning world champions, England, were beaten 3-2 in extra time by the team they had turned over on that glorious sunny afternoon at Wembley in 1966.

These players had medals and trophies. In my case the glories stopped with the odd bit of praise as I pulled off a save. One incident sticks in my mind. We were on the Rec and I was having a good game, using my highly secret method of keeping my eye on the ball and trying to remember exactly where the posts were as I kept looking forward. As another well timed rocket headed in my direction I threw myself up and took the ball as it dipped for the corner. Skidding and rolling within sight of a clump of thistles, I held on tight and staggered up without once letting go of the ball. This move put bruises on your elbows, but it looked great when Gordon Banks did it. Today, the experience of years of watching the game tells me that the move is great because it allows a goalie to demonstrate his mastery and power in the area. The stubborn refusal to loosen the grip on the ball as you recover from the save tells the world, along with any opposing forwards, that they didn't get past this time and the next move is yours.

On that day I remember clearly that Mr Bell's reaction was to say, 'You're a regular Gary Sprake this afternoon'. Sprake was the goalie in Don Revie's Leeds team who were in the infancy of their dominance of the English game, having just beaten Arsenal in the League Cup final. He was also well into his 11 year stint as a regular keeper for Wales. For all this, I remember this little incident because the thought of being Gary Sprake didn't appeal then or now. If I was going to 'be' anyone that afternoon I'd have settled for Gordon Banks, Alex Stepney or . . . Alan Ross.

Never mind that Sprake was the only one to whom I had any kind of resemblance with his tufty shock of blonde hair, and famed ability to drop the odd clanger. I must have been eight years old, still gazing in awe at pictures of footballers in the paper and snatching the odd glimpse on television. Not really old enough to have any kind of role model and just starting to put the whole thing into some kind of order that involved more than remembering names, colours of shirts, and the grounds at which these teams played.

Gordon Banks, then as now, was a giant amongst goalies. With a face more suited to a character role in a seriously grim Western, he set standards that are envied to this day. Alongside the agility, anticipation and sure hands that make the reputation of most goalies, Banks had an air of impregnability which relied in part on his uncanny ability to hold a ball as his body went through every stage of a save. It is a measure of Banks' class that Alex Stepney - an agile and fearsomely brave stopper with Manchester United - only gained one full England cap. Banks and Stepney were regulars in the papers, even my Dad's *Guardian*, which treated sport then with marginally more respect than needlework. They also made it to the pages of boys' comics, and by the time I'd graduated from the kids stuff to the real deal offered by the likes of comics like *Jag* and *Joe 90*, the football heroes were a regular part of my life.

Alan Ross on the other hand . . . I'd not really thought much about wanting to be · Alan Ross. He wasn't in the comics or *The Guardian*. In fact the other pictures that were carefully clipped from the decent tabloids read by the other kids' Dads didn't feature Ross either. Alan Ross, you see, was the regular first choice keeper at Carlisle United. My images of Ross included only the vaguest notions of how he moved and how he shut out the best the Second Division could offer. This was the start of a gradual slide into an addiction that would stay with me for life.

Thinking back all these years later, the reasons for the start of this addiction are not totally clear. One serious factor in the equation was the way that the Carlisle players slowly assumed a legendary status in my life. Their absence from all but the local papers was probably a factor in this. I never saw them play on television, so whilst the legend that was Gordon Banks appeared in stark black and white on telly at the back of the leaking disaster that was the Stoke City defence, the legend that was Alan Ross only moved in my mind. His saves and agile command of his area were described by the people to whom I looked up to. Geraint's big brother, Gavin, for one.

Gavin was old enough to have been to Brunton Park. He once lovingly drew a picture of the ground on a sheet of A4 paper which ended up in my pocket and stayed there for almost a year. I remember it was in my coat pocket on the day that I finally made it through the turnstiles for the first time. In a crude way, the sketchy picture of an empty football ground was all the more powerful for its lack of detail. I had to put in the spectators and the action on the pitch and in my mind the blue shirts of Carlisle United swept up the pitch like a whirlwind.

If my generation added anything to football support - apart from an impressive capacity for mindless violence - it was a genuinely unrealistic element in our romantic love of local teams. The deal on the fringes of rural West Cumbria was that you supported some big team of achievers and also got behind the local team - Carlisle or Workington. We were also raised on a diet of Bobby Moore holding the World Cup high in the air. We were, briefly, the best in the world, and to a generation of schoolboys brought up with that awareness, the romance of a World Cup win trickled down into ludicrous claims about the capabilities of smaller teams. Hell if England could do it then anything you could dream was possible.

My own memories of the Sixties include the ever present figure of Harold Wilson on the news in his raincoat, pictures and models of mini cars with union jack roofs, and the chunky figure of World Cup Willie, the mascot of the tournament in England. That and the obligatory dive for cover behind the settee when anyone threatened Dr Who.

Along with the things that I took for granted, like having a telly and a plentiful supply of Corgi toys and comics when the news was on, came a few observations from the senior members of the clan, my grandparents in particular, who could remember what people did before television. The Dunkirk spirit and the notion of people banging away on pianos into the long dark Northern nights never rang completely true to me, but I did buy the general idea that they'd made their own entertainment. It was just that the entertainment in question struck me as seriously low grade. Talking, reading, and going down the pub. Come on! Any eight year old will tell you that every option on that list is crap.

Hindsight tells me differently. Each generation makes the most of the options it has, and my own family find some of my history hard to fathom. Seven year old Thom Nixon can't remember a time before the internet and his appearance at Carlisle United games has to be carefully negotiated around a dazzling range of options which include indoor play areas to rival the special forces training grounds of 30 years ago and interactive entertainment that pitches him into realities that dissolve and reform at the press of one key. No wonder he struggles with the entertainment value of kick and run football on a rain sodden pitch. It does leave me speculating about what Thom's kids may have available and how his early years might appear dull and pointless in their eyes.

The truth is that we are moving steadily towards a more self centred world where the choices are limited only by our wallets, our imagination, and the ability of those charged with inventing things to link the two in some product. With computer generated legends like Lara Croft available in the secluded comfort of your own home, the 'legendary' status of a local football team is under serious

17

threat. In the old days, in the absence of Big Red Racing and Thomas The Tank Engine on video, I made my own entertainment. At least, that's the way I tell it now. My generation were constantly reminded by our parents that we were lucky and that we would have opportunities they had never seen. Perhaps that gave us more freedom to dream. The basis of the dreams wasn't interactive but that did leave more space for your imagination.

That much would be obvious if you could go back to a school playground of the late Sixties or early Seventies. Take a copy of that week's *Shoot* and you might just see some ten year old striking the same action pose that featured in a football pin-up. I can recall particular pictures of stars and pathetic attempts at replicating them.

Sir Geoff Hurst has worked in insurance. I bet he wouldn't appreciate a hefty pile of lawsuits causing him to gag over his Corn Flakes. It's just about possible because a regular footy picture of the time was a side on shot of Hurst in full airborne flight as he struck home the last of his Wembley hat-trick in 1966. What the picture didn't tell you was that an uncoordinated nine year old attempting to fly and strike a ball at the same time was more than likely to end up grazed and battered by his Mum as she faced another fun night making her own entertainment by way of sowing up his school trousers. To this day there may be limping forty-somethings with carbon fibre knee joints who blame it all on a misguided attempt to copy that all out Hursty pose complete with puffed out cheeks, right leg fully extended, and head slightly down. Then again, it was a hell of a picture and you can't blame a kid for being inspired.

In the period between England's World Cup triumph in 1966 and their ignominious exit in 1970, I became a fully fledged football fan and a blooded member of the active support of Carlisle United. What started as a normal enough love of football developed into a period of gathering any scrap of information I could, took a detour into gathering these scraps into a mental picture, and re-emerged as an ability to talk in detail about the heroes I'd never seen.

This period certainly had its humour value to outsiders and I took a few baitings from people who really knew what they were on about. In the playground things could get seriously dodgy if you couldn't tell the truth from fiction. There were loads of stories flying around. Some were complete bollocks such as there was a match between 'Fleccy' (Fletchertown) and Leeds and Fleccy won.

Others, believed to be bollocks, were completely true. Such as Carlisle getting stuffed by a bunch of non-leaguers the year they won the Third Division.

I'd figured the non-league stuffing as complete bollocks on the grounds that everyone who told me the story struggled to name the non-league team in question. I was stunned to find out for sure that Crook Town had dumped us out of the FA Cup in my own lifetime and that story was added to the armoury for impressive facts to dredge up whilst fishing chunks of gristle out of the gloop.

My memories of the 1966 World Cup tell me that, at six years old, I really hadn't got the plot at all. I was devastated at the result and the way the final went for me. Honestly, I had a stinker of a game. It all went wrong the first time I saw the German forward, Wolfgang Overath. In the way that six year olds make sense of the world around them by imposing familiar pictures on the new things they see, I liked Overath from the start. It was logical enough. He reminded me of Bobby Bell who lived at the farm up the road and came round once a week with the butcher's van delivering meat. I liked Bobby because he had a way of winking and acknowledging a passing kid, and because he brought the stuff, sausages and the rest, that I could really appreciate.

I'm not sure if my Dad got hacked off when I told him that Bobby Bell was playing or when my pleasure at the first German goal became obvious. I got my marching orders sometime in the first half and I honestly don't remember registering the importance of the result that day. My Dad didn't go to matches and his passion for England was a combination of romance and an appreciation of a damn fine performance. He'd had a great game once little Neil had been banished to the kitchen.

In the following months and years - as my awareness of football grew - I came to recognise the true significance of that 4-2 victory. At the same time I was getting a sense of the excitement of a real game from the few people I knew who went to Brunton Park on a regular basis. Gavin Bell for one. He'd been often enough to run through players' nicknames and he had the time to describe the action. Gavin, my best mate Geraint, and their headmaster dad would occasionally go to Brunton Park together. Geraint and I were inseparable at the time and we'd gone through several important firsts together from discovering *Thunderbirds* and arguing the toss about our favourite Tracey brother to staying over at each others' houses - and even an aborted attempt to sleep out in the wood at the back of my parents' house. It was natural enough that I'd take in my first game in their company. The only realistic alternative was a trip to the dreaded Borough Park and 90 minutes in the company of Workington Reds.

If Gavin Bell's stories of Carlisle United fired my imagination ahead of the first visit, there was an equal importance in the things I heard about Workington. Laura Irving from the village had grown up with my Mum and she baby-sat me and my sister on a few occasions. When she did, I remember her husband Bob heading off to Workington and never coming back happy. His face looked bleak enough on one occasion and I assumed Workington had lost. In fact they'd managed a 1-1 draw. Laura asked Bob whether it had been a decent game and he could only look into the middle distance and mutter, 'Poor . . . poor . . . '

That summed it up. Workington were poor. Some of my Southern friends think Vic Reeves and Bob Mortimore invented 'poor" as a catchphrase. They have no idea. It's been a standard in Cumbria from as far back as I can remember, and the legend of Workington in my mind was built on that word. Workington were poor. That is 'poor' in a solid northern accent with a deep sound and flat 'ooh' in the middle leading to an 'R' sound that stumbles from your lips and falls into a great sorry puddle on the floor. Gavin Bell and others who had been schooled in the arts of Workington support would tell it like that. I remember an argument about consistency in football and Gavin chipping in with a one liner about Workington being the most consistent team he'd ever seen. Seven times he'd been and they were never less than complete rubbish.

The only two Workington players I remember from my schooldays with any clarity are Frank Rogan and John Burridge, both goalies. Their outfield, by contrast to the legends of Carlisle, seemed to exist as a shapeless bunch of interchangeable red shirts skilled in holding panic at bay on the odd occasions they had possession. Like the man said, consistent rubbish. Workington were legendary in another way. There was a game we played in the school playground, a version of football with one team defending and another team trying to score - in other words half the players at any time had no chance of scoring. The name of this defensive game was . . . Workington.

So really there was no choice, it had to be Carlisle, and on March the 31st, 1970, I finally made it through the turnstiles to see players who had already assumed a legendary status in my eyes. The game, against Bristol City, was the third last home encounter of the season and had been rendered meaningless by the hopeless mid table position of both clubs. In the end we would finish two points above them so a reversal of the score that night would have reversed our two mid table positions, nothing more. Then again, the team I went to see had got within 90 minutes of Wembley and actually went to West Brom in the second leg of their League Cup semi-final carrying a 1-0 lead. They had sold out the 27,500 places at Brunton Park for a storming FA Cup fifth round collision with Middlesborough. They may have lost this clash by the odd goal in three, but earlier in the same competition they'd seen off top flight opposition in the shape of Nottingham Forest. In that season Carlisle had continued to impress the football world with their ability to raise their game on the big occasion and pull passionate performances from an improbably thin first team squad. This level of performance was fairly new to the long timers but my growing awareness of the club went hand in hand with their best days. The third place finish in Division 2 in 1967 had almost pitched them into the top flight and their mid table finishes in the following years had maintained their reputation as a tough and well organised outfit with clear potential.

On that first venture through the turnstiles, I drank in a heady mix of atmosphere, excitement and potent football skill. In reality this marked just about the lowest point of the season. The team played out an encounter they knew to be unimportant on a cool midweek evening in front of 6,000 of the truly committed, a smattering of Bristolians, and me. The things that most astonished me were the sounds, sights and smells, and the fact that I heard one fan around my own age chanting 'Alan, Alan, Alan Clarke!!!!!', as in Alan 'Sniffer" Clarke, Leeds and England centre forward.

In those days you could get into any part of Brunton Park quite easily and we headed in at the Waterworks End before wandering round to the scratching shed. Both were known haunts of away fans, but the red scarved Bristol contingent were in short supply and we mixed easily enough. The Waterworks was, then as now, the only section of the ground lacking any roof, and the icy blackness of the sky above amazed me. The piercing white of the floodlights in an evening kick-off spreads a light that puts a gloss on the night sky as you look up into the blackness. This more than anything else stuck with me from that night. Well that and the way the pitch almost glowed. A stage fit for legends.

In my mind Carlisle were inspired and superior to anything Bristol City could manage and I expected the skilful moves from televised games. 30 yard rocket goals, saves that rivalled Olympic gymnastics, and George Best levels of possession that split defences. What I recall most clearly is the pace, the sounds of tackles, and the closeness to the action from my vantage point hanging over the perimeter wall. With space to wander on the terraces, Geraint and I had found a position as close to the pitch as possible, within sight of his dad and big brother, but most assuredly our own place. Winger George McVitie ran flat out with awesome power, and as he ran at the Waterworks End goal I could hear the churning of the turf and the ball skidding just ahead of him. In all of the times I'd stuck my oar in at school in football arguments, I'd never imagined these sounds or sights. More than anything, it was the power and pace of the game that caught me that night.

And finally, there was Alan Ross. My goalkeeping career had progressed to owning a proper football kit and 'training.' The training consisted of persuading anyone gullible enough to bang a succession of shots in my direction as I threw myself at supersonic speeds through the air to deflect them with as much needless overacting as I could manage. The action pictures of great goalies in *Shoot* were a useful source of tips here, and when one of my uncles or some work friend of my Dad's had drawn the short straw I could put the pictures to good use.

The similarity between my uncles and Dad's colleagues was the precise and polite way they'd hammer the shots in my direction. They were humouring me and their killer instincts were probably blunted by outright boredom and the thoughts of their coffee going cold in the house as they punted a few balls in my direction on the lawn. The beauty of their blunted strikes was that they came from predictable angles and with enough delay between shots to allow me to fix mentally on some treasured picture of a goalie in action. As the shot came in my direction I could concentrate my energies on assuming the same mid-air shape as Gordon Banks in full flight and smother the slowly trundling ball with an accurate impersonation of the master at work. Banksie, like Geoff Hurst, could puff out his cheeks like a hamster with a bicycle pump in its mouth. I got that one down to a fine art and grabbed at skidding balls before staggering to my feet and blowing out a huge breath.

If you were around in the Seventies you'll remember the impersonations of Mike Yarwood that took televisual mimicry to new levels of accuracy. Did it ever strike you as odd that Yarwood could do just about everyone, but he never took off a famous goalie? I'd like to think he was scared of his young rival in Cumbria. The one guy who could wipe the floor with him in accurate impersonations of the top stoppers. Then again, I'd like to think that nobody laughed at the day I proved my ignorance by asking a lesbian for a date.

For me at ten years old, the glamour of goalkeeping had also intruded into high profile clothing. Those all important gloves. Way back then your average Cumbrian sports shop was the size of a shoe box and was stocked with the few things the world weary owner knew he could shift on a slow and steady basis, like football boots. Goalie gloves for the likes of me came from a proper clothes shop and bore a striking resemblance to low grade leather gloves worn for everything other than goalkeeping. Apart from the pose value, their main advantage was the thick insides which probably resulted from some bored and underpaid factory hand failing to shave the last pound of fat off the sheepskin lining.

The pose value was exhausted once you'd milked a full ten seconds of performance out of studying the gloves in the playground and putting them on with enough care and attention to suggest you were a goalkeeping genius inspecting the top notch tools of the trade. The pose value was exhausted so soon because once the gloves were wet they were useless for stopping anything approaching you from the side. These tricky balls would skid through your hands, take a deflection and leave you just enough time to watch them fly into the goal at some impossible angle. I swear I was one of the first kids in school to be labelled a 'tosser.' For years I thought I was being accused of tossing these skidding balls into the back of my own goal.

The practical advantage of the gloves was the way they took the sting off a fast moving ball on a freezing day. You could stop a direct shot with a flat palm and still manage the all important Gordon Banks exhale, and you could painlessly punch anything above head height. The punching just about made up for the slips on the skidding shots because you could head out for anything in the air and, once it was obvious you'd elected to punch, it was in everyone else's interest to keep their heads out of the way. An added advantage was the fact that a playground is much shorter than a proper pitch and football games amongst ten year olds involve a lot of people within a few feet of the ball. In these circumstances a well punched ball could lay on a stunning break out of defence and a chance for one of your team to smack in a well angled shot that would be fumbled by the other goalie with his low grade leather gloves.

So, back to Alan Ross. I knew everything about goalkeeping down to the properties of pathetic gloves until the night I saw Alan Ross play. Ross was class. Gavin said so, Geraint agreed, and the local papers made it obvious. The reports I read so carefully described the teamwork and flashes of inspiration that had turned over the likes of Nottingham Forest and West Brom. Each member of the outfield would get occasional praise. One day 'Tot' Winstanly would head off the line, another time a well timed Bob Hatton strike would have left the opposition goalie sprawling and hopeless. The one man who always seemed to get a mention though was Ross.

By the time I saw him in action I'd learned to cherish newspaper lines like, 'Ross pulled off a fine save'. If the icy sky, churning of feet on the turf, and the pace and fury of the whole spectacle was inspiring, the real revelation was Ross. This man was known to be a top quality keeper. He'd trained with Scotland, others named him as a player who could transfer into the First Division someday. But none of these things made him a revelation that first night. What stunned me was the fact that the great Alan Ross didn't wear gloves! That night, I swear, he did it all with bare hands. I heard well struck balls smack off his palms, saw him deflect one corner of the net bound shot off his bare fingertips, and never once saw him flinch.

I saw Chris Balderstone run the midfield with skill and commitment that ignored the meaninglessness of the match, saw George McVitie storm off after loose balls and bury one in the Bristol net, grumbled at the absence of Bob Hatton and 'Tot' Winstanly, howled for at least three penalties, and came home happy that we'd won 2-1. None of this, however, looked like football on the telly. Down low to the pitch it was fast and furious and I had to take some cues from the crowd because I couldn't see all the action in front of the Warwick Road end. The one thing I did see in spectacular detail was the legendary Alan Ross in full flight. Gloveless, lightning quick, brave beyond belief, and almost unbeatable. Most of what I'd imagined about the game was little more than a combination of school boy wish, television clips, and *Shoot* action shots. The real thing wasn't exactly a disappointment but it was certainly different to expectations. Ross was a revelation. Better than I could have imagined. He stood just yards away from me as the game rumbled around the midfield, and I saw him read it, position himself, and dive into action when it came his way.

Your average football addicted schoolboy has a favourite player to go with a favourite team and I'd veered from Balderstone to Hatton to Ross in the gristle from the gloop lunch-time conversations. Inspired by the sharp flavour of the cheese pie we had at least 17 times a week, I'd even ramble on about Frank Barton. But all that was in the past.

As of March the 31st, 1970, there was only one player in the frame for me and that man was Alan Ross. A lifetime of support later and he still has no rival. I'd like to think that I detected in his inspired touches that night a clear sign that he would go on to make 466 appearances for Carlisle, setting an all time record for the club in the process and continually scuppering the best efforts of highly rated strikers. Then again I'd like to think that the six numbers on my lottery ticket will come up the next time there is a triple roll over jackpot.

In all probability my lifetime of admiration for the man comes down to one thing. In his performance that night I saw him do the things I thought I could do, the things I wanted desperately to do. Alan Ross had it. Whatever it took to be a great goalkeeper was there in that average game in the mid-table of the old Second Division. The man on the pitch was doing the things that one schoolboy standing yards away could only dream of doing. His commitment, positioning and the fact that he so obviously revelled in everything he was doing were a genuine inspiration. The man was born to keep goal for my team and - from that day to this - my life is better because of him. And it is because of those experiences and people like Alan Ross that many of us go to football matches. And it is because of those experiences and those people that we should go and keep on going.

When I left Brunton Park that night I knew one thing for sure. I was going back.

Blue Nightmare #2

'CAPTAIN SLOGG, STARDATE Easter, 1971, these are the voyages of the Starship 4-4-2. Its endless mission to voyage in the manner of a terminal ground-hopper, to seek out new games and new variations on the basic meat and potato pie, to boldly go into split infinitives and reeking dressing rooms.'

On the bridge of the Starship, Captain Slogg enters wearing the distinctive yellow Everton away shirt. His pointy eared side-kick, Mr Spack, the sheen on his hair matching the sheen on his replica Chelsea shirt, is already glaring into a cheap looking cardboard tube with a coloured bulb at the end. Spack acts as if the cheap prop is clever enough to fool a television audience into thinking it is an advanced piece of scientific equipment.

'MMMMMMMMmmmmmm,' mumbles Spack.

'You constipated again or have you found something?' grunts Captain Slogg.

'MMMMMMMmmmmmmmost illogical,' says Spack, refusing to rise to the cheap toilet humour.

'What is it, tell me Spack.'

'I'm in the vicinity of Brunton Park, Carlisle. It appears to me that a player has just passed the ball and performed a bizarre kind of body swerve. He appeared to be going in two directions at once.'

'Impossible,' shouts Slogg. 'Name the creature Spack, bring its likeness up on the screen.'

The entire bridge of the Starship watches as the inanely grinning features of a cross between a malnourished orphan child of the previous century and the menacing child/man/demon characters of gaudy Nineties horror videos appears on screen.

'Spack, Spack, give this . . this . . . thing a name,' cries Slogg.

'Sensors and data banks agree we have encountered the Stanley Webb, Captain. Born in Middlesbrough, England, December the 6th 1947, height . . . '

'Forget that crap,' yells Slogg. 'What do you make of this thing? I've never encountered anything like it.'

'Hmmm,' grunts Spack carefully. His gaze rests directly on the screen for several seconds. 'It's life Jim, but not as we know it.'

25

Chapter Two - Stan Webb

MENTIONED FOR THE FIRST TIME IN THIS CHAPTER:

Peter Beardsley - Yup, he started with us!

John Gorman - Speedy full-back, tough tackler, good distributor of the ball and sometime assistant to Glenn Hoddle and Howard Wilkinson when they formed the England management team. A landmark achievement for a Scotsman.

Matt Jansen - Slender and slippery forward, possessed of obvious class even as a teenage prodigy in the United reserves. Amongst his many claims to fame is the fact that he turned down a move to Manchester United twice before his 21st birthday.

Dennis Martin - Fast winger, former West Brom player and long-term favourite at Brunton Park.

Bobby Owen - Attack minded midfielder, signed from Manchester City.

Stan Webb - Short lived but well remembered striker signed from Middlesbrough 1971 sold to Brentford 1972.

'STAN WEBB, MIGHT be a reet mongul features, but he gets goals.' Keith Easterbrook had spoken and I knew he had a point. A polite translation of his words might read: 'Stanley Webb bears an uncanny likeness to a person with serious educational problems, but his prowess in front of goal suggests that his faculties, both physical and mental, are in superb working order.'
    Keith was a couple of years older than me, lived in the house 100 yards up the road which his parents had bought from my uncle Tom, and messed around with me and what passed for a gang around our way. We weren't exactly kindred spirits, and time would show just how far apart we were. Keith went on to join the police and eventually got a job in the motorcycle division where his life was cruelly cut short at 36 at an accident black spot on the road to Cockermouth. It was, as I recall, the job he'd always wanted. I went on to write a 'comedy' first novel in which a trio of psychopathic thugs beat the police to a pulp, and, in the heat of one battle, actually conspired to eat a constable. Not exactly the job I'd expected when I was 11 years old.

But back to Stan Webb. I now felt confident enough to talk about personalities, skills and specific games. Still in the company of Geraint and his family, I was making a few trips to Brunton Park and by the summer of 1971 Geraint and I had graduated to heading off there together and stumping up a mighty 15 pence to stand in the boys pen in the front left hand corner of the Warwick Road end. With programmes at 5p, this was just about affordable. Throw in crisps and a Bovril and we had the makings of a serious day out.

I saw Stan Webb, and a few other new faces that season. By now I was getting used to the games, the pattern of play, the genius that was Alan Ross, and a few other favourites in the team. Webb truly was a strange phenomena and holding a discussion about him with Keith underlined my growing confidence as a Carlisle supporter. Hell, I knew plenty about Webb because I'd heard the rumbles and grumbles coming out of the Warwick.

One book on United reports a famous Webb incident. I wasn't there, but it must have been a hell of a challenge that left Stan stunned on the pitch. This guy bounced off gorillas in the opposition defence with no obvious ill effects, and so when he was upended by one of his former team mates as Carlisle played away at Boro even the Cumbrians joined in the fun with a chant of 'Don't bother with the trainer, just go and fetch the vet.' The book recording the incident is one of the few books ever written about Carlisle, and this, along with the conversation I remember only in parts, highlights the difficulty in being accurate about incidents so long ago. If the chant broke out spontaneously as Webb played away at Boro, then it had to be in his final match for The Cumbrians in September, 1972. This game, when he came on as a sub, was his only run out in a Carlisle shirt against the Teesiders.

For all that, I remember similar chants and conversations about Stan well before this. I also remember one seriously great Webb performance I saw from the boys pen. The end of the 1970/71 season left us with no hope of promotion, but every hope of finishing impressively. Our last game was at home to Sheffield Wednesday and we hammered them 3-0, with our Stanley finding the net twice in a typically deceptive performance. Webb had a diminutive presence, the face of a cheerful schoolboy from some inbred pre-war back street community, and a haircut that suggested his barber still had a pudding basin in the back. There were times he'd run straight at goal and the defenders forced to stop him would misjudge their tackles.

I was still naive enough to think pushing up against the perimeter wall was smart, and so for me the boys pen offered a view at little more than pitch height and turned Stan Webb into a bizarre spectacle. On a few occasions, and certainly against Sheffield Wednesday, Webb's body would appear to be heading in one direction whilst the ball would leave his feet and head off at an angle. The trick, and maybe the legend has grown in my mind over the years, was that Webb's legs would then follow the ball whilst his upper body would continue to look as if it was

27

heading off in the other direction. Defenders acting on instinct could be thrown in the split seconds it took them to register that Webb's body wasn't wired in the same pattern as everyone else. The confusion might be short lived, but it left enough time for Stan to get round and bang in a shot. Stunningly imaginative attacks, in the manner of Eric Cantona, were not a Webb speciality, but his unorthodox moves did produce a few goals, and on that May day in 1971 he hit more than one goal for the only time as a Carlisle player.

He also helped me in my ability to put serious arguments together concerning Carlisle. I could counter Keith's 'Reet mongul features' line with several of my own. I wasn't exactly smart enough to work out what it was about Webb that was so unusual, but I was sharp enough to listen to the old timers on the edge of the Warwick who would scream, pass comments, and casually impart wisdom that was snapped up eagerly by some of the youngsters in front. As I recall it, the main difference between Webb and several of the others was that Stanley's slips were often greeted with gasps of despair along the lines of 'Fuckin' pillock'. You might get the same abuse hurled at someone else, but on the rare occasions that Frank Barton lost the ball in the same circumstances, it might be 'Barton, you fuckin' pillock.' The difference - and it matters here - is that people were hacked off with a skilful player like Barton because they figured he could help it. Webb, and for all I know the guy is about to win a Nobel prize for a great discovery, was given the benefit of the doubt on the grounds that he couldn't help it.

Having built some sort of familiarity with Carlisle and their support I was now starting to get the feelings and familiarity that went with the whole caper. The Webb experience is all the clearer in my mind over almost three decades later because I didn't understand it then, and that meant I worked all the harder at trying to make some sense of it. It just felt so damn good to be encouraging Webb. Hindsight tells me that what I was getting was some sense of community. Not understanding exactly why I found his unpredictable goalward runs so bloody entertaining, I'd listen out for Webb talk and hear a mixture of encouragement, abuse and strange comments along the lines of 'the lad' not being able to help it. In short, he might have been a nutter, but he was our nutter.

I'd never experienced that kind of community feeling before and I didn't understand it. It was something between watching a favourite pet out running without a care in the world and marvelling at the native skill of some tribesman you'd just encountered in a jungle clearing. For all I know the whole thing was totally misguided. In 1982 I saw one other man in a Carlisle shirt with a facial expression that suggested he would struggle to hold a newspaper the right way up, and a touch on a football that suggested some bizarre genius lurking beneath the surface. I remember thinking then he might be another Stan Webb. He turned out to be the truly unique Peter Beardsley, arguably the best player ever to wear a Carlisle shirt in a senior game, certainly one of the best football brains we ever

28

employed and a man targeted and chased as a potential player/coach for Carlisle in 1998. The new Stan Webb! What the hell did I know?

As a bizarre footnote to the enigma that was Stanley Webb, the generally trustworthy *Lads In Blue*, Paul Harrison's definitive history of the club, records his birth date as December the 6th, 1917! Making the man 53 years old on his United debut. All that and he still looked like a 12 year old! Assuming this definitive reference is accurate, Webb might now present the truly baffling combination of a man sporting a bus pass, coming up to his first shave and preparing to make football history with a truly unique blend of experience and football ability. Since the birthdate puts Webb well past 80 years old, the 'experience' in question may well include power runs dodging Nazi bombs as they rained down on Teesside, and a lifetime watching and playing the game covering the Matthew's Cup final of 1953, Alf Ramsey's World Cup winning wingless wonders, and, of course, that all important stint in the hard and testing run to fourth place in Division Two with Carlisle in 1971. For all this to be true Webb would have to exist on some kind of strange ageing timetable, like a dog which ages seven canine years for every human year, or so I was told once. If your average 'Webb year' ran for nearly four and half human years the guy could sign a professional contract for the best part of two decades, smash Peter Shilton's all time appearance record, and become the first professional since Pele to run in a goal tally into four figures.

Maybe the 1917 birth date really is true. Maybe Webb was a bizarre biological experiment dumped near to Sellafield in the hope that nobody would notice. If you think I'm ranting into total lunacy, you never saw Stan Webb! Frankly, the discovery that the birth date is accurate would be a surprise, but a small one. It is generally accepted that Webb was born in 1947, but if anything was going to go wrong in the definitive history of Carlisle United you could almost bet on Stan Webb being the source of the confusion. Striker with strange gifts or a medical experiment unique in human history, your guess is as good as mine. Where Stan Webb is concerned nothing would truly surprise me.

Webb went on to Brentford in 1972 and I couldn't tell you what happened after that. He and a handful of others made a real impression on me that 70-71 season, and after Webb's great game I was over the wall for the first time and onto the pitch, running for the tunnel to mob the side that had finished fourth in the old Second Division. I grabbed myself a lump of turf and spent time over the next few days in a futile attempt to grow it at home. Geraint already had a lump that was struggling for life at his place.

The fourth place finish made little difference then. Today we'd have been in with a late season shout at securing promotion on such a finish, and I'd have been in for some serious begging at home involving distant relatives, Wembley tickets and a massive financial outlay on the part of my parents. The one thing that finish did secure was a feeling of involvement between the team and me. I could recount

Webb talk in Keith Easterbrook's attic bedroom. I knew the players and their strengths and weaknesses. I'd seen a young full-back called John Gorman come on that season and on that final day of the season I'd found myself in the half-time food queue with his mum. I'd just bought a few player pictures from the flimsy mobile that served as a club shop then, and managed a picture of Gorman amongst them. His mother, clocking the Gorman picture in my hand as I headed for the crisps, had commented on it and I'd managed a few lines about his passing being solid in the first half and nothing much getting the better of him. She seemed knocked out that there were schoolboys out there who admired her son. I was knocked out that I knew my way around this football business and it felt to bloody good.

Geraint and I had managed to gather an impressive body of football knowledge, and a few genuine connections to Carlisle by this time. First and foremost was the 1100 car, I can't remember if it was the Austin or Morris version, but I do remember that the previous owner was a certain Robert Owen from Manchester. Bobby Owen had signed for Carlisle in the Summer of 1970 and appeared to have spent some of his new found wealth on a better set of wheels than the 1100. Geraint's Mum and Dad bought Bobby's old one. Our connection with Bobby Owen was further strengthened by the presence of his wife in the area of the Warwick just behind the boy's pen. She got well into the games, screaming 'Come on Bobby!' along with the rest of the assembled masses.

I couldn't match Geraint's car connection, but I did know my stuff with regard to Owen as a result of having collected an entire album of football stickers the year before. Bobby Owen had featured in the Manchester City line up and the biography underneath had noted his memorable debut, scoring with his first touch in a senior game. I could also quote chapter and verse on winger Dennis Martin since he appeared in the same sticker album chasing a ball in the colours of West Brom. Chapter and verse in this case might have been limited to the 70 words or so the makers of my sticker album could fit under the picture of Martin, but added to a few well gleaned comments from *Match of the Day* and my own imagination, it was enough.

High in Keith's attic bedroom that summer I could let rip with the deep knowledge I'd gained. 'Martin's better off with us, they've built that West Brom team around Jeff Astle, Martin roams around too much, he's on the wing and then he's cutting inside. He's got too many ideas for a team like West Brom, and too much competition for a place. He's fine with us.'

There was a lot to admire in that team and the fourth place finish meant I could compare them favourably to the First Division outfits supported by some of the others at school. Football was still a big player in the conversations at school and the Leeds bubble was in the process of a slow burst. They still had a Cup win and some European glory nights in them, but Arsenal had risen from the ashes to dominate the English game in 1971. In the complicated football politics of one little Cumbrian school, that meant that most of the lads were backing losing teams. Arsenal being Southern, out of the glory for a few years, and the product of Bertie Mee (a 'sensible' manager if ever such a creature existed) lacked glamour, and were hardly prime candidates for support amongst the population of the Thomlinson Junior School in Wigton. Add to this the League Cup victory of Spurs, and northern glory was thin on the ground in the domestic game. Chelsea took the Cup Winners Cup and the only consolation for those in the school who supported the northern clubs was a victory for the well supported Leeds in the Fairs Cup (the 1971 version of the UEFA Cup). There were loads of lads in the school who backed popular and unsuccessful teams that year. At least I'd been to a handful of games in the second most successful league season Carlisle had ever enjoyed.

I'd moved from the local village school when my Mum had taken a deputy head mistress job in 1970, and by 1971 I was finishing junior school in the bursting metropolis of Wigton. It might be a village to any southerners reading this book, and I've met at least one American who'd claim to own a ranch bigger than Wigton, but to a kid used to a village school the place pulsated with life, crawled with cosmopolitan types and existed several light years in the future. Hell, you needed a proper football kit when you turned out in the games lessons and the school even had an upstairs.

If parting from Carlisle United was painful, it had nothing on the last day in junior school which included a massive fight at lunch-time. I got jumped on in the playground and, having fought my way back to my feet, ended up in a furious one to one with Edwin Sharp, a kid with a fighting reputation and a wish to leave the junior school on a high. I remember it as a full on 15 rounder that would have put Ali and Frazier to shame. My adult self wandering into the playground would have seen two kids trading powerless punches for a few minutes. Either way, I came out on top when Sharp got tired of taking the punishment and headed home.

The inquest in the headmasters office was another lengthy affair. He'd given pretty well when we were trading punches and I'd hit him with everything I had. Okay, at 11 years old I didn't have that much, but I still hit him with all of it. He might have run off, but he didn't go down. None of that punishment matched a caning for sheer terror. Given the uncertainty of the whole inquest I thought I was going to get whipped senseless with the bamboo for the first time in my life. I was let off, on the grounds I'd been defending myself. The others weren't. Despite everything, I could still manage some sympathy for Edwin Sharp as I disappeared out of harms way as fast as I could.

I didn't ever go looking for trouble, but probably by virtue of being just about the tallest kid in the year, I'd been jumped on a few times just for the hell of it. This had been fun of sorts, but the all out humdinger that had ended junior school had been a learning experience to top anything they'd taught me in the last term. Edwin Sharp was hard, everyone knew that, and I'd just found it out. For the first time in my life I realised that you could get hurt in fight. This might have been obvious to the smaller kids, including the poor sap I'd thrown clean over a table within weeks of arriving at the new school, but it finally hit me why that poor sap had got up with a mixture of hate and confusion in his eyes.

The real world was closing in that Summer with the Nelson Thomlinson Comprehensive looming in September and the certainty that, biggest in the year or not, I'd be part of the smallest bunch in the big school. That prospect was daunting enough, but the grimmest twist of all was the fact that the Nelson Thom had a reputation as a rugby school and that meant playing the game for the first term of the year. I didn't know it then, but life was lining itself up to give me more insight into the workings of education than I could ever imagine, or want. What I had to face that summer was the usual dilemma of the sensitive middle class kid heading for the psychopathic fear factory. Okay, it wasn't that bad, but you've got a few choices and a few escape routes in this situation. First off you can behave like a complete wanker, talk posh, flaunt it and line yourself up for a serious kicking on a regular basis. This way you spend the next five years of your life without having a slash during the hours of daylight between Monday and Friday. This way you get to talk about your innermost feelings on a regular basis, but many of these innermost feelings come from the serious internal injuries you get after admitting you're a sensitive type.

I was never stupid enough to go down that route and the one comforting thought I could draw on coming up to that September was that there would be other people who were that stupid and therefore more likely to take a serious kicking. I was never gonna cut it when street cred involved a full-blown Cumbrian accent and helping your Dad up the road on Friday night because he wasn't fit to walk. There was a survivable alternative that involved keeping my head down a bit, trying like hell in games lessons even when I knew I was crap, and knowing enough of what mattered to get by. I could just about survive on this score and I didn't have to fake anything in the area of Carlisle United. Where others could remember names I'd seen them and I bloody cared enough to have taken on board loads in the way of useful knowledge. Given the compact nature of the boys pen, I also knew by sight the handful of faces from the school who had made trips there when I was around.

This was just about enough and I managed to enjoy the asylum more than I dared expect. Lets get this one in perspective though. I wouldn't honestly say I ever *enjoyed* school, but there were some decent surprises along the way. Managing to enjoy some of the work was one surprise. I had mates, a halfway decent brain, and a better life in terms of material comforts than most of the kids I knew. By the end of my first term I'd started throwing parties combining my crowd and my little sister's mates. These end of term blow outs would become a regular feature of our lives until we left school.

In the first couple of years - known as the 'Lower School' - I took a bit of stick, had one more furious fight which I was slowly losing until a senior prefect stepped in to break the whole thing up, and also got a few insights into life that weren't on the subject list for exams. Okay, I was a lippy loudmouth who could give back more to the teachers than I was supposed to, and there were times when I didn't much care who I was hacking off, but, hey, that's why you're there at the age of 12, right?

For all that it still came as a surprise that one or two people around the place seemed to have a serious down on me. This made more sense after a stilted conversation with one of the hard crowd. Fuck knows how it started, we may have been talking Carlisle United for all I know. He threw a few insults my way suggesting I spoke like something off the BBC News, and I threw a few back that linked his family bloodline to stuff you'd find in a zoo. In boxing terms, I was storming round after round. He was wading in with the predictable 'cunt' and 'twat' jabs and I was giving it the old Ali shuffle, dazzling the crowd - well, two or three bystanders - with inventive cutting remarks about what was on top of his old lady the night he got started and the long metal trough that saw service as the family dinner table. I was on a winner because It was all going predictably to form until - like Mike Tyson wading in with the only good punch he had left - he dropped a line linking his out and out hatred of me to my Dad's Jag. This git had a down on me bordering on outright hatred because my Dad drove a Jag! We're talking prejudice here and it dawned on me in a few seconds that drew themselves out into hours that he meant it. This stunned me as much as getting hurt in that fight at the end of the junior school.

It had all been clear enough to me before. You got your crowd, slagged off everyone else's and got by like that, more or less. It hadn't really occurred to me that people really did hate each other. Sure, I knew we'd been in a few wars, and there were pitched battles at football games and the rest, but none of that had actually touched me. But on that day in my second year, the git had a serious down on me, and I wasn't winning the slanging match at all. Every insult I could dream up only gave him more reason to hate the lippy middle class kid. In the face of this hatred my suggestion that his little sister was up for shearing was putting my life in danger. This was scary, first off because I didn't understand where this hate came from, and second because that much aggression suggests your head is gonna come off your shoulders soon. So what if he was smaller than me. He meant it, I was just taking the piss.

I learned this lesson around the time I encountered prejudice on a wider scale at Brunton Park. Two incidents stand out. One October day I remember Geraint and I heading off to see United take on Burnley with his Mum cheerfully predicting a 3-2 Carlisle win. A tense first half struggle with some impressive goal keeping at either end saw us hitting the Bovril and crisps after 45 minutes with 0-0 on the board. We debated the chances of sneaking a winner, but within an hour we were stumbling, stunned, out towards Warwick Road, having seen United crumble to three second half goals without reply. We did our best to score, but Peter Mellor, an opposing goalie who would come back to haunt us in a truly significant match for United, maintained his form.

In the absence of local league rivals, Burnley are as close to anyone as 'the enemy' at Brunton Park. This may need a little explaining to those of you brought up on genuine local rivalry. The real local rivals were the only other league team from Cumbria, Workington, but this rivalry had all but ended on the pitch by the time I was a regular supporter. Before my first appearance on the terraces, Carlisle had last played Workington in anger the day after my eighth birthday when the red scum dumped us out of the League Cup at Brunton Park. Workington's major fight was now the one against applying for re-election. Carlisle v Workington 'friendlies' were still a pre-season feature, but these games pushed the envelope on animosity and qualified as classic battles only in the annals of the Cumbria police. We might have last played them 'in anger' in the Sixties, but the friendlies were 'in anger' on the terraces. 'Unfriendlies' might be a better name for these games.

In one famous instance at Borough Park, Alan Ross was heard to bawl out a mob who had spilled into his penalty area by telling them he just wanted to get the game over so he could go home and watch the boxing on telly! A quarter of a century later, we sometimes play Workington in the Cumberland Cup. This is a knockout for non-league sides in which Carlisle traditionally field the reserves. The last time I saw a game in this competition, Carlisle's side featured a mix of young hopefuls and some senior reserves as Gretna raised their game to beat us in a hard fought encounter. There was no local rivalry promoting any terrace fighting. In fact, there wasn't much of anything happening off the pitch. That game remains memorable only as my first sighting of Matt Jansen.

Geographically speaking the nearest senior team to Carlisle is Queen of the South, based in Dumfries, and placed in the middle of the senior league structure in Scotland. Willing takers of a few United cast offs over the years, but in terms of gates and tradition, about as credible as 'local' rivals as Workington. The only senior English team within 60 miles is Newcastle United who have traditionally fought out well attended and passionate battles with us. As our paths have diverged over the years though, only a long shot Cup draw has threatened to put the fashionable Premier League outfit on the same pitch. But we still need someone to hate.

Burnley, Preston, Wigan and a handful of other Lancashire teams have therefore formed a regular revolving hate list for United fans. Trips to these grounds won't leave you with much change out of 200 miles by the time you've found parking spaces and pulled up for a stop on the way back. The close concentration of teams in Lancashire also means that these teams all have genuine local rivals and don't always need to hate Carlisle the way we hate them.

Every fan has a hate list and so the only unusual thing about our revolving list of Lancashire teams is the distance on the map between us and our 'local' rivals. The traditional hatred reflects a mixture of jealousy and frustration on our part. Burnley and Preston in particular have a longer and more celebrated past than ours with more major achievements, international players, and regular fans to their name than Carlisle.

The Warwick went mental with Burnley pissing on us that day in 1971. They had a good reason. The differences on the pitch didn't merit the gap in the scores. Peter Mellor looked like something from the Hitler Youth with his improbably blonde locks and a level of agility that foiled even the pace and vision of Dennis Martin, the bizarre inventions of Stan Webb, and the ever dependable Bobby Owen. Mellor's presence in front of the Carlisle fans was bait for the worst insults that could be dredged from 3,000 reeling brains. The usual chants of 'You'll never take the Warwick!', 'You're gonna get your fucking heads kicked in!', and 'You're going home in a Carlisle ambulance!' gave way to some free flowing insults directed at Mellor and the Burnley crowd in the Scratching Shed.

With certain defeat staring us in the face, a few carelessly tossed missiles started to fly and the police around the perimeter fence took an interest in the terraces. It was probably a welcome relief from the failure of our final passes to connect on the pitch. There was some trouble outside the ground, a few missiles and some general attitude stuff, although Geraint and I passed well away from it. In the end, the 'local' enemy had done us over impressively and given us one more beating to avenge.

I don't know if it was in the same season or the following year when Orient came to Brunton Park and featured Laurie Cunningham in the team. The game in question is best remembered for an incident in which Cunningham had his shorts ripped and had to change them on the pitch. Cunningham, as some of you will remember, was a black player in an era when such people were a genuine novelty. My football sticker album featured 440 cards and, I think, only one black player, West Ham's Clyde Best.

Laurie Cunningham was a blinding prospect with pace, vision and the kind of masochistic streak that left him able to take the abuse that opposing crowds in northern outposts seemed capable of dishing out. When Cunningham ripped his shorts at Brunton Park the old pair were removed to reveal a dazzling white pair of underpants that would have put a Persil ad to shame. Throw into this collection Cunningham's almost ebony black skin and the mentality of the section of the crowd that would make monkey noises, and you've got a recipe for one liners that pass as witty or illegal, depending on your view point. Let's just say the incident remains memorable for those who were there.

Out and out hatred, the us and them mentality of football, is central to the game. Without the wish for our lot to 'do' the opposition there really isn't that much point. You could argue that the beautiful game is a celebration of athleticism and the combined skill of a team of men playing at the very peak of their abilities. You could argue that, but how the hell you could use this argument to explain the stuff that took place on the pitch in Workington's final league seasons beats me. Deep down we go for the tribal stuff and when all else has gone we still have the tribal instinct, and we still keep going. Workington's fans in the Seventies paid good money because they wanted, against all the odds, to see their boys turn over the opposition. Carlisle would eventually force me into the same grim mind-set in which I was throwing my money over the turnstiles out of nothing more than hope and habit.

I'm supposed to be smarter now than I was when Burnley stuffed us and Laurie Cunningham ripped his shorts. These days I've got pieces of paper and everything to back up the claim that I'm educated and employed to use my brain once in a while. Hell, I even write books! The truth is I'm older and wiser only when I'm away from a game. Three days before I started work on this chapter we won 1-0 away, sneaking a result we hardly deserved and scrambling away several chances that threatened our goal. I realised somewhere on the way out of that game that I'd almost lost my voice. The same sort of things happened when I was eleven.

Political correctness these days would say I should condemn anyone who hurled abuse at Laurie Cunningham and threw a stone at the Burnley crowd. That's an easy line to take and, to my mind at least, it is as much complete bollocks as the kind of narrow minded thinking that passes the same stuff off as harmless fun. The racist 'fun' back then was so harmless that the first black players to risk the main stage were known to advise their families to stay at home. There wasn't much joy in it for them, sitting and listening to ten thousand ape grunts every time their man got the ball.

That kid who hated my middle class life right down to the Jag in the driveway probably taught me the most important lesson of the entire year in school. He taught me that deep down we can all hate, and when we do hate no amount of clever reasoning is going to change things. I didn't feel too happy with it at the time because I just couldn't understand the hate. It makes more sense to me now because I've seen more of life, and yet the problem of who we hate and why we hate has beaten the best minds of every generation.

It is important in football, the us against them bit. Without that there is no competition and without the competition the passion is gone. It's this need to keep the passion that makes the whole hate mentality so hard to remove from football. And however you try and change things, the main problem with the crowd violence and the racist chants is that football lends itself to the whole affair so well.

I've seen changes over the years, but it's easy to fool yourself that these changes have meant a lot. Laurie Cunningham faced some serious abuse from crowds in the days when virtually every other player was white. Years later our black striker, Keith Walwyn, muscled his way into opposing defences and the Blue Army chanted, 'We've got Pele!' It might be tempting to think we were celebrating a hard working black player in our front row, but look at that chant from another angle and all it really says is that black players look alike. A sentiment which verges on racism. Think about it, we didn't consider chanting, 'We've got George Best!' every time Frank Barton got the ball. Despite the similarity in the Best and Barton styles, we could tell those two apart.

Football violence didn't reach its heyday until after the early Seventies. It was simply more visible then because you got it on the terraces and occasionally this could even spill over into *Match Of The Day* where the whole country would see it. Carlisle got its fair share of aggro at that time because we were in our prime as a high profile club and the numbers we could muster gave us confidence. Our worst excesses in the violence department are a lot more recent ,and thankfully most of them take place away from the pitch these days. The matches of the Seventies matter to me more because I was there at a time when the whole business of hating the opposition made a lot less sense to me. For the most part I'd put down the abuse as harmless, but it's too easy to dismiss the whole thing that way, and flying bricks don't really come into the harmless category anyway. Despite this, I came away from the Burnley match well able to hold a conversation with anyone about why we hated Burnley. Hell, I'd got reason enough having seen ten lucky bastards and one inspired goalie stuff us with three goals at home. Street cred in the school meant knowing about football and being involved in it. The stuff I heard shouted at the Burnley mob that afternoon, and the stuffing they gave us, could be trotted out later on over a massive helping of cheese pie and mashed spuds.

I never really got it with the racist stuff. I understood it easily enough. Anyone who was black was different and that made it okay to grunt and suggest they were apes in coloured shirts. When I say I didn't get it, I mean it never felt right. I'd have to give my Dad credit for that one. He had a way of questioning and throwing out the odd one liner that gradually taught me that you couldn't divide the world on skin colour. Whilst the messages I was getting from overhearing the Warwick Road End suggested life was that simple, my Dad told me a few other things that clouded the picture.

On the other hand, maybe there was another reason I wasn't happy with the racist crap. That git with a down on me had given me a taste of prejudice from the other end. He and I might have been the same colour but apart from that it was the same as racism.

So, in those few years spanning the end of junior school and the start of the real deal in the comprehensive, life taught me a little and confused me a lot. Every

37

seemingly simple thing had a darker side that was never going to make sense. A hate list of 'local' teams that could be re-jigged every time one of them gave us a serious stuffing, the growing knowledge that we were all brothers under the skin, and the discovery that the line between taking the piss and hating enough to do damage was just about invisible when what you really needed was an unmissable set of warning lights. Somehow the increasing confusion made sense at a football match. It wasn't so much that I could stand back and compare life to football, but that the more complicated life got the more football simply felt great.

I'd like to think I was sharp enough to see all the links between football and the rest of life there and then. Then again, I'd like to think that Alex Ferguson is so sick of winning trophies the easy way that he'd be up for a real challenge before he retires, like bringing the FA Cup to Brunton Park.

Looking back, I'd be lying to say it made any real sense to me then. But almost everything I remember about the games mentioned in this chapter and a pile of others featuring that team is good. The crowds were big enough to feel like crowds, and in the safety of the boys pen you could just about get swept off your feet, crunch into the perimeter wall and shout and cry along with the old hands pushing against the fence behind you. Okay, the freedom from adult company, the junk food and the presence on the pitch of a team that were famously hard to beat were pretty important. But my adult self says it felt good for other reasons. If life was confusing then, football had a way of letting you feel good about being confused. You could hate a guy playing for his club and love him the second he scored for England. You could swear you'd kill someone from a town you'd never visited, and then shut up if you found them waiting to cross the road beside you on the way out of the ground.

Above all, you could argue the toss with anybody who said it was just a game. But, when you think about it, football manages to mean so much because at the core it remains just a game. The competition, the uncertainty, the rules that allow everyone to use the same skills and tactics, are all part of a game. The second it loses the passion and competition, all the other meanings - from tribal to appreciating the whole thing as art - are out of the window too.

It makes more sense now than it did then. Right then it just felt great, and that sense of being part of something, drinking it in from the pitch and the terraces behind me, was electric. It never felt better than when we'd put one over on the opposition, and the best experience of the lot was that day at the end of the 70/71 season when we hammered Sheffield Wednesday. We stuck it to a big city club, finished within sight of Division One, and played out a match we knew didn't really matter with passion and skill. Up front Stan Webb pulled the moves that only he seemed capable of pulling, and we celebrated his goals and his unique talent by crashing into each other, the wall and the fences.

At the heart of this there was a real contradiction. It was hard to tell whether we were celebrating or patronising this most unique of strikers. Putting the 'get the vet' chant down on paper makes it all the more obvious that Stanley boy was supported and abused in the same breath. And yet it felt so damn good. It felt good because every one liner, every chant, and every blissful moment celebrating a goal brought a sense that you could belong to the whole thing. There were things to share and things to know, and in Stan Webb there was a football phenomena to behold. Mere words didn't seem to do the guy justice. You just had to be there. Even if it didn't make sense, it was still an experience that mattered.

Like the boy said that day, 'Stan Webb, might be a reet mongul features, but he gets goals.'

Blue Nightmare #3

TAKING A BREAK from grinding out his book on Carlisle United, Neil heads out for the kind of rest and recreation that always works wonders. Within half an hour he is entering one of several second hand record shops in which he is on friendly terms with the owner.

OWNER - Alright Neil?

NEIL - Alright?

SHOP OWNER - Hey, before you start looking in the racks, I've got something down here that might interest you.

NEIL - Oh aye.

SHOP OWNER - Yeah, some kid came in the other day, said his dad had cleared off and his mum was chucking out all the junk from the attic. I got a few corkers off him, Jefferson Airplane's *Surrealistic Pillow*, you know the first version without *White Rabbit*, a pile of Beefheart, plenty of bluesy stuff, The Groundhogs, Hard Meat and this . . .

(RETRIEVING A DOG-EARED AND DUSTY COVER, THE OWNER HANDS NEIL THE RELIC WHILST SLIPPING OUT THE WELL WORN DISC FROM THE PLAIN WHITE INNER SLEEVE. STUDYING THE BACK OF THE COVER NEIL IS STRUCK BY THE CHEAP LETTERING OF THE NAME)

NEIL - Bugger me!

SHOP OWNER - Look you're a decent customer, don't get me wrong, but I draw the line at . . .

(NEIL IS OBLIVIOUS, HE STARES IN AWE AT THE NAME EMBLAZONED ABOVE THE FOUR HAIRY GORILLAS STANDING ON A SMALL STAGE, HUNCHED OVER THEIR INSTRUMENTS. THESE MEN ARE . . . THE STALWARTS!!!!!! A BAND HIDDEN SO DEEP IN LEGEND EVEN NEIL DIDN'T BELIEVE IN THEIR EXISTENCE)

NEIL - BUGGER ME!!!!

SHOP OWNER - No, I bloody won't. Llook, we've both got families, and anyway, I can't forgive you for starting off your book with that cheap joke about still standing like Elton John! Those homophobic jokes are so bloody old, you wouldn't catch me getting involved in one.

NEIL - Yeah, it wasn't worth a laugh was it. Hey, what does this thing sound like?

SHOP OWNER - I gave it a spin the other day, early Seventies stuff, bit blues, bit heavy, little bit flashy. Atomic Rooster, Sabbath, you know.

(WITHOUT ANOTHER WORD THE OWNER SLIPS ON THE DISC, AND HE AND NEIL STAND IN SILENCE AS THE CRACKLES GIVE WAY

40

TO A THROBBING BASS GUITAR, THUDDING DRUMS AND A HARD EDGED PLODDING RIFF SIMILAR IN STYLE TO EARLY BLACK SABBATH. THE SINGER WADES IN WITH A BEER SOAKED GROWL THAT MANAGES SOME POWER AND AUTHORITY. THERE MAY BE AN ALBUM'S WORTH OF MATERIAL HERE, BUT WITHIN THE FIRST 30 SECONDS IT IS OBVIOUS THAT THE PRODUCTION AND AMBITION ANCHOR THIS SOUND JUST OUTSIDE THE BIG LEAGUE. CLOSE, AS THEY SAY, BUT NO CIGAR)

NEIL - [STILL SCANNING THE BACK COVER] - You know anything about this lot?

OWNER - Nah, nothing. I thought I knew my music as well.

NEIL - Yeah, me too, couldn't tell you a thing about . . . WHAT?!!!!

(NEIL'S EYES WIDEN, HIS HANDS START TO SHAKE AND HIS GAZE STAYS ROOTED ON THE BOTTOM CORNER OF THE RECORD SLEEVE)

OWNER - You alright?

NEIL - This thing is on Scratching Shed Records.

OWNER - I've never heard of them, have you?

NEIL - No, but I remember a Scratching Shed, it was many years ago, I was so much younger then . . .

OWNER - Skip it, I've got a shop to run. Look, I'll do you that for a fiver. It's pretty consistent, lets rip in places. But overall it's a pile of brainless grind . . . your kind of crap for sure, erm . . . I mean, I figured you'd appreciate its rarity value . . .

(NEIL HANDS OVER THE FIVER AS THE SHOP OWNER ALWAYS KNEW HE WOULD)

OWNER - I've never heard of Scratching Shed Records either, must have been some little independent that went bust after releasing that pile of shit . . . I mean, that album that could only appeal to the most discerning rock fan. Front cover wasn't much help, there's just this stupid picture of . . .

(NEIL TURNS OVER TO THE FRONT COVER AS HE SPEAKS)

OWNER.....a football team.

NEIL - WHAT?!!!!!!!!!!!!!!!!

OWNER - You alright?

NEIL - It's them! Carlisle, look this is the 1971 team picture! I don't believe it. I've finally found The Stalwarts album and it has a picture of Carlisle United on the cover, this is unreal.

OWNER - They're never a football team, that big lad in the number 11 shorts has right meaty legs, he looks more like a bank manager.

NEIL - That's Chris Balderstone, he could run the midfield like . . .

OWNER - Gazza?

NEIL - Well, not exactly.

OWNER - Look at that one with the crap haircut, he's a reet mongul features.

41

NEIL - That's Stan Webb and he couldn't half score goals.

(THE OWNER SPOTS THE PLAYER CROUCHED DOWN AT ONE END OF THE FRONT ROW)

OWNER - Bloody hell, what a haircut, Art Garfunkel meets The Stray Cats.

NEIL - Leave it will ya, that's Bobby Owen, my best mate's Mum and Dad bought his old car.

OWNER - Half of this lot belong in a Barnados home and the rest look like they could make better money as extras in *The Sweeny*.

NEIL - They were my team and they could play. Most of this lot took us to fourth place in the old Second Division. That would be good enough for a play-off shot at the Premiership today. See him, the one with the hair and the sideburns. That's Stan Bowles, a bloody legend he was.

OWNER - Yeah, I remember him. If he could have passed a betting shop the way he passed the ball, he could have been a millionaire.

NEIL - Bog off, I've heard it.

OWNER - Hey, that one looks about 12 years old, is that his uncle next to him.

NEIL - The little one is Ray Train, midfield dynamo he was, and buying him put us on course to having the best side and best midfield we'd ever known. The 'uncle' is John Gorman and he was the first Scotsman to manage England.

OWNER - What?

NEIL - Yeah, assistant to Glenn Hoddle and Howard Wilkinson.

OWNER - So, you saw this lot? They are a real team?

NEIL - Yeah, my team, hard working, bit heavy, bit flashy, very early Seventies a proper bunch of . . . .

OWNER - Stalwarts?

NEIL - Yeah, stalwarts. That's the word.

(THEY STAND IN SILENCE AS THE FIRST TRACK ON THE ALBUM WHICH IS STILL PLAYING GRUMBLES TO A HALT. AFTER A FEW SECONDS OF FIZZING SURFACE NOISE THE SECOND TRACK ON THE STALWARTS ALBUM PUNCHES IN WITH A SENSE OF PURPOSE AND ENERGY. THE DATED SOUND IS STARTING TO GROW ON NEIL AND THE SHOP OWNER)

OWNER - They had something?

NEIL - Who, the band or the team?

OWNER - Both of them.

NEIL - Yeah, they did.

OWNER - We've got a few other things in the Indie section you might like. A CD by some tossers called Penis Burger. Sounds like four gorillas with their balls dipped in turpentine let loose on electric guitars from Woolworths. Your kind of stuff for sure.

(NEIL STANDS AND THINKS)

42

NEIL - Maybe next time, I've got to get home and give this one a listen. I'll never top this, it's unbelievable.

(HE HEADS TOWARDS THE DOOR)

NEIL - Hey, how come you call this place 'Sounds Perfect' when half the stuff you sell is old vinyl that sounds so dodgy you'd swear there was someone cooking chips between the tracks?

OWNER - Bog off, I've heard it . . .

Chapter Three - Joe Laidlaw

MENTIONED FOR THE FIRST TIME IN THIS CHAPTER

Alan Ashman - Arguably the best manager we ever had, and beyond dispute as the most successful in the post. Ashman started his second spell in charge of team affairs in the late summer of 1972.

Stanley Bowles - Stylish, long-haired midfielder with a blinding first touch. Spent almost a year at Brunton Park, headed South, never heard of again!

Frank Clarke - Deceptively effective goal machine signed from Ipswich in August, 1973, brother of Alan and no relation to more famous Frank Clarke, hang-dog faced full back and manager.

Kevin Hegarty - Seldom seen outfield player. Utility player for sure given that six of his seven senior appearances took place in the number 12 shirt. Best remembered as a bloke with an uncanny resemblance to Alan Ross when the light caught him in the right way.

Joe Laidlaw - Flying blonde tresses, droopy moustache and just a hint of a gut. The aerodynamic 'Flying Pig' of the mid-Seventies strike force and a Brunton Park legend.

Ian MacFarlane - 'The Big Man' and manager who took us to fourth place in Division Two in 1971. Carlisle United gave him his managerial break and also left him - and plenty of us on the terraces - stunned when they sacked him to almost universal surprise.

Hughie McIlmoyle - Firm favourite, a striker who spent three terms at Brunton Park including a return to the club in his mid thirties for one last hurrah in the top flight.

Jean-Claud Pagal - Former Cameroon international who featured briefly in 97-98 campaign, making his debut with fetching dread-locked pig tails at Gillingham.

Ray Train - Comically named, diminutive fresh faced midfielder signed from Walsall in 1971. Hard-working, tricky opponent sometimes upended by frustrated opposing players.

ALONGSIDE STAN WEBB, another enigma trod the Brunton Park turf between 1971 and 1972. He briefly added a new dimension to our lives. The two Stans - Webb and Bowles - might have been on the same pitch, but they offered different visions of the game and appealed to die-hard supporters in totally different ways. So different in fact that this chapter will overlap seasons with the previous one. I'm not trying to confuse things, far from it. These guys taught me different things and appear to this day in different parts of my life. I'll swap Webb stories with long time supporters and Bowles stories with people who dismiss Carlisle as a team who've never meant anything to them.

History records that Stan Bowles hit the very top in football terms, playing for England and scoring a goal for his country whilst also on the books of a QPR team that boasted a young inspirational captain by the name of Gerry Francis, an assured goalkeeper of international class in Phil Parks, and the dazzling skills of winger Dave Thomas. Bowles midfield play-making, defence splitting passes and well-timed assaults on goal were a notable feature of the London team's success in the mid-Seventies.

They were also briefly a central part of Carlisle United's storming runs to seriously average league positions in Division Two. Bowles opened his account with us in a perfunctory 2-1 defeat of Oxford at the end of October, 1971, which for all the world resembled the Bristol City game with which I'd opened my account as a supporter. Two mid-table stalwarts going at it with speed and occasional fury in a game that in all probability wouldn't make the slightest difference at the end of the season. It didn't, we ended that season in tenth place, Oxford finished five places and five points behind.

The most significant thing about that encounter was the sight of Stan Bowles in the blue number 10 shirt. That shirt mattered more to me than young Stan - a £13,000 capture from Crewe Alexandra - could have known. Since I'd become an active member of the Blue Army, the number 10 shirt had been the on-field property of Chris Balderstone, Bobby Owen and . . . Bob Hatton. I knew well enough that just before my arrival on the terraces the legendary goal-getter, Hughie McIlmoyle, had made that shirt his own during his second spell with the Cumbrians.

Now this long haired-bargain basement hopeful from the kind of team that everyone had heard of and nobody I knew had ever seen was out there with number 10 on his back. He did just enough before his substitution to suggest that his skills could add a new dimension to our hard-fighting, fast running and solid performances. It wasn't that Bowles did much in that game - in fact, it was Bobby Owen who scored both of our goals to turn round a 1-0 half-time deficit. It was Bowles' presence on the pitch - slight, long haired and positively alien by Cumbrian standards - that spoke volumes about the changes he would briefly bring. Speaking

45

of the 'positively alien' bit, when Bowles was substituted that day Stan Webb took his place. I'd love to repeat the barrage of killing one line jokes that exploded around the Warwick Road End, suggesting that Ian MacFarlane had brought off a girl and sent on a gorilla, but . . . there weren't any. Just a few comments about the 'not bad' start. Like most debuts, Bowles performance had lacked understanding, included some well placed but hopeless off the ball runs, and presented the spectacle of a man with some idea and a long way to go.

I've seen others start in a similar way. In 1998, former Cameroon international, Jean-Claude Pagal, combined moments of inspiration with the sorry spectacle of a bloke whose understanding of the game failed to connect with the other 21 players on the pitch. Pagal had Bowles touches, but in his early thirties he was on the way down when we signed him. Bowles was 22 the first time he stepped out at Brunton Park. He ghosted, glided and mis-read the game in equal amounts, but when the cheerful chunk of mindless, meandering mirth that was Stanley Webb slapped hands with Bowles and trotted onto make his contribution, we knew Bowles had arrived.

Confident in the conversations at school I might have been, but I still had a lot to learn and Bowles debut just hinted at some of the things still to be discovered. Looking back all these years later, it's tempting to suggest that it all came so naturally. That each bit of football philosophy, each vivid memory of a move or a goal, and each one liner from the Warwick, overheard and understood, simply had to happen. It's tempting, but it is also complete bollocks. I was making progress alright by the time Bowles arrived. I'd just about got it with Stan Webb, and Bowles, like Webb, offered an experience. His fresh features, long hair and sideburns in the stock shot featured by Border TV didn't begin to tell the story. As with Webb, you had to be there. For someone my age, a bare 12 when Bowles started, being there meant a pile of contradictions and a lot of uncertainty. We've done the contradictions with Stan Webb, so let's do the uncertainty.

Every time United took to the pitch there was going to be some uncertainty. In my mind, shaped by the tales I'd heard before I went, and the achievements of being 90 minutes from Wembley in 1970 and two places from Division One in 1971, we were a formidable team. From the pitch height vantage point of the boys pen we were battling in the 70-71 season and not always getting the best of it.

We fought Oxford and gave it some serious stalwart grunt in the second half. Bobby Owen who had commitment even when the first touch deserted him was the difference on the day. Bowles wasn't your average stalwart player. Speaking of which, does anyone use the word 'stalwart' outside of football writing? This has occurred to me from time to time, but I've not found much evidence of it. Think about it. It's not as if there were ever a rock band called The Stalwarts. Hell, we've had every other name under the sun. I pride myself on knowing something about music and - to the best of my knowledge - no band has taken on that name.

46

They've gone for more obvious and attractive monikers like Toad The Wet Sprocket [of which there have been UK and US versions], The Glaxo Babies, Jesus Christ And The Nail Knockers, Acme Sewage Co, Rancid Hell Spawn, The Moors Murderers, The Strawberry Alarm Clock, The Snivelling Shits, Smegma and Bogshed. I should know, I bought records by many of those on the list! I live in hope of finding the ever elusive album by The Stalwarts.

I swear there are some old fashioned words I know only because I read *Shoot*, *Football Monthly* and the few other magazines that made it to either of the two newsagents' shops in Wigton. 'Redoubtable' is another such word. For me it conjures up sweaty pictures of defenders like Manchester United's Tony Dunne, a no nonsense Irishman who clocked up over 30 appearances for his country in an international career that spanned nearly 15 years. In other words he wasn't exactly a regular first choice for all that time but he was always a tryer. Carlisle's game was based on effort and organisation making us a bunch of redoubtable stalwarts. A team who would never say die even when we were dead and buried.

Bob Hatton had been in that league. The problem was he wanted to be in the First Division. When he left us in October of 1971 for Birmingham there were a few grumbles around and a few comments to the effect that we'd finished well above them the previous season and Hatton didn't know where his best chance of top flight action lay. They were wrong of course. Birmingham, and Bob Hatton, took second place and promotion behind Norwich City that season. I'd been on the terraces often enough to feel an attachment to the team and Hatton's departure was a blow. The guy could score goals with clinical efficiency and his skillful touches on the way to goal suggested class.

It was a turning point for me in another way. Along with the sense of belonging to something there was uncertainty. The battling performance against Oxford was only the start. I knew this team could lose, I even knew they could leak three goals at home inside 45 minutes. But in the first 45 minutes?

A miserable December Saturday. A team struggling for form and looking shapeless. Some touches that looked purposeful until the self-assured players of QPR pounced on our errors and stuffed us for three by half-time. I've had that sinking feeling at half-time many times since. I've even had it when we were four goals down at the same stage of a game. But the first time lingers. That sinking feeling, that trapped, purposeless 'I've spent my money and I'm stuck with it' feeling. At 12 years old and not exactly wealthy, entry to a football match, even the cheapest corner of the terraces, comes expensive. Throw in shit weather and the recent departure of your reliable goal machine for a team that were looking serious promotion contenders and you've got a sick, miserable half-time drag to the 'refreshments'. They didn't refresh much. In those circumstances, parting with cash for anything seemed to make the situation worse. This is one thing that has changed with time. These days, in the face of a pathetic first half, unassailable opposition lead and a lack of inspiration at our end of the pitch, I can throw myself into a frenzy of tepid coffee, low grade snacks and those old stalwarts of the chocolate kingdom, the Mars Bar and Kit Kat. I can also comfort myself with the philosophical slant that comes with age and think long-term, even into next season if I have to.

Back then, I was thinking a week ahead and other priorities were coming into my life. I was noticing girls, listening to music and making attempts to look stylish (by early Seventies standards anyway). Stuck in a queue for crisps at half-time, I thought better of it and read my programme. I didn't want to part with any more cash that day at Brunton Park. QPR could have refreshed their half-time with a fag, a pint and a legendary Brunton Park scotch pie, and we still wouldn't have got back into that game.

I knew enough by then to have heard the cliches that football's great thinkers could trot out. 'Eleven men against eleven, game of two halves,' etc. A fat lot of bloody good on December the 11th, 1971. Our eleven men trotted out for the second half and managed marginally more shape, but that was about it. Incidentally, this game is also notable for another small slip in the definitive record. According to *The Lads In Blue,* Kevin Hegarty ran on as substitute but nobody is indicated on the team list with an asterisk, suggesting that nobody went off. That might just explain the confusion we produced on the pitch. Maybe Stan Webb pulled his unique trick by making it appear as if his legs were heading off before fooling everyone when his body moved in a mysterious way to remain on. With 12 on the pitch we were probably cacking it big time with everyone worried that we'd be reported to the FA and relegated an entire division for our front! Frankly, I don't remember and I don't much care to remember. We drew the second half 1-1 giving us an overall aggregate score of 1-4 on the 90 minutes, me a sinking feeling as I dragged myself out, and the biting cold a chance to get into my well worn Parka jacket.

I'd been abroad by this time in my life, wandered round some foreign cities on my own, and even been caught up in massive crowds. A few months before the 9,250 people shuffled grumbling into the dank Cumbrian night after that defeat, I'd stood in the centre of Leichtenstein in a much bigger crowd whilst their prince mumbled something about everyone enjoying his birthday. The only words I got from his speech - in German I think, not that it mattered to me - were the ones that related to fireworks before the place went mad for it with a display that shook me to the core and sent out pulsating explosions that thumped me in the chest. A summer night in a foreign country, a country I could barely find on a map, stood in the middle of a massive crowd, rattled by massive explosions, with a vague idea that I'd meet my parents back at the van once the display was over. I took it all in, decided it was okay and calmly set about finding my way through the strange, heaving town in a country whose name I couldn't even spell with any confidence.

48

A few months later I was in Carlisle. I knew the town, knew my way back up Warwick Road, and I felt scared. Rattled by the whole uncertain mess of seeing a team that had a battling reputation as a tight footballing side ripped apart by a team that displayed our familiar qualities in the kind of quantities we could only stand back and respect. This all happened at the same time I was developing a sense of belonging to Carlisle, but in my mind this experience is in another time. I see myself alone, although it would be much later that I'd start heading off alone to games, and I remember finding out that standing and watching a defeat could thump you right in the guts. It was a different sinking feeling to losing a game in which you'd played. Our shapeless and occasionally desperate football that season taught me the hopeless frustration of throwing money at this kind of 'entertainment' and then standing, stomping and lashing out at a concrete wall when you got a lesson in football from some well groomed Southern outfit who knew they were better than you from the kick-off.

We're talking, gutted, cold, miserable, lonely and scared. Like I said, character building. Thank fuck for Stan Bowles. If you want an image of that season it is Bowles running, spraying sweeping passes and turning with his hair flowing behind him. He typified that season, not in his play, which was amongst the best in a blue shirt, but in the varied numbers (6-10-11) he carried. This says something about the search for a tactical plan that went on in the face of injuries, squad changes and determined opposition from the likes of QPR, Birmingham, Norwich, Blackpool and Burnley. Clubs who thought themselves better than us and - as I was starting to realise - who probably had a point.

1971-72 was a turning point for me. The romance was gone for long expanses of the games and my own interests were broadening. By Christmas, 1971, I owned records. T-Rex were massive, having taken two singles to the top that year. Bolan won me over the day I saw the footage of him playing *Jeepster* live in concert which was used to promote the single. Around the same time I'd discovered Deep Purple for myself, mainly through their regular mention in the *Pop Gossip* section of my sister's *Jackie* magazine. By the time I'd seen them giving it ten tenths on *Top of the Pops,* performing the title track from the *Fireball* album, I was hooked. That single was hardly off the turn-table of my first record player that I'd acquired that Christmas. It would soon be followed by a steady stream of Purple albums. Then there were girls, although they didn't go to football matches as far as I could see, apart from Bobby Owen's wife who was still a vocal presence behind us in the Warwick Road end.

There was never any real chance that I was going to quit on Carlisle, despite their middling league form, but my life was slowly becoming more complicated and most of my idle moments in school were spent thinking about the girls around the place. Within a year of starting the Nelson, Thom most of my ambitions would revolve around music and most of my other thoughts took in those girls. Although

49

I'd moved from a Junior to a Comprehensive school in the same small town, the new school contained many more kids my own age on account of its role of taking in the kids from all the local village schools for miles around. You'd be struggling to find Newton Arlosh on a decent road map, but I'd been there many times because my folks had friends out that side. I'd never once encountered Kathleen Graham until she walked into my life in that first year at school. The idle speculation on her account would eventually turn into action of a sort, the kind of thing that early teenagers do well, kidding on they don't care but still sticking around in each other's lives and within sight and earshot at school. Within a year we'd be cosying up at parties, falling apart over nothing in particular, and making up at the next party. By the second year of school we'd even managed to find ourselves in the same class which allowed her to pass notes to me. I'd kid on they didn't matter much, but I'm writing this years later and I can still remember what was in them. Kate - as she was from the second year onwards - is the strongest memory I have of those first two years at school. We would be in and out of each other's lives for the next ten years and I'm still in touch with her. The last time I saw Mrs Harding, as she is now, she was 40 and still gorgeous. She definitely did more of the chasing at the start, but I had a choice and I also had a vague awareness that this was a new part of life. Choice wise I deserve some credit. You'll remember your first serious kiss for life and they don't come any better than Kate's. The rest doesn't matter that much in a book about Carlisle United, but most of it was great, in that teenage confused way. Which means that, looking back, I remember brilliant moments.

To put this up against the subject of this book, the start of that love affair, like the other love affair which started with that 2-1 defeat of Bristol City, felt so damn good. In the football crowd there were confusions. Especially with the inconsistent form and the sense that we weren't going anywhere. The same confusions were around at school. Kate sat in front of me for most of the time in the infamous 2.14 second year class. The main difference was that you could give yourself totally in the football crowd. Win, lose or draw, I'd perfected the kick against the concrete wall for the bad moments. It was easier to get down there and kick it because the on/off form had thinned out the crowds. I'd also got pretty good at the chants, scarf waving and abuse hurling. Giving yourself to the opposite sex in full view of everyone at school was a totally different proposition. Hell, it was hard enough at a party and the ready cash available didn't quite extend to full-blown dating.

Having just about perfected the rituals of being a football fan, I was struggling with the all-together more complicated business of getting to know Kate and girls in general. But in reality, there was only one who really mattered. Giving yourself totally in this area wasn't an option mainly because keeping up the appearance of not being too bothered seemed to be a big part of the deal. Unlike football, I didn't have a bunch of old timers and those in the know standing behind me and barking out one liners that I could use to build my understanding. Let's give my parents their due though. By Cumbrian standards they were liberal and easy going to the point of being almost embarrassing. I was, in all probability, the first boy in my year to understand the facts of life, and knowledge like that isn't a whole lot of good unless you get to use it. Enough said.

Oh yeah, football. Carlisle United and I were still at it and Stanley Bowles appearances were doing something to keep me interested. Our tenth place in 1972 owed a lot to Stan. The inconsistent form suggested we deserved the mid-table mediocrity of tenth place, but it could have been so much worse without stalwart performances in mid-season when we went seven games without defeat. This run immediately followed the annihilation at Brunton Park at the hands QPR and - true to our inconsistent form - started with a comprehensive destruction of Norwich City in which we'd stung the stylish side with two goals by half-time and then hung on before striking with clinical accuracy one more time in the second half. They might have been champions in May, but they were a sorry sight at twenty to five on the Saturday before Christmas Day. Stanley Bowles netted a hat-trick that day for the one and only time in a Carlisle shirt and he kept on eluding defenders and scoring goals for most of the season.

Geraint and I were there when Tottenham came to Fortress Brunton in the third round of the Cup after a hard fought 1-1 draw at White Hart Lane. I'd been excited at the prospect of watching two seriously good players that day. Martin Peters and Pat Jennings, as I recall, both played. They were simply outclassed by Stan Bowles and Alan Ross though, despite Spurs beating us 1-3 on the day. In a redoubtable, stalwart, passionate United performance, Bowles was drawing comparisons with George Best - at least from our end of the crowd. Not such a fanciful suggestion. He could take him on in the off the pitch action stakes for sure!

Bowles made one of his confusing appearances in the number six shirt. The varying shirt numbers added to the exotic mystery along with Bowles' ability to ghost and glide past opposing players, like Martin Peters at his best. The George Best comparisons were not made lightly. Hell, we thought we had our answer to George Best in the form of Frank Barton. The difference between Barton and Bowles is significant in considering Carlisle United during that era. Looking back it also puts clarity into some of the thoughts that run through this chapter.

Barton was ever present that season, eventually leaving us in the summer of 1972 to cut through the middle of the park and make the play at Blackpool. In a memorable article in the *Cumberland Gazette* during the previous summer, somebody - it may well have been Chris Balderstone - leaked our secret plan for winning the Watney Cup. This might need some explaining so stick with this diversion into the Watney Cup and we'll get back to Barton, Bowles and Best.

The Watney Cup was one of those non-competitions that attract sponsorship, give glory to the also rans, and often fizzle into nothing within a few seasons. I used to think I understood how to qualify for the Watney Cup until I tried to explain it to somebody at work. If I remember rightly, the eight teams in the competition, which ran pre-season, were made up of the highest two finishers in all four divisions who hadn't won anything. So, Carlisle United's fourth place in the previous season and the pitch invasion which had seen Geraint and I over the wall had achieved something. We'd made it to the mighty Watney Cup!

In doing so we had the tasty pre-season prospect of playing Crewe Alexandra in the first round at the end of July. I was doing the middle class bit, piling into the family caravette for a trek round Europe. I remember being mightily unimpressed with the Mona Lisa and visiting my grandparents in Carlisle just before we left where I read the secret plan, the plan which was shared only with the truly initiated, like the 44,000 readers of Cumberland's premier free-sheet newspaper. The plan was simple enough. When we made it to the final, as we surely would, Frank Barton would do a man for man job on the priceless George Best, marking the greatest player in the English game out of action and bringing the silverware to Carlisle. We must have gone on holiday on July the 31st that year because I remember taking the paper off my Dad at the motorway services and reading about how this plan came to grief. Halifax Town threw the whole lot into touch when they took out Manchester United, Best, Charlton, Law and Stepney amongst them with a 2-1 shocker of a result at The Shay. When I got home Geraint filled me in on the rest. We'd gone out to Crewe in the semi-final.

I don't remember who won and the whole competition mattered so little that my *News of the World Football Annual* doesn't record the winners. It does record all the winners of the Simod Cup and I can't remember how the hell you got into that one either. Perhaps, if they ever bring *Mastermind* back to the telly, some anorak will choose the Sherpa Van Trophy and other football non-events as a specialist subject. I'd love to see that guy's face (I'm not being sexist here, just trust me it would have to be a bloke!) when he was asked how exactly you qualified for the Leyland Daf Trophy. Following a full and comprehensive answer he would be staggered when Magnus said, 'I'm sorry, you are incorrect, the right answer is . . . WHO CARES????!!!!

So, we were talking about Frank Barton. The logic behind the Barton plan was that he and Bestie were ball players with pace, acceleration, an ability to hold onto a weaving ball in open play, and a reputation for finding the target from odd angles. Barton wasn't that good though. His man to man job on Best would have revolved around superior fitness and an ability to guess what George was gonna do, but not match it. Barton was your average stalwart George Best impersonator. His droopy moustache and abundant crop of hair might have hinted at a wish to hit the fashion heights of the early Seventies, but there was a hint of thinning beneath the thatch, a working class honesty about the way he rolled his sleeves up in the thick of the action, and a plodding quality behind the shimmies that marked the man out as a grafter with a good touch. George Best was all touch and class, like our Stanley

Bowles. Up against the top flight in the form of Spurs, Barton had to sweat, and got caught in possession if he didn't go like hell. Bowles, young and still looking slightly dazzled in the floodlights, glided and passed and drew a few comments from the old timers about his short term status at Carlisle. Our £13,000 was going to turn into someone else's big price tag.

We slogged out the '71/'72 season on the strength of the seven match unbeaten run in the middle. The last seven matches by comparison saw only two wins and a draw. That summer stays in my mind more than the records I was buying. I'd got Deep Purple's *Machine Head* and by the following season my expanding Purple collection included the *Fireball* and *In Rock* collections. The acquisition of these treasured items and the start of my regular subscription to the music press was rudely interrupted by the sudden departure of Ian MacFarlane, the 'Big Man' who'd managed us to fourth and tenth places in Division Two in successive seasons.

His departure ranks as one of the most unsavoury in our history and only the welcome return of Alan Ashman to the helm could have made up for it. The official histories suggest that MacFarlane had a straight talking style that didn't impress those further up the chain of command. My own very unofficial history would like to record that this guy bought Stan Bowles and Ray Train - a diminutive midfielder who looked like a cheery twelve year old and wiped the mocking smiles of defenders as he ran past them with no respect. Anyone who saw the potential in these two and got change from twenty grand had to be alright. He also bought Stan Webb and so we've got to give him credit as a crowd pleaser. And finally, it was his team and their high finish that got me onto the pitch for the first time, top man, The Big Man.

Just a few weeks after MacFarlane's departure, I was back at school for the start of the second year. I remember that day well enough. Kate was in my form and the timetable they gave us was unbelievable. One by one a who's who of teachers not exactly famed for their capabilities in the area of riot control was read out as our timetable was dictated to an increasingly disbelieving and surprisingly small number of people. The only unknown quantities were the new arrivals, one of whom, Mr Godfrey, was the form tutor. Glances were exchanged, fists clenched in triumph and heads were sent spinning at the dizzying prospects that lay before us. One teacher wasn't even there to start the year because he was still recovering from a nervous breakdown.

I can't prove any of the following, most of which came second hand from tame teachers and others likely to know. I'm not claiming any of this as fact. But . . . the 'genius' thinking that created 2.14 may, just possibly, have been linked to two problems both of which had their roots in the recent combining of grammar and secondary schools to make the mighty comprehensive. Some of the grammar school teachers were not relishing the prospect of the new lunatic asylum and the nervous breakdown that had reputedly seen off the English teacher who was due to join 2.14 that year was merely the tip of the iceberg.

The new crowd in the school included certain characters, the likes of which they'd never previously encountered and, as I understand it, the 'genius' solution of 2.14 involved loading in a smallish number of self-starters who might work more co-operatively with the teachers. These teachers could then be hand-picked from the ranks of those who were dodging missiles as the grim reality of the meaning of the word 'comprehensive' dawned upon them. My abiding memories of that year involve Kate passing me notes and physically ejecting her mate, Lorraine, from the chair in front of me so she could have it, me getting caught fixing a metal dustbin to land on a teacher's head as he entered the room, the detailed knowledge of music I gained from reading *Disc* whilst the teachers tried their best, and the way I shamelessly buried myself in English literature with a passion. Hell, you'd be passionate if you'd just discovered *The Sex and Savagry Of the Hell's Angels*, *Angels From Hell* and . . . well, great books the lot of them.

What the hell the poor saps up the front were on about beats me. I can remember quite a lot of what I learned before and after, but '72/'73 goes by in my mind in a blur that starts with Marc Bolan strutting *Children Of The Revolution* on *Top Of The Pops* and comes to a grinding halt the following summer with me stretched out on my bed reading a real trash corker of a book and debating whether Alice Cooper's *Billion Dollar Babies* or *One And One Is One* by Medicine Head would be best as a background noise. The only real memory of the lessons involves either prevailing on the improbably good natured Mr Godfrey to look after the albums I regularly swapped for a week or two with my mate Noddy - his Free for my Deep Purple - or getting hit in the back of the head by a misdirected missile as Mr Leaky tried to maintain order. Years later I would find myself working in a factory job over the summer with Mr Leakey's son. 'He doesn't work in state schools anymore,' said Richard Leakey. Smart move if you ask me.

2.14 may have grown in legend over the years, and perhaps if my adult self walked back into that class I'd be amazed at the fact that it looked like any class in any school and little else. However, it should be remembered that a few unsullied academic careers came off the rails that year, and that people who entered that class with impressive records of good marks went on the following year to open their educational accounts in less demanding company. I know for I was that soldier, or one of them. It should also be remembered that the experiment was never repeated whilst I had anything to do with the school.

But so what if my education was heading away from the stars and into the toilet at 13. I'd had a great year, I could name you every musician who had ever been a working part of Deep Purple, I knew the running order on every album from *In Rock* to *Who Do We Think We Are* (and most of the lyrics), I had Kate within note passing distance five days a week, and the sun shone without a break in those far off and carefree Cumberland days.

I don't know who dreamed up the 'experimental' form, but in the immortal words of songwriter, Barry Mann, 'Who was that man, I'd like to shake his hand, he made my baby fall in love with me.'

I was getting older and life was now about planning events. Heading off from home into Carlisle with my mate, Peter McCall, I'd planned all week to pick up *Billion Dollar Babies*. The *Disc* reviewer reviewer had suggested his copy ruined his weekend and that was just the bait I needed to grab my copy. I'd progressed by this point to avoiding the likes of Smiths and Woolies where possible in favour of the independent more sussed and altogether cooler Pink Panther record shop in Rosemary Lane. There were also school discos to add to the parties I was throwing and a few others had got into the act. And as the owner of more records than most of my mates, I got to slap a lot of vinyl on in the background as I got into close proximity with Kate and tried to figure out what else I should be doing.

At school I got it totally wrong one hot sunny day when Kate and Lorraine were watching us playing football. I managed to turn a diving header into a complete somersault in which my knee went crashing into my hand, which then swelled up to impressive proportions - the first serious sprain I'd ever had. This football disaster was in all probability down to the fact that I couldn't see a moving ball well enough without my glasses. Whatever, the lack of football skill didn't matter to me as much as the hand injury. Hell, I was gonna need my hands in that rock music career I was planning.

If life was about events, and I was entering that self-centred stage when I was out for all I could get, then football had to fit inside the new demands. Jeremy Higham had the misfortune to be the son of two teachers at the Nelson Thom, not the easiest gig on the planet. His thirteenth birthday fell not long after mine and his Dad took him to his first football match, mob handed. Mr Higham, a History teacher who would eventually take me to one of the most improbable A-level pass grades in history stumped up serious cash to take a handful of Jeremy's mates to the Brunton Park clash with high flying Blackpool, a team with promotion pretensions and current internationals in their ranks (okay, we're talking Welshmen, but international is international, right?).

This match was an event. For starters we got into the stands, proper seats and a panoramic view of the pitch. We also got there seriously early. So early that we were stood beside the Blackpool team coach and collecting autographs as the players went in. The autograph bit had obviously mattered to Jeremy because I remember him idly talking about wandering onto the pitch to get the players autographs before the start. Like I said, I think it was his first time at a real match! We played hard, gave it the stalwart come headless chicken treatment, and ran out 3-2 losers. As a regular of more years standing than the rest of the party I remember blaming it on the absence of Ian MacFarlane from the manager's office and the recent sales of Stan Webb and Stanley Bowles. The implication being that Alan Ashman hadn't got the tactics right and the recently acquired Joe Laidlaw, who had scored that day, was no match for Stan Webb. I was of course talking complete shit, a speciality in which I was virtually unbeatable at the time.

Another event was the visit of Arsenal in the Cup. *Match Of The Day* came to that one and saw us fight like hell from our lowly league position only to go out of the competition by the odd goal in three, a gift of a goal at that. Joe Laidlaw, who had missed the 2-1 humbling of Sheffield United which had put us into the fifth round, had a mixed game, and the defence let in Frank McLintock to score the Arsenal winner. Frank bloody McLintock! A centre half! We'd done well though and the highlights on *Match of the Day* suggested an even game. Arsenal stood on top of the league that day and they only beat us because we slipped up. I saw myself on television into the bargain. One advantage of the boys' pen was its pitch side proximity to the Warwick Road goal, and that coupled with thinner crowds allowed you to see yourself on the very odd occasion that the cameras bothered to come.

Our eventual 18th place and my increasing interest in other bits of life saw me drifting away from Carlisle United, although I stayed in touch well enough to get to a few games and notice the improvement in 1973-74. With a third promotion place on offer into the First Division, Geraint and I speculated early on that United might yet see top flight action. If the place had been on offer in 1967 we'd have made it. Come the middle of September with one point from the first six games and an away defeat at Luton on the record, we were 6-0 down by half time! Things didn't look so bright.

In the odd way that Carlisle seemed to mirror my own life I was also up against it. Years three and four at school meant the Middle School, a windswept stalag with all the architectural appeal of downtown Berlin in May, 1945. With its long corridors, flaking white paint job and the deep black floors that rendered the blood invisible once it had congealed, the place would have needed a serious makeover to qualify as depressing. The mile long corridors magnified every sound from the stairwells and on most days you could hear the blood curdling screams of another poor sap being ripped limb from limb over the bannisters.

The sounds echoed down the corridors and visitors to the school would often find green midgets ferreting around in the cloakrooms. On closer inspection these creatures would turn out to be amongst the brainy elements of the new third years, resplendent in their bottle green blazers, their lack of height due to the fact that they were reduced to walking on their hands, pushing the top half their bodies along and leaving trails of blood from the ragged stumps that hung from their waists. I remember one day heading into my Civics class, which was held in the hidden room next to the cloakroom, and finding one poor specimen lying flat on his back, pale from the lack of blood and almost ready to expire. With the feeble strength left in the top half of his body, he bent one skinned knuckle and beckoned me over. I had to crouch low to his face to hear his last dying words. As his eyes dimmed and shut that kid whispered, 'Where in shitting crikey are my legs?' I hadn't the heart to tell him that I'd seen the 'progress' class toasting them on a bonfire two hours earlier.

Teachers experienced in the softer climes of the grammar school, kids positively allergic to education, and a building fit only to be an SAS training ground. What could you expect?

TEACHER - For the last time, will one of you cretins explain to me why this boy bled to death in the cloakroom?

BORED LAD IN CLASS - His aunty gave him a Toblerone and he wouldn't share it with the rest of us.

Well, it made sense at the time.

The generations before us might have had a scrap or two with the Germans, but I'm tellin' ya. In Wigton, 1973, we had it rough.

My league form had slipped in the second year and I'd hit a relegation position that rendered me Set 2 material for the start of the Middle School. In plain English that means saveable but lazy. My own pre-season training for the demands of the Middle School wrestling championships involved some serious tactical thinking. The ambush central architecture was a known danger and - in this environment - it was permanent open season on mouthy posh gits. Fair enough I suppose, it was too far to walk to the chip shop at lunchtime, the weather was usually crap and you needed some indoor entertainment. My tactical master plan involved shutting the fuck up, watching my back, and trying to talk my Dad into buying a rusty Ford Transit for the odd occasions when he ran us to school. Results wise, I guess two out of three ain't bad.

After a low key and under-confident start I got the tactics sorted and started to feel comfortable. I saw some real relegation candidates turn in worse performances than me. The third year allowed for new faces to join us from Aspatria and Silloth, legendary outposts on the very fringes of civilisation. Silloth once achieved national fame when it was celebrated as the worst holiday resort in the whole country by BBC *Nationwide*. These new faces had been sent to Wigton to allow them to take O-levels in vast numbers whilst their less fortunate companions stayed behind at the infamous institutions at Beacon Hill, Aspatria and Silloth, and sewed mail bags until their fingers bled. I saw one or two new faces being rearranged before things settled down.

By the end of the third year I remained untouched, my work was improving, I'd got Kate Graham's phone number and she'd been round to my house. That Summer I started heading into school in a scruffy blue jacket that just about

57

matched one of the stripes in the school tie. Mr James, a History teacher with a stiff upper lip and a reputation as a fighter ace in the Second World War, cornered me in the dinner queue and made it clear he was unimpressed. The gist of his rant was that standards had fallen badly enough amongst the rest of the school without the saveable types falling to their scruffy depths. He didn't know it, but he'd just paid me the greatest compliment I'd ever had from a teacher. I'd pulled it off, I was keeping up the work well enough to be a contender, and looking dozy enough to count as a real person. Thanks, Sir!

It was a stalwart performance on my part built on consistency. Carlisle United had responded to the blood chilling nightmare of one point from their first twelve - remember, we're still talking two points for a win at this stage. The unflashy consistency of Frank Clarke, striker brother of 'Sniffer' Alan and a £35,000 buy at the start of the season, was providing regular goals. Joe Laidlaw, the self same striker I'd run down on my first sighting of him against Blackpool, was also proving his worth. This guy was a crowd pleaser with real character and a worthy successor to the mighty Stan Webb. I was still getting to the odd game, but it was the games I was missing that really put the fire back into my love of the whole thing.

We beat Orient 3-0 in February, and with both teams chasing promotion *Match of the Day* deemed it worth a 700 mile round trip to cover the events. They got their money's worth with a diving header from Joe Laidlaw cannoning into the Orient goal. With his flowing blonde hair, the all important aerodynamic rounded front with the hint of a beer gut, and an approach to the game that combined equal amounts of bravery and skill, Laidlaw was always likely to connect with a ball in a crowded goal mouth. And the results, although unpredictable, could often be spectacular. They didn't come any better than that goal and I'd only seen it on TV. I was missing out and reduced to the same state I'd been in at the age of nine.

In my absence that February afternoon, 'The Flying Pig' had dived into Brunton Park legend. Laidlaw was a grafter in the great Carlisle tradition and his performances, along with the rest of the team had been blended into an outfit every bit as formidable as the great teams of the past. A stalwart outfit for sure, but winners. 5-1 winners over Swindon, a game I missed, 2-1 winners over Nottingham Forest another game I missed, and 1-0 winners over promotion chasing Sunderland, another game I missed. Sunderland was the last straw. The report on Border Television described a hard-fought encounter, with Chris Balderstone keeping his cool from the penalty spot to score the only goal whilst Alan Ross performed heroics in the other goal mouth to keep Sunderland out.

Balderstone was another stalwart, like Laidlaw, who'd come through. His very Carlisle team place had been threatened at the start of the season when he'd seen out the cricket season with Leicestershire and been fined by Alan Ashman on his return to Brunton Park.

58

That report on Border did it. I could hear the roars as the penalty went in, feel the tension of the last minutes ticking away and it wasn't really so different to my nine year old self hanging on to Gavin Bell's stories of the legends who wore the blue shirt. Hell, some of the players were still the same, and in that Sunderland game Balderstone and Ross - players I'd idolised from the start - had made all the difference.

I was watching television on Friday, May the 3rd, missing out on another match, but this game was in Birmingham. Border Television were carrying the news. The previous Saturday we had beaten Aston Villa to finish our season standing in third place, Orient were two points behind with Villa to face in their final game. An Orient win could take them past us and into the top flight. Despite their lowly position, Villa had made us sweat for the 2-0 victory and on May the 3rd they held Orient to a 1-1 draw.

That result with Orient said everything about the fighting spirit of Aston Villa. That game secured 14th place for Aston Villa, condemned Orient to fourth, and left us safe in third and secure in the knowledge that we were a Division One outfit. It also sent me tearing around the house on a lap of honour. Being a posh git we're talking a sizeable house here, so this was quite a gesture!

With my parents out at the folk club in Ireby and my sister suitably unimpressed, it was a lonely and pathetic celebration for the greatest moment in my club's history, but at that moment it felt good. It felt totally bloody improbable and more than anything else it put the love of the whole thing back into my life. I didn't deserve them, I'd wandered away and missed some of the games that would now be legendary, but the feeling I got was a small dose of guilt to a huge explosion of love for the team and what they'd done.

I may have wandered, but I was going back. I wanted everything else in my life and, frankly, I couldn't help myself wandering in the direction of Kate, but I'd left Carlisle too far out of my life. I knew better now. Writing this years later, a few other things strike me about this historic moment. Carlisle got to the First Division the only way they could ever have made it. They played solid, well organised football with a manager who knew the flow of a game and the strengths of his players. Stanley Bowles may have dazzled us, but we knew we couldn't hang on to him. Joe Laidlaw and Frank Clarke headed, booted and scrambled us up, Alan Ross threw himself at net bursting shots, and the midfield blend of youth and experience that pitted the little ferret-faced Ray Train and the sophisticated Chris Balderstone into the same area of the park, kept the play moving and the opposition chasing shadows. Grafters first and stars when the moves came together, United were a stalwart team in the great tradition.

If you needed someone to use as an image then, just possibly, Joe Laidlaw was your man. He'd looked pretty damn ordinary in a hard-working but defeated team the first time I'd seen him from the stands in that 3-2 defeat by Blackpool. Against

59

Aston Villa in April, 1974, he was a goal hungry strike machine who'd hit home before half-time to settle United's nerves. 'The Flying Pig' was a stalwart who'd needed service and luck, but he worked hard to get on the end of anything that flew goalwards and he'd scatter defenders to make the all important touch.

Like me, he'd started the season poorly and left serious doubts about his ability to cope in the thick of it. He didn't miss a game, but he'd left it till mid-October to score his first goal. By the end of the season he'd got the blend right. As far as the goal tally went, he was getting the results that suggested he was a real contender, but he still looked dozy enough to count as a real person. I recognised that combination well enough. I'd found myself another hero, a role model for sure, and he'd done it so deceptively that I had to give him real credit for the way he'd crept up in my affections. On a good day Laidlaw could teach Stan Webb something about crowd pleasing and that meant he'd already taught me something about writing off footballers, and football teams, too soon.

Blue Nightmare #4

MANY PEOPLE HAVE asked over the years, 'Whatever happened to Joe Laidlaw?' The famous 'Flying pig' of Carlisle United legend, the man with the gut that parted the air and the ability to score from almost anywhere.

Stories circulate to this day about the diving header that left Orient flagging, the way the Luton Town defence split like a rotten log as Laidlaw took a run at goal, and the ageing First Division defender who collapsed with exhaustion as he tried to dribble around Laidlaw's ample form.

We can exclusively reveal that a man with unsurpassed crowd pleasing abilities and aerial 'skills' that might best be described as 'unique' has finally found the right niche in life.

Uncredited and unrecognised by the foreign crowds to whom he displays his best moves night after night, Laidlaw has spent well over a decade in the employ of rock giants, Pink Floyd. As the band weave their magical musical spell and the lasers cut the air all around the stage, only one thing can complete the performance. As the music builds to a storming peak each night, Laidlaw sets off on his own journey, trundling above the heads of the crowd on a wire drawing spellbound gasps, some smiles of recognition and many guffaws of affectionate laughter. Things are really little changed since he displayed the same skills in front of his adoring Brunton Park public. In those days the name Laidlaw appeared on the programme. That name would be unfamiliar to the hordes who pay to watch Pink Floyd, but the man remains a legend, a one-off amongst entertainers, and an experience to be savoured. Pink Floyd fans may not know the name of Joe Laidlaw, but everyone has heard of The Flying Pig.

Chapter Four - Les O'Neill

MENTIONED FOR THE FIRST TIME IN THIS CHAPTER

Peter Carr - Fair-haired defender with a moustach. Athletic, handy with a swift punt upfield, and usually reliable in his understanding with Alan Ross . . . usually reliable!

Bill Green - Tall centre back and captain. Disciplined, not known to respect the feelings or bodies of highly rated opposing forwards.

Les O' Neill - Diminutive playmaker with distribution, vision and a surprising amount of class for an ungainly little feller.

Bobby Parker - Defender with good positional sense, good commitment and impressive sense of being a team-player. One of three ever present players during the '74-'75 season, and a great servant to the club. Leaving eventually in 1984 to local football with almost 400 Carlisle United games to his credit.

Eddie Prudham - Forward signed from Sheffield Wednesday with a view to strengthening the First Division squad. So injury prone, 'Weakness' could have been his middle name. Less than 20 appearances in three seasons.

Stan Ternent - No nonsense diminutive defender. Good reader of the game, hard worker and not known for respecting reputations. Went on to forge a tough management career based on teaching diminutive clubs - like Bury - to stop respecting the reputations of bigger clubs.

'REANEY, YOU SECOND hand slimy bastard!'
It was the end of November, 1974, and following a dream start to the season we were falling down the league alarmingly fast. On that day in November our fast running, effort-based game came up against a great side who were themselves on a downward slope. Leeds United came to Brunton Park. We lined up, ran around and gave a debut to young Eddie Prudham, a capture from Sheffield Wednesday who'd been drafted in to strengthen the creaking forward line. We needed more pace and movement. We got it until Eddie's slight frame collided with one too many Leeds defenders, and he left the field. That game was the first real inclination I had that things were not going to work out and in response I was letting rip big style.

The swearing was one of the best things about that First Division season. I'd got a few corkers revved up and ready to go. Many of these had started life at school years before. The 'Second hand slimy bastard' one for sure. I owed these one liners to Peter Scillicone, or 'Skilly' to his mates, which didn't include me. When I was in the second year, Skilly had been a fifth former with an attitude a mile wide. As we all trooped up to the bus stop that year it appeared to me that Skilly's entire purpose in life was to make the life of a boy known as 'Joe 90' a complete and utter misery. Joe's complexion indicated that he was one of life's slightly unfortunates. Add a pair of plastic framed glasses to the reddened cheeks and mini pus tales which erupted from them, and you have enough angst to trouble your average 16 year old. Put Skilly on his back every night as he trooped up to the bus stop and you've got a teenage torment of wrist-slashing dimensions.

Joe 90, a predictably unimaginative nickname for a bespectacled kid in the mid-Seventies, crossed my path off and on for years. The strange thing about him was, away from Skilly, he looked pretty average and he remained a decent kid and then bloke. Cowering before the withering blast of abuse on the way to the bus stop, I'd swear his face sprouted acres of spots and his back seemed to arch and bend him forward. Hindsight and a bit of *Guardian* reading over the years tells me that abuse on this scale is a life changing trauma from which some never recover. My memory tells me that Skilly was the best entertainment on offer at ten to four under a drizzling, leaden Cumbrian sky. His ability to create a free-form stream of non-stop swearing bordered on full-blown Tourettes syndrome and I could only marvel from a distance at the volume, timing and invention that kept the act alive for an entire year before I moved to the Middle School. Years later as a comedy writer who was being paid handsomely to push the envelope on attitude, I would spend long evening hours in search of the same linguistic invention that made Skilly a giant amongst fifth formers. The fact that I'm still in work owes everything to Skilly and to those first blasts of abuse on the Brunton Park terraces.

It also owes something to Leeds United. They were the first team to make it obvious that we were going to struggle. Man for man, pass for pass, we were a match for them. We fell apart in the cynical upending challenge department. I'd had higher expectations of a team that was still packed with the players who'd brought a League Championship, an FA Cup and European glory to Elland Road. These were dashed in a performance that saw crunching tackles, breaking our rhythm and convincing Eddie Prudham that enough was enough.

The First Division dream had started so well. What I mean is it started well for the team and several thousand supporters. I missed the start of the whole adventure, like I'd missed the Watney Cup and a brief European excursion in the Anglo-Italian Cup in 1972 on account of being on holiday with the family. The usual pattern involved a long caravette trip across Europe with plenty of culture on offer and a close look at some out of the way places. With the kind of irony that only hits you

63

years later, I realised that I'd missed Carlisle United's only foray into Europe because I'd gone to Scotland in 1972.

I didn't get the joke at all when I came back to the UK at the end of August, 1974, and, talking to Geraint, got the lowdown on how we'd achieved the greatest feat in the club's history. As I recall it we landed back in the UK on August the 25th. First priority for me was a look at the Sunday papers and an inspection of the league position and the match reports. With no reference point I started scanning at the bottom of the First Division, couldn't find Carlisle, started moving up and up and . . . WHAT!!!!!

If you're a Cumbrian you know the rest, if not, you're the sort of person with whom I'd love to bet. Because, whether you are prepared to believe it or not, on August the 25th, 1974, after three games in Division One, Carlisle had three wins to their name and stood on top of the entire Football League. Remember, this is the League in 'old money.' There was no Premier Division. We were first, there were 91 clubs below us, and three of those clubs - Chelsea, Middlesbrough and Tottenham Hotspur - were already regretting the day they'd met us. Alan Ross had kept three clean sheets and Les O' Neill had three of our five goals to his credit. What a week, what a team, what a midfield dynamo, what a shit time to be wandering round a French camp site.

Let's hear it for Les O' Neill. Alongside the class and experience of Chris Balderstone and the endless darting energy of Ray Train, the touch and vision of Les O' Neill got us to the top of the heap that late Summer. Not especially tall or athletic, Les O' Neill had the kind of deceptive class that makes the likes of Paddy Crerand and Ray Parlour into star players. His class was the understated blend of hard work, accuracy and anticipation that puts heart into a team and makes a mockery of over-priced transfer fees and high profile reputations amongst opposing players.

Throughout most of that season it was the journeymen with a sense of their own self-worth who gave Carlisle United a pride and a shape on the pitch. Defenders, Bill Green and Bobby Parker, and little Ray Train in the middle of the field didn't miss a single game between them, Cup ties included. They all displayed that understated class, but Les O' Neill held a hell of a lot together. His inheritance of the number four shirt also cast him in a tradition of diminutive hard workers who could impose their personality on a team. Admittedly it was a short tradition, but Stan Ternent had previously inhabited the shirt, and in the season before the First Division, O' Neill and Ternent briefly traded the number four.

Ternent remains a name known to hardcore football afficanados to this day on the strength of his reputation as a manager who'll forge teams on a shoe-string budget and teach them tenacity in the face of classy opposition. In 1974, Ternent was a name known to Carlisle fans for displaying those same qualities on the pitch. Tough little Stan had departed for Sunderland at the end of the 73/74 season, and it was going to take a major talent to impose his personality on the team. O' Neill played a slightly different game, was similarly useful on the left side, and expanded his game to fit the gap created that Summer before we kicked off in the top flight. He was never better that in the First Division season, 74/75, and the rest of the team were rarely better than Les O' Neill. Maybe if he'd played in every game . . .

O' Neill missed almost all of October, and by the time he returned, our slips - which started with a home loss to Boro in the fourth game - were starting to look a little worrying. For me this worrying slide could be seen from two angles. On the one hand, sense dictated that we were surrounded by some serious teams and there weren't that many pundits who fancied us to stay up. We could just sit back and enjoy the ride, the unfamiliar experience of seeing current internationals at Brunton Park at almost every game, and the distinct chance of television cameras at a game. On the other hand we were already in unreal territory and, given the start to the season, anything was possible.

Hell, I was passing a few personal milestones, at parties, close up with some female company, in the things I was getting up to and getting away with. Life held opportunities, and the Neil who returned that season to Brunton Park to howl at skilful international players on opposing teams was a boy old enough to know what life could offer and too young to be scared of some of the consequences.

Given all of this, I could manage an optimistic slant to the pre-match conversations with Geraint, who went off and on by the name of 'Geg' from this point in his life. 'Geg', Phil - the copper's kid who'd done the preamble to the holes talk - and me, were also making reasonable fist of playing music together. Phil's love of country rock and the presence in his family of a big brother who was on the verge of a semi-pro break in music gave the musical direction to a loose outfit that would gather to murder the best tunes that The Eagles, America and several others could write. We thought we were okay, the tapes skulking somewhere close to my desk suggest otherwise. But, as I said, life was full of possibilities.

It was possible we could have beaten West Ham, Chelsea, Leeds and Newcastle, but they all turned us over. At least I had my growing habit of grabbing life's opportunities to sustain me. Geg and I saw out the West Ham match in the Scratching Shed, surrounded by Hammers, and chatting cheerfully away to the members of some Scottish rock band who were killing the afternoon before gigging in town that night. I swigged away at the wine they passed round and discussed the midfield skills of Les O' Neill. One of the Scots had rightfully identified O' Neill's work rate and central midfield position as a key to our attempts at keeping our place in the game once West Ham had scored what would turn out to be the only goal that afternoon. We may have lost, but there was hope at that stage and I was still new enough to alcohol to leave the game feeling heady and satisfied, having chatted away about music and football with blokes old enough to know them well.

65

We never quit on the top flight and on our day we had it, ask Arsenal, or more importantly Everton. They finished fourth that season, four points away from being champions. We took four points out of them with home and away wins. We've never played them since giving us a 100% league record against them. We took three points off Derby County who went on to be champions. But, in the way that these things work, we lost twice to Luton, who looked relegation candidates from day one, and eventually took the dive back down.

Luton had come up with us the previous season and their form was a good guide to our own progress. Their 2-1 destruction of us in mid-March was one game in which my positive attitude failed me big time. Despite his heroics which included our goal that afternoon, I think even Joe Laidlaw came in for some of the flack. Geg and I stood on the Waterworks end for that one, and I can distinctly remember walking up and heading for the exit as the game still raged. I didn't leave, but it was as close as I've come to heading out of the gate whilst the action was still going on. When all is said and done, my middle class pretensions hide the spirit of a true tight Northern bastard and the thought of leaving a game without my money's worth makes no real sense to me.

This game - I think - is notable as the encounter in which my own eyes watered as Hughie McIlmoyle took a thump right between the legs and collapsed in front of the Waterworks end. Even the one liners from the crowd were desperate, and I remember feeling sympathetic pains right where it hurts as the trainer ran on and applied the freezing sponge. McIlmoyle had been drafted in to strengthen the squad, he was already 34 at the start of the season, and in what would prove to be his third and final stint with the Cumbrians he scored twice and never played again after that Luton game.

I was hitching to games on a regular basis from this point and Geg started around the same time. Lucky git, he got the real nutters including a transit load of headcases from West Cumbria who were prepared to punch each other's lights out in a row about the letters on Smartie tops. Saving bus fairs meant money for food, and twice in this season my love of a decent snack put me as close to a genuine football ruck as I'd been up to that point. I got my scarf ripped off heading into a Carlisle supermarket, and on another occasion, Geg and I got hassled heading for a city centre chip shop. Kids stuff that one, we pushed past and that was the end of it.

Our close personal friendship with all things Burnley was in fine form, and with the cause near enough, lost Carlisle did manage to pay them back at Brunton Park, but I missed this game - and the home annihilation of Everton, as I was bobbing along the Caledonian Canal with the rest of the family doing the old exploring the world and expanding my mind bit. We scored seven goals in my absence as we staged a very late rally, stuffing Burnley and Everton. Liverpool, with their eyes on the championship put it beyond doubt when they beat us an Anfield in front of the biggest crowd we'd see that season, over 46,000.

We were 22nd by this point anyway, and my foul-mouthed rants had done little to turn back the tide of tricky opposing forwards who'd swarmed on the edge of the United penalty box in the latter part of the season. With only pride at stake and spaces visible all round the ground, the team lined up in the centre of the pitch before the kick-off against Wolves in mid-April. They waved to the crowd and turned round to target every part of the ground. Belligerent, stroppy and headstrong I might have been, but I almost choked on what I felt watching them in that unexpected moment. They were still my team, and Alan Ross and Chris Balderstone - men who'd been around at Carlisle long enough to know how hard everyone had worked simply to have this season - were both in the line-up. I didn't know it then, but it was the last time I'd see Chris Balderstone play.

At that moment I felt an honest, almost painful pride. This team had nothing to be ashamed of and they couldn't have tried harder. At times that season it was, frankly, painful in other ways. Hughie McIlmoyle might have been a legend, but against Newcastle he'd looked short of pace and I'd had a sense of a man willing but out of his depth. Chris Balderstone could size up situations and spray out passes, but there were teams in that league that moved quickly enough to leave these skills redundant.

We were beaten but there was pride in the team and what we'd achieved. The pundits who had stated we were relegation certs couldn't take that much pride in their predictions. Many of the same people had simply been trying to make up for the fact that they'd said we would never make it in the first place. I didn't feel too despondent at the relegation, despite caring more than I had for years about that team. I was having good moments in my life and I'd stood munching my way through the sharp crusty round tops of legendary Brunton Scotch pies as I watched the very best the English game had to offer that season. Incidentally, those pies were probably about the best the game had to offer in that department. When I think of that season now I remember moments which seemed to define it all.

We beat Ipswich 2-1 in a display of passion which took on and trashed a well organised outfit under the direction of Bobby Robson. I remember watching from the Waterworks as we lined up and missed a penalty. The ref decided the goalie had moved and ordered a re-take. Having left the ground and gone into explosions of curses at the first miss, I was screaming my heart out about the referee being a Cumbrian. We lined up the penalty again and missed the fucker a second time! ARGHHHHH!!!!!!!!! The result meant nothing to us in the long run, but Ipswich finished third, two points behind the champions Derby with a superior goal tally! But for that game they could have been Champions, a situation that might have given Bobby Robson an earlier shot at England management and our national team a shot at qualification for the 1978 World Cup. Well, it's a thought, eh? Joe Laidlaw scored the goal that secured both points that day. These days 'The Flying Pig' can be encountered still indulging his love for adventure off the ground as he

67

plies his trade as a roofer around Portsmouth. I wonder if it has ever occurred to him that he delayed the appointment of an obvious England manager, ensured the gloom of a country as Italy dumped Don Revie and his detailed dossiers on the opposition out the tournament, and allowed Bill Shankly to turn up on television and pronounce the Italian goal that dumped us out at the group stage to be 'The goal of the century.' I'll bet that line gladdened a few Scottish hearts.

Laidlaw made history as our leading scorer that season. If he'd missed the target and allowed Ipswich into the game maybe history as a whole would have been different. Worth turning over in your mind as you slip a few new slates on a roof I reckon. Then again, leaving Brunton Park in the middle of January with that 2-1 victory - missed penalty into the bargain - all that occurred to me was that we still might pull off the Division 1 survival.

The slide out of Division 1 was slow, steady and scattered with 2-1 victories over Ipswich and other hope building events. Even when we were relegated this fitted into my great scheme of things to a survivable degree. I cared about Carlisle United and I would happily argue my case with anyone and everyone, along with the arguments about favourite rock bands, the genius of the Monty Python team and the like. But that Summer there were foreign exchange students, parties, more drink than a 15 year old had a right to expect, and many other good things in life. For the most part I was back as a regular supporter and Carlisle were back in my life. I'd got through a losing season relatively unscathed and I could justifiably hold a pride in my team. In answer to the usual taunts about United being useless, I could always fire back that I'd been there, Revie's Leeds were psychos and United had fought their corner in a tough division.

Well, I could almost always argue that. If you were there that season you've probably spotted the obvious missing game from this account. The 90 minute hell ride from which we staggered bloodied and disheartened. I know I've got to mention it, so let's go. March the 8th, 1975, our first - and still our only - excursion into the quarter finals of the FA Cup. Carlisle United 0 Fulham 1. Fulham. Second Division Fulham. Bobby Moore and Alan Mullery in defence and Peter-Fucking-Mellor in goal. The self-same Mellor who'd denied us as we leaked three second half goals against Burnley in 1971. The baby-faced, improbably blonde stopper who bore a vague resemblance to something out of the Hitler Youth.

The Cup mattered, historically, in a way that still gave it precedence over the League in the minds of casual fans. You could go the cynical route and suggest that casual Cup fans have fewer tickets to buy, but that isn't the point. Ask Chelsea, Manchester City or Nottingham Forest, teams with pretensions and a record to be proud of. Teams who'd all come to Cup grief at our hands during my spell as a supporter. The move up to the top flight had simply confirmed our 'as good as those bastards' mentality for a season. Our presence in the Sixth round of the Cup, with Wembley almost in sight and some seriously good teams already out of the running, was a real boost in a tough season. Fulham were a division below us, not likely to get promoted, and from London into the bargain.

This was a time for the casual and regular support to get together. Statistically speaking, the difference between the two at Carlisle is awesome. We're moving a little ahead of the game here, but Michael Knighton's 'genius' in taking over the frankly pathetic remnants of the once great Carlisle in the early Nineties and attempting to harness the club's potential rested squarely on a few ideas. The acreage of land owned by the club close to the main motorway link is one feature that a guy with a background in property development could appreciate, but so is the army of latent support out there. People in Cumbria are pretty much the same as people everywhere. The key difference in their casual support is that they have nowhere much else to go. If Bury have a good Cup run they could put bodies on the gate at Gigg Lane, but those same bodies have Old Trafford, Main Road, The Reebok Stadium and Ewood Park within easy striking distance. Then there's rugby league, a decent motor racing track at Oulton Park, clubs, cinemas and . . . yeah, well, Carlisle isn't quite that well off. When he took over, Knighton compared us to Norwich City and it isn't such a ridiculous comparison. Two clubs marooned in a large rural area. Get them performing and the people will come. Give them a Cup run and the people will come in serious numbers, and they'll sing about their undying loyalty.

In the 73-74 season, Geg and I had gone along to watch the eventual winners, Liverpool, dump us out of the Cup. The following Monday at school I got a graphic lesson in the loyalty and pride that the casual support of Carlisle United could muster. Jeremy Higham, son of two teachers and the kid whose birthday party had put me in the stands for the first time, pledged his loyalty to Liverpool. Okay, so far, most of us had grown up supporting some flash club and Carlisle. What Jeremy did that stepped out of the unwritten rules was to turn up to the Cup tie wearing Liverpool gear and walk in with the Liverpool fans. Seeing him get his head kicked in the following Monday at school taught me a useful lesson. I knew the kids dishing out the punishment and I also knew that I didn't see them on a regular basis at Brunton Park. They sure as hell weren't around the following season when I went to most of the home games. This lot were not regular Carlisle supporters, but they could be mustered, and if you stepped out of line their punches connected with the same force as the regular supporters in the Warwick Road end.

The Liverpool crowd had been huge - over 21,000 according to the records. A year later against Fulham, the crowd was around the same size. The following week to the Fulham game we played out that dire encounter with Luton in front of less than 9,000. Like I was saying, the difference between casual and regular support is a wide gulf in Cumbria.

I'm waffling, wandering around the point, hell I don't want to go back to that place, well over half my life ago, and I'm telling you, this hurts, really bad, it hurts.

Geg and I were once again in the Waterworks end and close up to the action. This put Peter Mellor in front of us in the first half and allowed for discussions that this was the same guy who'd done it for Burnley in front of us a few years back. We already knew that the FA Cup was our only hope of glory that season and from the start we set about reminding Fulham that they had no place standing in our way. The stuff we threw at them would have humbled anyone. Hell, we'd done half as much to stuff Ipswich and they were Championship material. I read reports after the game and I've read books since. They will tell you that Mellor denied Les O' Neill, Bobby Owen and Joe Laidlaw. That doesn't begin to describe it. The midfield of Ray Train, O' Neill and Balderstone spent most of the game pumping balls forward, running into space, twisting to make passes and letting in Owen and Laidlaw. Forget the ones that nearly hit the back, the whole game was alive with chances and moves. We penned them back in the first half which put Fulham and their fear-eyed defence within easy sight and abuse hurling range of the Waterworks end. Trust me here, they knew they had a game on! Every move, every pass to a running blue, every corner, was greeted with roars of approval. The only things that didn't go down well were the leaps, twists and suicidal dives into crowds of players that left the ball in Peter Mellor's hands. Forget the bloody score for a minute, we were brilliant, worthy of Wembley, worthy of anything and I know cos I was bloody well there.

The half-time scores were an opportunity to discuss the next round, the possibility of drawing West Ham who hadn't been that far above us in class in the league game and to agree that Fulham just couldn't bloody last another 45 minutes like the last one. To give Fulham their due, the old heads at the back were keeping things calm, but there must have been white shirted defenders cradled in Bobby Moore's arms in that dressing room at half-time. 'Please Bobby, please, don't make me go out there again!'

Alec Stock, a bloke who'd always struck me as an unlikely manager given his schoolmasterly distance and seeming lack of emotional involvement, was in charge of Fulham. He must have said enough to get their shattered nerves back in shape because they emerged for the second half. And they got more of the same. To put this in context, this was the opening of *Saving Private Ryan*, those white shirted Londoners were storming the beach and our gunners were picking them off at will. Shots, headers, corners, all now at the far end from Geg and I, were raining in.

Then they got a break . . . I don't want to go there . . . please don't make me write this. Peter Carr's defensive skills were never the equal of an Emlyn Hughes, but he was usually sharp, fast on his feet and capable of clearing a dangerous ball into the midfield even if he wasn't going to run it there himself as opponents trailed in his wake. Like Bobby Parker, he was redoubtable, a stalwart, and he'd take on an attacker with a reputation. We didn't have the best defence on the planet, but they pulled for each other. Until that second half. Carr and Alan Ross misread each other with a dangerous, but containable ball heading towards the Waterworks goal. The misunderstanding left Ross stranded and stretching to hold it at the last minute. He didn't smother it, he pushed it out into the path of . . . .

I remember seeing it hit the back of the net, I was probably too stunned to look away. It took months in my mind, but the television replay on ITV the following day confirmed that ball moving pretty damn quick. I don't think any single goal conceded has ever gutted me as much. I'm old enough to know better these days and like waking up the following morning with someone you can't believe beside you, like the stunts I've pulled drunk and regretted sober, like my worst moments of blindness and stupidity - trust me on this I was the only bloke on the planet who didn't know she was a lesbian and I asked her out!!!! - like every moment that could just come back to haunt me, and like the worst cold sweat, stomach churning embarrassment of your life, the one you might think of now if I ask you to, that goal lives on in my mind as strong, sickening and downright bloody undeserved as it was that day in March, 1975. Carlisle United 0 Fulham 1, and it was our Cup that year. The same team that we humbled for 89 minutes that year made it to Wembley where, in one of the most one sided and least entertaining Cup finals of the Seventies, they were deservedly beaten by West Ham 2-0. West Ham were mid-table mediocrity on legs that season, even if they did do the double over us. If they were good enough for Wembley and Europe, then we were good enough too.

I think Geg's mum was still driving the 1100 at that time. I have a vague recollection of heading home, full of chips, still feeling empty inside and listening to the round-up on the radio. The bit I remember as if it was yesterday is 'Diddy' David Hamilton, Radio 1 DJ, 'celebrity' Fulham fan and gloating, spewmongus Southern git, talking gleefully about the FA Cup result and how it had been well worth his while hiring a plane with a few mates to come all the way to Brunton Park to see it. The obvious follow up story, the one about how the staff at Carlisle airport had covered the runway in wet mud, given the fire brigade the rest of the day off, and wreaked a small amount of playful vengeance for a massive injustice was sadly absent from the radio.

'Diddy' David was never exactly required listening for anyone this side of complete sad bastard status, but his show did have the unusual habit of playing some class country rock amongst the lightweight garbage. The odd Eagles, Poco or Doobie Brothers track was no longer worth the grief, and I gave up on the swine from that day. I guess he and his pals felt deflated enough wandering away from Wembley that year, but then they'd seen justice done on the pitch. West Ham were worth their win in the final, while Fulham weren't worth their place in the velvet bag for the semi-final draw.

Alan Ross was the master of understatement and, frankly, his skills on the pitch didn't extend to glamour or charisma in an interview situation. Speaking to *The Big Match* the following day he simply said, 'I let the lads down.' Well, maybe. I find it hard to blame Ross considering how much he gave to the club and me over the years. Ross made one slip, Peter Mellor was outstanding to an unbelievable / cold sweat nightmare degree. Somewhere along the line things got seriously screwed up and having not wanted to write about it at all I now can't stop going on about that game and what should've been. A year or so before, Poland had effectively dumped England out of the 1974 World Cup finals with a performance that included improbable goalkeeping theatrics from Jan Tomashowski - a man dubbed a 'clown' by Brian Clough. Incidentally, I haven't a clue how to spell the Polish guy's surname, but if you saw that match I'll bet you still remember him. Well, Carlisle v Fulham was injustice on that scale!

So, that First Division excursion was a season of slow sliding torment with added agony and injustice but it had its good moments. I was back in the fold, I cared about this team and I belonged on those terraces, every one of them. I stood on every part of the ground at some point that season. I was growing up and the First Division adventure went hand in hand with adventures into unexplored territory in other areas of my life. In football and life there was plenty effort and when these efforts delivered results they were brilliant. I saw so many games that season, but it is the moments in this chapter that stick with me. Eddie Prudham crocked first time out, carried off against Chelsea and never likely to shoot us out of trouble after that. Hughie McIlmoyle, a legend with heart but short of pace. Alan Ross brave to the point of heartbreaking and still a hero to us all, but blaming himself for the Cup exit. Passing round the wine and talking midfield dynamos at the West Ham game. And the well of emotion I can still touch from watching that team stand in the centre circle and salute the 9,000 odd diehards who'd come to see them beat Wolves when there was nothing but pride to play for. We'd been there with them and felt it all.

Somewhere along the line I'd found a way of belonging to that team that would see me through my life from this point on. Older and not so romantic, I still cared enough to hurt over the results, but I was also realistic enough to know what was going on. On balance we deserved that relegation. Not as much as some pundits would suggest, but we'd made our own mistakes and the lack of a squad big enough to sustain a reserve team really told on us when key players - like Les O' Neill - were out. I could see this, but I still cared. The love for this team that had started with something like infatuation for the legends was older and more mature. I could see the faults, and when the rumour spread that we'd turned down £110,000 for Laidlaw I could manage outright shock. He might have been our leading scorer, but £110,000 for Joe Laidlaw? I'd cheer him on because he was our 'Flying Pig', but I knew in reality he was at the right level at Brunton Park.

So this was an older, more realistic love at a pretty unrealistic time of my life. To put this in perspective, my idea of romance at the end of that season involved turning up at some party populated with foreign exchange students, downing enough alcohol to get me heady before the first side of the progressive rock masterpiece slapped on the deck by the sixth formers came to an end, and then heading off to extend international relations without the aid of conversation. Looking back on the whole thing, the football love was easily the better part of the bargain. It taught me how to build a love that would last. Accept the faults, work on the good bits and keep on reminding yourself why it matters. By contrast the only thing that my approach to relations with the opposite sex taught me was that the world was surprisingly full of girls who were as desperate as me.

And finally . . . if you're a true blue don't do the anorak bit and go out of your way to remind me that the crowd at that Wolves game was nearly 10,000. 9,707 according to the generally definitive *Lads In Blue*. I know, and three people told me I'd got the crowd figure wrong before this book even went to the printers. I didn't get it wrong, I just took away a few hundred to allow for the Wolves fans. There were an amazing amount of them around that day and I know cos I bloody well saw them. I'd give them four hundred at least, maybe more. Which means, allowing for a few casual observers, our bed rock, First Division support who came when it didn't matter any more must have been around 9,000. Okay? Now quit bothering me!

Blue Nightmare #5

IT IS AUGUST the 16th, 1977, and *Border News and Look Around* is building to its usual frenetic climax with the nail biting will he / won't he lost tabby cat story to close the news round up, when the chubby form of Alan Cartner - yeah, remember him Cumbrians?!!!! - is handed a piece of paper. With his usual unflappable delivery, Alan continues the broadcast.

'Some late news just in. A Carlisle shopkeeper was injured today when she was hit by a flying coin thrown by a man attempting to pay for a newspaper. This report from the scene . . . .'

The picture cuts to shocked looking shopkeeper with an assistant holding a towel to her face and attempting to stem the flow of blood. The shopkeeper is pale and rambling. The reporter can't get in a question before the shopkeeper starts.

'He was average size, looking young and fairly fit. He'd already got the paper, but he insisted on standing back thirty yards to shoot the change at me. He could have passed it, there were people in a better position to hand me the change, but he shot it at me with all the force he could manage. He was almost on target but look at me.'

The assistant dabs away with the towel. The Border TV reporter gets in a question and manages the investigative depth beloved of tea time viewers to local television all over the country. 'So you got a look at this man. Could you describe him?'

'Too right,' gulps the shop keeper. 'Scrawny growth of beard, blue shirt with a huge wide white stripe, fit looking bloke. I'd reckon he could fend off a challenge. When he lined up to shoot I knew there was no stopping him. I'm telling you it was HIM!!!! You know HIM!!!!!!!! ARGHHHH!!!!!!!!!!!'

She crumbles in a heap, the reporter muscling in front to say something, but the shot cuts back to the studio where Alan Cartner has managed more animation in his expression than most viewers believed possible. Alan looks into the camera lens like a man confronted by the imminent certainty of his own worst life and death nightmare. A dark shadow falls over Alan's face and the shape of a man moves into shot, too close to the camera to make out, and carrying heavy bundles under both arms. The man moves in close to the speechless form of the bulky presenter and grunts six chilling words . . . 'Like a pie, don't you Alan?'

Cartner remains speechless as the man, out of focus but clearly in Carlisle kit, shuffles backwards. He is soon out of shot, but the fading sounds of his studs on the studio floor and Cartner's mute-faced death watch give his position away. He must be all of 35 five yards back before the onslaught starts. A hail of Brunton Park scotch pies reign in on the presenter's pudgy face in quick succession. Cartner's

74

terror is obvious, but the aim is ever so slightly off and the pies glance off his chubby cheeks, spatter his shirt and smack into his forehead.

'Nooo!!!!!!,' he screams into the endless hail of missiles before scooping chunks of minced beef and gravy off his face and clothing and forcing them into his mouth. Within a minute his screams are muffled by the mulch in his mouth, each thick gurgle dislodging a plug of half chewed pie and spattering his desk in brown goo. The hail from a distance continues, pies bouncing off the Border TV Michelin Man as his increasingly frenzied attempts to down the lot hasten the approach of the grim reaper. Less than five minutes from the start of the assault, Cartner is collapsed on his desk, shovelling in pies with both hands and taking slightly off target hits to the head. He appears to be choking, the end must be close, the screen fades to blackness. Cartner gasps through cheekfuls of pies . . . 'It's HIM, it's HIM!!!! . . . '

The following day several thousand Cumbrians swear blind they saw the death of Elvis screened live from Carlisle.

Chapter Five - Mike Barry

MENTIONED FOR THE FIRST TIME IN THIS CHAPTER

Mike Barry - Midfielder with fierce shot, some positional sense and an occasional lust for glory.

Mick McCartney - Short on finesse, strong on being strong. Midfield forward thinking player with ability to score goals.

Ian McDonald - Lanky centre-half, willing and sometimes able.

Bobby Moncur - Formerly famous as captain of Newcastle United. He had a contract with us that required him to manage.

Billy Rafferty - Big centre forward, good at the skilful stuff and handy in a goalmouth bundle. Some of the best news in a generally poor period at Brunton Park.

Trevor Swinburne - A goalie. Shared the number 1 shirt with Alan Ross from this point on.

'FOOKIN 'ELL.'

WUZZELL had spoken. It was somewhere in early August, 1978, in the changing cabin that stood on the edge of the main fitting shop in the old section of the British Sidac factory in Wigton. I'd been working at Sidac since mid-July. A Summer job to stock-pile cash before continuing my education in the hope of finally learning to read and write. Well, a Cumbrian is nowt without ambition, right?

'Fookin 'ell, what's with that then?'

I wasn't ignoring him, I just didn't realise he was talking about me. I knew I'd dropped my cheque book and once I'd got my boiler suit piled onto the bench I was going to pick up the cheque book, stuff it in the top pocket of my denim jacket and head off into town to get some cash. This is Wigton, 1978. Rumour has it that *Tomorrow's World*'s feature on the cash dispenser was edited from the edition of the programme shown in West Cumbria in case it provoked a mass panic. Imagine it, getting cash out of a wall with no hope of stopping to chat with the person doling it out. In the first two years of automatic cash machines being introduced to my part of the world - I think we're talking somewhere around 1995 - there were 53 reported incidents of people breaking bones in their hand after they cuffed cash machines for failing to answer back when asked 'Hows't tha doin'?' One man is still in secure psychiatric care after he spent three hours talking to a cash machine in Maryport. 'I don't get it,' he told the ambulancemen who prized him off the machine. 'That bastard went to school with my l'al brother and now he won't fookin' speak to me.'

Cumbrians. We're big on the human contact bit, but some of us get confused pretty quick.

'Fookin' 'ell,' so back to Wuzzel. I can't honestly remember where he came from. I'd been to school with a lot of the lads in the factory, but I don't remember Wuzzel. This would put him - probably - in school around Silloth or Aspatria. Whatever, it finally dawned on me that he was interested in my cheque book. The thing that interested him wasn't the obvious bit about it hitting the floor. It was the pictures on the cheques. A dormouse, a badger, a woodpecker and some other animal I can't recall. I'd requested a pictorial cheque book because each one issued put a pathetic amount of money into animal charities and - what with lining myself up for college and all - my poncey posh-git liberal tendencies were starting to show.

On the other hand this chequebook was different and that made it fair play for a laugh. By the end of the afternoon the joke had developed and everyone was getting in on the act.

'You can get a cheque book for owt now. Shirtlifters have their own l'al chequebook with a fookin' great lump of lead stuck to it with a chain. You're bent over so long with your arse stuck out trying to pick it up that . . . '

Hilarity ensued.

How we've moved from the shuffle out of the First Division in 1975 to my first stint in the factory will take some explaining, but in reality, this shift is down to one thing as far as this book goes. My life, and the part of it I devoted to Carlisle United, appears to exist in moments over these three years. We're talking teenage years; wilful depravity, uncessesary sex, drugs and rock 'n' roll, and Carlisle United somewhere at hand most of the time. But we're talking moments. Key moments that seem to define my life at this time. One of them put me in the fitting shop, slopping grease out of the cracks in my hand with Swarfeager and heading up into town for a lunchtime pint. I was never likely to work my entire life in a factory. Statistically speaking, mouthy posh gits are in short supply in fitting shops. By the time I stepped into the shop I'd completed my A' levels, put in an application for University and read at least one book with no pictures in it. I'd pulled off this and the ability to survive the knock about, hammer weilding, humour of the factory because I'd thrown myself into other things apart from football. In a fitting shop, labelled as a posh student slumming it for the money, you can easily go over the line. The line of being different, you know, like insisting on having little badgers drawn in your chequebook. Too far over this line and the playful ribbing turns into

77

grease down your underpants. I avoided that and made it through the first of a handful of factory stints the same way I'd made it through school.

If Carlisle United helped me grow into the ass-whupping psychopathic jungle of the Nelson Thomlinson School then by the start of the fifth year there were experiences I needed to get some other way. Or I *chose* to get some other way. I'd been up and down with the team and the emotional bond forged in that top flight season was there for my whole life, but the prospect of Second Division football, the looming excitement of other things in my life, the total lack of passionate football fans amongst the best looking girls in the school, and the fierce relationship between my increasing income and the rapidly growing list of vicarious pleasures available for cash, left Carlisle United holding their own in a competitive market.

They were there, like my parents were there, like the school buildings were there, like my stereo was there. In later years I'd be obliged to read massive and worthy books full of sociological jargon attempting to describe the experience of being a teenager. At one point I figured on writing my own book which I whittled down to less than twenty words. It would read:

When you're a teenager
Stuff is there
You deal with it
Sometimes life is brilliant
Sometimes it's shit

That about sums it up for me. Now let's talk about moments, and Carlisle United. Moments wise those difficult teenage years were packed. It wasn't all sex, drugs and rock 'n' roll, but I remember those things better than I remember the Geography lessons on the ins and outs of the climate of East Anglia. The sex was the usual predictable stuff, discovering that there were girls out there who liked me and who weren't drunk and desperate when they said it. Figuring I could sustain something approaching a relationship and getting involved with all the usual head on collision of out and out sincerity and out and out lies that it involves in those years. Like I said, we're talking about moments - good and bad.

A GOOD HONEST ONE
NEIL - I've always liked you.
A GIRL - Really?
NEIL - Yeah, I just never had the courage to say it.
(SNOG!!!!!!)

You can mock all you like, she was lovely, what I said was true, we had a handful of beautiful months together and were still in touch until we were about thirty.

A BAD DISHONEST ONE

A GIRL - Do you always come so quick?

NEIL - No, it's never happened to me before.

A GIRL - You mean that?

NEIL - Sure, it didn't happen any of the other 2,742 times I've done it!

Of course, it wasn't all sex and drugs and rock 'n' roll. Sex wise it was happening, not as often as I wanted, but it was happening. Rock 'n' roll wise, I went to my first proper gig - The Sutherland Brothers and Quiver - in Carlisle in December, 1975. Within a year I was a gig regular, there to see anyone who dared play in the city. By the time I left school and entered into discussions about animal cheque books at British Sidac, my album collection was getting pretty varied and well into three figures. Drugs wise, the opportunity would have been a decent thing. Hell, I was sixteen before I saw anything passing around the school and I was in the lower sixth before I saw any gear worth buying!

Life's rich tapestry was spreading before me in West Cumbrian pubs, clubs and the occasional bedroom . . . and Brunton Park was still standing. It took less time than I thought to change things. Carlisle's fall into the old Second Division coincided with my own fall back to the main school building. Here prefects stalked a building where the floors lacked the blood concealment properties of the middle school and there was some semblance of law and order. You could read books in the library and rumour had it that some kids actually did some work!

Carlisle and myself had both returned to familiar territory. We both proceeded to have our moments. My first sighting of the new squad - pretty much the old squad - was on *Match of the Day*. Away at Chelsea they took a 3-1 pasting in a game that marked the halfway point of a four match losing streak that left us with one point from five games and, I think, 21 teams above us in the division. Chris Balderstone had left and the midfield was missing his calming influence but, more than anything, the stalwart team were lacking shape and passion. But, there were moments. In the Chelsea game, Mike Barry picked up the ball in the middle of their half, lined up, took aim and proceeded to unleash a thunderbolt of a shot that would see action for months in the opening sequence of ITV's *The Big Match*, win their goal of the month competition and figure highly in their goal of the season consideration. What a moment! Shame about the result.

As I write this I would say that the best goal I ever saw a Carlisle player score from the point of view of being a paying customer came in October, 1994. The best goal I've ever seen a Carlisle player score anytime, anywhere, left Mike Barry's boot and screamed into the back of the Chelsea net on August the 23rd, 1975. My Dad's birthday.

In October, Alan Ashman left Carlisle and Dick Young took charge of the team. Let's do the anorak bit here. Dick Young had never managed a senior side before and he was 58 years old when he took charge. This - if I'm correct - makes him the oldest management debutant in Football League history and gives Carlisle the curious distinction of having the oldest and youngest first time managers in the League at various times in their history. Ivor Broadis became the youngest ever football league manager when he moved to Carlisle in August, 1946, at the age of 23. He also became the first manager to officially transer himself when he moved to Sunderland as a player in 1949. Not that I gave a toss about Ivor in the growing gloom of the Autumn of 1975.

Results on the park weren't shaping up. On some Saturdays my loyalties were seriously divided between Brunton Park, Pink Panther Records and the four screen cinema down at the bottom of Botchergate. Life in Carlisle eh, so much action, so few hours on a Saturday afternoon!

I never seriously thought we'd go down, even when the league table screamed 'relegation!' at anyone who'd got eyes to read. Dick Young had been there or thereabouts at Carlisle for as long as I'd been going. He'd been the trainer before taking over the team and although he couldn't produce much magic on the pitch, he changed things around enough to get some fight out of some of the players some of the time. This was still the same team that had matched the best in the country stride for stride 12 months before. Curiously, it wasn't The Flying Pig, Ray Train or Les O' Neill who really got stuck in. O' Neill would finish his professional career in his early thirties at the end of that season, and once our new found status as second string plodders in search of shape and rhythm was well established, it was open season for bets on when and where Ray Train, Joe Laidlaw and a few of the others would go. To their eternal credit, Alan Ross, Dennis Martin, and Bobby Owen stuck it out. One way and another, Ross had a nightmare start to the new season. Out of condition and favour, he didn't play until the winter had well and truly set in. Whatever, Ross, Martin and Owen had never let me down and they didn't start that season.

With Carlisle United flailing in search of shape, there was a lot of furious chasing of off-target passes. A lot of standing, staring and head shaking as York and Oldham ran into spaces that were never made available to the likes of Everton and Arsenal. In the face of this it was the unlikely lads in our squad who stood out. The visions of Eddie Prudham I can most easily conjure in my mind have his injury prone body collapsed on the Brunton Park turf after eye watering challenges in the First Division games against Leeds and Chelsea. However, if I really try, I can picture him chasing everything and bundling the ball into the back of the Portsmouth net the day after my sixteenth birthday when we finally managed a league win in our sixth game of the campaign. Mike Barry's screamer of a goal ranks as another sublime moment from a player who'd existed on the fringes of the First Division squad.

If you'd blinked in the First Division you could have missed Mick McCartney's contribution to the campaign, but Dick Young drafted him in to add some bite to the front end of midfield the following season. He managed a few goals and by the end of that season the shaggy main and odd shaped body of young Phil Bonnyman had also added itself to the squad.

Maybe it was my life, maybe what I remember is true, but that team stand out in my mind as an outfit that put in a serious amount of running, passing, shouting and sweat to almost no useful purpose. Stand on the terraces and follow John Gorman, Alan Ross or Bobby Owen with your eyes and you'd see a decent player, working hard and doing all the right things. Watch the shape of the game and you'd see a team with enough skill and class to hold most in the Second Division being humbled by lesser mortals with more sense of purpose and organisation. Lots of effort, some brilliant moments, long way to go. That was Carlisle United 75/76 and my life as well. Which means that looking back all these years later it wasn't so bad.

I've forgotten the boring Friday nights stuck in front of *Starsky and Hutch* waiting for my life to start, but I can still remember the odd events, like the Saturday lunchtime in March when I staggered out of Carlisle station and found myself amongst a mob of Midland accents. The Carlisle scarf was well enough out of sight to keep these Nottingham Forest supporters off my back, but I wasn't prepared for the odd experience of bumping into a bunch of suits standing on the pavement. The strange thing was the presence of the odd black face amongst the well dressed young blokes. On this evidence alone I knew they weren't Cumbrians. And then I spotted Cloughie. I kid you not. Right there, within easy bricking distance of his own supporters, stood Cloughie surrounded by his team. It was the first week of March, 1976. What they were doing there I don't know. Perhaps train travel with the fans was a necessary economy given the massive wage bill involved in keeping Larry Lloyd and Viv Anderson on the same pitch. Perhaps their coach had broken down, maybe Brian fancied a swig of best quality British Rail whisky on his way to that intimidating date with destiny in Carlisle. Either way it is one of those moments that stands in my mind. It was also one of our better performances that season. Not exactly classy but certainly committed, we held the future European champions 1-1 at Fortress Brunton. Although, the whole idea of Fortress Brunton was starting to look pathetic. Beaten at home by Notts County and Leyton Bloody Orient, come on.

If you want a measure of how far we fell in terms of fighting spirit that year it is worth looking at the knock out competitions. Dumped out of the FA Cup at the first hurdle and staggering into the second round of the League Cup mainly on the strength of a pathetic own goal that killed off the impressive fighting spirit of Gillingham. 1-0 and they were still up for a fight. Everton - over whom we'd done the double the previous season - put paid to the League Cup hopes. Add the FA Cup and League Cup 'runs' together and we scored three goals in three games.

Look a bit harder at these figures and the only one of those three goals credited to a Carlisle player was Joe Laidlaw's opening strike against hard working Gillingham. I can remember Gillingham scurrying around like hell at Brunton Park with every hope that they'd level the score. I'm struggling to remember the Flying Pig's all important first strike. Given the scarcity of United goals that year and my usually reliable memory this maybe says something about the quality of Laidlaw's goal. Think a bit deeper and this says we weren't that bloody impressive the season after we fell from the top flight.

I still found some things to cheer and - pretentious as it sounds - some things to relate to. The first signs of this were in that Division Two season. In the first stages of a few important things in life, puffing away on the odd Malboro, swilling a few cans of bitter here and there and discovering that the the dog eared copy of *The Joy Of Sex* I'd aquired in a second hand shop within weeks of its publication was indeed anatomically correct, I'd hit that teenage alchemy stage. The stage when you realise that all of this stuff works but - on the odd occasion it works for you - you're not sure how exactly you pulled it off!

Sorry, I know that pun was a stinker. Anyway, the popular view of alchemy is that these mystical sorts sweated away in damp smelling laboratories, following a mixture of magic and instinct and occasionally discovering something worthwhile in their pursuit of the ever elusive method of turning base metals into pure gold. In a manner of speaking your average teenager hits the same thing. Gold, for a teenager, is someone to get really close to, being monumentally pissed, doing something seriously out of order, the usual teenage kicks. The alchemy bit is that you can try the same stunts in the same way three days later and come off looking like a total loser. Sometimes, a good hard look at life will show you that you are not alone. Briefly, I got this from Carlisle United in that Division Two season after the big one. It would happen a little like this.

A few hard passes out of defence. John Gorman teeth bared, running away down the left and laying it off to Dennis Martin. Martin looking for space. The confidence and shape of Division One wasn't there, but you'd still cheer the speed and the attempt. With Frank Clarke running for space up front, Martin would see the oncoming defender, lay it off to Mike Barry and . . . 'Shit no, he's gonna shoot again!'

Somewhere nearby an Iraqi, freezing and miserable in Carlisle as he completed his pilot training at our friendly local 'airport', would be grasping the wheel of a light aircraft, taking the controls for the first time in his life. Flying clear of the city over local fields he would see the oncoming projectile, register inside a split second that it was a football, and fill his newly acquired Marks and Spencer's thermal underwear as the spinning hunk of leather and wind rattled his windscreen and put grey hairs in his lovingly combed moustache. Whiter than he would ever believe possible he would turn to his instructor and say, 'Please, how does it happen?'

82

'It happen because Mike Barry can't forget the screaming thunderbolt he netted against Chelsea.'

'Please, what is Mike Barry?'

'Never you mind, son. Just forget it and fly the fuckin' plane, there's a good lad.' Mike Barry and me had more in common during those days than I'd care to admit today. A history of memorable moments, spectacular success in small amounts, and a habit of trying to repeat the greatest moments and coming off looking like a total tosser. Apart from the totally unexpected sight of Cloughie and the lads at the Citadel, my clearest memories of that season are Dick Young urging the team forward in the final minutes regardless of the score, a lot of effort to less effect than the previous season, the general hope that we'd get a result, and Mike Barry blasting up, wide and across in fruitless attempts to stage another encore to that magical *Big Match* moment at Chelsea. The number of good moves wrecked by his attempts at an encore doesn't bear thinking about. Then again, it was one hell of a goal.

Over 90 minutes we weren't that bad. At least not as far as I could see. We never lost by more than a single goal at home. Over a month we were worse because of the consistent habit of letting points slip away and the occasional habit of just lying down and playing dead. Over a season we were genuinely worrying. 19th place might have been safe from relegation, but the presence of Hull, Orient and Plymouth above us said it all. In comparision to the previous season, we were unrecognisable despite most of the same faces and the same shirt.

Mike Barry's attempts to rekindle his greatest moment provided one link between my life and the team. However, like Carlisle United 12 months after the top flight adventure, the main change in my life was the company I kept. I don't know exactly when it happened. Somewhere between the desperate and hard fought and packed out home draw with Sunderland (in which Mike Barry managed another goal, but one that would never make goal of the season), and the acres of space on the terraces 4-2 hammering dished out to the similarly shapeless Bristol Rovers. But whenever, Geraint stopped speaking to me. I've got to get this one into context.

Since our early adventures to games we'd changed a little, but - by and large - we'd stayed together. We were in the same 'band,' a motley assortment who'd meet at my place, gather round the piano and bash away on our cheap and cherished guitars and dish out ritual murder to country rock standards before plumbing the real depths by performing our own compositions. The last time I tried to play the reel to reel tape of these sessions, the drive belt on my machine broke before facing a test the technicians at Tandberg could never have imagined. Geraint was now 'Geg.' He brewed his own lager, sat next to me in the generally saveable set who were destined for O-levels, owned a passable Yamaha acoustic, expressed a fondness for Neil Young before I'd really got it with the great man, and generally hung out like one of the gang. One day in 1976, he simply quit speaking to me. I still can't tell you why.

To the best of my knowledge his girlfriend didn't howl my name at the height of their most mind-blowing physical moments. Incidentally, I went out with her off and on much later in life, and the only time I heard her really howl my name out loud she was bawling me out for forgetting to tell her to turn off a main road. All other speculation here is pretty damn pointless. Geg and my other good mate Phil Nelson would often rib each other mercilessly, and Phil laid off speaking to me the same day, but by that afternoon he was back on side and we stayed mates until he left school later that year.

Geg just quit speaking and that was that. Years later, with a bunch of mutual friends and Geg just back from his latest covert stay in the USA, we headed out to see the blindingly brilliant *Rust Never Sleeps*, Neil Young's second movie. Geg was back in the gang and the last to be picked up. There was some general discussion on the way to his house about whether he'd speak to me. We were 22 by this point and the general agreement was that he would. I think it was Chris Storey who brought it up when we arrived, Geg mumbled something that sounded like 'Yes', and I got in a reasonable one liner. 'So, Geg, how've you been for the last six years?'

So anyway, 19th place and a mate that used to be. The 75/76 season.

That summer, on the strength of about one week's hard revision for my O-levels I headed into the sixth form. Geg headed to the local Tech and work as an electrician, and the football team we both loved headed for some serious changes. The team that had chased and closed down the best the Second Division could offer no more than two years before were dismantled within a matter of weeks. Bill Green went in one direction to West Ham, Joe Laidlaw went in another to Doncaster. Ray Train had already joined Sunderland, playing his last game for Carlisle the day I collided with Cloughie. The team that took the field in early September, 1976, to play Hull couldn't, in all honesty, claim to be the same team that had taken us into the First Division. We fought out a draw, looked less than impressive and - true to form - Mike Barry managed a spectacular moment of skill in the third game of the season to hammer home our only goal of the 90 minutes. Then again, *The Big Match* were never keen on dour encounters between unfashionable teams and that strike would exist for posterity in no more than 6,000 minds.

The Neil that took to the sixth form around the same time was also a changed animal. Rock music had delivered more seriously mind blowing thrills than Carlisle United in the previous season and the priorities were slowly shifting. The dawn of the sixth form was also the dawn of serious party time, hell I was getting served in pubs, getting somewhere with the opposite sex and getting a sense of what life had to offer. The love affair with Carlisle United was a comfortable constant in a changing world.

A comfortable constant that took me to a smattering of games over two seasons in which we plodded and occasionally burned our way through the Second Division. Those next two seasons and years at school were real flurries of moments. The way it makes sense to me now is that the stuff that normally gives your life some kind of shape and direction was pretty much out of the window for me. There was this vague idea that the A-levels I was doing would lead me somewhere, although in all honesty I hadn't much idea where. There was a timetable for the week at school, the added commitment of part-time work (mainly at Stan Palmer's Filling Station near the throbbing all action urban sprawl of Bolton Low Houses - well, it does have a decent pub), and the problem of finding time to spend the wages and any other cash I could earn. None of these things really forced my life into any kind of regular shape and my main commitment for the two years of the sixth form was to having a decent time. On a good day I was something of a party animal, on a bad day I was somewhere the other side of out of order. The final verdict on those years - decent parties, shame about the A-level results. The final verdict on those two seasons at Brunton Park - decent moments, shame about the league positions. We'll get to the football in a minute, but I didn't get to it anywhere near as much as I wanted or used to. It was there, like my bedroom was there, familiar, comforting, occasionally surprising and, once in a while, the source of earthmoving and memorable moments.

I've got to give my parents their due. One thing that happened during those decent partying years was a steady stream of my mates who kept coming around to our house. This isn't as mundane as it sounds. 'My house' was out in the country, over half a mile from the nearest village, over four miles from anything you'd call a town and more than seven miles from Wigton where I went to school. It would, quite frankly, always have been easier for me to go to them. My folks were brilliant. That is brilliant as in tolerant, generally non-interfering and a stable influence. Years later, in the same position myself, I'd come to appreciate just how good they were. More than anything they cared about me and my sister and we never doubted that.

As bad as it got was my Dad once saying to me he thought I might have 'grown out' out getting up early to be in The Pink Panther the second their Summer sale opened in 1977. I think he was really hacked off that this involved him giving me a lift as far as Wigton. In the great scheme of teenage traumas I've encountered in other people, this ranks on a par with a broken fingernail in terms of its devastating effects on my sanity. No wonder my remote country mansion was a prime hang out. My parents actually moved to the other end of the house around the time my sister and I hit the noisy stage and left us our own end for years. We threw some decent parties, had people round all the time, and repaid my parents' kindness by leaving everything standing. There was some serious damage done, but it was almost entirely concentrated on people. The house is still there.

85

Peter Crossman was one of those people. Drunk to the point of complete insensibility, he left one of our parties in the back of a car and stayed comatose with a few mumbles thrown in for effect. The poor saps trying to return him to his loving home were reduced to scouring Wigton phone boxes for a directory in the hope of locating Crossman Towers. Eventually they managed this, but their loving care ran short when it came to unloading the dead weight from the car. Smacking the back of his head on the door sill and the pavement, Peter ended up with a headache to remember. Years later I'd encounter him ordering a pint for a jelly baby which stuck out of his overcoat, convincing the assembled masses in the Wigton's only Chinese takeaway that he was a complete lunatic and then deepening his understanding of mental disorders in general by taking a long term job as a mental nurse. I'd like to think that a lifetime in which craziness would figure large was aided and abetted by the insane moments he and others managed to conjure up in my house. Then again, I'd like to think that I can still run ten miles without feeling the effects.

I can remember getting pretty close to my girlfriend upstairs at one party and hearing a massive ruck starting outside which involved a gang running Peter Crossman to ground and him screaming 'You'll never take me alive.' Great days, even better nights.

I could still rouse myself to go to Brunton Park, although working many Saturdays in the filling station left me pumping petrol into cars sporting blue scarves from the windows. In the season to May, 1977, I spent as much time talking to Carlisle fans as I filled up their cars as I did standing with them on the terraces. The following year I probably managed more time talking at the filling station than I did at Brunton Park. Whilst I was getting up to speed in other areas of enjoyment I was falling behind in terms of football and the problem was complicated by having friends who generally gave something less than a shit about Carlisle United.

My first sightings of the new signings were often accompanied by the kind of hard listening to others on the terraces that had been a feature of the first forays into this territory a few years before. One new signing needed no introduction. George McVitie had been a favourite in the first team I'd seen before heading off to West Brom. In 1976 he was back. The mantle of Hughie McIlmoyle, Bob Hatton and Joe Laidlaw had now fallen on Billy Rafferty, a summer of 1976 signing from Plymouth Argyle. Big, effective and clinical in close, he could score, even if he couldn't always chase back and rob the opposition in midfield.

He was on target when we stuffed it to Sheffield United in February. A 4-1 win by our lowly placed team. Our dominance that day was so great that Bobby Parker netted the second goal. Parker played almost 400 games for Carlisle, including some serious stalwart stuff into and out of Division One, but scoring was never his strong point. This was the only time I saw him score and he only managed half a dozen goals in a career with us that went from the mid-Seventies to mid-Eighties.

His longest goal famine lasted over five years. You might usefully say he was 'pacing' his forays up front so that day was a treat.

The following weekend, if memory serves me correctly, was the day that Geg headed off to an away game with Michael Asbridge. Despite his genuine Cumbrian pedigree, Michael had a darker skin that your average puce coloured Northern specimen and with the kindness, keen observation and rigid adherance to politically correct codes of behaviour for which Cumbrians are famed the world over, we'd nicknamed him 'Paki'. Whatever, he and Geg headed off to Burnley where in addition to watching us plummet to a 2-0 defeat, Geg got hit by a chunk of masonry which served as a calling card at Turf Moor. Our paths still crossed, like the odd occasion I'd find myself filling up his motorbike with two stroke petrol. He'd grunt rather than talk on these occasions, and he wasn't big on eye to eye contact. My presence at the pumps probably gave Geg some problems. Stan Palmer's was, and still is, a good filling station and it wasn't everyone around the area who sold two stroke.

On the evidence of the acres of concrete visible at the Sheffield United match there were more people than me missing out on games. There were days I was glad to be away from it. The 6-0 home defeat to mid-table Southampton was one such occasion. Martin Burleigh had replaced Alan Ross in goal for the middle part of the season. He leaked 12 goals in January and I wanted to think that my return along with Alan Ross for the 4-1 stuffing of Sheffield United marked a new start in that miserable season. It didn't.

Saddled with those odd, hard to fathom patterns of bogey teams, coincidences and omens, that dog football teams, we continued our downward progress. The early March visit of Nottingham Forest brought the same game at the same time of the year as the previous season with the same result, 1-1, and the same scorer, Dennis Martin. Not a great day out, but better than the crunch match I missed through work in May when Bristol Rovers, whom we'd seen humbled in a season saving performance at the end of the previous campaign, turned up for the last home game. Both of us were in the same relegation mire we'd faced the season before. 2-0 up at half-time, we'd saved our season in 45 minutes. I filled cars for some miserable people that night and got the same story. The disbelief in what they'd witnessed in that second half. The papers recorded Jimmy Hamilton, Bristol's attack minded winger as man of the match and the architect of a season saving second half in which Bristol Rovers scored three goals. The people to whom I spoke reckoned we should have closed them down, penned them back and / or broken Jimmy Hamilton's legs.

Based on a handful of games and a lot of talk over the pumping of petrol, I reckoned it was mainly a defensive problem. My target for major blame was lanky centre back, Ian McDonald, who committed the unforgivable crime of not being Bill Green. Bobby Moncur's management, which had started in the winter of 1976, didn't much impress me either. I moaned to the few friends of mine who cared about football that the best decisions Moncur made all season involved dropping himself after January and retiring as a player at the end of the season. Moncur's last game was also Martin Burleigh's last and that miserable January was unquestionably the worst time I'd known as a Carlisle fan.

We were deservedly relegated on goals with the two teams above us also fronting a pathetic 34 points. Billy Rafferty, and George McVitie had found the net often enough. We'd simply leaked like a sieve at the back despite the presence of John Gorman and Bobby Parker.

There were changes that summer. Including the departure of Mike Barry. Following the strike against Chelsea the man couldn't find himself with a ball and a yard of grass without the idea of a shooting opportunity entering his head. Okay, the Blue Nightmare which opened this chapter is a bit unfair, but ask a long standing Blues fan to this day, and Mike Barry means long range shot with the possibility of spectacularly successful results. A nightmare on the occasions when there was a blue shirt unmarked up front. On other occasions the nearest thing we had to a genuine crowd pleaser after Joe Laidlaw. Rafferty could get a crowd going with a goal, but Mike Barry was Mr Entertainment in the great Stan Webb and Joe Laidlaw tradition.

I could pretend I continued at the same level of support the following season with the Division Three fixture list promising the dubious delights of Chester City, Walsall, Exeter City and Lincoln City. The truth is that anyone who shared a sixth form class, dark corner at a party, back of a car, or comfy corner of a pub with me at this time won't recall me as a Carlisle United supporter. The depths of the 76/77 season were eased by the highs of some decent smoking mixtures, the presence of some good people around me and tankerloads of alcohol. I'll pull a few punches to protect the guilty and spare you a long-winded account of nights spent talking complete bollocks under the influence of various stimulants. But my love affair with the adrenaline pumping-life changing delights of Brunton Park was seriously threatened by my playing away with other adrenaline-pumping life changing delights.

Of the bits that matter, I ended up getting booted out of school twice. Once for a pretty serious suspension which lasted five weeks and resulted from a lunch-time excursion to a local offie followed by some decent drinking. The mistake we'd made was to take somebody who didn't swill the same quantities as the rest of the gang. Those of us with an income fit to sustain a drink habit had been regulars in this department for ages and finally getting rumbled at the start of the upper sixth was a shock mainly because we'd got used to shipping a few pints in this manner. Currys from the local Chinese were also a favourite of mine and there were drugs around in the school too.

There were drugs around in my body on a semi-regular basis. The whole caper started when a mate of mine had totalled a borrowed motorbike. In the convoluted logic that followed this event, the rightful owner of the said bike had been obliged to play innocent, leaving my mate copping the responsibility for taking the machine without the owners permission. The said owner then made it all up to my mate by way of off-loading a lump of dope fit to stone a regiment. Spread over many sunny afternoons at the end of the lower sixth, it regularly did the business for a handful of us and as the high summer of punk roared into top gear I could be found stoned, smiling and loving every living thing to the sounds of Pink Floyd, John Martyn and pixie-era T.Rex. Who needed Mike Barry with this lot on offer?

The rest is pretty predictable. I was banned from one pub before I was legally old enough to drink. Given the feat I was attempting to deserve this ban the night I got really out of order, I was lucky to get off so lightly. A few days later I missed the trip to casualty I really deserved by mere seconds when Paki and I dived for cover behind a wall to avoid a speeding car and its murderous occupants. Adrenaline pumping, life changing and more exciting than 90 minutes at Brunton Park!

Another time that sticks in my mind is a party, the only all-lads party I ever went to, in which my drug buddy and myself ate our way through a decent size plug of gear. I don't remember everything that night, but one thing that sticks in my mind is my crawling over the floor to tell him that the stuff I'd eaten 90 minutes earlier was kicking in big time, and my mate splitting the remaining gear and each of us swallowing half of it. Later on, I'd hear snatches of conversation, close my eyes and marvel as my mind flew off in a thousand directions at warp speed. Every half-baked, pretentious sixth form philosophy idea resolved itself in my mind into a myriad of possibilities each of which I could see in total clarity. I saw the futility of the arguments because cosmic consciousness was upon me big time. Every time I tried to open my eyes and join in I couldn't put my mouth in gear beyond a dull mumble, and the fact that it was taking me ten minutes of pathetic slobbering to tell everyone else that I was - cosmically speaking - several light years ahead of them was a source of serious amusement.

Things turned nasty later on when the second plug hit the top of my head and scrambled my brain to death-trip levels of paranoia. The speeding thought that I'd got so much poison inside me that I might not get out of the experience in the same shape I entered it was a serious bummer and a topic of conversation long after the two days it took me to get my head straight. And that gear was classified as a 'soft' drug. The hard stuff turned up later. Been there, done it, worth a look and I'm not gonna talk about it here.

In the steadily expanding world of debauchery and the collecting of memories which would assume legendary status in our gang, the night of cosmic consciousness, and several others, would be re-lived on a regular basis. With limits being steadily pushed, the odd wander down Warwick Road acted like an anchor to a safe world that existed somewhere outside my little envelope. Like eating a sherbet dab, it was a happy throwback to a different time, but not the place that was gonna change my life anymore.

The thing that strikes me now thinking back to that mid-table Third Division season, is the odd familiarity it offered in a sea of things that were changing. Speaking of familiarity, I saw Carlisle score one goal that season and it was good old George McVitie who struck home against Colchester. Shame about the three goals the opposition scored in the same game. On another occasion, well into the mind expanding period, I watched Peterborough and Carlisle bore each other stupid into a 0-0 draw over 90 minutes. I'd challenge any member of the Blue Army present that day to honestly recall anything that would qualify as a highlight. Between these two games Alan Ross managed a 15 match spell in goal, but Trevor Swinburne was the latest in a long line of the great man's understudies trying his best to get a regular sniff of the action. I was tuned in enough to credit his performances as workmanlike and lacking the class of the great Scotsman. Ross was highly visible on the two occasions when we played stunning football that season.

We'd managed to avoid Manchester United throughout our entire history. No Cup ties and never in the same division. If this sounds confusing to you younger readers then the story of how we avoided them is worth chasing up. Six years after they won the European Cup, the mighty Manchester United were humbled to the point that their last game of the season represented a 90 minute battle against relegation. To make matters worse, the opposition that day were Manchester City. In a scenario that a film producer would reject on the grounds of improbability, the bitter local rivals dumped the once proud European champions out of the top flight and the killer blow was struck when a veteran striker, who had a golden end to his career with City, struck home with the United defence beaten. That striker was Dennis Law, a former United legend and the one notable absentee from the side which had won Europe's highest football honour at Wembley in 1968. His goal condemned United to the final relegation place. And what a goal it was, an instinctive strike with his back to goal. Law's reaction to this was a mixture of shock and dejection, and he was substituted immediately.

That same season, Cumbria's finest won promotion to top flight and so the two legendary clubs spent a season in unfamiliar surroundings. Manchester United won the Second Division in 1975 and we - as has already been established - finished bottom of the First. And the moral of this story - for you youngsters out there - is that nobody has a divine right to the top flight and the greatest club of this era were slumming it within living memory.

The first meeting of the two clubs in competition came in the third round of the FA Cup, 1978. The pull of Brunton Park was still alive for me. My presence at the filling station that day suggests I didn't care anymore, but you don't know how hard I fought the urge to phone in sick. Living in an anonymous city it would have been easier to swing that one. I reasoned - rightly - that the tie would be televised. Nobody had reckoned on the complications that reduced *Match of the Day* to coverage of one half of the game. Still the 1-1 result guaranteed a replay and *Sportsnight* managed coverage of all six goals. 2-0 down at half-time, we played United to a hard fought 4-2 defeat - in other words we took them on goal for goal in the second half and looked for all the world like a team that enjoyed the prospect of turning over highly rated opposition. This Man Utd side had finished FA Cup Runners' Up in 1976 and gone on to win the same trophy in 1977 with a classic fluke of a goal. All told, it isn't too surprising that they opened their account the following season by dumping us out. The surprise was that it took a replay. Those televised matches got the old adrenaline pumping more than any visit to Brunton Park that season.

I was still playing the odd bit of football, and despite the drink and drugs, I was also heading off for the odd jog down the country lanes. The great thing about being this age is the way you can combine the lot and still manage to feel human. At least most of the time you can anyway. The first serious suggestion that I might be mortal hit me - quite literally - as the result of combining too much sex, drugs and rock 'n' roll with an attempt to be healthy. The drugs and rock 'n' roll had come the night before and I still opted for athletics in favour of cricket in the sun drenched PE session the following day. Knackered as I was, I headed off into the wooded undergrowth of the country with a girl and managed some serious physical closeness. Given that we hardly knew each other it was all a bit nervous, and somewhere on the other side of the big moment my reserves ran totally dry. She was just at the first stages of checking out if it had been alright for me when I got serious cramp. It was agony then, 20 years later it strikes me as hilarious. From my side it was obvious enough, I was moaning in agony trying to stuff one foot into the soft ground to stop the pain. I didn't know her well enough to say I'd got cramp. From her side it looked like I was still grunting in ecstasy and moving around for an instant replay. Since I'd accidentally convinced her that the Earth wouldn't stop moving for me, I couldn't come clean about what was really going on. Given that neither of us had exactly cracked the black belt in full blown sex by that point she probably took what I was doing for normal behaviour. I hope she wasn't too disappointed when she realised that some blokes just lie there and don't move afterwards.

So much for the edited highlights of the sixth form. Just trust me here, the truly outrageous bits are better off in my mind than on this page. The whole predictable point here is that the years from 16 to 19 taught me that football is a constant in a changing world. They also left me somewhere in the Premier League of party animals and turning in a steady GM Vauxhall Conference performance in the

Academic Giants League. Whilst I was finishing these competitions at the top and the bottom, Carlisle were mediocre to the point of being invisible. Tenth in the old Third Division is about as uninteresting as football can get. Without the Man Utd Cup tie that season, we were in danger of dying of apathy.

At the end of this time my highest intellectual achievement was two sorry A-levels, one of which was General Studies - an unseen exam on a range of topics that was manna from heaven to mouthy posh gits everywhere. I have a theory about this A-level. I reckon a few education minded types with studies full of books and houses full of dope smoking waster kids once got together and tried to figure a way of saving the academic futures of their offspring. Rightly figuring that the only things their kids could do well was ponce on about life, the universe, and everything, they invented A-level General Studies, stuffed it full of essay questions about life, the universe, and everything, and sat back to reap the rewards of their kids who would clean up their lives somewhere after university and go on to be a credit to the family. Hell, it worked for me!

The only proper subject I managed was an E grade in History and both myself and my mate, Jonty, counted ourselves lucky to have pulled this off. Two days after the results came out we headed off for our usual pint or twelve at Wigton Rugby Club. Dave Everett, History teacher, all round good bloke, and one teacher I'd always rated even when I was bunking off his lessons for a session of bonking and cramp in the woods, was also cradling a pint of bitter in the Rugby Club. He clocked me and Jonty, we clocked him. He knew the score well enough, he'd had us sussed as a couple of pint swilling borderline cases from the start of the sixth form. Let's give Dave Everett his due, he was an excellent judge of character. 'You lucky bastards,' he said. And he was right.

Within weeks I was at the factory stashing the cash that would keep me in beer, gear and the occasional text book at college. The conversation about the animals in the cheque book which opened this chapter said a lot about how far things had gone in a few years. You could get all pretentious and talk about the conflict of the dope smoking liberal values and my upbringing in a working class Cumbrian stronghold. In reality, life was just getting more out there in every way and I'd packed in a fair bit during the two years of the sixth form. There were many more things to choose from and life was throwing these things at me as fast as I was throwing myself in the other direction.

I still cared about Carlisle United, but life was more crowded and the things I was chasing hardest were the new experiences, like cramp free sex. What was wrong with football was the way you had to stand back and watch. What was right with sex, drugs and the rest, was the way they were so close you could touch them or feel them wandering around inside your head. I was never stupid enough to think any of it would drop the meaning of life in my face for the minimum of effort, but it was worth a look.

Blue Nightmare #6

NEIL - **I'll have a cheese and ham roll and some of that soup over there.**

GIRL IN SHOP - Alright.

BLOKE IN QUEUE (LOUDLY) - Where ye from, like?

NEIL - I live up Chester Road.

BLOKE IN QUEUE - I can tell that by ye posh student accent, don't get funny with me, pal. I asked where ye were from?

NEIL (QUIETLY) - Carlisle.

MAN IN QUEUE - We piss on them blue bastards.

NEIL - You didn't the day Chris Balderstone's penalty buried your promotion hopes and we went on to get to Division 1.

A FEW DAYS LATER

CORONER - And then the deceased was heard to mention Chris Balderstone, a certain penalty and a depressing day in the history of Sunderland AFC. He did this within earshot and full view of several ship builders who were queuing for sandwiches. I would also like to add that the deceased was a student and lacked a convincing regional accent to suggest any kind of empathy with the rugged working types in this queue.

JUDGE - And his torso was completely severed from his limbs?

CORONER - More or less, M'lud. One arm did remain loosely attached by a strip of skin, but when the police arrived the shipbuilders were within seconds of gnawing their way through that.

JUDGE - He definitely said that about Chris Balderstone's penalty?

CORONER - Yes.

JUDGE - To a man who'd already identified himself as a Sunderland fan?

CORONER - Yes.

JUDGE - A verdict of suicide would appear the only logical conclusion.

CORONER - I rather think so M'lud. Fancy a pint?

JUDGE - Yeah, why not.

CORONER - That penalty was a sickener wasn't it?

JUDGE - Too right we should have gone up that year, that game could have gone either way.

Chapter Six - Paul Bannon

MENTIONED FOR THE FIRST TIME IN THIS CHAPTER

Paul Bannon - Occasional goal getter, all round character. Started 78/79, established the following year and holder of permanent place in my heart.

Peter Beardsley - Okay, we've mentioned him already. But, his stint as a Carlisle player starts here.

Phil Bonnyman - Scots born midfield / defensive minded player. Acquired during shapeless 75/76 campaign, went on to become regular in later seasons. Scored a few, including one at .

Paul Haigh - Pricey, unflashy and ultimately dependable defender. Signed in the dark days of Third Division struggle, stuck around long enough to see a few highs and lows.

Jim Hamilton - Lanky forward-playing journeyman who netted a few in the Beardsley era team.

Bryan 'Pop' Robson - Chunky, ageing, goal-getter drafted in during grim-survival campaign of 80-81.

Gordon Staniforth - Perm, tache, tight tight shorts, fashion guru and sometime scorer in late Seventies and early Eighties. Record signing - £120,000 - from York City.

Bob Stokoe - Next to Alan Ashman, the only other contender for best manager at Brunton Park, ever! Gritty, realistic and capable of working with a little to achieve a lot.

I FIRST ENCOUNTERED Sunderland Polytechnic in a newspaper ad concerning their newish Communication Studies degree. Slapping in a late application, I got a late interview and found myself confronted by a handful of confused looking lecturer types all hell bent on having a coffee break.
None of them especially keen to grill me on anything academic. We waffled for a few seconds about my A-levels, got on to talk about climbing mountains and skirted round films, the meaning of life and the quality of the common room coffee.

I knew deep down I'd found some kindred spirits. Rumour had it that there was at least one researcher around the place who could spell 'academic rigour', but you shouldn't trust rumours.

In the first year I was there, the college bookshop put ring-binders on sale that spelled Polytechnic as 'Polytecnic', and by the time I'd got there the stocks had been hastily returned. The folders in question had passed through enough hands to suggest there should have been some kind of quality control, but the thing that had alerted everyone to the embarrassing mistake was their inexplicable popularity amongst the students. Never before had the college's own brand sold on this scale. Every one of those ring-binders stood a sporting chance of becoming a treasured souvenir.

As for my admission, we could have saved ourselves some time. All they had to do was take my pulse. The ability to stand up, breathe and say you actually wanted to come to Sunderland seemed fairly high on the admissions criteria, in my opinion at least. I should stress at this point that my opinion is not the opinion of my publisher, Terrace Banter. It should also be noted that we have already established that I wasn't very bright at 18 years old. In fact, I was so blinkered that, in all probability, I was too thick to realise I was surrounded by academic excellence in Sunderland.

I knew something about it. My mate Pup had shared a few adventures and rounds of drinks at school and, by virtue of using his considerable brain-power, had made it to the highly rated Pharmacy course at the Poly. Sunderland had its academic high spots, but it also had jokes in the rag mag.

TUTOR - So, how many A- levels have you got?
COMMUNICATION STUDIES STUDENT - 27.
TUTOR - You're taking the piss.
COMMUNICATION STUDIES STUDENT - You started it.

Oh how those of us the Communication Studies course laughed at that joke - once someone from the Science Department had explained it to us.

Culturally it was a shock. Never more so than on the first Saturday when I went out mob handed with a bunch of virtual strangers and headed for a few pubs. Semi-sozzled and considering a disco to finish the evening, I staggered out of a town centre pub around half ten and found myself standing between two fights. I passed a few more scraps on the way back to my bedroom in the Polytechnic Precinct and figured the whole place was the largest open prison in the country. I'd seen this kind of stuff before, I once found myself in the thick of a fight in a Keswick disco and ended up leaning against a door alongside a bouncer as we listened to the morons on the other side beating the shit out of each other. Stuck together in this hilarious and scary situation, me and the bouncer had briefly discussed Carlisle's impending relegation from Division Two, the way you do when there is a skull thumping the other side of the door a couple of inches away from your own head. As a football fan I'd also seen some serious rucks going down inside and outside the grounds. What hit me about Sunderland was the scale of the whole thing.

Within a few weeks I'd got a handle on it. If they didn't know you you were okay, most of the time. A lot of the aggro was people settling scores from the week before. You know, close knit community stuff. Two blokes meet, one gives the other a gentle talking to in the form of a serious kicking, an ambulance ride and a limp that lasts the best part of a month. A fortnight later they're in the same pub and the one who can walk without a limp casually says, 'You fixing to stuff your hands up my little sister's bra again?'

The limping one cradles his pint, makes as if he's weighing up the matter deeply and grunts, 'Way, Man, I'll gi' it a miss from now on.' Everyone is happy again and the talk turns round to Sunderland's weighty task of coming away from Anfield with the points that will ensure their First Division survival. In these 21st century days of electronic communication, faceless bureaucracy and endless shopping malls, I miss those old earthy values, don't you?

Some places were off limits. The Royalty pub for one. There were odd skirmishes with the locals, but as often as not these involved instances of suicidal stupidity, like a student in some pub ordering a gin and tonic. I knew the form quite well, and I survived three years without incident. As bad as it got was some guy giving me serious lip in a chip shop. I got out of that one by discussing football. This was pretty rich really because my presence in Sunderland, Carlisle's presence in the old Third Division, and my presence in the student financial bracket left me little chance of seeing United in the flesh. It wasn't exactly the end of an era, but the sixth form tradition of indulging other interests at the expense of football really took hold whilst I was at college.

Carlisle got along well enough without me. In my first year at college they topped out sixth in the Third Division, a feat they repeated the following year before plummeting to 19th in 1981. I wasn't a total absentee, but I was reduced to keeping up to date on the odd weekend I was home and, given the fleeting visits to my folks, it would be taking the piss to cynically stage each weekend around a match. 'Hi ya, I'll just dump my stuff, head off to Brunton Park and I'll be back for my tea around half six. You'd better make it snappy though cos me and Ian are out for a pint around half seven.'

Holidays were a different matter and four goals in two home games in March, 1980, went down well enough. The opposition were Blackpool and Plymouth, both of whom were beaten with confidence. Given the complete break I'd had from Cumbria let alone Brunton Park, there were a few changes. Unfamiliar faces on the park, and the whole place seemed to have shrunk. Then again, I had passed Roker

Park on a regular basis by this time and the landscape of Sunderland generally made Carlisle look smaller. Another shrinking feature of Carlisle United were the crowds. You could see bare concrete on the Warwick by this time.

Life had taken a few strange turns by this point. I'd moved in with Dawn and broken up with her, and I'd taken a couple of trips back to Cumbria to 'get my head together'. The whole romance had started out somewhere near *Nine and a Half Weeks* and ended up around the final scenes of *Fatal Attraction*. Quite how Dawn had gone from an upbringing that had seen her rubbing shoulders with the seriously wealthy, living in Nassau and being a fully fledged member of the Junior Jet Club (in other words air travel was commonplace in her very young life) to starting a couple of degree courses in windblown, grey-skied Sunderland is a book in itself. What matters is that our lives passed each other in that first year, we got together late in that year, and by that Summer, Dawn was facing the uncertain prospect of looking around for a course having failed to make it past year one of Combined Arts. She started an English Studies course which allowed us to move into a big house with a handful of others including Rich who would - a decade later - become my brother-in-law. He was already going fairly seriously with my sister, having got together with her when I brought him home for a weekend in Cumbria.

Somewhere on the far side of Dawn's panic about her future, things got really serious between us and for a brief period there wasn't that much else in the world for me. Dawn was more devoted, caring and loving than anyone I'd met, or dared imagine I could meet. It was intense, and the ins and outs of the whole thing don't matter much in the history of my longer lasting love affair with Carlisle United. When I ended it all in the early part of 1980 the situation in the house showed up your average big budget TV psychological drama for the shallow, half-baked bilge it usually is. My future brother-in-law, Rich, was practical to the end, God bless him. I remember having a serious conversation with him in the library at the Poly one Saturday afternoon, the gist of which was me saying I had to end it and, more or less, picking his brains on the whole idea. Rich's practical advice included leaving it until after tea to tell her because it was Dawn's turn to cook that night!

To leave it quite like this really isn't fair to Dawn. I'd discovered more in the previous nine months about building your life around someone and thinking about that person all the time than I'd believed possible. 'Significant' doesn't do it justice and both of our lives took seriously different turns as a result. Nobody talked about post-traumatic anything in 1980, but we suffered from it though.

This matters in the great history of my lifelong love of Carlisle simply because it changed me and that, in turn, changed what I was doing watching my team. Having already noted that Carlisle United were there in the manner of many other familiar things, there was a time around Easter, 1980, when those comfortable and familiar things started looking more attractive than they had for a hell of a long time. I'd pushed the envelope to the point of coming up hard against the real limits of sanity and survival. Given the way I was feeling, the comforting sight of Brunton Park was a welcome relief and the matches around March and April, 1980, were all the better for the fact that this was a team with some pretensions of achieving things. What I needed most in my life was a sense of hope and the idea that there was something - anything! - in the future.

From my early teenage years I'd often gone to things I wanted to see on my own. I'd discovered early on in life that some of my tastes were at odds with the rest of the world. Initially this had something to do with the way that I'd laugh at things that made others wince. This progressed to a realisation that there was nobody around at school who would seriously consider dub reggae as decent music, treat books about UFOs as worthy of interest, or give a shit about what passed for cult TV in those times. The first time I saw Aussie headcase and chat show host, Norman Gunston, on TV I was almost helpless with laughter. What cracked me up most of all was his item on disaster movie birthday cakes. His *Towering Inferno* number, constructed of alternate layers of firelighters and marzipan, was demonstrated complete with desperate screams from the falling and soon to be deceased victims. I discovered later that almost everyone I knew who'd seen it had reckoned the guy a total loser or simply switched off in a mixture of disgust and / or apathy. Pretty soon I'd make the odd solo sortie to take in oddball films, gigs by transparent basket-cases of musicians, and other lame attempts at entertainment.

But around Easter of 1980 I took this solitary behaviour into another dimension. I started heading off on my own to football matches. Given the intimate atmosphere generated by three and half thousand fans, I soon got chatting away to the other Blues around, but in the social atmosphere of a football match this was still an odd move and it felt strange turning up alone. The familiarity of the ground was welcome and regular reading of the *Sunday Sun* and other sports coverage available in Sunderland had kept me in touch with team changes. Familiarity wise Ian McDonald, Trevor Swinburne, Phil Bonnyman and George McVitie were still around. Given the Third Division opposition, McDonald was well able to cope. He was as effective as Bill Green had been an entire division above this level. The strength at the back was improved by a familiar looking figure in an unfamiliar beard. Ageing and a little slower on the ground he might have been, but 'Tot' Winstanly was back with some experience and a greater readiness to upend anyone quick enough to try to run around him. Tot's imposing presence and McDonald's deceptive speed were a useful combination. I have to admit it, Trevor Swinburne was pretty good, and I wasn't going to get full blown nostalgia because Alan Ross had retired at the end of the previous season so I might as well get used to the new situation. All good things come to an end, but sometimes this brings new beginnings.

The team carrying the mighty reputation forward in the third season of Third Division action were an effective outfit who managed the shape and direction of

98

previous years and were just about managing to cut it as a credible footballing side. Fortress Brunton was almost worthy of the name, but this fearsome reputation had something to do with the less than fearsome opposition. Hell, I'm not saying that the Third Division was weak that season, but that jumped up bunch of nobody's from London - Wimbledon - the rank amateurs who'd taken the place of Workington in 1977, had fought their way into Division Three. They fought us to two draws that year and finished bottom of the division. It was obvious Wimbledon would never amount to anything as a football club!

There were some new faces to me in that Carlisle squad. I'd missed Jim Hamilton the season before and his height up front had its uses. The buzz, such as it was amongst so few people, concerned the little youngster up front, Peter Beardsley. I've got to admit, on first sight I didn't really get it. Sure, he was fast and he had the skill to get round defenders. He even had a first touch that put confidence into those around him and a lay off that generally delivered the ball into the right place, but the guy was so bloody short that he could be overturned by any decent size lump of blubber in the opposing defence and his rate of running to contributions in the game wasn't that brilliant. So I reckoned anyway.

Then again, Beardsley's flashing strike in the first half against Plymouth which set us up for our second win in four days was a moment of lightning reaction class, and I was airborne in response to it. Don't get me wrong, I didn't have anything against him - I just saw solid journeyman goal getters all over the pitch at Brunton Park and I wasn't sure that this youngster was completely out of their league.

Paul Bannon on the other hand. What was great about Bannon was his mournful look. He looked like some world-weary police constable jogging around his beat in the total certainty that life's darker side would present itself at any second. A natural athlete only up to a point, Bannon oozed character in a subtle way. I'd managed to miss him the previous season. Not hard given his lack of action. He came on as a substitute for the new wonder boy, Gordon Staniforth. Staniforth had the Keegan perm, the obligatory tache and a sense that the cameras were on him all the time. Bannon had the tache, the long hair and a totally different aura - he was the anti-Gordon Staniforth. It all came clear for me, still trying to get up to speed with the new faces, when Bannon jogged on as sub and somebody close by shouted out, 'Smile you miserable twat, you've got a game.'

He didn't smile, I'm not sure he managed much of a smirk when he scored. But I'd found another crowd pleaser, even if he had to convince the rest of the crowd. Thinking back on this, it probably had something to do with the shout as he came on. It may even have had something to do with the time I'd spent at college. Academically, I was still definitely in the GM Vauxhall Conference of brain power. In other words I'd do what I had to and then head off in the direction of a pub, record shop or wherever once I'd got the basics delivered. Despite this, I was also in the student mentality of looking for meanings and messages wherever I could find them. Give me a few like minded pals, something stimulating to help the evening pass, and I led the conversation into hitherto undreamed of interpretations of anything and everything. Paul Bannon, with his combination of seething miserable undercurrent and the essentially positive role of a goal hunting forward player, had the same hard to fathom combination of opposites as the soft spoken clinical killers played by Clint Eastwood. At least, that was the way I told it back at college.

More to the point. I went to two games to get grounded in old familiar surroundings and Paul Bannon scored in both. He sure as hell had something. He bagged another brace, with concrete still visible on the Warwick in mid-April, and you could still catch sight of him walking back from an attack or wandering into position from a set piece with his head down, sunken cheeks and an expression that suggested either that he read Jean Paul Sartre for kicks or that each moment of reflection put him in touch with some terrible secret.

Maybe I just needed Bannon, given the turns my own life had taken and the company I was keeping. In an era when I was obliged to start reading those novels with grey and green spines, and contemplating the messages for us all cooked up by miserable French writers with too much time on their hands and a history of not being held enough as babies, Paul Bannon was a revelation. For starters, he embodied existentialism in an accessible way. Albert Camus, Joseph Conrad and the great Sartre himself should have met the guy.

Just relax here, I'm not going to start poncing on about all those self-centred deep and meaningful writers, or compare and contrast existential and nihilist approaches. I did enough of that at college. Bannon and Camus would have got on because they both knew football. Camus, who could write about alienation, the human condition and futility, saw it all first hand from between the goalposts. He even managed one international appearance as a goalie. Given the absence of video coverage of Camus' appearance for the Algerian national side, I guess it is useful that we can still buy paperback copies of *The Outsider*, but, take it from me, it is possible to combine professional football and an all pervading sense of isolation. Bannon managed to carry that same world weary essence onto the pitch. Peter Beardsley, by contrast, existed somewhere between the philosophical schools of depth fronted by Emlyn Hughes and Bonnie Langford.

If we contrast their two styles we could say that Bannon's head down, sunken cheek expression says to us, 'The goal is merely a fleeting moment in a journey of abject and unavoidable pointlessness.'

Beardsley's scurrying, fast flowing passing and lay-off game of the time also had a message for the world which read, 'Hey I'm enjoying my football and I can't wait for my beans on toast afterwards.'

Beardsley and Bannon got totally different treatment from the crowd. Bannon was never a favourite and, despite almost five years at Brunton Park, he took frequent stick. For my money, he combined the same qualities as favourites like

Billy Rafferty. In other words he wasn't a touch player, but he was effective and his strike record wasn't that bad considering that he achieved some of this under the management of Bobby Moncur and most of it within a team that generally assumed levels of mid-table mediocrity. Bobby Moncur was never a manager to think laterally when dour predictability would do. Even if I'm half right about Bannon, those team talks at the end of the Moncur era must have been a riot.

MONCUR - So the scouting is pretty solid. They're weak in the left side of defence. What we're looking for is this: Georgie I'm looking to you to carry the ball into their back left. Beardo, every time George is running forward with the ball in their half you cut in right from wherever you are, and when George delivers the ball turn your man and flash it over the box. Stanny and Paul should be running on and if we move fast enough there will be space in the middle because they'll have to pull men out of position to cover the weak space on the left. Any questions?

BANNON - Why?

MONCUR - Cos they're weak there. There's no mobility on the left side of their defence.

BANNON - But why?

MONCUR - Cos they've got injury problems. We can exploit their . . .

BANNON - Why boss, why?

MONCUR - Eh?

BANNON - Why are we here, what is it all for?

MONCUR - Cos I'm payin' you decent money to play football.

BANNON - But what does it all mean?

MONCUR - Mean?

BANNON - Yeah, life and that. What does it mean?

MONCUR - There's something wrong wi' you Bannon, I dunno what it is but I'm gonna get to the bottom of it if it's the last thing I do.

BANNON - It's all bottom, there's no such thing as 'top'. In the end everything is futile.

SQUAD - Fucking hell, Bannon, shut up!

Bannon and Beardsley first played together under the functional and frequently ineffective management of Bobby Moncur. Bobby Moncur, to the best of my knowledge, never did fathom the enigma that was Paul Bannon. The last thing Moncur did at Carlisle was part company with the club around the time Dawn and I had headed our separate ways. He went on to manage Hearts and take them to a similar level of stumbling mediocrity as the Carlisle team he left behind. Who or what he is managing now, I don't know. If your local supermarket opens an area of listless displays, special offers that offer nothing special, and an attitude to customer satisfaction that suggests they are doing you a favour simply by opening the shop, it might be worth looking at the pictures of the managers they like to display out front. You never know.

Martin Harvey was in charge by March, 1980. Harvey's main weapon in the new tactical armoury appeared to have been to turn up the speed control. Where Moncur's 'tactics' appeared to involve people holding positions, running into predictable gaps and generally shouting through a megaphone to tell the opposition what was coming, Harvey had gone for the revolutionary idea that you could actually enjoy football. Tactically we weren't that different, but the added speed, the odd bit of invention and the extra yard of pace that comes from having a good time was a welcome change. Carlisle and myself both pulled ourselves out of the depths as the cold wet winter of 1980 turned into the cold wet spring before taking a headlong Joe Laidlaw style dive into a wet summer with the odd cold day.

One week after Easter we bagged five goals in two home games, Bannon got three of them and still took stick from the terraces in both games. Promotion was a mathematical possibility and still the crowds didn't come. A logical look at the presence of Sheffield Wednesday and Blackburn Rovers at the top of the table would suggest that there were bigger clubs likely to grab the promotion places, and our position in mid-table for most of the season hadn't done much to inspire confidence, but my faith was returning in large enough doses. More to the point, Martin Harvey's team took crowd pleasing seriously, and in the second half against fellow promotion outsiders, Reading, we ran hard and fast in search of both points. Behind for a good part of the game, an unremarkable but highly effective Bannon strike finally secured a point. I didn't see any of the final three games, including a Bannon brace in the final home game in which we humbled another top of the table team - Colchester.

On the odd occasion in which I found a football fan at college, I'd talk about Carlisle but I was always up against it in terms of talking familiar faces. This was an era when Trevor Brooking, Kevin Keegan and Kenny Dalglish existed as the pinnacle of football achievement and Liverpool just held off Manchester United's championship challenge. The Third Division - the 'Turd' Division as I once heard it labelled - didn't really rate. I was, after all, living most of the time in a hotbed of football passion, Sunderland. I met a lot of people from Sunderland, but even more from 'SUNNERLAND.' That is 'Sunnerland' as shouted fast and loud with a sharp stop at the end of it.

I briefly had something going with a third year student at the college who lived just off Roker Avenue in the shadow of the mighty stadium. Sunderland's level at the time was at the lower end of the First Division and their precarious status combined with the passion they could muster put Carlisle to shame. Whilst I've seen books about Carlisle lovingly chronicle a few stuffings handed out to Sunderland and seen these accounts praise the Blue Army, I've never seen Carlisle match some of the things I saw that year. My whole idea of football crowds was changed the day I tried to get to my girlfriend's place and found myself walking against the crowd heading into Roker Park. Carlisle were dishing out their late surge stuffings in front of 3,500 fans on a good day. Sunderland were fighting for their top flight survival in front of ten times that number. Walking against a tide of humanity that filled an entire street brought home the sheer scale of support that gathers itself behind a bigger club. Sunderland, with a population of 300,000, was listed as Britain's biggest town. It is now a city. In those pre-Taylor report days, the Roker Park support would stand to watch a game. I'd been conditioned to Carlisle's scale of things and the values of a city stuck in the middle of a huge rural area. Sunderland was a different proposition. Sprawling, industrial, built up and - although a town - still home to more people than the county in which I'd grown up.

Sunderland put the dwindling crowds and the futile last minute scramble for a Third Division promotion miracle I'd seen at Brunton Park into perspective. Despite this, that season ended on a positive feeling for me because Carlisle had been there for me at a time when I needed them, and the familiarity of the ground, the shirts, the crowd and the rest had been part of that healing process.

1980/81 dawned with me alone at home. My little sister was giving it some Inter-rail action with Rich and my folks were taking a seriously long break in the motor caravan. My major responsibility in mid-August was looking after the dog. Given the sprint up the table the previous season and the presence of hopelessly small outposts like Newport, Brentford, Exeter and Chester in the division, we were definitely up for promotion.

It's twenty to five on August, the 16th, I'm facing the prospect of a long bus ride with a walk on the end only to be savaged by a neglected dog. Was it worth it? Carlisle United 0 Sheffield United 3. I'm not saying we were complete shapeless shit with a death wish thrown in, but two weeks later the crowd for a league game on a Saturday afternoon in bloody August was down below 3,000. That day - our fourth match without a win - we were complete shapeless shit with a death wish thrown in and the 4-1 hammering we suffered at home to the mighty Newport County was verging on a let off. Hell, earlier that year me and Carlisle had both hauled ourselves from unaccustomed deep holes. I thought we'd turned a corner together. Newport! I mean, Newport bloody County, come on. They put four past us.

A month later I'd turned twenty one, headed off for my final year at college and moved back for a year in Sunderland. There was a complete lack of Third Division teams within striking distance. I might have been living in a hot bed of football support, but Darlington and Hartlepool were well below Carlisle. Middlesbrough, Sunderland and Newcastle United were out of sight way above us. The closest games were in Carlisle and in one of them the week after I went back to college, a Carlisle team containing Peter Beardsley and a couple of old-timers who'd seen much better days - Bobby Parker and George McVitie - took an almighty stuffing at

Fortress Brunton. Chesterfield ran out 6-2 winners, sticking three goals without reply in the Carlisle net in the second half. I could still talk up Paul Bannon to the handful of my fellow students who gave a shit, but there was a grim security in all of this. I could say what I wanted because the few football fans I knew didn't care at all about Carlisle. A few people remembered the Division One season or the well deserved reputation as a hard outfit to crack in knock out competitions, but Carlisle's position as a punch bag for the high flying likes of Chesterfield and Newport bloody County rendered them invisible to most football fans.

I was happier talking about Joe Laidlaw than the league position that presented itself in the *Sunday Sun* as that autumn dragged on. I was also happier in general than I'd been for the best part of a year. The main reason for this was another serious revelation that hit me around this time. We'll get to the revelation, by way of a little detour.

There used to be a joke in the spate of 'Irish' humour that hit England in the Seventies. A bloke goes into a brain shop and starts haggling about adding some extra memory to his own bonce. He is shown an increasingly expensive sets of grey matter until the shopkeeper pulls out the best he has, a ludicrously expensive Irish brain. 'How come that is so expensive?' asks the bloke, remembering the famous Irish reputation.

'Listen,' says the shopkeeper going in for the killer sales pitch. 'The previous owner of this brain was an Irishman. He had this brain his whole lifetime and he didn't use it once.'

Hilarious eh?

Incidentally, the real killer in the Irish humour craze is that the jokes really show up the seriously limited historical knowledge of the English. Irish people are thick in Irish jokes because there was a long period in English history when we saw massive amounts of semi-skilled and often uneducated Irish people. They'd arrive mob-handed, to build railways, bridges, and roads, and be seen mob-handed at the end of the week as they headed out for a well deserved pint. The English that encountered them soon clocked that half of this lot couldn't read and write and the rest weren't much on long winded conversation. They built an image on this and didn't think hard enough to realise that most countries can scramble a gang of uneducated muscle on demand.

Try telling jokes about the thick Irish in New York. If you're lucky you might still be breathing as they drag you out of the ambulance for a last desperate attempt to save your life in intensive care. The truth here is that most countries have their targets for thick humour and most of these targets came into being because there was some mob - either local or imported - who could be relied on to turn in a good day's work for shit pay and some beer at the end of the week. Things are never exactly as they seem. There are deep rooted reasons for the most inexplicable and surprising twists that life throws at us.

The reason I know this and I can earn a crust explaining some of these twists is down to the revelation that struck me late on in 1980. Carlisle United were plumbing depths that were becoming depressingly familiar but - for once - I was heading in the other direction. The revelation that hit me that year was that I wasn't thick after all.

Then again, up to that point, I'd never been so sure. Had my brain been in that shop it would certainly have been in the bargain basement. Worth something because it hadn't been used, but marked down on general wear and tear. Maybe the shopkeeper would have kept it under the counter and pulled it out for the occasional trick. For starters he could have squeezed it into a bucket before drinking the resulting liquid and pronouncing it to be a decent pint of bitter.

Thinking about my situation as part of the intellectual elite of the country, I reasoned it a bit like this. My O-levels had been conjuring tricks of a sort. Slap in a week's hard revision and even the maths started to make sense. All you have to do at that level is rehearse a few arguments and jump through hoops. My sixth form party time had been saved by some decent blagging in the History exam and the ray of hope offered to all bullshitters in the form of A-level General Studies. With around seven months of the degree course remaining, I knew that I'd have to learn something if I was going to make it out with a qualification.

Having opted for a GM Vauxhall Conference level course, I'd finished my second season as a student staring relegation into the Unibond Premier League full in the face. One tutor, tearing apart an essay that had involved a whole hour's effort on my part, informed me that he'd left the mark where it was because another one percent off would have left me failing a module and, frankly, he couldn't be arsed wading through more of the same shit if I was forced to re-submit for his part of the course.

Somehow or other I had to turn this around or fail. The only person who'd managed to get me into the library on a regular basis had been Dawn. At the end of 1980 I started hauling myself down there. I started building a collection of hardbacked, thick and serious books in my room. I'd always had a few - well, they're handy for skinning up when you don't want to crease your record sleeves - but now the collection expanded. Having figured I'd actually have to read the bloody things if I was going to make anything of being a student, I set about catching up on two and a half years of work.

The first signs that something was seriously wrong came that Christmas. I took home essay titles which weren't due in for weeks and spent entire afternoons writing. I'd been able to gauge the time I was taking on essays before by the number of albums I got through. I wasn't kidding about the 60 minutes for the shite essay that reduced my tutor to insults. If I remember that one correctly it took both sides of the second Clash albums and around one side of the first Undertones album. Now, I left essays unfinished after an entire afternoon, went back for more in the evening and even took more than one day over getting them right.

Given the way our lives kept shadowing each other, Carlisle United duly responded by beating Burnley 3-2 at home on Boxing Day. Shit season so far, scrappy game, decent Beardsley goal to seal the points and a promising recruit at the back. Paul Haigh should've been decent. £121,000 on Gordon Staniforth was serious money by Carlisle standards, but the £100,000 we paid to acquire Haigh's defensive skills meant that there were two players out there who cost almost a quarter of a million between them. This was 1980 and we were at the arse end of the Third Division facing relegation into the bottom flight. Even today teams in that position fill their trousers in the face of six figure transfer fees.

The signing of Paul Haigh was immediately followed by some serious stuffings. Carlisle United reacted by telling Martin Harvey to get stuffed and then calling in the dependable and experienced management talent of Bob Stokoe. I had a soft spot for Martin Harvey, mainly because he wasn't Bobby Moncur. I also valued the boost his team had given me earlier that year. Harvey had been offered a coaching position beside Bob Stokoe and he told United where to stick it. He was certainly better than the league position in September, 1980, suggested, but it's a hell of a lot easier to argue that from the safe distance of 20 years than it is to watch a once great team teetering on the edge of the lowest division.

In the face of a panic situation the one guy you would want on your side is Bob Stokoe. After leaving Carlisle for Blackpool, he'd seen higher highs and lower lows than Carlisle had managed in over 50 years. He'd taken Sunderland to a Cup victory that defied belief, and a season later he'd been sacked by the same club when the Second Division narrowly failed to crumble before the Cup winners and allow them a promotion place.

As with the departure of Ian McFarlane before him, Martin Harvey's leaving left some of us with decidedly mixed feelings. The incoming man was, once again, a former hero and there were some suggestions that Stokoe could do an Alan Ashman and produce miracles. He didn't. The Boxing Day scramble to victory was pretty much par for the course for a season in which we fought for survival and ended up - survivably - in 19th place. The lowest league position 'enjoyed' by any Carlisle team since my blooding as a supporter. More typical performances than Boxing Day took place in two home games over Easter. Two draws, one goal, plenty of kick and rush football and a first sighting - during my residence in Cumbria - of Bryan 'Pop' Robson.

With his comb-over strand flapping above his balding head and his shirt sleeves rolled up, Robson looked like a down-market Bobby Charlton. He was 35, packing a body that could never be described as athletic, and signed - in all probability - as a result of Stokoe's Sunderland connections. Having played out his highest profile years at Newcastle United and West Ham, 'Pop' had come back to the North East and starred in the Second Division outfit at Roker Park. With Sunderland clinging on to top flight action, Robson wasn't figuring in the plans.

In reality there are these local arrangements all over the place in football. Tranmere has seen ageing Liverpool legends, Bury has played host to former Manchester United and City stars. What bothered me was that I'd been brought up on the idea that the Brunton Park traffic was mainly the other way. Eddie Prudham went to Workington like a few before him. When we signed players from the higher flying North East clubs in the past, I'd seen young hopefuls - like Stan Webb - getting a chance of first team action.

Like a prize fighter at the end of his career, 'Pop' had the moves - in a rusty sense - and he had retained the one thing that had always seen him through, his punch. 'Pop' was an out and out striker and the down-market Charlton idea isn't too wide of the mark. Where Charlton was deadly with a run and shot starting 40 yards out, Robson could do the same from 18 yards. We needed goals, we lacked shape, and we could scramble attacks in an unpredictable fashion. If the tactical master plan showed the failings of a team built on two expensive signings and a bunch of journeymen and grafters, at least we had 'Pop' Robson. There was no sense of dominance on the pitch that season, but the half way effective machine could still put the odd ball deep into opposition territory and muster a charging wall of blue shirts to chase it. So long as the rotund form of 'Pop' Robson was thereabouts at the time, there was a chance that an accurate strike would fly goalwards from somewhere in the box. Like Ian Rush, the guy could score goals as if his life depended on it. And, like Rushy, you'd be struggling to argue the merits of many of them as classics. The nineteenth place we'd managed was survival, just.

To put Robson's impact into perspective it is worth looking at the final positions. Four clubs finished that season on 41 points. We were third in that list of four. Our goal scoring performance was poor - Walsall, below us, were only one goal worse. 40 points or less and you were in the shit. Remember, these were still the days of two points for a win, so the totals that year were slightly higher than average in the Third Division drop zone. We were one point from disaster in that curious end of season table. Proof that it could happen to us and that bottom flight was staring us in the face. As we stumbled through three straight league defeats in our final games, we were faced with the worrying sight of bigger clubs with bigger histories shambling along below us.

I saw nothing after Easter when 'Pop' Robson hammered home an unmemorable and vital strike against Exeter. We got a point that day. Two places below us Sheffield United finished with 40 points and a goal difference that would have done credit to a mid-table side. Remember, they'd run in three of those goals in August, stuffing a Carlisle side that bordered on complete shapeless shit with a death wish! We scrambled a point away in Sheffield when the deep, indescribable enigma that was Paul Bannon scored our second goal in the second half. I wasn't there but I'll bet he didn't smile.

So let's give 'Pop' his due. He played nine games, scored six goals and managed in that total to net two winning goals and two that sealed 1-1 draws. Take any one of those goals away and we were dead meat. Paul Bannon only managed the same goal tally and he played all season. Disaster was only an inch, a split second's hesitation or a mis-timed challenge away. 'Pop' Robson wasn't exactly classy, but he was on target, decisive, and not known to shirk a tackle.

I'd teetered into the 'dead meat' area myself, academically speaking. Having bordered on academic oblivion before turning it round, I finished the college season with a better string of results than three straight defeats. In reality I was only going to scrape a passable degree. Some of the final grade of the course depended on second year work, and I'd done sod all during my second year. I got stuck into the coursework with a vengeance and discovered that my brain worked better than I'd dared expect. The transformation was - roughly speaking - the difference between riding a bike without gears and riding a Harley. I hit speeds and levels of performance I'd only dared dream about and all I'd done was start treating the course as if it mattered. Submitting essays ahead of time, doing the reading that the lecturers suggested, and actually planning something before I put it on paper. I'd also bought a typewriter to help with my fledgling sideline as a music journalist.

Given the handicap I'd given myself by way of missed second year marks, there wasn't a hope in hell I'd catch up all the way, but I was getting marks that dragged my previous relegation performance comfortably into mid-table. At the end of the course I was coming up fast in the current form league, an earlier start at the same level of performance and I'd have been challenging for a place in Europe. You get the general idea.

I ended up with a 2.2 and got an invitation from my auntie Eden to chill out in with her in Sussex. She'd earned a 2.2 herself and told me it was a 'sociable' person's degree. Too bloody right it was! If they'd given out a PHD in Party Animal Research I might have been a star performer. As it was, I'd scrambled out of trouble and finally learned something worth knowing. I was capable of hard work!

This blinding revelation and a piece of paper that said I was a graduate would have to equip me for the life, the universe and the prospect of another season in Division Three. I had one familiar experience left, another summer in the factory. I'd had a fairly easy ride for a student during the shutdowns at the factory. Our general role was helping out with maintenance whilst the old side of the factory was shut down to allow access to all the machinery.

I made serious money one day when the heir to the throne decided to get married and the nation took a holiday. The students at the factory opted to work. They couldn't give us a day off in lieu because we were only there for six weeks and so we got triple time. One student came out of the gents and announced he'd earned the price of a pint just having a shit. Hey, thanks very much Your Highness! I spent half a week doing maintenance on acid baths, saw two boiler suits rot in two days, and got holes in my jeans as a result of the second such incident. British Sidac coughed up a third boiler suit in a week and the money for some new jeans. Six years later, I was still wearing the trendy ripped ones which had dissolved under the powdered acid when I went to gigs.

These were pretty hollow victories. I was going to have to do something about doing something and, after the factory, the real world was closing fast. 15 miles down the road from my country home Bob Stokoe was thinking about doing something to keep a once proud football team out of Division Four.

Blue Nightmare #7

THE GOSPEL ACCORDING to Stokoe, chapter one verse one

Bring me your tired, your poor and your hungry. I will forge them a land and give them a place to be, a job to keep a roof over their heads and the companionship of their fellow men.

No case is too desperate, no out of contract run of the mill centre forward too clumsy to be beyond my gaze. Their weakness alone can be their strength together. For in each pathetically pointless run, each clumsy tackle I see only the effort and the will to achieve. I see the loose lay-offs of the halfway decent midfield general and I will combine them with the furious goalward runs of the ungainly striker. Together we will strive to create a shape, an army and a campaign so that the world - or at least one poxy division in a generally unremarkable era for the British game - will know my name. For I am Stokoe, champion of the oppressed, motivator of the underpaid and tactical genius in the face of limited resources. I am Stokoe, holder of the Carlisle hotseat for all eternity and a day, compared to Martin Harvey at any rate.

It won't be pretty, son, but we'll get results.

Chapter Seven - Jack Ashurst

MENTIONED FOR THE FIRST TIME IN THIS CHAPTER

Jack Ashurst - Mr No Nonsense, dependable defender. A stalwart worthy of selection in any era at Brunton Park.

Tommy Craig - Been around, seen it all, so he decided on Brunton Park. Arguably the best manager we never had!

Bob Lee - He looked like a centre forward, sometimes displayed the mobility of a hot air balloon marooned in quicksand, and still put it about well enough to score a dozen goals in two seasons.

Thomas Ritchie - Another Scot in the ranks, loaned from Sunderland to add some decent passing to a team blended in battle, since August, 1981. Stayed a few months in 1982.

Dave Rushbury - Not as fast as his name would suggest. Thin, angular, occasionally clattering, defender.

SO, AT LAST, it was time for the real world. The world in which results mattered and you had to work to make yourself a winner. The Football League responded to my new found position as a person in search of results by instigating a system in which every win was worth three points. Looking at the previous season's results suggested there would be little change in Carlisle's league position, but the points total might go up by a dozen or so.

Carlisle had however been busy in the transfer market. Given the lowly league position of the previous season our pulling power was reduced, but then again we had Stokoe, a man who had already proven his worth as a signer of talent.

At the back, during the previous season, we'd leaked like John F Kennedy's head on its way to hospital. In search of composure we'd run around in circles and shouted at each other. In August, 1981, we acquired Jack Ashurst and Dave Rushbury. Ashurst from the tragic Blackpool, a team so desperate they'd finished below us in the Third Division the previous year. Rushbury from Swansea.

Dave had the same strange angular features as Paul Bannon, Ashurst looked like Beardsley's more sensible big brother. Given the strange angular features of goalie Trevor Swinburne, I wouldn't have been surprised to hear rumours of inbreeding linked to the team. Imagine a gaggle of Greg Russedski faces and you've got the general idea on the odd occasion that Bannon, Rushbury and Swinburne combined in a move. Then again, the curious similarities might have meant we were on the receiving end of constructed footballing robots all being cast from the same mould. The limited movement and dinosaur quick reactions of the blatantly mechanical Bob Lee - a summer signing from the hopelessly free-falling Bristol Rovers - gave some credence to this rumour.

As August rolled into September, I was stumbling towards job applications, making the odd visit to my mate Ian who was starting his PHD in Liverpool, and happy in the knowledge that the traditional disasterous start to the season hadn't materialised. 'Pop' Robson popped one home in each of the opening games which left us with a truly middling position and a record of W-1, D-1, L-1 goals for 6, goals against 6. Hell, at least we weren't bottom.

On my 22nd birthday, Carlisle and I celebrated the first win, 3-2 over Southend. The short, stocky and decidedly human presence of Beardsley, Robson and Ashurst on the same pitch gave the team an odd look. Their physical similarity meant that there were two groups of three people in the team who looked like close relatives to each other. The truly individual Paul Bannon was however missing, in fact he didn't get a run out until the end of November.

I stumbled around in search of work, knocked out some writing and a few job applications on my typewriter and wandered into everything from an unpaid stint in local radio to some semi-regular kick arounds with a few old school mates. My luck changed when my good luck charm appeared to predictable jeers. Bannon bagged three goals in his first two games as November turned into December, and around the same time I'd hit lucky, if you'd call it that, by scoring a job.

The advert in the local paper said 'Lecturer in Communications' at Carlisle Technical College, my degree was in Communication Studies and I slapped in an application. Around the same time, my Dad's mate, Mike, who worked at West Cumbria College in Workington and Whitehaven, mentioned they were short of staff and desperately short of a lecturer to teach Body Systems. I was doing nothing and felt up for it once I discovered that the hourly rates put most other casual employment around the place to absolute shame.

The idea of teaching Body Systems was a riot. I'd taken A-level Biology and failed it. So had my little sister. The one thing Lesley had over me was a neat set of notes which were still lying around the house. A week after Mike mentioned they were looking for someone, I jogged onto the turf to face a packed house of Social Care students in Workington. The crowd was well into double figures which put it on a par with anything at Borough Park that season. By this point I was also on the books at Carlisle where they'd dropped me into midfield for their team who were teaching Communications and General Studies.

From here the learning curve was seriously steep. The Communication Studies soon expanded to work in Workington teaching a cracker of a subject, Social And

Life Skills. There was an element of being dropped right in at the deep end by this point, but a couple of things were obvious. By and large I was teaching kids on the new YTS scheme. The need for new staff owed a lot to the fact that some of the old timers wanted nothing to do with this influx of the young jobless into their domain and there was more than one of them who intimated to me that I wasn't so much a lecturer as a riot control officer.

What the hell, I needed the money. Within a few weeks it dawned on me that I could actually do the job. It wasn't that bad and there was the odd ironic twist in the whole thing that turned it into an adventure. With that all important West Cumbrian humour that could see a belly laugh where your average punter could see only the lifeless body of the racing driver being helicoptered away to the morgue, I managed to find amusement, education, and a sense of satisfaction in what I was doing. The biggest laugh of all was the notion of me teaching Social And Life Skills. The gist of this was that I had to know enough about everything from the services available at the Post Office to the greatest hits amongst the local amenities. In return I got to teach a steady stream of students all loosely grouped around vocational choices - Mechanical Engineering, Social Care . . .

Social And Life Skills teaching contained a decent belly laugh simply because you have to question the 'wisdom' of putting a former mouthy posh git with a newly acquired degree in front of a bunch of streetwise kids. Remember, I was there to teach them how to survive. There is a serious ironic twist in some of the situations I remember. On one occasion I was well into the exploration of the action packed city of Carlisle. Shuffling around the threadbare excitement of the old Tullie House museum, I was spinning out the stuffed birds to add another 20 minutes to the riveting 'lesson' when one of the YTS kids launched into an informed discussion on several unsolved local crimes and the likely culprits. This kid knew every criminal at large in the city. And I was there to teach him Social And Life Skills!

These 'kids' were more streetwise than I could ever hope to be and more informed on survival than the people who put together programmes on Communication Studies and Social And Life Skills. Some of them also knew Carlisle United and one route to respect in the slick county town college was to discuss the players and high flying First Division team I'd seen. Whilst I'd been on the terraces, these kids were still drawing matchstick pictures of their mums in their first school books. In Workington I had to survive more on my wits, but once we'd exhausted the meagre local attractions, there was at least a roller disco.

I was working hard to grind out results, but there was a developing shape to my play and I came away with something in most of the encounters. I'd been thrown in with a group of welders on a Friday evening. These guys were third years and they'd seen off a steady stream of part-time staff in their time. By the ninth week I'd struggled through most of the obvious stuff and I hadn't a hope in hell of talking about the services in the local Post Office. We were plumbing the depths of

113

depravity in discussions, and running our way through the handful of worthy and outdated films in the possession of the college, when one of the students pointed out to me that nobody had lasted as long in their company as I had. Given the stunts they were famous for pulling, including walking from room to room above the ground floor by utilising the outside the building, I wasn't totally convinced of this fact. Later on, one of their tutors confirmed that it was true. If I could survive this, maybe I had a future in this game.

If I was grinding out results and improving my game plans, so were Carlisle. By Christmas we were well established as front runners with an ability to slog it out rather than impress with our class. Bob Stokoe's fighting spirit and sublime ability to blend a tactical plan with the most limited of resources was showing the others in that limited Division the way home.

Peter Beardsley was showing signs of being exceptionally good, but he was also wildly inconsistent. I'd realised some time before that he was genuine class, but that is a mixed blessing in the lower divisions where ageing, limited and frustrated defenders take a perverse delight in attempting to end the games and reproductive capabilities of nippy young hopefuls. Beardsley's lack of height always put him in the firing line for such attention, but probably the worst challenge he faced that season came from a young defender by the name of Steve Bruce. As the fierce December weather set in with a vengeance, Bruce left Beardsley pole-axed on the Brunton Park turf with a challenge that would have been ruled out of order in a Bruce Lee movie. That day in December it was two young hopefuls colliding in front of a handful of supporters. The same challenge eight years later would have put around 15 million pounds worth of talent in danger of crippling injury.

As the weather went from bad to newsworthy, Carlisle found themselves lucky enough to have the only fixture playing in the Third Division on December the 19th. The South West around Bristol had escaped the worst of the freeze and we were scheduled away in that area. Bristol Rovers were having a fairly pathetic season and duly obliged by letting us win with a Bob Lee goal. I wasn't there, I can only assume it was a mud bath because fast moving runs which glided past defenders were not exactly a Bob Lee speciality. Furious flailing mud-spattered surges at goal on the other hand . . . Yeah, it must have been a heavy pitch and shit home defence at Bristol because Bob Lee scored. Against his old team as well. Maybe they just stood back and laughed as he ran at them with his usual mixture of bluster and incompetence.

Before Lee was covered in mud, he bore a passing resemblence to Bob Latchford, sometime Birmingham, Everton and England centre forward. Okay, he lacked the beard and hairstyle, but he was the same shape. If they'd made a prototype Bob Latchford, he might have turned out like Bob Lee. Perhaps in some lonely outpost, on a windswept beach kept free from prying eyes by a massive sand dune and a squad of guard dogs, there had been boffins at work. One boffin fingered the radio controls whilst the other took notes. On the sand a slighty bulky figure ran with a football at its feet.

BOFFIN 1 - Make him turn.

BOFFIN 2 - He's responding but we'll have to do something with that mobility. Look at the stop watch, it took him seven full seconds to turn to the right and we still couldn't make him strike the ball cleanly.

BOFFIN 1 - I agree, we've got to go for all round improvements, in speed, mobility, reaction time and cleanly striking the ball.

BOFFIN 2 - The name is a stinker too, Bob Lee sounds like a dustman or a miner.

BOFFIN 1 - Ah, I've been thinking about that. I think we go for something with the same letter sounds but more distinction, like Latchford.

BOFFIN 2 - Oh yes, I agree. What are we going to do with this prototype?

BOFFIN 1 - I've no idea. Let's list the positives and have a think.

BOFFIN 2 - The positives . . . well, he looks like a centre forward.

BOFFIN 1 - He looks alright in that blue shirt too.

BOFFIN 2 - So we pawn him off on a shit team that play in blue. Let's have a look in the book . . . nothing under A, nothing under B, C - Cardiff, no they're too good, Carlisle . . .

BOFFIN 1 - Oh yes, lonely outpost, shit football, blue shirts. Hell, if his electronics fuse up there and he spends 90 minutes running round in circles, they'll still think he's human. They've seen some sights up there you know. Stan Webb played at Carlisle.

BOFFIN 2 - Stan Webb, the one we built from surgical off-cuts and the mould we used for Gilbert O' Sullivan's head?

BOFFIN 1 - The very same.

BOFFIN 2 - We've come a long way since that abomination, eh?

BOFFIN 1 - You could say. Then again, we're still a long way short of making a credible footballing robot. You'd have to be pretty desperate if you were fooled into thinking Bob Lee was the real thing.

BOFFIN 2 - How desperate are the footballing public in Carlisle?

BOFFIN 1 - Pretty desperate. They were one goal away from relegation to the bottom flight in 80/81 and they reckon 'Pop' Robson is an acceptable striker.

BOFFIN 2 - So Carlisle it is then?

BOFFIN 1 - I think so.

Mechanical Bob Lee's strike mattered because those points in the absence of any other game in the same Division put us right up there on top of the table. The first time we'd been top of a table since August, 1974, when we'd been top of bloody everything.

115

The Christmas encounter with Lincoln City was a top of the table clash and, naturally enough, the millions thronged to Brunton Park. Well, not exactly. Less than four thousand for what amounted to the most serious game the Division would see that holiday period. We won it, Paul Bannon buried the winner, and he looked strangely depressed after scoring the single goal in a game that kept us up there and confirmed our superiority over the rest. But, that's the wacky, manic depressive, world of Paul Bannon for you. Then again, maybe he had a point. He is credited with the goal. In truth all he had to do to score it was to get in the way of a clearance and watch the ball hit the back of the net. It was a Paul Bannon sort of moment and doubtless he pondered it with his usual abject misery.

BANNON - What is man, what does he do but fill a certain space at a certain time in the generally futile hope that he might achieve something by accident?
THE REST OF THE DRESSING ROOM - Shut up you twat, we're top of the league.

And so it went. Carlisle grinding out results with a team built from a range of misfits and hopefuls. There was promising young talent - the most promising of which, Peter Beardsley, played his last game for us in February, 1982, before generating a club record fee of £275,000 on his way to Vancouver Whitecaps. Rumour had it he would return. The next time he stepped into my life he caused me nightmares, but that was in 1998 and we've got a few adventures to share before that game.

Amongst the journeymen there was the solid defensive confidence of Jack Ashurst. Club captain and taker of shit from no man. Paul Haigh, the man whose six figure transfer fee had put several pins in the Martin Harvey voodoo doll, which remained hidden under a seat in the director's box, also came good under the watchful eye of solid Jack Ashurst. 'Pop' Robson kept popping and Paul Bannon plied his world weary trade scoring improbable goals which looked like they were dying of apathy even as they crossed the line. Bobby Parker - the only link with the First Division - had his best season since the top flight and Trevor Swinburn's athletic impersonations of Alan Ross became ever more convincing.

Never pretty, barely athletic in some quarters, this was a team built to sweat, and in an average season, surrounded by average opposition, the tactical master plans of Bob Stokoe gradually began to tell. The veteran Scots campaigner, Tommy Craig, joined the midfield for the later half of the season, and Thomas Ritchie - another Scot - arrived, allegedly as interpreter for Craig. In all probability, Ritchie was there to add to the percentage of passes that hit the target. Five draws in six games over February and March took the edge off the manic surge to the top, but we kept scoring as Ashurst ran the defence like his own personal protection mafia.

116

Physically, philosphically and in terms of hairstyles, Bannon and 'Pop' didn't exist in the same universe. Somehow they managed to forge a partnership on the pitch that rattled in goals in the face of desperate last ditch defensive tackles. The lanky and deep one with the tache, and the jovial, baldy little side-kick picking up the crumbs and mimicking the behavior of the other. It had proven itself a killer combination once before, but let's not drag up Hitler and Mussolini this late in the day eh?

Speaking of dragging up history and horror, the 81/82 season brought another twist in the on-going fortunes of Carlisle and Workington. A futile attempt to play out an FA Cup tie with the mighty Bishop Auckland ended in a swamp at Brunton Park, and with a serious winter setting in and fixture congestion piling up, somebody looked at the map, realised Sellafield was close by and reckoned on the radioactive warmth of the Solway solving the problem. And so it was that Borough Park, Workington, heaved under the crush of four and half thousand bodies and saw a professional team in the shape of Carlisle fight out a hurricane lashed encounter with non-league minnows. Heavy pitch, furious encounter and - naturally enough - a Bob Lee deciding goal. It could have been, should have been a mad head-down charge on the Bishop Auckland goal with elbows flailing, mud flying and defenders taking flight and landing amongst the tightly huddled supporters. Instead it was a header in enough space to allow the slow wits of the god of gormless goal-getting to get a gormless goal, in a god-like way. Bob Lee and Borough Park, they belonged together.

Following the fixture slow-down, we came to grief at promotion chasing Fulham when we leaked three in the first half and ended up 4-1 losers. Around this time I was also slowing down. The repeating of the same old stuff in class left me thinking seriously about the game plans. Hell, I could do it, that much was obvious. The real question was how badly I wanted it. There were serious changes going on in my life. One of them had created some suspicion. The previous November I'd been out with the gang I'd joined after coming home from college. Hitting the Sunset Inn at Silloth we'd done the usual few pints, few dances, and unwinding after a hard week. I was meeting the same people on Sundays for a semi-regular attempt at playing football and this would soon develop into scratch matches against other hopeless local outfits.

Anyway, I can recall the moment quite well. I was sitting alone at a table with a pint in front of me, once I'd downed this one I'd got almost a gallon on board and I was near enough stone cold sober. I remember my Dad once telling me about 'celebrating' his 21st birthday in the Royal Artillery. Marooned somewhere on the far side of nowhere, he and a couple of others downed a bottle of whisky - each! There was, apparently, a peculiar biological quirk in the clan which gave us a tolerance for alcohol that was almost unreal. Let's get this in perspective. I've been drunk in my life. On several celebrated nights this has extended to spectacular levels of drunkeness, including passing out and being carried around as a trophy by others at the same party, before finding out about it the following morning. All I knew about that one was that I woke up and wondered how the fuck I'd got home. I got drunk enough to throw up on my 21st. But, slow the rate down to manageable proportions and I could knock the stuff back all night and still read a book before I fell asleep.

I was sat at the Sunset Inn that night watching a gorgeous girl on the dance floor who bore more than a passing resemblance to Angie Dodd on my degree course. It struck me that I was clear headed enough to drive her home although I'd got enough beer on board to give a blood sample with a head on top. I started giving my brain maths problems, mentally replaying classic Carlisle goals and generally searching out the stuff that needed concentration. Anything I wanted from any part of my brain was still there and I was well into my seventh pint.

It started with a decision to stop drinking for a month. The purpose of this was to lose some of the tolerance and allow myself to get spectacularly drunk this side of a second mortgage. Honest, I never intended it to last the rest of my life when I started. It's just that I never really missed it. In terms of a satisfying, mind-bending experiences, drink was always a poor second to sex and drugs. Allegedly.

Since this time I've downed the odd drink that has been shoved into my hand, a situation that means half the alcohol I've shifted since 1981 is champagne, and all the alcohol I've shifted since then would amount to three average nights between 1979 and 1981. A few years later, seriously in love, I headed out for a week's holiday on Rhodes and found myself at the opening night of a bar and plied with enough free brandy to constitute embarrasing hospitality. I walked home sober that night as well, but by that time I was living inside a seriously different body.

I've been quietly asked if I was a reformed alcoholic, whether I was taking powerful medication for some serious and life threatening condition, and more than one person has simply asked me what was wrong. I quit drinking, okay? I also started seeing Kate Graham again, sometimes at the Sunset and, since she knew the DJ, I often ended up in the booth with her and Barry, the said DJ. This allowed me to slip in the odd record at the bottom of Barry's stack as he lined the singles up for the turntables. My tastes had headed in every bizaree musical direction I could find over the previous few years, but the Sunset crowd were unresponsive to anything but the familiar. The best I managed was a regular play for Pigbag's *Papa's Got A Brand New Pigbag*. This crowd liked it straight, uncomplicated and heavily smattered with chart fodder.

A few months after I'd stopped frequenting The Sunset, the mighty John Peel did a gig there and found himself obliged to squeeze his chubby frame through a toilet window before the end of the night's festivities. This undignified escape owed everything to the fact that the chart sounds crowd were attempting to lynch him for the crime of playing unpopular, bizarre, mysterious and intelligent records. I've loved Peel for decades for these very qualities, and it would be fair to say he's opened my ears to sounds that have changed my life. Now, with Peel rightfully honoured by both his fellow professionals and the Queen, the full story of that night can be told.

The Sunset demands club membership and in the Summer of 1982 they asked these members questions about what they wanted to see in the place. I voted for Peel and, if memory serves me correctly, some of the rest of the gang also did the same. The management of The Sunset spotted the trend in their market research and booked Peel, but by the night in question several of the gang, myself included, were employed many miles away. Most of the Peel listeners I knew in Cumbria were not Sunset members and only heard about the gig after the near riot. To most of the Sunset members the words 'Radio 1 DJ' on a poster meant chart sounds and smooth chat. Peel's night-time radio show coincided with their telly watching and most of them wouldn't have known the guy if he hit them over the head with a Rip Rig And Panic 12".

Sorry John, I'd have gone if I hadn't been hundreds of miles away. You've changed lives and you deserved better than that. The people of that little outpost are not all blood hungry savages and a few months earlier we'd have raised a posse that would have given that gig a result. Maybe you should've stuck to wall to wall Pigbag! I'm writing this 16 years after that fateful night and John Peel is still on my stereo. He's playing Pavement, 'the first record by an American band to mention a wicket keeper'. These records, his show and the observations about Pavement still matter to me. They matter so much I'm working in a study heaving with records I first heard on Peel's show. The man is a legend, but maybe not in Silloth.

My new healthy lifestyle included a reasonable amount of time in Kate's company and close attention to Carlisle United. Bob Lee's regular selection was an insight into the true quality of the side, and a side that had to rely on the dinosaur reflexes and cretinous levels of invention in the box that were the Bob Lee trademark was always going to struggle to produce class. But this was a Stokoe team! That is to say, 11 men of varying abilities blended into a fighting machine built around the strengths identified by the great man in the dugout. When we'd gone top he'd honestly expressed the opinion that our performances weren't that good. Like I say, the 'great man', never one to be fooled easily.

There were moments, Bobby Parker had two against Millwall. One of them he put through our net and the other splattered a Millwall defender's scrotum over 18 square yards of pitch. With the poor sod practically into an out of body experience of agony, Tommy Craig netted the rebounding ball and the home crowd celebrated whilst simultaneously clutching their own nuts in sympathy. In a game which had so obviously reminded us of the frailty of all human flesh and, by implication, the impending death of every human, the only person fit to score a winner was Paul Bannon. He duly delivered. There was a sense that life was changing as spring broke over Cumbria. The habits of a lifetime were changing. I was tee-total and the home crowd were right behind my man, Bannon! The hopeless Southern upstarts who had dared to replace Workington came to Carlisle. Wimbledon and their generally shapeless football were duly sent packing at the start of May and the whole affair was made sweeter because the points put Carlisle - potentially - one win away from automatic promotion with five games still to play. Wimbledon had even managed to score our winning goal themselves. Let's face it, this lot from the London suburbs were a complete disgrace, they'd never amount to anything, and their place in the Third Division was rightfully under threat.

Our position, 'one game from promotion', depended on Lincoln taking a defeat and the other teams round about failing to knock in cricket scores, but this far from the end of the season near certain promotion was a cheering thought as the war escalated in the South Atlantic and a decidedly predictable England squad played warm ups for the World Cup finals. Three away games generated one point at Reading and the jitters really struck home when we faced the Southern scum at Wimbledon. They'd happily engineered their own defeat at our place, but they stuffed us convincingly at Plough Lane. With the opposition closing fast, we were running out of games.

Boring Bob Lee was dropped for the last home game against his old club, Bristol Rovers. We had a perfect warm May day to pick up the three points that would ensure promotion and leave us needing only a draw from the final away game to go up as champions. I managed to rekindle some of the old feeling, more so because the team ran to the centre of the pitch and staged the same wave to the crowd that had ended the First Division season.

The Division that year had been dire all round which was why such a mediocre Carlisle side could stride out to win promotion in this way. The next 90 minutes would be all about one result. So long as Carlisle gave a Bristol team hopelessly stuck in mid-table a good run around we could all go home happy. We didn't of course. We were shit. So bad that Bob Lee would have improved things. Solid and gormless as he was, he could have been useful. The rest of the team could have picked him up and used him as a battering ram to clear a path to the Bristol goal. It took £120,000 of Staniforth striking talent to score our only goal and that was from the penalty spot.

The second half saw fast moves snatching their way past the Bristol goal. The only fluid movements were filling the trousers of disbelieving Cumbrians as chance after chance went begging. We put pressure on their defence, made the spaces and shot at low flying aircraft. The spirit of Mike Barry was alive and well just when we needed it least.

I didn't go to the last match at Chester. Still there was hope. Bristol Rovers may have staged a late revival that made a mockery of their safe but unimpressive

120

position, but surely, we could do it at Chester. They were after all the bottom club. We won, with another unremarkable looking goal from the one player old and experienced enough to have seen many bigger games. Thanks 'Pop', you made all the difference. The same thing you'd achieved the previous season. 12 months before you'd earned us survival in the Third, this time you got us out of it. Given the end of season nerves, I for one wouldn't have been surprised to see the team that crumbled in front of Rovers facing the same lowly opposition for another season.

So it was the Summer of 1982, and Carlisle United faced big changes and a step up in the class of their work. And I was bunging in the odd job application myself.

Blue Nightmare #8

ONCE UPON A time a man was in London. On a station platform he spied a poster. The poster said, 'ENJOY CARLISLE.'

'Oh that looks a lovely place,' said the man studying the picture of a castle on the poster. 'I must go there.'

So, the man bought a ticket to Carlisle. As he was walking along the platform at Carlisle the man saw a poster. The poster said, 'LONDON IS LOVELY.'

'Oh yes', thought the man. 'I would really enjoy a visit to London,' so he bought himself a ticket and got back on the train.

But when he got to London he saw the first poster again with its lovely castle. Once more he headed straight for the ticket office and waited his turn before saying 'A single to Carlisle.'

The man's odd behaviour continued for several days. Although he was reasonably well off, his bank account soon began to run down because the journey between the two cities isn't exactly cheap. This story unfolded in the distant days of British Rail. Their services may have been more punctual than Virgin on this route, but they were not known for offering cheap fares.

On his 13th visit to Carlisle station the man got a nasty surprise when the ticket man said to him, 'I'm not taking another bloody cheque, the one you gave me yesterday bounced. Oh, by the way, they've just put a stop on your Access card as well.'

'Oh dear,' thought the man. 'And I so wanted to go to London. It looks exciting on the poster.'

A few hours later the man was rudely awoken by a British Rail guard who discovered him stowing away in the guard's van of a Carlisle to London express.

'Right Pal, you're out on yer arse at the next station,' said the guard showing no respect for the fact that this man was the best private customer that BR had ever seen over a seven day period. When they got to Crewe he kept his promise and flung the man out.

Dusting himself down on the platform the man headed for the gents to wash up. As he did so he passed a poster. It had a picture of the rough end of Crewe on it. It read, 'DON'T COME TO CREWE COS IT IS CRAP. IF YOU'VE GOT ANY SENSE YOU'LL GO TO LONDON OR CARLISLE.'

Chapter Eight - Don O'Riordan

MENTIONED FOR THE FIRST TIME IN THIS CHAPTER

Kevin Carr - Goalkeeping's answer to the chocolate teapot.

Russell Coughlin - Welsh midfield wizard. 99 parts graft to one part magic.

Scott Endersby - So impressive when playing against us for Swindon that Stokoe signed him. A welcome sight after Kevin Carr.

Gary Fulbrook - Six, little remembered, games 87/88. Our first black player.

Tony Fyfe - The kind of 'star' striker to which we were reduced by the late Eighties. The guy has been known to command an opposition penalty area and score goals, but he was playing for Penrith at the time.

Harry Gregg - A manager with heart, no money and a patchy squad. We needed a miracle worker, Harry was a grafter. Maybe in better times . . .

John Halpin - Fast, skilful and passionate about the game. The best news of the 84/85 season. Just about the only good news after that.

Brent Hetherington - Skilfully challenged, forward playing scorer of a handful of goals. Signed from Workington, managed to cope with the step up in class. Then again, by the late Eighties there wasn't much of a step up in class from Workington to Carlisle.

Dean Holdsworth - Yes, he played for us. It was over pretty quickly.

Garry MacDonald - Striker, so unspeakably crap he proved that even Stokoe's astute buying had it's failures.

Dave McKellar - Signed from the dole, the best goalie we'd seen since Alan Ross and an impressive servant to the club for years.

Clive Middlemass - Yup, things were getting desperate in late '87. So desperate we needed a manager who'd seen similar depths. Middlemass had played for Workington. He knew how to cope with desperation.

Eric Nixon - Same name as my Dad, quality keeper signed on loan who made 16 appearances for Carlisle.

Malcolm Poskett - He came, he scored 40 goals, he went. He came back, he scored 20 goals, he went.

Jason Prins - Look, just don't ask! Don't even go there, alright? His 15 minutes of fame are coming up much later, he gets a name check in this chapter.

Don O' Riordan - Another in the great crowd pleasing tradition. The man may be a certifiable schitzophrenic. Listed as a defender, but in truth, much given to leading everyone on the pitch through the most positive of examples and then punctuating such performances with shameless attempts to kick opposing strikers over the main stand.

Wesley Saunders - Solid and unfussy. Sadly, he wasn't another Don O' Riordan.

Alan Shoulder - Former Newcastle striker, famously signed for the Geordies from non-league soccer and gave up his coalmining job for professional football.

Rod Thomas - Another one making a premature appearance in this chapter. Light years ahead of Jason Prins and worthy of more than 15 minutes of fame.

Jim Tolmie - ARGHHHHHHH!!!!!!!!!!!!!!!!

SO WE WERE stepping up a gear. I'd attempted as much myself by putting applications around in response to job adverts for lecturers and other vacancies. As for the 'other' vacancies in question there were openings at junior levels all over the media, but none of them seemed to want me.
The problem was you needed experience to get the job and you couldn't get a job without experience. There are two ways around this in the media. Firstly you know someone and they get you in. Secondly, you needed to find somebody who would let you work for free to gain experience. My best hope was the latter, but living in Cumbria the chances were limited. I'd managed to put in some time at BBC Radio Carlisle where I'd had a stint in most areas, including the pleasure of getting seriously pissed on by rain as a farmer tried to string a sentence together about the price of lambs at an agricultural show.

I'd worked with a few other students at BBC Radio Newcastle whilst I was still studying. Some of this stuff had been completely kicking and I'd been let loose with portable recording equipment to carry out interviews and put together features.

124

All great stuff, but I needed to earn a living. I'd had the odd review and article published, and in 1982 I placed my first piece of rabid fiction in a magazine, but this wasn't exactly a living either.

I spent some time trying a few other things that summer. I dropped in on a few communes in search of seriously different people and in the hope of finding free love and the rest. Less than an hour after meeting a girl at one place down South I found free love and more. A few days later we were at her London flat, around the start of the new football season. Carlisle were stepping up a gear, and I was surrounded by the stuff since she earned a crust flogging it! This was an eye opening experience that left me heading back for more a week later. I linked up in London with my future brother-in-law, Rich, who was starting his own career down there but still holding things together with my sister. Just as well.

In my absence I'd got an interview and the people at Thurrock Technical College had contacted me in the hope I could turn up. Unable to get through to me, my folks had rung Rich in the hope that he could stop me coming home and tell me about the interview.

I hadn't a clue where Thurrock was, but I knew that I would get a train fare for simply turning up. And so just before Carlisle opened their account with a convincing stuffing of Derby at the Baseball Ground, I waited my turn to talk to a bunch of blokes in suits at a college that served some scruffy industrial wasteland within sight of the Thames.

The main thing I took to that interview was the ability to start work the following week. I figured they must have been desperate - let's face it, they were talking to me. There were six of us there in all and the first thing they told us was that there were two jobs on offer. We divided ourselves into two groups and I was up against a couple of blokes, one of whom wore a loud check suit and couldn't seem to talk about anything but athletics. I knew I was in with a chance and I left there that afternoon with the offer of a job. A week later - along with Carlisle United - I was stepping up a level. I had a full-time job and a range of opposition, some of which was likely to give me a serious test.

Carlisle started the season with a similar set of contradictions to the previous year. Three games in they'd won, drawn and lost, humbling a Derby County side who had been awesome within the recent past, losing out to the odd goal in five at Grimsby and fighting to a 1-1 standstill with Burnley. Given the hurried return, the packing of bags and the long journey to the North Bank of the Thames, there wasn't much time to take on board the new team or the new star striker. Malcolm Poskett looked like the sweaty, skinny one hanging in the background in some low budget American movie just before the rednecks in the bar commit some terrible crime.

In ordinary times we'd never have seen Poskett because Watford would have hung on to him. But, with the money that Elton John was pumping into the team, Poskett found himself surplus to requirements. Alan Shoulder joined the strike force from Newcastle, continuing the great 'Pop' tradition of North Eastern players slumming their final declining years at Brunton Park. Whatever, Soulder and Poskett scored all the goals in the 3-0 demolition of Derby that opened the account.

I was dropped in at the deep end for sure. I had everything from 'ESN' (you were still allowed to say 'Educationally sub-normal' in those days) to mature engineers who needed demanding Communications work. With wall to wall YTS making up most of the other hours, I was really thrown in to the job. Almost everything was new and the location took some figuring out. Grays Thurrock is basically nowhere in particular and its current claim to fame - the proximity of the Lakeside shopping complex - was nowhere to be seen in 1982. There was simply an almighty hole in the ground.

Watching Carlisle in this situation was going to demand locating and visiting away grounds. The Second Division that year offered Crystal Palace, Charlton, QPR, Fulham, and Chelsea. Palace visited Carlisle in mid-September. I'd been at the hard end of the job a week and I combined getting ready for the next gruelling five days with a short exploration of the delights of Grays Thurrock. 350 miles up the road from Grays, we won 4-1 with Poskett scoring the lot. Hell, I'd have loved to be at Brunton Park for that one. Full-time jobs, they really fuck up your life!

The straight hard working world was indeed upon me with a vengeance. The free love life of a few months before was well and truly in the past. I'd had one almighty indication that - just maybe - I was meant to be straight during that summer. I was exercising my chemical consciousness on a mind expanding walk that took in a few beautiful sunset colurs, a darkening sky and some impressive dark clouds. I'd been amazed when a huge flash of light hit the seaside street down which I was wandering with a decidedly sober mate. I'd just registered the fact that I was on the receiving end of some good gear when it struck me that the guy with me was staring wide eyed and open mouthed into the space above us. He could hardly get out the words. 'Did you see that?' he gasped before explaining that lightning had hit an electric wire over our heads and run a sheet of flame across the street.

All I had seen was the flash and I'd put that down to something else entirely. Without the wire the lightning could have hit the street, or earthed itself through the nearest avaiable conductors, like people! So there you have it, my mate gets a life altering, mind-bending experience. I take a trip and miss out. There may be a message in there for us all.

The 4-1 victory suggested Carlisle would survive when dropped in at the deep end. The fact that I was getting laughs, getting people to write things down and getting out of classrooms alive suggested I was up to the professional job as well. The bulk of my working life involved facing groups of YTS who were faced with an unemployment blackspot for a home area, a handful of qualifications to their name, and the prospect of a life built around menial labour and general education in return for £25 a week for the best part of a year. Naturally, what these people needed to make their lives complete was a liberal amount of my time and a scheme of work based around all the skills they hated at school!

In fact it worked out reasonably well since I was new to the whole caper as well, and the monumental three and four hour sessions I'd been given with them allowed for trips into town, visits to anywhere local that would have us, and the odd venture further afield in a mini bus. As to whether any of this would benefit their lives further down the line I was dubious.

We did get to talk football though. The general verdict on Carlisle was that the inhabitants of Grays knew them like they knew Stenhousemuir - a name on the football results or the pools coupon. West Ham, and Spurs all drew fans from this crowd and those with an active interest talked in detail about the ICF and West Ham's travelling army. Since our dizzy heights in the recent past had only included lining up against the might of Chesterfield and Grimsby, I could only respond with stories of the last time I'd seen West Ham in action, all those years ago when I'd shared wine, chat and an appreciation of Les O' Neill with that travelling rock band at Brunton Park. But this much was the basis of a conversation and probably amounted to more a meaningful educational experience than the stuff I covered about the exciting range of services at Grays Post Office.

Within a month it struck me I could cope with this for a living. I was - at best - ambivalent about whether it was the right thing. But, having started my stumbling and confused mid-life crisis somewhere around 14 years old, it also struck me that confusion on this scale was normal and I might as well have been earning a living whilst I was still deciding what I really wanted to do to earn a living. I was still banging away with the writing and, since the new job demanded handouts, schemes of work and the rest, I was spending some nights late in the staff room. Here I was banging out page after page on the typewriter, starting with one job and working my way through two or three others by the end of the night. Then it was simply a necessity, now it strikes me as an important period in terms of cracking the discipline of writing for a living.

My boss, Tony Mulvihill, found himself on the receiving end of a fair amount of distrust and rumour. He didn't share a lot on a personal basis, but to this day I'm still learning from the examples he used to lead us. When our paths finally went in different ways, I thanked Tony for teaching me that looking after number one was sometimes the best policy for everyone. It got a laugh from the people we'd worked with, but I meant it and it does hold true in many situations.

Workwise the next few years would teach me a lot about what I'd fallen into. Your local college may well be peopled with more misfits than the average workplace. What this means in real terms is that Further Education - which usually means something you do after school, most of which is not at any higher level than work offered by schools - is staffed by people who have arrived from a bewildering number of directions. In a school or university you'll generally meet a teaching staff who intended to teach in those places. In an FE college you'll meet everyone from the truly gifted teacher, who sees the unwilling English retake crowd as a challenge of evangelical proportions, to a smattering of refugees from a range of trades who are looking for a living wage and an escape from the nerve shredding realities of the real world. Like I said, misfits.

Virtually none of the people with whom I worked in that first institution had honestly intended to be FE lecturers when they left school. Some of them were still working on escape plans and an impressive contingent had well developed activities on the side. Like the varied and unpredictable crew of students we drew from the surrounding area, our staff had come from everywhere for every reason. I might have been trying to figure out why I was there, but in reality, that wasn't exceptional. The only slightly odd things I brought were an in-depth knowledge of Cumbrian issues and my youth. At 22, I was a baby in such company and to this day I haven't met a full-time lecturer in the same business younger than I was on the day I signed up.

The other great trend in FE colleges was, and remains, the way they respond to changes in the world around them with a combination of missionary zeal, absolute desperation for business and surly cynicism in the face of a massive boot up the rear end from the government. The differing responses arise because different people in the organisation have different things to gain and lose. In the case of management there is a constant battle to gain and keep a market share. As fast as you tooled up the colleges to teach welders in the Eighties, the jobs vanished, leaving echoing workshops as the growing areas of Performing Arts and Media Studies staged epics in cramped classrooms with paint peeling off the walls. Look at this situation from the point of view of someone trying to balance the books and an initiative like the YTS starts to look exciting. Part of the beauty of these students was the chance they offered to put more work into existing areas, like skilled trades. Another attraction was the influx of 'new' money attached to the scheme.

There were people committed to making the whole thing work. Some because they genuinely cared, some because they cared what they could get out of it. Elsewhere there were people who already had jobs and who regarded this new type of student as something akin to letting the supporters loose at a football club and fielding a team drawn from the terraces. These people also had a point.

If you'd spent 20 years teaching Motor Vehicle Studies to a steady stream of those born to dismantle engines and then found yourself confronted by a group of people who'd only decided they wanted to dismantle engines when the other options on the form included working on circuit boards or learning the rudiments of landscape gardening, you might start to doubt the wisdom of the YTS. At worst - and its no names no pack drill at this point - Motor Vehicle Studies on the YTS meant taking in a student who might be taught something in a college, but would be trusted with nothing more dangerous than a hosepipe by the time he arrived at the local bus garage. The bosses at that end of the process wanted the buses to start and arrive at their stops on time. They might have been willing to offer a work placement but they also wanted mechanics who could be left alone to repair engines.

From one perspective the YTS was a noble scheme to skill those in most need and offer genuine opportunities. From another viewpoint it put slave labour back on the agenda and clean buses on the streets. Somewhere in the middle of this I spent half of my first full-time year trying to get the lives of these people into some shape. In terms of my encounters with the same crowd we'll call the whole thing a score draw. Like the YTS in Carlisle, these lads - and they were all lads in my groups - could teach me everything about local crime, second hand tellies available in pub car parks, and using three cushions to pot an impossible black on a pool table. I had the edge on basic literacy and how to cope when you just have to send that telegram. Somewhere in the middle we all managed to negotiate a pace of work and a pattern to the week that allowed for all round survival and allowed the students in question to understand one end of a bank account from another.

Within a few months I'd got on top of things to the point that the Second Division fixture list offered some reasonable options for the weekends. Reasonable that was until twenty to five in the afternoon. Heading off to Brunton Park on my own was one thing. Negotiating London with an A-Z in search of the less fashionable grounds was different. The biggest change was the sheer volume of supporters travelling through the main stations and the absolute absence of Carlisle supporters in these crowds.

I played it close to home when confronted by the trip to Loftus Road in November or The Valley in March. There were Carlisle fans at both games, both involved convoluted train journeys for me and both ended up as disappointing results. Queens Park Rangers who finished top of the division that season were barely worth their 1-0 win over us and the game was barely worth the effort of going. We were struggling at the lower end of the division and Rangers were always fancied to go up. However, I was in over my head and still surviving, I expected to see Carlisle doing the same.

There was some of this in evidence at Charlton. You could probably see The Valley from the top of the five story tower at Thurrock Technical College. Getting there without taking the car is another story. Charlton were basically in the same situation as us. Skilfully challenged, short on fans and used to having to fight where other teams could flow. A winter's day, some hard fought football in front of a pathetically small crowd, and no goals to show for it. Somewhere, in the perverse mix of emotions which had hit me as a result of moving South to earn a living, there was a happy glow. It came from the thought that here in an unremarkable corner of London there was a pocket of football activity that resembled Carlisle, right down to the misfit team, the fighting spirit and the desperate choke of the star striker in front of goal.

I was in unfamiliar territory. I was working hard to hang on to the things that made me that loveable mass of confusion, sick humour, inconsideration and crass stupidity I had always been. Carlisle United were one such thing and their trips South offered opportunities to hold it together. The McEwan-Younger logo on the strips was a new departure and it struck me, since I was tee-total, that the sponsors were wasting their money as far as I was concerned. It also struck me that the team looked oddly unfamiliar away from home. In fact the whole thing was a new perspective. A snatched conversation on a train with an opposing supporter was - as likely as not - to take in his sightings of Malcolm Poskett before he'd pulled on a Carlisle shirt.

CHARLTON FAN - 'Well, they wuz a decent side Watford, but Poskett wasn't up with the pace the day they come dahn 'ere.

NEIL - He bangs them in at Brunton Park.

CHARLTON FAN - Brunton Park, oh yeah, I wuz tryin' to remember the name of your gaff.

In the hard fought scoreless encounter with Charlton, Russell Coughlin's beefy frame fought off enough challenges to impress a bunch of cold and apathetic supporters. Coughlin looked like a creature who belonged in an inconsequential scrap of a game. Where Poskett had a killer instinct and a deceptive level of invention - hell, the guy threw in a creative back-heel the day we hammered Palace for four - Coughlin simply ran, passed, sweated and collided with the opposition. Slap a tartan shirt on him and you'd swear he was a plumber who shifted pies and sausage rolls like they were going out of style.

The slings and arrows of the life of an away supporter came home to me in a legendary story which - I think - relates to this season. I didn't make the trip to Stamford Bridge in March, 1983. Chris Storey did. Chris had been a couple of years above me at school, started off at art college and shared with me a love of Carlisle, Neil Young and stories about the paranormal. Probably because we tended to finish each other's sentences or repeat the same arguments, we'd managed friendship but didn't exactly hang out together the whole time. On a famous occasion Chris went to a Chelsea v Carlisle game on his own and got set upon by Carlisle supporters at the tube station. The story I heard came third hand and may have grown in the telling. I considered checking it out for this book. I figured that to be a bad idea, partly because of Chris's current residence in Japan, but mainly because of the danger that the truth would turn about to be less interesting than the version I know well.

130

We'd gone down in a six goal encounter because Chelsea - despite their own pathetic position within sight of the drop zone - had put two past us in each half. Chris, alone on the platform, was set upon by a mob of Carlisle supporters who had him figured for a Londoner. When the jostling got to knocking him off his feet, he started shouting about his history as a Carlisle fan. This made things worse since - to the Cumbrian contingent who were about to send him to Casualty - he'd announced himself as a soft Southern shite. Quite simply, they didn't believe him at first, but once he'd recited a few legendary Carlisle names they realised he was a genuine Cumbrian and this - in turn - put the pummeling they were dishing out into a different light. Laying off and helping Chris straighten himself out they shuffled about a bit, mumbled 'Sorry, Lad,' and - according to one report - insisted Chris came out for the longest and least enjoyable pint of his life. The last I heard about Chris was that he was living in Japan, in Kobe. He didn't make the news reports about the earthquake so that has to be good news. Either way, it's a long way from Bothel where he grew up. And I thought the South East of England was a lonely outpost for Carlisle fans.

By May of 1983 we'd ensured survival in the form of mid-table mediocrity and I was investigating the whereabouts of Craven Cottage for the first time in my life. With two games to go in the league we faced our last away encounter of the season against a team that could, mathematically at least, make it to promotion. In front of a heaving crowd we got a lesson in finishing. Shoulder and Poskett didn't get a look in as the London outfit put one past us in each half. The absence of Jack Ashurst and the mighty Paul Bannon would have given me the basis of an excuse if anyone at my work had cared to bring up the subject of the game, but they didn't.

By this point I'd mapped out a life in and around London to go with my work on the fringes of the city. I'd got together with Tricia, a Scot from Kirkaldy who'd been down in the capital long enough to work her way through a succession of jobs and find herself employed by a book publisher. We could get out most weekends and see something in the city, although her interest in football only extended to knowing that Raith Rovers were her local club. As Carlisle survived a season back in the Second Division, I finished the academic season somewhere above mid-table mediocrity. I'd performed well enough against the opposition to earn support from the manager and a lengthy discussion of skills and tactical plans for the following year. Like Carlisle, these tactical options had to be drawn from a limited choice. The options, however, included getting involved in new courses and working to make them successful. Up to now I'd simply been dropped into stuff that was already running and expected to carry it on.

350 miles up the road, Bob Stokoe was also making similar decisions based on limited options. He drafted in an unemployed recruit, Dave McKellar, as the new first choice goalie. Trevor Swinburne headed for Brentford. No doubt his first days

in the new club were a riot as the backroom staff and team members all asked him the same thing.

'What is it with Stan Webb? Where the hell did Carlisle find him?'

McKellar's 'unemployment' became a legend - remember these were the days of Margaret Thatcher's economic miracle which involved rising numbers of jobless. In fact, McKellar had faced retirement from the game due to a back injury. Swinburne had gone to Brentford and it was Brentford who were prepared to place McKellar on the scrap heap. Bob Stokoe knew form and players with a depth few others could understand. If Hollywood can make millions with Robert Redford playing *The Horse Whisperer* what fortune awaits the screenplay and ageing 'name' actor who plays the title role in *Bob*. The movie about the football manager who can see form and class, even in those invalided out of the game? If they ever make the movie, the chances are that the location catering budget alone will be more than Stokoe had available in the Summer of 1983 to build a team for an assualt on the Second Division.

Dave McKellar would come and go twice from Brunton Park. Years after being consigned to the soccer scrap heap he would sign for Rangers. He might have been second choice in Glasgow, but when the reserve matches included runs out against Celtic the crowds were respectable. In one game McKellar played in front of over 10,000. Bad back or not, he played in every Carlisle game bar two for the next two seasons.

I weighed up a few options that Summer. I had a full-time job and I could survive well enough in that environment. Having started the whole thing at a week's notice and without any qualification to suggest I could do it, I was now faced with one day a week off over two years to get that qualification. The time off aspect was attractive in those days. There were marathon runners in the same college clocking up mileage during the daylight hours, there were other people running businesses on the side, and the main job of educating people was getting done to a high enough standard to keep the students coming year after year.

I weighed up my own position. All told, I had a few things going for me and several stacked against me. I wasn't going to get a massive advance from a publisher overnight. In fact I'd be lucky to get one at all. I didn't know anyone in the writing business apart from Tricia. In any case, her job revolved around a company who turned out limited editions of highly priced collectables. The Jackson Pollock sketchbook she showed me one day was a snip at £300. This was 1983, that book was worth half the price of my current car!

There were compensations to working in colleges, one of which included the chance to develop things you knew you could do well. You had time to do your own things and do the job well. Against this you had to weigh up the fact that others in the education business regarded colleges as a Micky Mouse operation.

They were wrong, but they had evidence every time we jumped to respond to a new trend and continually redrew our own boundaries.

On a personal level I had some shortcomings to consider. Mainly the fact that I'd partied my way through an education that had left me qualified in mid-table mediocrity and facing an uphill struggle to achieve anything much in life. Having near enough drifted into a job that was starting to look like a longer term prospect than I planned, I had to do something about making this whole caper work for me and my employers. The 'star player' potential was there, but then it is there in most youngsters who get dropped into the deep end and survive. Hell, years later in a Carlisle side that were skilfully challenged only on the days they were also truly inspired, we'd look at anyone short of twenty five years old and hope they had potential. Even Jason Prins.

On the plus side I was starting to discover the qualities that I would need to put extra money in the bank and phone numbers in the address book. Yes, we had address books in those days. The Filofax and the database existed in primitive forms, but pens and paper were what really mattered. I was writing on a typewriter and so was everyone else in 1983.

There are only two things you really need if you want to write for a living, self-discipline and ambition. I've heard people talk about talent and inspiration, but these are hard to quantify. In fact, they are about as hard to quantify in the writing world as they are on a football field. Let's take talent. At the top end there are players apparently bursting with it. Players who can hold a ball, evade tackles and place the resulting pass onto any given blade of grass if required. Every generation has such wonderous men; Stanley Matthews, George Best, Diego Maradona, Rod Thomas. Men of talent and inspiration, but - in truth - they are nothing without the context and the structure around them. The same is true of writers or anyone trying to make their living from a profession that needs ideas and tactical thinking.

George Best needed Bill Foulks. In fact that monumental Euro glory team needed his uncomplicated defensive approach, his total lack of respect for the most expensive strikers the best European teams could muster, and his experience. Forgotten amongst the giants of his own team, it is worth rembering that when Manchester United beat Real Madrid in the match that finally sealed their first appearance in the European Cup Final, it was Bill Foulkes running onto a George Best pass who scored the goal that took United to that historic game at Wembley in 1968.

Alex Ferguson might just have assembled a team of equal merit by 1999, but once again the 'inspired' striking partnership of Yorke and Cole was based on one man who had been labelled 'crap' on a fairly regular basis by a large section of the fan base. A man who'd missed a one on one chance against West Ham with a Championship at stake, and found himself some unwanted affection from Blackburn supporters as a result. Cole could forage, scrap, run, blast and head in all over the box. One player like him is containable, two like him with the small matter of passes laid off from the accurate feet of David Beckham and you have a strike force that need fear no opposition. Andy Cole is brilliant, first and foremost, because he works hard and wants to succeed. Alex Ferguson gave him the opportunity to strike his way into history.

In 1983, I had begun to discover a level of self-discipline and ambition that nobody who'd ever taught me had believed possible. The most obvious sign came on the longest day of the year when I headed out to complete the 'Four Peaks' marathon in the Lake District. Having taken up jogging around the time I quit drinking, I had progressed to buying decent running shoes, upping the mileage and making it a regular part of the week. I'd always gone fell walking and that summer, somebody, probably my mate Ian, had suggested a crack at the suicidal 49 mile trek around the four highest peaks in Lakeland. A few weeks before the event I'd come badly unstuck scouting out the thin path that counted as the climbers traverse around Broad Stand. A short cut to the top of one of the highest mountains, a route generally used by people who are running up and down the small rock faces around Scafell. At first I thought I'd broken my ankle. I'd only sprained it, but I'd done enough damage to leave me hobbling down from 3,000 feet. Three weeks before the big day my chances of playing were shot - or were they?

Short of training and fitness on the day, I did it. Somewhere around 36 miles, coming off the worst section of the lot on the mind numbing grassy slopes that make up the back of High Raise, I realised it was on. Stumbling into the check point at Steel End, with another 3,000 footer to go, I ran into the rest of the mob. Rich and Ian hadn't any excuse. They were fit and I'd caught them up. Three weeks before, the day after I'd almost broken my ankle, I couldn't even walk properly. We slogged our way over the last mountain and back to Keswick. The secret? Not inspiration, not natural ability, I just wanted it badly enough. If you want something badly enough you can overcome the obstacles, assuming you get the chance. Ask Dave McKellar and Bob Stokoe.

From that Summer things established a pattern that has - more or less stayed the same for me. Carlisle United set about establishing a similar pattern and almost achieved the impossible in 12 months. In the same period, I worked hard at getting fit, writing anything I could place in print and getting on top of the problems and opportunities offered by the day job.

Using the paltry sums available, Bob Stokoe set about building a team to challenge for promotion. In addition to McKellar, he brought in Don O' Riordon, a defender so disciplined he put the unfussy efficiency of Jack Ashurst to shame. I wasn't to know it that summer, but Paul Bannon's days in a Carlisle shirt were numbered. Just as well then that as one of my heroes departed, Stokoe acquired a man with the crowd pleasing skills of Stan Webb or Joe Laidlaw. O'Riordan wasn't a man to let his feet do the talking when there was a team-mate within earshot.

'Inspirational' barely does the guy justice. Lob a troubling ball into the Carlisle box and it would be Don who killed it with his first touch, blustered past two opposing players and scrambled a clearance to the feet of a breaking Blue to start something. The guy made Peter Shilton's outbursts at team mates look restrained, and could turn up anywhere on the pitch with a telling touch. He was a defender and he bagged almost 20 goals in two seasons! Telling touches out of position all of them.

The man was class to his very bootlaces and yet he hid a character trait that raised his crowd pleasing antics to the levels few will ever touch. Deep down, O' Riordan possessed a psychopathic tendency that left opposing strikers airborne and stunned, and left Carlisle fans with sore throats as we screamed with absolutely no conviction, 'He fucking dived.'

The really entertaining aspect of this trait was its total unpredictability. Faced with an incisive run on the Carlisle goal, Don could tackle fairly for the ball, lay it off and lay into the rest of the defence with an encouraging fury that would tighten things up and leave the opposition no chance for the rest of the game. Faced with an acre of space, a 50-50 ball and the certainty of a 2-0 lead already in the bag, O' Riordan could win the ball, slip his man and then respond to a second challenge with an all out assault that would leave the sound of cracking bones echoing chillingly around the ground, until the Blue Army waded in with the predictable claims that the convulsing specimen writhing on the pitch had taken a dive.

Don was a find in the great tradition of Carlisle characters. By placing O' Riordan next to Ashurst and putting David McKellar behind the pair of them, Stokoe had excelled himself. To put this in context, in 82/83 we conceded 70 goals. The following season we let in 41. Bob Stokoe, genius on a shoestring. I rest my case.

If I was facing a future of Further Education then my life was also going to take the shape dictated by the area in which I had found a job. I've never grown to love the South East and even people in the South East would struggle to like Grays Thurrock. If you're a Cumbrian reading this book you're unlikely to care that much. Just take it from me, we're talking Cleator Moor on Thames. Nuff said. The proximity to London was a major plus though. From this point on, my life as a Carlisle supporter would be shaped by the dates on which the fixture lists placed South Eastern encounters, the unpredictability of Cup competitions and the chances of getting to a match on my visits home. Add to this an inordinate interest in the promotion and relegation of teams I'd never considered in the past, and you've got the picture.

All in all, it is a life that revolves around getting results on the back of good planning, but being constantly reminded that the bigger picture is totally in control of someone else. This mirrors Further Education and also the way Carlisle continued to perform throughout the Eighties. In a good season I could easily make a quarter of the games. Despite this, by May I'd find myself with some curious emotion amongst the predictable reactions to Carlisle's fate. At the end of a good season, like the Summer of 1984, I was sad at the relegation of Cambridge United and, therefore, the lost chance to walk into the Abbey Stadium by way of the allotments. Such is the lot of the expatriate fan.

The net result of this is that I've taken the attitude of many of the Cumbrian expats I've met down South. We're stuck in limbo, nostalgic for the sights and sounds of home and - paradoxically - more Cumbrian because of our distance from the place. It's a situation on a par with ethnic minorities with an added twist. Because we aren't any kind of ethnic minority, the only people who'd begin to see us as different are ourselves. Put a group of Scots or Irish together in a big city bar outside their home countries and the results are predictable. Cumbrians are the same but nobody outside of Cumbria recognises us or knows what it is that makes us special. We're a minority and we're totally invisible. There aren't even enough of us to mob up in most places. In the face of this, we cling on to the things that make us special, one of which is our only league football team.

Time and again I've chatted away to some Cumbrian at a game and, after the usual discussion of current league form, the predictable 'Crap down here' slamming of whatever Southern outpost we're visiting, and the equally predictable crack about what we do for a living, we can get into enjoying the football. In those early Eighties days I hadn't much to offer in these conversations. I'd barely made a life for myself in the South and it ached every time I headed South after a good break in Cumbria. It still does, but in the immortal words of Bob Dylan, 'I've never gotten used to it, I've just learned to turn it off.'

We're never likely to be Southerners and - given our desertion of home - we're not really Cumbrians. If we're caught midway between the two, that leaves us stranded in Crewe, and that place really is a toilet. I was stranded in Crewe once, halfway down the motorway to the South with the big ends all but knocked out of the car. So, just maybe, my view of the place is skewed by a shit experience, a shit garage and a shit car.

Sticking it out for the job, the cash and the proximity to London, my life quickly established a pattern. The fixture list for 83/84 offered some real bonuses. Two home games in quick succession at the end of August whilst I was at home. The only goal of the two games hit the Carlisle net, but we had shape, commitment and O' Riordan. The return to Charlton offered better weather, a worse crowd and a better result than the previous season. It was also the last sighting of Paul Bannon in a Carlisle shirt in the South. He only played in four games that season, twice as sub and twice from the start. On the occasions he started, he was hauled off and subbed.

At Charlton, short of pace, a telling first touch and much involvement in the proceedings, his performance had finally caught up with his sullen facial features. It was all the more obvious because elsewhere we were giving a good account. Substituted, Bannon finally let rip with what he'd wanted to say all those years.

Bursting into the directors box he held up a banner which screamed 'THE WAY OF ALL FLESH IS TO DECAY AND DEATH, JUST LOOK AT MY FUCKING PERFORMANCE THESE DAYS.'

Luckily the stewards restrained him just before he got the gun to his temple. Had he pulled the trigger he'd definitely have been charged with bringing the game into disrepute.

We surged through the season hitting the top three after a 15 match unbeaten run. I never saw Carlisle lose in the South in that campaign. Crystal Palace and Cambridge leaked two apiece and Chelsea and Fulham were fought to 0-0 standstills. Chelsea were a seriously good side in a strong Second Division. This Division was so strong that Newcastle outspent half of the First Division and still barely scraped promotion. In the face of performances like these and the good feelings every time I'd met the double challenge of surviving a nerve shredding 90 minutes as we fought out a point and finding the ground and getting in and out alive, I could feel I'd come away with a result. The absence of promotion to the First Division and our eventual 7th place was a mixed blessing. Had we kept up the top three position - we were third in the middle of March - I'd have felt I was really missing out living so far away. I'd also have feared for our safety facing the clinical midfield at Anfield or the fearsome pace at Old Trafford. Seventh in the circumstances was creditable and probably about fair. This team were not the equal of the 73/74 side and the top flight had got harder in the decade since we'd scrambled into that level. At least, that was the way I worked it out in my own mind.

Having got the job and the other distractions under control, I could start enjoying things again. Travelling out of London and back again at night had really cut down the amount of time I spent on other things. This was brought home to me one Saturday afternoon when Carlisle were playing at home and I was record shopping. I heard this record being played in the shop with a riff that leapt from the speakers, a drum sound that rattled out far enough ahead of the beat to keep you wide awake for the duration, and a lyric that combined hilarity and depth to achieve something little short of brilliance. I bought The Smith's *This Charming Man* on the spot, but the fact that I'd been so far away from John Peel's show and the music press meant I was just about the last person alive to pick up on this band. Bloody shameful. I was also struggling to get anyone else interested. The first time they made the *NME* cover, Tricia drew a cartoon figure looking over Morrissey's shoulder and added the words, 'Wot, no talent!' Lovely girl, but she hadn't a clue on The Smiths. It was a North of Birmingham thing for sure, but the appeal seemed to miss a lot of females. They were The Byrds with the hippie pretensions replaced by dour Northern wit. The bastard sons of George Formby. John Lennon's dying wish. They were fucking brilliant and remain - to this day - one of the best live acts I've ever seen.

137

It matters in a book about Carlisle because there are parallels in football and the things we want from the game. Carlisle could provide moments of escape. In the form of Don O' Riordan, they had a Morrissey figure. A genuine talent for sure but someone who would do it his way, try and enforce his will on others and explode into surprising action. Like Morrissey he had a hard time convincing Southerners he was funny. Then again, if he was attempting to put your star striker into orbit, you'd be pissed off.

Busier than I'd ever been, writing and running seriously in my spare time, and still following football, I'd reduced Carlisle to something on a par with my other loves, but they were still there for me and, to a Cumbrian stranded in The South, they mattered. These were pre-internet, pre-satellite TV days. Hunting down game reports on Carlisle sometimes involved scanning every paper on a Sunday.

Some of the news came late. Paul Bannon's departure for Bristol Rovers at the start of 1984 was inexplicably left off the front pages. The *Daily Mirror* could have given their savaging of Margaret Thatcher a miss for a day to give that coverage. Bristol Rovers seemed a reasonable home for the one-man enigma. Apart from anything else this team had employed the questionable 'talents' of Bob Lee and that proved the football supporting public of that city had a taste for strikers with their own unique angle on being human.

Speaking of Lee, he had also departed. His destination, Hong Kong. This left the worrying thought that Bob Lee was still - just about - on the same side of the planet. At least he wasn't within sight of Brunton Park and it would take a major injury crisis to put him back in a blue shirt. On the evidence of his 'style' and his strike a couple of years before in the Borough Park mud, he was - in all probability - made for Workington. Maybe the shame of this thought sent him packing to Hong Kong. People joined the French foreign legion because they wanted 'to forget'. If you closed your eyes and pictured yourself in a Solway gale that cut through your flesh to chill the very marrow of your bones as you blundered around on a quagmire, stumbling and graceless in the mud. Well, maybe you'd deny your true nature and run away to Hong Kong.

The Summer of 1984 gave us a heatwave, me a holiday of unbelievable proportions and Bob Stokoe the same old headache on trying to build a credible side on the strength of loose change. Whilst the contractors toiled at Thurrock College to strip asbestos from the ceilings, I sweated out hard road miles in the heat. I'd entered a race in Essex to get a feel for the whole competitive end of running and that Summer I entered two up in Cumbria. The first, the annual pre-season training fun run at Brunton Park pitted me against some of the players and saw me finishing with a sprint in front of the paddock with a few blue shirts in the pack behind me. My first half marathon in Workington a few weeks later sealed it. I could handle this.

I could handle it a hell of a lot better than the merciless stuffing I saw at Brunton Park when Brighton turned up to get in some target practice in the first league game of the season. They'd scored all the goals in the game - all fucking three of them - by half-time. To make matters worse our new 'star' striker, Garry MacDonald, was beached out of reach of a decent pass somewhere in no man's land. The *News And Star* said he was a striker. Anyone could slap on a shirt and say they were a forward, but then Adolf Hitler said he was an artist. Garry MacDonald never scored for Carlisle and a matter of weeks after joining us from Middlesbrough he jumped ship and found his true level at Darlington. The Hitler comparison isn't so far from the truth in the case of Garry bloody MacDonald. On the evidence of his non-performance against Brighton he had something in common with great dictators like Augusto Pinochet. For starters, he seemed to think that people herded themselves into football grounds for the sole purpose of being tortured.

By the time we were taking four points in two home games at the start of September, my world was changing on a major scale. Starting the second year of my lecturer training course, I was stuck in the canteen of an agricultural college as the new first year group arrived. My mates Eric and Chris were 'talent spotting' amongst the new group and all three of us noticed one of the new intake in particular. The lack of seats obliged the new crowd to split up, and once we'd persuaded her to join us, Eric waded in with a pile of up front questions. Name, age, where she lived. From where I was sitting I soon sussed that she wasn't wild about this subtle as a flying mallet approach.

I also got her name. Jane Wilson. A few nights later we were together on the dance floor at Dukes, the nearest thing Chelmsford had to a nightspot. Jane and I had managed a romantic night for two because the other 12 who'd turned up trying to get in had still got on their scruffy jeans and bale twine belts from the Barn Dance we'd held at the agricultural college.

Soon after that I was round at her place for the first time and meeting the rest of the outfit. Three year old Owen was sitting on the kitchen worktop, spinning the water off some lettuce and eyeing the unfamiliar man in the room. Within minutes I was messing about on the settee with him, and, all told, things went on quickly from there. Which, in a round about way, explains my limited presence at Carlisle games over the next couple of seasons.

The results ground out whilst I was in Chelmsford took Carlisle into the top end of the table although we never got above seventh, our finishing position the previous year. The rot set in after that whilst my life just got better and better. At least I was back in the frozen North by Boxing Day. Little had changed. We still lost 3-0, we just spread the leaks out over 90 minutes as Boro gave us a lesson in passion, clinical finishing and all round organisation.

The Boxing Day crowd was pathetic, with good reason. Three days earlier a Carlisle supporter had taken a fatal blow to the head after being struck by a missile hurled by a Blackburn fan. The guy from Blackburn served a term for manslaughter. The incident took place in the car park behind the main stand at Brunton Park. It made national news headlines. A few weeks later, it was a talking point with the students when I got back to work. Those that cared about football had noticed the story and it got us talking about Carlisle.

Carlisle have a hard element to rival most teams. The only real difference is the lack of numbers compared to the bigger teams. But the rivalry with Wigan, Blackpool or Burnely can bring them out. Years later, a Carlisle supporter, Paul Dodd, celebrated by the tabloids as the worst hooligan in the country and banned from Brunton Park, would publish his own account of football violence. *England's Number One* is the one Carlisle book I've never seen in the club shop. It's a page turner and it'll give you an insight into a part of the Carlisle crowd that don't appear in this book. Blackburn might have killed one Carlisle supporter at the end of 1984, but we've been involved in causing trouble ourselves on a regular basis. Apart from acres of terrace space that Boxing Day, the biggest change I noticed as a result of the tragedy at the Blackburn game was the slight increase in awareness of Carlisle amongst the students I was facing in the South East.

'Can your mob fight then?' being a fairly regular question.

Yeah they can. Trouble in various forms has been there or thereabouts for most of my life as a football fan. I've seen some, usually as I was running away from it. The most involvement I've had is going over the wall on several occasions. The lower in the league you go the easier the walls are to clear and the slower the stewards are to clear you off on the other side. The last time I went over the wall onto a pitch I was well into my thirties and old enough - apparantly - to know better. In fact, it was the smartest thing I could have done. Standing still in front of a pitch invasion would have got me trampled.

Boring bastard that I am, I tend to go for the law abiding approach. Where I tend to differ from a lot of the things written about trouble at the games is that I've got less against the troublemakers than many fans. One thing that doesn't get written on a regular basis is that the worst troublemakers still pose very little threat to the 'scarfers.' I guess I'd just about qualify as a 'scarfer' in that I'll usually sport colours and I've never thrown a brick. I've never knowingly met Paul Dodd and, really, there is no reason why I should. If we ever did strike up a conversation the most pressing thing I've got to tell him is that I couldn't put his book down and I finished it inside a day. He'll organise a ruck in a car park, and I'll be well on my way to the station when it kicks off. If we ever rubbed shoulders in the queue for pies, he left me well alone and that is just fine.

Take away everyone who ever got involved in a fight and you lose half the noise, a hell of a lot of the income and some decent one liners from every game. Take these people out of the Second and Third Divisions and you've got part-time football for certain at a couple of dozen clubs. This is not a defence of every stitched cut and thrown brick, it is simply a recognition of the fact that our national game is a rallying point for a range of emotions.

The solution to the trouble problem isn't simple, and anyone who thinks it is now solved because games are more lawful than they were 25 years ago is missing the point. The middle class 'designer' football fan can disappear as easily as he arrived and the hard element are still there. They just fight in a different place. If football prices itself out of the market or lowly teams lose their appeal to the point that financial ruin threatens an entire Division, the people who are going to keep a club like Carlisle afloat will include the same people who are mobbing up in 'away' pubs ahead of the game. It may be an uncomfortable thought but, to my reckoning at least, it is the truth.

Short of giving people employment, a sense of their own self worth and some ambition, you'll never get rid of the causes of football violence. A handful of the worst offenders have all of these things, they just like the adrenaline rush that goes with a good ruck. Tackling the causes of the problems would be so horrendously expensive it would create more problems and a hell of a lot of resentment. Short of a social change bigger than any of us can imagine, we've got trouble on the fringes of football long into the future. It may be a curse, but in reality it is a mixed blessing. I don't think I'm the only one who shrugs it off as part of the territory and feels relieved that the problems tend to erupt on seafronts, in car parks and anywhere else two mobs can arrange a meeting.

Speaking of mixed blessings, the acres of terrace space available that Boxing Day may have been due to the fatal fight, but a bit of thought could have told anyone that this was likely to be best policing of the season. Maybe if we'd allocated a few coppers to the Boro attack we'd have come away happier. On the plus side this was my first sighting of John Halpin. Fast, committed to the point of foolishness, and running hard from the moment he came on as sub to the end of the game. The league position bordered on worrying. Halpin suggested Stokoe's touch was back after the disgrace of Garry Fucking MacDonald.

It has to be said, from this point on my weekends belonged to Jane. By the end of that season I'd registered the 2-1 away win at Craven Cottage, including Don O' Riordan capping a man of the match performance with a goal. Carlisle wise, this was about it. I'd also registered a feeling of belonging and sharing things I'd never known before. The ins and outs of this don't matter too much in the story of my unconditional love for Carlisle except that, for a time, I had to work at something else that was more important. I don't know how early on I knew this was the real thing, but I'd suspected it almost from the start. I'd never thought of myself as relating to children before, but Owen and I hit it off immediately. It opened up a world that I'd never imagined. Adding a new dimension to my life, seeing things through a child's eyes, inevitably shrank the time I had for other things. Owen was three years and two months old when I met him. At this stage in his life we were never going to share stories of Chris Balderstone passes or Don O' Riordan's entertaining combination of defensive mastery and spontaneous attempts to murder opposing strikers. Within a few months of knowing Jane and Owen, I was dreaming that I might get the chance.

When Carlisle put together a nine point bonanza coming up to Easter, a sequence that included a 6-1 smattering of that Southern abomination of a team that had stolen Workington's place, I was impressed. I was struggling to talk to Jane about it, there just seemed to be more important things to talk about. Years before, I'd spent a period falling in love with Carlisle United. As a kid I'd allowed them to fill my thoughts and shape my imagination. Jane was now doing that, more than I'd thought possible.

It started with simply trying to figure a few things out. Jane's husband had left to go off with someone else. I alternated between doubting his sanity and wondering who could have convinced him that his time was better spent away from Jane and Owen. Within a matter of weeks none of this mattered. Jane and I were working at making it work, it took some effort in the circumstances, but the will was there on both sides. The weeks became months and we managed a week away on Rhodes the following Easter. That sealed it, and by the following Summer I was helping her to move into the first house she'd bought on her own. I thought then that the next time she moved we might be going in together on the mortgage.

As for the long term love affair I'd had with Carlisle, things were probably falling apart more than I'd like to admit. I wasn't working at this one except when it was on a plate. The following Summer I was up at home, but organising the timings around families and missing out on the pre-season friendlies and the opening skirmishes.

Carlisle and I didn't part company, but in the way of a romance that is neglected, our distance from each other allowed things between us to cool badly. Then again, you can't blame the few quid of mine that they missed for sending them into a dive in the 85/86 season. Whatever could go wrong did go wrong. Tommy Craig had been an inspiration on the pitch. Even when his legs couldn't do the job you knew the other players respected him. Many closer to the club than me reckoned he should have been manager after being player-coach. Bob Stokoe moved aside in the early part of 85/86 to give 'Pop' Robson the manager's chair. Craig went off earlier in 1985. A few shit results and 'Pop' legged it. You'd have to struggle to get any positives from his 15 minutes in the hot seat.

Being really optimistic you could say the 90 minutes it took to beat Oldham and achieve his only victory provided a good afternoon. Being hopelessly optimistic you could say that his two month stumble through the bog end of the division cast the managerial careers of Martin Harvey and Ian McFarlane in a better light. Being honest you'd have to say he was shit. He turned his managerial career around years later running the reserve team at Manchester United. That made us all feel really good in Carlisle.

Stokoe had earned his retirement and the undying affection of Carlisle fans. Still, he came back again. He didn't deserve the rest of that season. I saw some sights I'd sooner forget. Great little ground in a familiar dog-eared sense, the old Valley in Charlton. A home from hell in the face of a 3-0 hammering. We got off lightly. The goalkeeping that day was good. I never saw the accident prone Kevin Carr in goal. He'd come and gone by the time the travelling circus came to Charlton. In his place we'd hired Scott Endersby. In defence, the sublime skills of Don O'Riordan had been replaced by Wesley Saunders.

At the time I was working with a former football scout, Jim Cook. Jim had taken a job in Student Services at Thurrock and he told me to look out for Saunders. Fair enough, Wes was unfussy and solid. The problem was, he was surrounded by disorganisation. Jim Cook had also worked with a youngster who had incredible strength and playmaking skills by the name of Paul Gascoigne. Shame we didn't sign him!

We limped, we stumbled, we fell, and on Boxing Day I persuaded my mates, Bif and Ian, to come along to Brunton Park, 'for old time's sake'. We'd never been to Brunton Park together before, but the sentiment was there. We scrambled a 1-0 win over Boro which convinced nobody that we had a fighting chance of being much above the drop zone. John Halpin was magnificent and his bravery and work rate were rewarded with the only goal. The result bothered me, but elsewhere things were wonderful. I was settling in with Jane to something like a regular life and the family aspect was bringing back some of the magic of childhood. Maybe this more than anything left me needing less from the familiar sights and sounds of the past, like Carlisle United.

When you are pouring your emotions into other areas of life, working them up for 90 minutes on a terrace seems futile. Carlisle and I, it seemed, were heading away from each other. We were soon back on a parallel course. Around this time I saw the most unbelievable sight I had ever seen at a Carlisle game. My team and I both hit the bottom, both of us in free-fall. What happened on the pitch was painful. What happened off it still hurts me now.

It was desperate, we knew that. Two games to go and three points needed from the last home game to keep the slim hopes of Second Division survival together. The opposition that day, Charlton Athletic, needed a win to maintain their solid hopes of promotion. By now it was obvious why we'd scrambled the Boxing Day win over Boro. Those losers were as good as down. Against Charlton we were 2-0 up after 40 minutes, survival in our hands. The rest . . . oh hell!

Look, if you knew nothing about Carlisle before this book you may recognise what I'm going to tell you. Jim Tolmie was on our team. Who or what he was doesn't matter. He passed the ball back to Scott Endersby in goal. Tolmie passed back from half way. Nobody in their right mind would have expected the pass, or the height and force he attached to it. There was a wind, but that isn't any fucking excuse. Endersby was a trier, not exactly Alan Ross, but he had heart. He hadn't a bloody chance. The goal is a legend. I know that because three days ago - and now I'm talking early May, 1999 - Big Mick, a photographer who works with me told me so.

Mick follows Charlton, he knows the story because that goal prompted a second half revival in which they ran out 3-2 winners and, near enough, secured promotion. One place behind them were that lot who'd stolen Workington's place and discovered that their yo-yo lifestyle could be stopped with serious long balls. Wimbledon made the top flight in third place. One place above them Charlton were promoted, thanks in part to Jim Tolmie's own goal. We made Division Three in third last place. Wimbledon got up by playing a long ball game which would become their trademark. We committed suicide with one long ball that even they couldn't imagine.

I'd never heard my Dad say things like that before. It wasn't just that my Mum was ill. It was the way he said it and the things he'd done. She'd gone into hospital, he'd taken her some flowers from the wood. The three acre wood that we owned alongside the house. I knew it was bad from the uncertainty, the way he was clearly scared and the touching gesture with the flowers. Lesley and I went up from London together, and my Mum had changed totally from the person I'd seen a few weeks before. Frozen in part of her face, positive but so simple in her outlook that she didn't appear to be an adult anymore. There would be tests, things found out and things we didn't know, but I'd decided after a few minutes that this was it. I didn't really want to think that. Dad and Lesley seemed more hopeful and genuinely confused by what was happening. He rang Jane to ask her to tell me that the tests in Newcastle had found a brain tumour. Once I knew that, he rang me after the operation to tell me that they couldn't get it all and Mum had somewhere between three and six months to live.

I'd suspected something like this. I was 26, I already knew people, like Ian, who'd lost parents. Ian's Dad died just before Ian faced his final exams at Oxford. Knowing people who'd been through it didn't really help me then. For years we'd talked about being a close family. I knew and appreciated that I'd been blessed with parents who had never been judgemental. By the standards of their generation and the place in which I'd been raised they were inspired thinkers. They'd worked to make the lives they wanted. Creative and fulfilled lives. Coming from generations of more rigid minds and life chances that were more about obligations than opportunities, they'd inflicted nothing but free spirits on my sister and I. We had our rough moments, but they were fewer than most families. Now we'd have to test the bonds we had like never before.

The holidays in education were - in comparison to other jobs - obscenely good. I spent almost the whole Summer at home. I could say the things I needed to say. I could nurse my mother and deal with the worst that her condition could throw at me. I knew from the start of this that there was no hope for her. Despite that, it was a privilege to be there and to spend all of that time with her.

As the cancer spread, her awareness of what was happening loosened and changed. She remained unconcerned and almost serene in the face of life slipping away. She'd done more than anyone to hold our family together. She'd been there for us when my Dad was working away and, in a family that had been encouraged to pursue their talents, she'd been the one who'd made the most sacrifices. She could have been a professional musician. Instead of this, people would remember her as a music teacher. Sometimes, as she slipped in and out of consciousness, her hands would move to strike invisible piano keys.

The further away she slipped the more we pulled together to look after her. She'd done more than any of us to make this possible and, at the end, she would never know how well we coped. We owed so much of our strength in this situation to her. There were other things she'd never know. I was close enough to Jane and Owen to begin to understand what she had given to her children. I'd only started to talk to her about these things because I'd only started to see them. She died without knowing if Owen would ever become, in any sense, her grandchild. She died without knowing if she'd have any grandchildren at all. In the face of her death we were, quite simply, all the things she would have wanted us to be. None of which stopped it hurting. My mother died as the winter of 1986 began to take hold. There really wasn't anything much else that mattered at the time.

Bill Shankly, great man. He might have managed Liverpool to glory but he learned management at one school that could guarantee to teach him. The school of hard knocks at Brunton Park. As a rule, people forget that bit of his career. Like I said, a great man. But that famous quote, the one about football being more important than a matter of life and death. I hope he was kidding. Because if he wasn't, that great man hadn't a clue.

I'll tell you how much football mattered then. I was at home when Carlisle opened their home account in Division Three. At three o' clock on Saturday, August the 30th, I was pegging out the washing in the wood. After that, I went in to sit with my Mum.

As the months rolled by I headed up home, to spend time with my Dad. We went out fell walking. Slowly, we were learning the ways of a new relationship. I didn't think he'd really get over it. In all honesty, he didn't want to. But he still had things to live for. One of which was the local fells. By the following summer he was coming down to see Jane, Owen and me in Essex. Not really himself, but working at it. These things take time, a hell of a lot of time.

There are people who follow football, live around fixture lists, follow league positions and work out permutations as the matches tick away. They'd tell you they are worried. Three matches to go and you need seven points to avoid relegation. Oh yes, that's stress. But you see, if you're worrying about a football team like that, the chances are, the rest of your life is pretty stable. Stability of a sort was back with me the following summer.

By May, 1987, I'd seen something of Carlisle, none of it impressive. We were losing, we were in the drop zone, we got relegated and we bloody well deserved it. I managed to work up something of a reaction to this disaster. In the circumstances, this was a positive sign.

Another positive sign was the interest I'd got back in the ups, downs and issues of the whole football business. For 16 games in the previous season, Eric Nixon had kept goal for Carlisle. This was noticeable to me simply because the guy had the same name as my Dad. More significantly, Nixon was the kind of player we'd once attracted. Solid, confident, classy and adaptable. 'Adaptable' doesn't begin to do the guy justice. His stint at Carlisle helped him set a record that year. On the books at Manchester City he played for this club and four others including Carlisle, becoming, in the process, the only person ever to have played in all four Divisions of the English game in one season.

We were struggling to attract any real quality players and the loan signings made for inconsistency. They also made the gulf between the current side and that of the squad of 15 years before all the more obvious. The team I'd started to watch at Brunton Park had a goalie as good as Eric Nixon - by 1987 we could only get one when he was surplus to requirements at a bigger club.

At least I was back involved and planning my life around the fixture list. The current manager, Harry Gregg, had been given a small glimpse into football hell. I worked up some real sympathy and admiration for Gregg, but this was in 1998 when he gave one of the most emotional and heart-rending accounts of any event in sports history that I've ever heard. Harry had been on the Manchester United plane that failed to get off the runway in Munich and he'd pulled his team mates from the wreckage. On the 40th anniversary of the disaster his talk to BBC Radio about what he'd seen had a few million people spellbound with a story of simple heroism in the face of almost unbelievable horror.

On a smaller scale you could say the same about his time in charge at Brunton Park. No money to build a decent squad and a mixture of quality players on the way down, promising youngsters and a few journeymen who could, just about, argue their way in. Gregg hadn't the vision of Stokoe in his great days. But then, the Bob Stokoe who returned after 'Pop' Robson had popped off lacked that vision as well. From our point of view the only dependable good thing about the 87/88 season was the form of Newport County.

Maybe my memory has forgotten the exact figures, but I think the Newport team had an average age of twelve and their centre half was a 57 year old league novice, newly signed from a pub team. Either way, a team heavily reliant on people too young to vote belly flopped out of the starting gate that season and finally found their true potential when they hauled themselves up onto their knees. It was obvious from early on that Newport were an embarrasment of monumental proportions. It has happened since, notably at Doncaster, that a team built largely of YTS and old salts has been scrambled in the face of massive debts to fulfill a fixture list. To all intents and purposes, Newport were on the way out all season. We sealed our own escape from relegation into the Conference on April the 2nd, when we scrambled our second away win of the season, away at Newport, thanks to two Malcolm Poskett goals. It was our final away win that season and our first away win in five months.

Not that any of it mattered in terms of relegation, given the situation at Newport County. I didn't go to Newport, but I had developed a survival strategy for an exiled Cumbrian with family committments. Anywhere two hours from the Southern base was fine, any excuse to arrange a visit home to include a game or two at Brunton Park was better. With one notable change to the tactics, this is the strategy that has kept me going ever since.

Two hours from Chelmsford includes Cambridge, Colchester, Peterborough and London. It also includes Maidstone and Lincoln, but the Fourth Division didn't include either of those teams in that desperate season. Confined to away games, you get snapshots of the whole season. I missed Gary Fulbrook's historic half dozen runs out in a blue shirt. He played a few games, put in some decent tackles in defence and eventually returned to Bath City. Another one of the growing number of players being turned over at Brunton Park.

Historic because he was the first black player in our ranks. Dean Holdsworth didn't stay much longer, but he was just about the best news in our 4-1 stuffing at Leyton Orient. Away from home my snapshot was taking in some desperate form, empty football grounds and rapidly changing line-ups. Tony Fyfe came at the end of the season and - to me at least - looked useful in our final match at Cambridge. With nothing for either team to play for we won 2-1 and Fyfe and Brent Hetherington managed to scramble our goals in a game that everyone knew was pointless weeks before it took place. As at Colchester earlier in the season, I found myself pretty much the only punter in the whole place and the players took a break and sat down every time I went for a slash.

Hetherington and Fyfe combined in a clattering, unco-ordinated way to graft us a winning lead after being behind after 45 minutes. In reality it was a meaningless game fought out in a shoebox of a ground with allotments out back. Cambridge's insistence in naming the place the Abbey 'Stadium' was just about as ambitious as they got in those days. I was back on track, but this Carlisle 'team' were just a bunch

147

of blokes earning a crust for putting on a blue shirt. I could dream, but Tony Fyfe's contradictory presence on the pitch wasn't remotely close to the enigma of the mighty Paul Bannon. In the case of Fyfe the enigmatic appeal revolved around whether he could react to a pass without falling flat on his face, miss-timing his move, or swinging the wrong leg onto the ball by mistake. Brent Hetherington was Bob Lee firing on three cylinders and this was part of the dynamic strike force we would take into the next season.

Second bottom with another manager ousted, former Workington player, Clive Middlemass, at the helm, and about enough cash for a round of fruit gums in the bank, it was looking grim. We needed characters to make sense of the quagmire of mediocrity that threatened to overwhelm us. Somebody had to help us make sense of this. Unseen by the players and backroom staff at Brunton Park, I finally did my bit for the club. I became Don O' Riordan.

Oh yeah, and Workington won the FA Cup.

Blue Nightmare #9

Neil Nixon's all time Carlisle United Nightmare XI

1 - Mike Graham

2 - Mike Graham

3 - Mike Graham

4 - Mike Graham

5 - Mike Graham

6 - Mike Graham

7 - Mike Graham

8 - Mike Graham

9 - Mike Graham

10 - Mike Graham

11 - Mike Graham

Subs: Mike Graham, Mike Graham and Mike Graham

Director of Coaching - Bryan 'Pop' Robson

Assistant - Mike Graham, Player Coach

Opposition: Wycombe Wanderers away , FA Cup First Round

Chapter Nine - Mike Graham

MENTIONED FOR THE FIRST TIME IN THIS CHAPTER

Simon Davey - Promising midfielder signed from Swansea. Established himself 92/93, showed real class thereafter.

Darren Edmonson - Well fed product of the youth team. Went from Coniston to Huddersfield Town by way of an impressive stint at Brunton Park.

Paul Fitzpatrick - He tried to be inspirational in defence. On a good day he managed to tackle and clear the ball.

Ricardo Gabbiadini - Chunky and intermittent. I can confirm the rumours he had at least one good game. But he had some stinkers too.

Eric Gates - As mobile as a walrus stuck in treacle, but not quite as thin. He played for England you know.

Craig Goldsmith - A man who once earned his living as a professional footballer.

Mike Graham - 1988/90 - Willing, if predictable, defender.

Mike Graham - 1991/92 - Past his sell by date and easily passed by any opposing striker with two good legs.

Mike Graham - Febuary, the 12th, 1992 - a blue nightmare. The worst individual performance in the worst Carlisle team I've ever seen.

Mike Graham - 1999 - Seen in action amongst fellow members of Milnthorpe Corinthians. A team unlikely to trouble the higher reaches of the football pyramid.

Steve Harkness - A rarity, a decent and consistent performer in the 88/89 team.

John Holliday - Massive, misfiring, uncoordinated defensive enigma. To think, Bill Green once wore the same number on a blue shirt.

Mike Holmes - A passable member of a shit team in a shit season. Also, a footballer who once played for Carlisle United.

Simon Jeffels - A footballer who once played for Carlisle United. Also, a passable member of a shit team in a shit season.

Michael Knighton - Arguably the most controversial figure in the history of the club. Chairman from 1992 from which point there was seldom a dull moment, the scaling of heights and plumbing of depths came in quick succession and the man's matchless gifts for soundbites and inventive twists on the art of club ownership put United on front pages as well as the back of papers. A larger than life figure on his quietest days, more famous than any of his playing staff and a source of countless incredible tales told by fans, some of them possibly true.

Aiden McCaffery - One time player. Remembered mainly for managing the worst team in the history of the club.

David McCreery - Former Man Utd midfielder. First player-manager of the Knighton era.

Kelham O' Hanlon - 'Ireland's number one' goalie with an international cap and incredible reserves of motivation in the face of pathetic performances in front of his goal.

Paul Proudlock - He scored a few goals, we shouted his name a few times. A character who cared about the fans.

David Reeves - £121,000 record signing. Hard working centre forward, fan favourite, goal getter, always willing to put in 90 minutes graft.

Kevin Rose - Successor to transferred Dave McKellar in Clive Middlemass' greatest team. Had about half McKellar's class on a good day. Didn't have that many good days.

Nigel Saddington - Lanky, assured defender with scything tackle action when required, and sometimes when not required.

Richard Sendall - Almost a useful front player by the standards of the late Eighties, early Nineties. Then again, the competition included Tony Fyfe and Brent Hetherington.

Jeff Thorpe - Utility player brought through from youth ranks. A real prospect early on in his career. Injury prone later, but never faulted on effort.

Mick Wadsworth - A genuine coach. The best manager we'd had in ages. Appointed in the Summer of 1993. Delivering by the end of his first full season.

Derek Walsh - Scots midfielder who could score. Good enough for the plodding sides of late Eighties, early Nineties. After that a valued player at Gretna.

Keith Walwyn - All heart and always willing. Muscular striker, on the downward slope by the time he arrived at Brunton Park.

Andy Watson - Pretty much the only thing worth cheering outfield 91/92. Sold for a pittance the following season cos we were skint.

I DIDN'T START looking like Don O' Riordan. I didn't start dressing like him. It was more an attitude thing and a neccessity in the circumstances. Carlisle and I had drifted away from each other in some ways. As they'd plumbed the depths of the football league and finished in 91st place, I had headed in the other direction in terms of my performance. In the day job there were no YTS in sight and I'd written a new Media Studies programme which was gathering impressive student numbers. I'd also started teaching people to write. Not in the a-b-c sense, but in terms of Creative Writing, making a few quid and recording the things you always wanted to write down.

My writing course had gathered a mass of bodies. I was qualified to do this because I had also started collecting cheques and credits on a regular basis as a writer. After finishing my lecturer training I'd started a kind of literary 'target practice' period in which I'd line up material for any publication that looked likely and send it out. If they published it, I'd send more. If they didn't, I'd curse them for about five minutes and then figure out some way to recycle the ideas that had just been rejected.

The results had been interesting. In the same week that I cracked the worthy *Times Educational Supplement,* I also got my first jokes into *Viz* comic. *Viz* paid better and didn't butcher my copy, so I sent them some more stuff. The roots of this new branch of income went back to the end of the 1985/86 season. It was around this time I started letting rip with writing that began with little more than an idea of how to be funny. It drew on my experiences of being a Cumbrian, a football fan and a bloke with a seriously sick sense of humour.

On the last day of that relegation season, Carlisle United staged a pitch invasion and general ruck at Oldham. After the 2-1 defeat that ensured our drop into the Third Division, the police waded into the Carlisle end at Boundary Park, and Paul Dodd, amongst others, got coshed. I wasn't there, I just read the account in his book.

Carlisle were earning no friends with this approach to solving problems. The odd thing was, I was starting to write demented and sick prose that was finding friends who sat behind editor's desks. The closer I got to the literary equivalent of a football riot, the better the chance I had of getting my work accepted. I could fill entire paragraphs with little more than a tirade of obscenities and graphic descriptions of violence. In return I'd get a reasonable cheque. Hell, this was fun.

It was *Viz* and their ilk who turned me into Don O' Riordan. The great thing about Don was the mix of consummate professional skill and the fact that the Carlisle fans knew this leader of men, this classy motivation machine, hid the heart of an executioner. Don was a guy smart enough to have choices. He clearly enjoyed the lowest of tackles and the most pointless of fouls for their simple artistry. Part of the pleasure of watching him was the surprise of the opposing fans who didn't live with this guy on a regular basis and didn't see it coming. Don could wait over an hour for his first assault, lulling opposing fans into a false sense of security before . . . WHAM!

OPPOSITION FANS - 'Off, off, off, off, off, off!'
BLUE ARMY - He fuckin' dived.

I didn't write that much for *Viz,* but the success of this comic opened the floodgates for a raft of others. By 1988, *Viz* wasn't so open to a freelance writer. The management of the comic had gone into a deal with John Brown Publishing which left a lot of the administration in London and freed up the creators of the comic, who worked out of Newcastle, to do what they did to perfection. Let's give editor Chris Donald his due here, the bloke is near enough a genius. I never made that much money out of his publication, but without the stunning sales of *Viz* there would have been no *Brain Damage, Gas, Poot, Smut, Zit, Ziggy, Pulp, Acne, Gutter, Gutted, Elephant Parts* or *Head.* And I did okay out of that lot. Having sold stuff to *Viz* I could present myself as a credible writer to the competitors who sprang up, sometimes at a rate of one a month. Two years after selling my first item to *Viz* I was starting to cream it with the competition. This, in turn, presented one small problem.

At work, there were people who had earners on the side. These went from dealing car parts to taking pictures for soft porn mags. On one celebrated Monday morning, I ended up covering somebody's class because he'd just had an irate punter on the phone. The lecturer in question - who shall remain nameless - was jobbing as a carpenter and had managed to put on a roof repair over the weekend which had started leaking in the early hours of Monday morning. He nailed down the offending fabric and I flanneled in front of his students.

There was an uneasy acceptance of this moonlighting amongst those charged with managing us. In this context, my 'jokes' presented something of a moral problem. On one occasion a secretarial lecturer saw some of my work. She had no idea it was mine and she was so shocked she said she'd take the 'joke' to her church so they could pray for the people who read such garbage. Trust me, it wasn't that bad, you've heard worse 'jokes' if you go to football matches. But, for me at least, it was an insight. The smart move, in terms of keeping the day job under control, was not to blag too widely about what I was doing.

This had an added benefit which has kept me competitive to this day. The target audience for the jokes I was banging out were the students I faced on a regular basis. If I could work stuff into lessons and get honest feedback, I was in a better position to know what I should be writing. Taking the stuff into classes wasn't as shameless as it sounds. By this point I was teaching Media Studies. This involves studying a whole range of issues about the media world. One of the hardest to teach is the area of ownership and control. The main problem with this subject is that 16-19 year olds seldom express any real interest in the laws and controls on the media. Early on in this teaching, I cracked a way to get these issues across by looking at humour. I won't bore you with the classes here, but there are some obvious things to examine. Cruel stereotypes for one. *Milli Tant* in *Viz* might be a fat, humourless, man-hating lesbian, but I've seen her reduce hardened students to helpless laughter. That says more about the conflict between politically correct legislation and human nature than you can squeeze onto a page of a media text book.

So, in the time it took Carlisle to fall from staging a riot as they left the Second Division to staging a non-turnout as they fought out a pointless away win at Cambridge which ensured 91st place, I went from sending in hopeful copy to *Viz* comic to earning enough of a regular income to call myself a comedy writer. I also went 'underground' after a fashion. I was still the same person at work, but some of the things I was writing weren't getting discussed with my work mates. I was Don O' Riordan simply because the organised and methodical creature on the outside was giving way to the headcase inside who wrote as if he didn't give a shit.

When the comic competitors to *Viz* arrived they went all over the place in terms of style. Puerile, smutty and sick, sick, sick. So, writing for *Zit* wasn't the same as writing for *Ziggy*, but they all demanded regular piles of 'copy' every month. This meant turning it round at a phenomenal rate. For four years I would work for a couple of evenings a week, slap on some decent music, sit down with a pile of empty sheets of paper and knock it out. In the Eighties this still meant hammering it out with a typewriter. By the end of this period I'd bought myself a state of the art laptop computer.

To keep tabs on the output, I started by listing the titles of each item on sheets of paper. Later on, I shifted these lists onto a database. I realised I'd written around 2,500 'jokes' inside three and a half years. These 'jokes' could take the form of an article, script for a comic strip or any other item that would get a laugh from comic readers. A typical item would be the piece I wrote for *Viz* suggesting that Jimi Hendrix was alive and well and working in Chickpak's Carlisle plant. A 'joke' might also be a collection of 30 readers' letters or *Top Tips*. The Hendrix joke came from a pub conversation I'd had years before when a gang of us would compensate for the fact that nothing ever happened in Bothel by inventing things we'd seen. 'Lynyrd Skynyrd didn't die in a plane crash. I saw that Ronnie Van Zandt fixing tractors near Egremont the other day.'

You get the idea. Now, years later, I was getting paid for this. Carlisle United were never far away. They came in handy for two reasons. Firstly, the rate at which I was writing left me little time to do anything other than keep lists of the titles and send the stuff off to the various editors. Readers letters were a particular problem in this regard. One sentence, one joke and written inside half a minute. If they didn't make the comic until four months later I might not recognise them as mine. Since I was often expected to send invoices for my work when it was printed I had to find a way of spotting the stuff I could barely remember writing.

I took to filling my work with names I could spot a mile off. I got the names from the people on my degree course and my intimate knowledge of Carlisle United. For all of those years, Carlisle United players - past and present - cropped up regularly. In one edition of *Brain Damage* the entire letters page was written by the current Carlisle squad. A few months after that I noted Leeds United and Newcastle United names featuring prominently amongst the *Viz* letter writers and realised I might have started something.

I would sit down and knock out jokes from 5-30 to 9-30. The paper was blank and I'd start with an idea that occured to me there and then. Working at this pace, being in effect a sit-down comedian, I was bound to go back over ideas and themes that were already well established in my head. Carlisle United were everywhere. In the first edition of *Brain Damage* 'cash crisis club Carlisle United' re-signed one of their old players. The joke was that the player in question was 72 and he was obviously going to get massacred within seconds of his first kick-off. I'd based the player in question, I called him 'Stan Wilson', on Jimmy McConnell, a United legend from the first league days in Division Three North. Elsewhere I sold a joke questionnaire to another comic. In this one you had to decide whether your dad was a Third Division footballer. The questions asked things like what your dad was like on Saturday night and how he reacted when he saw Jan Molby on the telly. If he blurted out 'That useless fat bastard, I could spray out a few passes for the money he earns,' your dad probably was a Third Division footballer.

Okay, they weren't the greatest jokes on Earth, but the thing I soon discovered was that I could cut this stuff almost exactly to the needs of the different comics. Carlisle United were perfect subject material in each case and - sad to say it - they supported my attempts to work them into jokes with a pathetic start to the 88/89 campaign. Mid-table mediocrity hardly does it justice. Imagine if your team

155

managed their first league win on October the 15th. Imagine a mid-September situation of P-5, W-0, D-5, L-0. If you want to be charitable you could call it consistency.

This was a real parting of the ways for Carlisle and me. Compared to them, I was doing pretty well. Their place in my life was now something to do with maintaining the familiar feelings of being a Cumbrian and maintaining my loyalty. I learned something about how much I cared that season because we were almost as bad as the year before. There were encouraging signs in the organisation and a few useful touches on the park. Nigel Saddington's arrival in the defence had added some pace and an ability to read the game. Richard Sendall had a similar level of vision up front and we could always console ourselves with the thought that he wasn't Tony Fyfe or Brent Hetherington. Paul Proudlock had arrived by the end of the season. He scored goals with the odd rapid pounce on loose balls. Proudy could even slip an opposing defender or two.

But when all of these revelations in blue shirts were added together there was only one conclusion. A few years earlier we wouldn't even have considered most of these losers. To be fair to some of that team, they'd seen better days at other clubs. I've seen it argued elsewhere - like Mick Mitchell's book on Carlisle United - that Proudlock had real skill and would have shown it in a better team. Well . . . maybe.

I knew this team was limited, but I still cared more than I could say. I might have been writing jokes that regularly involved Carlisle, but the truth was they were in my thoughts so often that the ideas just kept coming. Stuck in Chelmsford I'd get to away games and see the odd bit of serious excitement. The 88/89 outfit only scored four goals on two occasions. Once they dumped Telford United out of the Cup and once they thrashed Peterborough. Hell, it was worth the run up from Chelmsford in January for that demolition of the Posh. John Halpin's leg was mended well enough for him to give the Peterborough midfield a lesson in creating space and we were so good that the chunky frame of Mike Graham got itself on the end of a telling strike on goal. It was plodding, percentage football all the way.

The opening of season nightmare of nine games without a win eventually gave way to a steadying of nerves and a general slog for points. The improved results owed a good deal to the return of Dave McKellar in goal. We briefly had a useful defender, Steve Harkness. He was there and gone so quickly I managed to miss him. He went to Liverpool in the end, all the reports said he was too good for us. Bill and Ben the Flowerpot Men would have been too good for the teams I saw in some games that season.

Early on in the campaign we chased Cambridge United around for 90 minutes. How the hell we scored two that day, I'll never know. Derek Walsh, a surging midfielder with an eye for goal, did have a decent game, but these things were relative. Walsh was a tryer in a generally turgid team. He might have been an attacking midfielder, but he was treading the turf in an attacking midfield tradition that included the likes of Chris Balderstone. Derek Walsh was well short of Balderstone's standard. I once saw Walsh play an inspirational game, masterminding attacks from midfield. This game was in 1995 and he was playing for Gretna. In a Carlisle shirt in 1989 he really had to sweat to stay with the play.

Carlisle were skint and Clive Middlemass had trodden this league road before with Workington. He was working hard to motivate and he did pull organised performances from a team that was thick with plodders. I'd managed to talk a few others into coming along to games. Jane's mate, Richard Courtney, for one. He hadn't been to a game for ages and worried about crowd trouble. Crowd trouble! That far south you were lucky to see a crowd in the Carlisle end. The Abbey Stadium, Cambridge, and Layer Road, Colchester, provided their predictable rattling emptiness. Colchester scrambled a point against us and fielded the fattest goalie in Christendom. I don't save programmes so I can't remember his name. I think it was Sumo.

We had a team who were trying, but clearly outclassed by anyone with 50 pence to buy decent players. I cared enough to go anywhere within striking distance of Chelmsford though in the hope of a miracle. It was worth the effort on my part. 4-1 at Peterboro was a miracle in those circumstances. I talked Richard Courtney along to the Colchester game and we had to jog the length of Layer Road to make the kick-off. In the car I talked great Carlisle teams and classic Cup ties. At the ground we got a low grade encounter with twice as much fury as there was skill.

The more Jane, Owen and I became a family the more I managed to work some football into our lives. We took Owen to his first football games at Chelmsford City. Chelmsford briefly had an out of contract Alan Brazil at the start of one season, but that was about as exciting as things got. Their 'stadium' was ten minutes walk from our front door on a bad day. I could sprint back from a game in time for the classified check on BBC1.

By 1988 we were leaving Chelmsford City and a few friends well behind. Jane and I had our moments, but we went in together on a house when she moved. Hacked off and bored with Further Education, she'd jumped ship in 1988 and landed a training management job with Kent County Council in Maidstone. This meant moving and we bought a house in Bearsted, on the edge of town and near the country. Jane had been ambivalent at best about Further Education colleges, she never completed the teacher training course which had brought us together in the first place.

In getting out she put the rest of us to shame. One odd feature of many of us who work in FE colleges is the amount of time we spend talking about getting out and doing something else. By and large, the biggest talkers about escaping are the ones who are still there ten years later. You'll see the same thing 'Oop North' and in the crowds supporting struggling teams.

Years later I'd see a pissed off Gillingham fan shuffle out of his ground announcing to the Carlisle supporters around him that this Gillingham side was the worst he'd ever seen. That man walked backwards to the turnstile, he still couldn't tear his eyes from the pitch. It's complicated beyond belief, the stuff that makes us curse and despise every moment we do something - and yet renders us totally incapable of changing the situation. The scriptwriters on *Coronation Street* have it down to a fine art. Time and time again someone tries to get on and everyone else in 'the street' whispers behind their backs. I've seen the same thing down South, usually at work, but it is an oddly Northern thing.

One reason we're, at best, ambivalent about our heroes up North is that these people remind us that we could all do it. If somebody starts off in Maryport and ends up on their own yacht in the Mediterranean it makes it bloody obvious that the 'No jobs around here' excuse his pals are using is a bit one dimensional. I'm not a Norman Tebbit 'On yer bike,' merchant. But, the people I've seen who really got on simply did the work and didn't fall back on the excuses.

I don't want to hang around with that Gillingham fan who cursed his team so badly. Anyone who'd leave a game complaining and still savouring the abomination of the team to which he directed his fury simply had to be a sad bastard at home.

Jane was never like that, and her positive and capable side took us to Maidstone, held us together, and gave us both a sense that this move was right. Cumbrian to the core, I was the one who had to be persuaded to have faith in change. We'd gone from falling in love to pulling together through a few challenges. The three of us were a family beyond any question by this point. We shared more than we had with anyone before and the problems, once sorted, helped us to keep on building. In the great Bob Stokoe tradition it wasn't always pretty, but we got results.

If you're writing jokes you have to start with some understanding of human nature. The whole point of humour is that it gives us permission to say things we can't say to our friends, workmates or family. In humour we can create incredible stories and still manage to be honest about the way things are. You'll hear this in football crowds all the time. I've heard it often enough when Carlisle are playing badly. Decent jokes work because they combine authority, timing and the right audience. Writing for comedy magazines I was getting my audience delivered to me. The rest I had to work at, but I'd had a decent training.

My Dad had something of the Don O' Riordan about him. He held down a professional career, earned some respect and still managed to hide a sense of humour that could find new angles on the worst tragedies. When I was nine, my Dad got a new job. I never really understood what he did. He was managing leadership training or something throughout Cumberland and Westmoreland - it only became Cumbria in 1974. He was eminent in a very limited field and as I got older I gradually became aware that some of the work he did was breaking new ground. On a fairly regular basis there were people dropping round the house who were professors of this, published authors, or simply people with some well developed but highly unusual talent. This started so early on in my life that it never really struck me as odd. It was only when other people were around that I was made aware of it. One totally bloody cringe-out of a moment came when my mate Anton was round and Melvyn Bragg followed my folks home from the pub one night. My Dad was showing some slides he'd taken at a local fair which included a couple of shots of Melvyn's daughter. Anton couldn't stop looking at Melvyn. He knew this guy had been on telly and ended up looking at him the way you'd look at an animal in zoo. In the end he whispered to me, 'Isn't Melvyn's hair nice!' I swear Melvyn heard it. I would've settled for the floor opening up for a minute.

The only time I ever saw my Dad nervous about working with people who were highly rated was when he ran a workshop with a guy called Carl Rogers. Rogers was an American who had near-enough founded a branch of therapy, and by 1978 when he was working with my Dad, was highly respected and pretty bloody old. I think the real worry on my Dad's part was whether the old lad could still cut it. I knew that one mattered because - amongst others things - my Dad asked me if I wanted to go. By and large he wasn't much for loading his work or achievements on me or Lesley. I think I gave Carl Rogers a miss to go to an AC/DC gig. Two years later, at college, I found Carl Rogers on the reading list for the second year of the course. Then again, AC/DC were brilliant and I got to see Bon Scott before he died. Maybe if Bon had blown out the gig in favour of some person centred counselling with old Carl he wouldn't have pegged out drunk and dead in his car a few months later.

Roughly speaking, I turned down the chance to meet a guy who did as much for counselling as Chuck Berry or Public Enemy did for music. Or Bill Green did for Carlisle United. Oddly, that doesn't bother me now. It bothers me more that I missed out on a chance to appreciate how good my Dad was at what he did best. I realise what a loss that was because, as I've got older, I've come to appreciate many of the things he passed on to me. One of which was his sense of humour. I didn't need to see him at work to appreciate this. Like I said, my Dad had a real touch of the Don O' Riordan's about him. The eminent contacts and imaginative work went hand in hand with an ability to see through a fair amount of bullshit and cut things down to size. This side of him would have been a surprise to some of the people he worked with. Especially anyone who was big on bullshit or getting carried away with their own importance. Just stick with this a minute or two longer - honest, we're coming back to football soon.

The best jokes are those that mix honesty with their authority. Don O' Riordan was funny because the flattening challenges contained a direct and honest approach.

159

They were a statement that the opposition were on his turf and they'd only got away with it for a while because he'd allowed them in. In the end, his stamping of authority put the situation into perspective and we loved him all the more for it. We wanted that solidarity at the back as much as he did. So, Don O' Riordan was funny, and I never felt dishonest abusing a ref for taking Don to task. Paul Fitzpatrick, Nigel Saddington and Darren Edmonson, on the other hand, could make me wince. A bit excitable was our Nigel.

My Dad once told me about a conversation he'd had with a mate who was partial to a bit of bird shooting. This mate of his once started on to my Dad about that adrenalin rush, the dry mouth and the tingle of anticipation he got knowing that the cannon fodder was just about to flutter in his direction.

'You should try it when they're firing back,' said my Dad.

I could picture that conversation. My Dad giving it a complete deadpan delivery and just letting the line hang there. In the circumstances the line was a comic gem because it had authority and honesty.

My Dad had tried it when they were firing back. 'They' were Japanese and the war was long over. The Japanese in question were hidden out in the jungle and they weren't up for being taken alive. Later on, my Dad took a boat load of them - all alive - back to repatriation. He had to go down to the hold amongst them, but he wasn't allowed to take so much as a revolver in case they got it off him and started blowing their own brains out. Yeah, come to think of it, there are worse jobs than teaching the YTS.

Put yourself into that kind of ridiculous situation. Those unseen psychos in the trees might announce themselves at any point with the chilling crack of rifle fire and the sight of your mate's head exploding. You can move in on them, but you're not supposed to kill them. As a lieutenant - which my Dad was at this point - you're obliged to carry out your orders, dangerous as they are. As a squaddie, under direction from the lieutenant, you probably don't give a shit and you just want one clear shot at the bloke in the tree. The more I think about that, the more I understand where my Dad developed his ability to see problems from several angles and appreciate the stunning ridiculousness of some aspects of life. In the circumstances humour is catharsis. It lets out the frustration and the feelings of helplessness. Without it you're insane. It's probably the most intelligent and useful weapon at your disposal.

You could be on a football terrace watching Eric Gates arrive three weeks too late for a decent pass. You could be emerging from the stinking hold of a ship whilst the Japanese prisoners stayed below deck. You could be facing the bunch of YTS students for the third time in a week. In all three cases you could be facing a situation that made you wonder whether you had the ability to make the right choices in life. Without humour, you wouldn't have much in those situations to give you a sense of your own self worth.

I was writing jokes at the end of the 'alternative comedy' period. A predictable quip from people who didn't get the alternative humour jokes was that the alternative to comedy is not being funny. Bollocks! The alternative to comedy is fascism. If you don't believe me, go up to the guy in the tree, the one who just shot the squaddie through the head, and try to tell him a joke.

So, my Dad could fire back at idiocy with the kind of intelligence and mockery it deserved. In the circumstances, it was a compassionate act. A celebration of all the things that make us human. Faced with the laws drafted in by John Major's government to halt assemblies of 'crusties' hell bent on scuppering road building, my Dad once staged a spontaneous demo of his own. A few coppers were hanging round the entrance to the forest track that ran down the side of Dad's house. The copper thought he'd gone there to break up any groups of hunt protesters that formed. He hadn't reckoned on getting more trouble from a bloke in his sixties. My Dad got talking to one of them about the unlawful assembly law. 'It's not right is it?' said Dad.

'Well, I wouldn't like to comment,' said the diplomatic cop.

At this point, my Dad's mate, Bill, came wandering down the road with his dog. 'There's two of us now,' said my Dad. 'Are you gonna break this up?'

Ten minutes later, having run through several of his friends who might just drop by if they received a phone call, asking for guidance on exactly how far he should stand away from everyone else and whether raising his hand to scratch his head amounted to a threatening gesture, my Dad gave it a rest and the copper got back to throwing threatening glances at anyone with dreads and a pair of combat pants.

Coppers eh? They hate it when you try and reason with them. Like I said, the alternative to comedy is fascism.

Roughly speaking, it's the same thing on a football terrace. Or it was during the early days of the Middlemass regime at Carlisle. Swearing, abuse, and some timeless one-liner humour. All of us in search of that cathartic moment, that release to capture the emotions we were feeling. Years before, I'd ranted at the mistakes of our greatest ever team as the First Division proved it was a class above some of their best ideas. I'd done it in a pathetic way, copying the phrases I'd heard at school and unleashing them word for word. By the Nineties, I was a bit sharper. I could see humour from all sides. Some of it because I'd had a decent teacher my whole life.

One of the best lines I ever heard came up at a Workington match. It was 1994, Workington were 2-0 down at half-time and the weather was shite. The bloke heading for the pies in front of me was mumbling to himself. He was unhappy, really unhappy. His mate looked him in the eye. 'Smile man,' he said, 'Yer a lang time dead!'

Too bloody right.

You had to be there. Hear the deep drawl in the voice. The dark tones that sounded like the grim reaper himself. I love West Cumbrian humour and when I got the chance to knock out 'jokes' by the truckload, it was the deep, dark West Cumbrian stuff that hit the paper. So, when I needed to sit down a knock out joke after grim joke it was there in my head. I could look at situations from enough angles to get a laugh. The stuff that poured out was the stuff that ran round my mind and a lot of it was linked to football. I might have based some of the jokes on Carlisle, but at the time, like most of the others on the terraces, I was coping with some problems on the pitch.

Middlemass was up against it. No money, not much competition for some of the places on the pitch and a smattering of ambitious teams with decent budgets in the same division. We needed humour badly between 1988 and 1993. It was the only antidote to the shuffling and sorry showers of shite we saw wearing the famous blue shirt. I don't want to go there in detail. When Carlisle needed me most, I was there. I parted with cash knowing full well that Mike Graham, Eric Gates, Tony Fyfe, and John Holliday were waiting on the other side of the turnstiles. If you saw these teams too you'll know what it took to stay loyal.

I'm going to bottle out here. I don't want to go through every mind-numbing dour encounter of those sorry seasons. I'll hit on a few games that say most of what matters.

Despite the 4-1 thrashing of Peterborough in January, 1989, a more definitive match that season was probably the late September encounter with Cambridge. Full of goals and incident. Mistakes played a big part in both. We battled, but we were no better than Cambridge and the full-on, blood, guts, and mistakes football ended with them 3-2 ahead. They wanted it more, so they won.

There were things to cheer that season, mainly the fact that Middlemass had put enough shape in the team to avoid the pathetic levels to which we'd been sinking 12 months before. But in the annals of Carlisle United, it was a mediocre season punctuated by one highlight. A massive crowd for a third round Cup tie with Liverpool at Brunton Park. Okay, Carlisle got stuffed 3-0, but in a season of non-events, this was a highlight.

The Liverpool match played a big part in another one off event which took place that season. With vouchers on offer for tickets to the Cup tie, the Boxing Day encounter with Rochdale at Brunton Park drew a crowd of over 10,000. Included in the throng was my future brother-in-law, Rich. To date, his only attendance at a Carlisle game. He'd come along for the experience, the bonding and the fun on offer. For some strange reason the freezing temperature, steady drizzle and complete fucking shambles on the pitch didn't grab him as great entertainment.

The massive crowd and our late arrival left us on the edge of the uncovered paddock and even the half-time Bovril struggled to cut through the cold. I had one over on them mainly because the three points we scrambled for a 1-0 win were a welcome addition to our middling total in a middling season. Presumably, Brunton Park in Lesley's mind is a windswept echoing hell hole populated by a solid mass of grunting fans all gazing intently as a slippery ball makes mock of the limited skills of 22 losers prepared to sacrifice pride in return for a liveable wage. Since that day, I've offered to take Lesley and Rich on sunny days, for pre-season friendlies, and for key matches played out by half-decent teams. You could describe their steady refusals as consistent performance. Carlisle were consistent performers that season. How consistent? Well, 1988/89 - P-46, W-15, L-15, D-16, goals for 53, goals against 52, pts 60, position 12th out of 24. Verdict - the very definition of mid-table mediocrity.

By the point at which we knew the final judgement on our mid-table fate, events had put this into another perspective. There had been some bad feeling in the crowd on Boxing Day, mainly to do with the lack of covered space, slowness of the half-time queues and the presence of some obvious 'fair weather' supporters who cared more about Liverpool than Carlisle. Some people thought this amounted to a problem. The pulling power of that Liverpool team would put our petty sqabbles into context a few months later when, with Wembley in sight, the team prepared to take on Nottingham Forest at Hillsborough in the FA Cup semi final. British football's greatest disaster sickened every true football fan, including those of us used to empty spaces on the terraces of the Fourth Division.

As Nick Hornby would later observe, there never had been a plan to prevent such a disaster. It could have been any of the massive First Division giants that day. Liverpool's fans were unlucky because their team had achieved such domination. Their regular presence in major games at 'neutral' grounds may have made them more likely to be the sacrifice that football was going to make before coming to its senses. It could have been , Manchester United or Spurs. Sooner or later, some massive crowd was going to fall foul of the fatal combination of fences and policing that equated thousands of fans with herds of cattle to be channelled and contained. By 1989, I'd been in crowds bigger than that assembled at Hillsborough, but I'd been watching rock stars at the time. I'd shuffled through tunnels thick with bodies pushing each other. I'd stood on stairways deep with row on row of people all ready to fall if someone made a slip.

At the end of a season that hardly warrants a mention in the official history of Carlisle United I'm willing to bet I did the same as many other Carlisle fans, by thinking long and hard about those people at Hillsborough. Like I said earlier, Bill Shankley was a great man. How ironic that it should be the club he led to greatness who would remind us that a game of football is a hell of a lot less important than a matter of life and death.

The 89/90 season showed that Middlemass had resolve and discipline. Okay, he also had some class. Dave McKellar still had what it took for sure - remember, he hadn't yet played that Rangers reserve match in front of 10,000 fans. On the scrapheap half a career before, he still had some of his best days ahead of him.

Some of his very best saves and some impressive domination of his area were there to behold as Carlisle, improbably, went to the top of the table.

I saw them win that year, I even saw them dominate. Oddly, the two defining matches that stick in my mind were both defeats. At Southend we attracted media interest. That morning I bought two papers which featured the top of the table clash. First against second at Roots Hall. Southend ran out 2-0 winners. We ran out 2-0 winners in the competition to have men sent off. Frankly, I didn't have a problem with either dismissal. Middlemass had a team that could channel agression and run on organisation. In the great Stokoe tradition, this was a team built around the players he had. Probably not the players he wanted. He got them working to their strengths. When they were outclassed, as they were by Southend, the frustration could boil over in an instant.

Still, for most of that year there were things to celebrate. Proudlock could run, McKellar's goalkeeping was dependable. Saddington and Fitzpatrick were a cause for confidence at the back. The muscular Keith Walwyn was committed to the point of pain. A stiker with some considerable mileage to his credit. A guy with real heart.

Walwyn's eventual fate is another of those dark ironies of football. He ended up playing non-league football for Kettering Town where his career was ended after the striker who was all heart suffered a heart attack on the pitch. One abiding memory I have of Walwyn is him chasing at full tilt when were already played out of the game at Southend. He pulled his hamstring. He hopped high into the air and it was obvious he'd got a serious injury. His face was screwed up in pain, but he was still looking at the ball as it rolled away. He might have been on the way down when we signed him, but Walwyn gave everything he could.

We chanted 'We've got Pele!' when he touched the ball. The point being, Walwyn was black. The fleeting Carlisle career of Gary Fulbrook hadn't done much to familiarise us with black players in a home shirt. That 'Pele' chant said a lot about our level of racial awareness as Cumbrians. As someone living and working in the multi-racial South I'd got a different take on this years before.

Let's get a few things straight here. I'm proud to be a Cumbrian. It is the only place on this Earth about which I care enough to feel genuine emotion when I arrive and when I leave. If I have any nationality, any sense of pride and identity I'm not English and not British. I'm a Cumbrian. When I die, wherever I might be living, I'm going back there. Over the years I applied for every believable job I could find in the county. I've attempted to argue my way into positions I wouldn't even consider in the South. I love the place in which I was born, and its people. In the way of real love, I love the place and people despite their faults. The weather doesn't bother me, I'll happily put up with travelling long distances to see decent gigs, and go on hot holidays. The only real frustration is the lack of decent jobs.

But it has to be said. Cumbria can be insular and inward looking. I've never known worse racism than the stuff I've encountered from Cumbrians.

I'm not sure which is worse, the abuse thrown at Laurie Cunningham when he was a forward scout for a future generation of black players or the way we treated Keith Walwyn. If you want a literal translation of the 'We've got Pele!' chant read Keith Walwyn is Pele because all blacks look alike. Like I said at the start of this book, we wouldn't have chanted 'We've got George Best' when Frank Barton was on the ball. The crowd chanting 'We've got Pele!' when Walwyn was on the pitch wouldn't have chanted 'We've got Beardsley back' when Paul Proudlock tried to shimmy past an opposing defender.

We've got to get this in perspective. Your average Cumbrian is as decent and reasonable as your average person from anywhere else. Every football ground has seen its share of racist chanting. Some of the worst racism of all, both football and non-football, is housed near to where I live and work in Kent. Welling, to be precise, where the BNP has its headquarters. The thing about Cumbria is that ignorance can survive because nothing challenges it.

So anyway, we had a hard working striker called Keith Walwyn, he was black, he was a crowd pleaser and he gave everything. In the end, it wasn't quite enough. The last game of the season pitted Carlisle against Maidstone United. We were in a play-off place, but the points situation was tight and Maidstone, one point behind us, needed to win to get a play-off place. There were a whole raft of teams challenging for the places that day and I tried to explain the ins and out of the maths involved to Owen as we drove to Dartford for the game. In another ironic twist in the history of my love affair with Carlisle United I'd moved to Maidstone in the year their team started a successful charge for league status. Maidstone United celebrated their achievement by selling their London Road ground and moving their home matches 30 miles up the road to Dartford. So, on a blazing May afternoon, Owen and I took our seats for the end of season showdown in Dartford. Along with the Southend match, that clash with Maidstone summed up everything about Clive Middlemass' greatest season.

Kevin Rose was in goal for the last sprint toward the play-off show down. Our league form and position had dipped from the top spot. I'd seen a true freak of a result when Colchester - who went on to finish bottom of bloody everything and get booted out of the league - hammered us 4-0 at Layer Road. Dave McKellar had been at Colchester. In fact, he was there for the sequence of six straight defeats that saw us drop from leaders of Division Four to one place outside the play-off zone. I've met a few football anoraks over the years, but nobody who could tell me the last time a league leading team suffered six straight defeats.

For all this, McKellar was still guarding the goal as well as he could. The balls hitting the back of the net were coming from opposing players with yards of space to run and strike. These players were getting possession because we'd surrendered the midfield and chosen to play Craig Goldsmith, a permed specimen who could disappear without trace for 90 minutes on a Saturday afternoon. I'm not saying it was all his fault, he just seemed to symbolise the growing problem. As other teams became more organised, the gaps in our planning and skill began to show. The fact we were prepared to sell McKellar to Kilmarnock said everything about our levels of ambition and ready cash.

On May the 5th, Maidstone had a younger, faster and more confident team and they charged at us with attitude from the start. We were a goal down before we knew what had hit us, but Walwyn's strength, fight and constant running got us even, at which point we were over the wall in numbers. 'We' in this case means the Blue Army, one of whom connected with Owen's head on his way across. Down the front and in seats, with Owen only eight years old, it struck me I'd got a problem. We were getting pasted on the pitch, despite the equaliser, and Carlisle did have an impressive track record of going over the wall when crucial games were going the wrong way. A Kent cop offered to get us out, I didn't want it, but the second time he offered I ended up making a real head versus heart decision and allowing the cop to find us a safer area . . . in with the Maidstone fans.

I'd checked before the game and been assured that there was standing space for away fans. On the day we were given one option of which part of the ground we filled. Terracing would have offered us a safe place out of line of the pitch invasions and surrounded by the comforting noise of the Blue Army. As it was, I got to stand in a less than full area with some of the most peaceful fans I've ever met. Unbelievably, this laid back pack were watching their team make the play-offs in their first league season. I think one of these 'home' fans managed to raise his hands and clap a couple of times. Well, by the time Maidstone had scored their fifth goal and broken our solid defensive line for the 20th time these Southern fans might have felt a vague stirring of passion.

Owen, had a great time chatting away to the home support and enjoying the quality strikes sailing past Kevin Rose. It has to be said, this was not a great team performance, but Kevin Rose was never the greatest goalie. The defence in particular were short on confidence. The running joke about Rose was an oldie but goodie. What did Kevin Rose and Michael Jackson have in common? They both wore gloves but nobody knew why.

We scored a second goal, not that it mattered. All we had to do was wait for the results from the other games which told us that Chesterfield had stolen the last play-off place. That summed it up really. Had we sneaked into the play-offs we could have made some useful money, but we'd never have made it to Wembley, let alone the Third Division. Had any miracle put us into a promotion place that season we would have been slaughtered in the league above. You could blame Middlemass, but he had achieved more with this bunch of journeymen than anyone could reasonably expect. The thoughts in my mind coming home from that game were a dark mixture. This team and this level of finance were marooned in the Fourth Division. Up against a team with some pretensions to class - like Maidstone or Southend - we looked bloody ordinary.

Craig Goldsmith had played as a sub in the Maidstone game. Or, to be exact, we'd seen Steve Norris go off and Goldsmith come on. From that point on we were down to ten men. Later that night, I turned on the TV and watched Sting playing a benefit gig for the reletives of the disappeared. He dedicated one song to the friends and family of Craig Goldsmith.

We didn't have anything to look forward to, but we still had a hero that day. 34 year old Keith Walwyn ran so hard in that final game that I have a picture of him fixed in my mind chasing a hopeful forward lob with almost no hope of connecting. He was breathing so hard I swear I could feel his breath hit me as he ran over the by-line at the end of another fruitless chase.

That was our greatest season under Clive Middlemass. The following season was a return to old ways. Newport County were long gone, but the press gangs were obviously raiding the infants schools in Wrexham, Aldershot and Halifax. Meanwhile in York, unemployed waitresses were begging any tea shop with spare change to offer them Saturday afternoon jobs. The alternative for the unemployed girls of the town was to be stuffed into the back of a van, roughly scrubbed over with boot black to create a fake five of clock shadow, and turned out in red from top to toe under the name of York City. Yes, the bottom of the league really was that bad in 90/91.

Thank fuck for the desperation in those teams because we weren't a lot better. To make matters worse there was no London team in the bottom flight and - apart from Maidstone and Gillingham - my nearest matches took in two hour plus trips to Peterborough, Northampton and Lincoln. As with Newport's monumental suicide run in 1988, our league survival depended completely on everyone else's tragedies. It was the sorry excuse for tactical master plans on offer at places like The Racecourse Ground, Doncaster, and The Shay, Halifax, that we had to thank for our 20th position.

As in 1988, we faced a last game on a balmy May afternoon with nothing to play for and a pathetic crowd gathered to watch. Sincil Bank, Lincoln, had been playing host to non-league football when we'd been holding a steady 91st place ahead of Newport in 1988. On the evidence of that season, when we'd come alive to hammer Cambridge on the last day, I thought I could expect another fighting performance in the face of a pointless game. I was wrong.

6-2. I mean, six fucking two, they beat us. I'd seen Carlisle let in five goals on the final Saturday of the previous season. At Lincoln they let in five goals in the second half!!!!! This was the bitter end, in more ways than one. John Halpin came off the bench, gave it some committment and walked out of lives to play for

Rochdale. Well, you can't fault him for wanting to go to a high flying club with ambition, eh?

Last game massacres were starting to look like a great tradition. The players got off lightly. From where I was standing it didn't look like they managed to wake up in the 90 minutes. For fuck's sake lads, its almost three hours each way from Chelmsford to Sincil Bank. You could've made an effort. I bloody did.

It's time to talk about the 91/92 assault on the Fourth Division title. Going there hurts about as much as revisiting the Fulham Cup defeat in that First Division season. You want to know how bad it was? Then let's go to the game that is, without doubt, my worst 90 minutes as a Carlisle United supporter. And let's talk about Mike Fucking Graham.

Graham had been there for a few years and he'd given a good account of himself. In the 89/90 side he'd worked manfully to hold back the tide of opposing strikers. But, on February the 12th, 1992, at Watling Street, Dartford, he stepped permanently into my nightmares to such an extent that I've made him pay for it ever since. Years have not mellowed the trauma in my mind and I will waste no opportunity to get even. When my little boy was so small that we thought it was cute to ask him questions and train him to give the right answers I started the indoctrination programme. Ask Thom today who was the worst player ever to pull on a Carlisle shirt and he will tell you, 'Mike Graham.'

Wander through the demented rant of my first novel and you'll find a character . . . 'Back-pedalling as furiously as full-back Mike Graham faced by tricky opposing strikers in the year Carlisle United finished bottom of bloody everything.'

I regularly take his name in vain and I'm not finished extacting retribution. It's personal between me and Mike and I'll purge the nightmare of that night until I'm over it. It may take years. It may take the rest of my life.

One reason I know I love Carlisle United is that what I'm about to tell you still hurts me. I am, supposedly, old enough and smart enough to be above all this. But it still bothers me that, in that season, we finished bottom of the league. Only the folding of Aldershot saved us from a certain exit. This was, unquestionably, the worst Carlisle team I've ever seen. The 5-1 hammering by Maidstone United on that freezing February night in Dartford was unquestionably the worst performance I saw that year and the 944 spectators who bothered to turn up amount to the worst crowd I've ever seen at a competitive Carlisle match.

On that night Mike Graham was unquestionably the saddest pile of festering garbage shuffling around in a blue shirt, and I'm forever haunted by the sight of his furious back-pedalling as, time and again, the golden shirts of Maidstone came forward and turned the slow-witted defender. Let's get this straight, Maidstone were not that great. Their passes lacked accuracy and their moves had a thin crust of confidence over a large amount of graft. That night a Carlisle team who lacked confidence, character, pride and all sense of decency, gifted a sorry squabble of a game to Maidstone United. Three years before, Maidstone had been a non-league outfit. In the summer of 1990, Maidstone had needed vision, effort and a hint of class to put five goals past us. That February night they only needed to turn up.

Mike Graham was a fucking nightmare. He hunched his portly shoulders forward, pounded like fury with his feet, spread his frame as wide as it would go, and still failed to make contact. Time and again his patch of defence was surrendered as the crosses rained in on Kelham's goal. Graham hadn't the pace or the skill to stop it happening. In the circumstances, Kelham didn't have such a bad game. It was the others who stood back and let Maidstone attack.

Maidstone were so bad that they finished the season 18th, one place and two points above the York team composed entirely of women press ganged out of the catering industry. Between Maidstone and ourselves were the mighty teams from those hot houses of football excellence in Halifax and Doncaster. My nightmare on Watling Street was compounded by the presence of a genuine ground hopper and his wife. Watling Street, the Dartford home of Maidstone United, was almost his last ground. He reverendly noted down the pathetic crowd number, taking real pleasure informing me that in over 90 football league grounds he'd never seen a crowd under a thousand. At least I got away from him at half-time. I headed for a cup of tea and a Mars Bar, and believe me, this was the greatest satisfaction on offer that night. The groundhopper stayed in his seat and shuffled in the big bag on his lap. Somewhere beneath his notebook, his torch and his ever ready copy of the *Rothman's Football Yearbook*, I thought he would have a flask. I was right.

In the Fourth Division, Aldershot folded. Weeks before this sad event it was obvious the end was in sight for them. So our league survival was assured. If you call that 'surviving'.

In the season prior to this, our leading scorer, Eric Gates, had displayed the mobility of a one legged zombie with his foot stuck in a wheel clamp. The 5-1 hammering in February, 1992, came after a very brief period of early season hope. Gates had gone and Doncaster were humiliated in an opening day of the season away victory. On the basis of these results, we'd been given a faint glimmer of hope. By the following February, it was obvious there wasn't much hope left.

'Depressed' doesn't do justice to my feelings on that night. I knew then, more than I'd ever known, that I was welded to this team and their fortunes for my whole life. If ever I could have walked away from Carlisle United it was in the days that followed that complete capitulation. Carlisle were in a hopeless situation with nothing but effort to fight the overwhelming tide. There was some skill, in the form of our new star striker, Andy Watson, and the calm and experience of Kelham O' Hanlon in goal. Kelham had seen it all, including international honours for the Republic of Ireland, but he'd never been down so low in terms of class. He had a work load to put his entire career in perspective. So did I.

By this point I'd got a job in Dartford. I'd risen into the management sector and taken on a team of staff. On my first day I was confronted by a desk two feet deep in unsorted paper and a filing cabinet neatly arranged in alphabetical order. The filing cabinet was a comforting sight until I looked into it and found it was totally empty. I didn't feel like I was picking up a new job. I felt like I was registering my predecessor's cry for help. I got stuck in as best I could. There are a lot of things you could say about this situation. I'll restrict myself to two. Firstly, it was obvious I'd got an uphill struggle on my hands. Secondly, I'm still working in the same place as I write this.

It appeared all the harder in Dartford because the previous six months had been the happiest of my working life. I'd been appointed as Publicity Officer at Thurrock College, my writing was getting published in large amounts every month, and there were opportunities being offered. There were adult humour comics coming out on every street corner, the buying public were 'mad for it' and every angle was covered. I'd struck deals with most of the main providers and I could easily get anything from a dozen to 20 decent sales a month. The more fragmented the market appeared to get, the more I could respond to each niche. In 1989 I was on board in the writing team for *Ziggy*, a magazine prepared to plumb the depths in search of the darkest laughs. How bad could it get? Well, *Ziggy* would openly suggest they should give a Brit award to everyone who smoked whilst poor old Roy Castle played his trumpet.

I saw the first edition of *Ziggy*, sent them some stuff and got hired. In the second edition they ran a comic strip story set in Palestine two thousand years ago, in which a dodgy sex criminal strapped angel's wings to his back and talked gullible housewives into bed. *Ziggy's* take on the virgin birth struck me as potentially offensive and I rang them up to check out how the hell they were getting away with it. The editor, who had a legal background, knew the ins and outs of offending people pretty well and he knew that he could defend his blasphemy on the grounds that it was funny and that the public were warned on the cover about the contents of the magazine. In any case, the rumbling furore about *The Satanic Verses* would complicate the issue. These were the days when Moslems everywhere were demanding instant and fatal justice for Salman Rushdie and the author was scurrying around the Brecon Beacons with his own private army ready to repel anyone who spotted him. If one tatty magazine was taken to court over a sleazy laugh, the Moslems in the UK were likely to kick legal ass over the denial of their rights to prosecute a serious and significant book. In short, *Ziggy* knew how far they could take it and they were up for going to the very limits.

As far as I could see, tabloid coverage would be welcomed and any unsolicited complaints simply confirmed to the editorial team that they were having an impact. I thought about their corporate mission for a few minutes and decided I was in. Within a few months, two interesting twists in my life took place. One of my 'jokes' formed the core of a shock/horror tabloid article slamming the sick magazine, and I got to meet my public on a large scale. In the case of the tabloid article there was a problem. The newspaper seemed to be genuinely offended and they refused to give *Ziggy* a name check. Hell, naming it could have been worth at least 10,000 sales on the next edition! *Ziggy* was going down well amongst the students at college and selling out in the few local newsagents brave enough to stock it. I'd met the odd reader of my stuff by this point, but in 1990 I did the Comic Art Convention in London, speaking to a few hundred people about writing sick jokes for a living. After the formal bit was over a few people hung around including two wide eyed and intense types who held out copies of *Ziggy* and said, 'You wrote *this!?*'

Having registered that they seemed impressed and weren't about to knife me for taking the bounds of good taste and stamping all over them, we got to chatting. It was reassuring to know that there were people out there, other than a handful of my Cumbrian mates, who could see the humour in the sickest twists of fate. This was doubly reassuring because by this point I'd also started writing about the paranormal and this had earned me some fan mail that bordered on the psychotic.

Month in, month out *Ziggy* would run sicko one liners:

Wouldn't it be funny if.....
Somebody shot off Paul McCartney's thumb the next time he stuck it up and grinned.
Somebody taught Canadian seals to club themselves to death.
Mike Tyson knocked out his next opponent and started eating him in the ring.

Amongst the milder stories which appeared in *Ziggy* were those which involved shocking claims, like the man who stole Helen Worth's chin. Elsewhere, every major disaster, horrific crime and celebrity death was ripe for a working over. The pub jokes you heard about Hungerford, Terry Waite, Lockerbie and Karen Carpenter may have started life in that magazine. It wasn't to everyone's taste. But, the people who loved it would accept no substitute and that was worth a few years of part-time work for me. I could work all day at college, write this stuff in the evenings, and come away feeling wide awake. Now that's what I call job satisfaction.

I moved on because a promotion offered itself, and offered me the chance of more money and no more travelling to the day job through the Dartford Tunnel. So, in one sense I'd worked myself up the ladder. Then again, that didn't necessarily make it feel better. Eight months into the new job, that night in February, 1992, depressed me all the more because I knew that, like my team, I was reduced to struggling against daunting odds with no gaurantee of getting the slightest result. Both of us, faced a long slog and the introduction of some new ideas and new faces before we turned round our problems.

By this point my favourite stress buster, in the form of my running was also on the skids. Here, I was also reduced to slogging rather than achieving. Through the Eighties I'd run more races than I could count. Three marathons and any half marathon, 10K or lesser race I could find. I'd been getting faster until 1987 when I had to admit that I'd found the training for one more marathon such a grind that I'd been bored into slowing down. I gave myself a break, got stuck back in as the winter came on and started planning some real adventures, like running the whole Four Peaks in the Lake District the following summer.

Knocking out faster winter times than I'd ever known I was within sight of the end of a run and just hitting a final sprint when something went, big time, near my right ankle. It was an achilles tendon injury, serious enough to put me out for six months. I didn't know it then, but it was the start of over seven years of problems that would keep me out of races until my mid-thirties and end any serious ambitions in this direction.

Just when I was clawing my way up around the bottom end of Division 1 as an athlete I got relegated. In an attempt to hang on to my athletes level of fitness, I set up a lunatic training schedule that involved mind numbing sessions on an exercise bike, more swimming than a sane person could handle, and sprints on a rowing machine. All of it useful but none of it a patch on the open air and the feel of rain on my face. The first injury happened the year Carlisle finished just above Newport County. Like my team, I was reduced to ceaseless hard work in the hope that one day I would get back to the levels I'd once enjoyed. Throughout the Middlemass years and beyond I was working hard to produce a performance that was all slog and little sparkle. Also like my team, this slog seemed all the worse because I could keep on believing there was some purpose in it.

Nature hadn't given me an athletes body. When I was a kid I had to visit the clinic in Aspatria for 'breathing exercises.' This meant, in reality, that people were worried that I might be ashmatic. I wasn't, but I sure as hell wasn't a natural athlete. When I got serious about running later on in life I had to contend with this lack of any natural talent, but I also came to realise that I had an athlete's brain, if not a body. At the start of *The Silence of the Lambs,* Jodie Foster slogs her way round an assault course and passes a sign that says 'Hurt, pain, agony, love it.' I did love it.

Thousands of miles and, until the injuries arrived, I managed to enjoy most of them. A big bonus in this depertment was the time I got to think without being bothered. Amongst other things, I got some of my best writing ideas whilst I was out training. The most lucrative idea I ever concocted for the humour comics was *Wor Jackie.* This item ran every month for a year and a half and presented a page in which Jackie Charlton would answer readers problems.

The whole idea came to me in an instant as I crossed a road near Thurrock College. Within the next hour on the run I'd worked out the whole first item and

Wor Jackie proved to be the most lucrative idea I'd ever had to that point. It was simple enough:

A young kid would write in and say that his dad was no fun since his uncle Gary had died. Jackie would suggest showing him a video of the 1972 Cup final and paying attention to Mick Jones forcing himself up the steps to get his winners medal with a dislocated elbow. His dad would learn something about committment from that video.

A bloke complained his wife had got fat, dirty and smelly since they got married. Jackie replied by saying the bloke should freight his wife to Jackie's home where he could keep her in a shed. She sounded like the ideal breeding ground for his fishing maggots.

It was easy enough to knock out 20 items a month, alongside any 'serious' journalism or other work I could manage. Coming up with the ideas was easy enough, often because football, and the characters of football, were hopelessly stuck in my head. When I was running, I could often plan out entire pieces of work in my mind. When I was reduced to slogging on the bike, they didn't come as easily.

So, like I said. My team and I were slogging. We could both remember days when there had been a sparkle to the whole thing. What sparkle there was as a Carlisle supporter often came from the company at the games. In that desperate 'bottom of the league season' I managed to enjoy two games. On Boxing Day, 1991, I finally persuaded my Dad to come to a game with me. They don't come much more hopeless than a bottom of the table encounter and Carlisle v Doncaster promised nothing for the discerning fan. For me and my Dad it was another part of the growing pattern of his life alone. Five years into being alone there was still a sadness in some of the things he did. He couldn't share anything with the person who'd mattered most. In the face of this, he did things he would never have been able to share with my Mum, because he'd never have talked her into them. A long trip to the Cape Verde Islands put him just about beyond civilisation and added adventures in self-reliance to rival his army days. By contrast, the trip to the Doncaster game was a minor skirmish. Carlisle won 1-0. The football was pathetic. Simon Jeffels got the only goal. Jeffels, like Paul Proudlock would end up in non-league football in his mid-twenties. Let's face it, this team was short on class.

What I got that day was a chance to talk to my Dad. We got decent seats in the main stand, I pointed out every other location at Brunton Park in which I'd stood and filled him in on a part of my life that he'd missed. He, in turn, marvelled at the quality of the view. A rugby man through and through, my Dad could appreciate a quality move and, looking down on the action, he got a few moments to applaud. Well, Kelham and Andy Watson added what class we had. What mattered most was being together and sharing some father and son time.

The strange thing was that, in an odd way, I was the dad. Brunton Park was new to him and he registered the potential importance of the result only because he understood the maths. To me it mattered emotionally that the score gave us some space over Doncaster and it might have kept us off the bottom at the end of the season. In the end it didn't matter at all. In May we chose to stage our traditional, last Saturday, full-blooded surrender. On May the 2nd we were second bottom in the morning and absolute bottom by twenty to five after play-off chasing Scunthorpe hammered us 4-0. Doncaster, bottom that morning, climbed into Carlisle United's traditional 'one off the bottom' league slot.

Carlisle were down to their loyal support. They hadn't much else to depend upon. I knew how they felt. Then again, my loyal support, Jane, had become my wife in the summer of 1991 and by the time I talked her into going along to the Gillingham away match in March we were expecting a baby. I'd like to think that Thom, the little boy in the big shirt on the front of this book, got his love of football from that game. In reality, this is garbage. He got it from growing up in the South and watching on television, talking Arsenal with his mates, and loving the proud red colours of the Arsenal shirt.

However, the first game Thom chose to attend was a Carlisle away match at Southend in 1997. He first went to a game inside his mother in 1992 as Carlisle played Gillingham. And we won. For years I would argue with other fans about this game and it would be over a season later, on a train back from Northampton, that I would finally find a fellow witness - a certain Phil Lorimer - who saw what I saw. Honest, it really happened, John Holliday had a good game. The misfiring man-mountain of moderate abilities managed to mess up the best that North Kent could throw in his direction. Sometimes his enthusiasm and unpredictability were achieving things by accident.

For starters, the Gills could hardly cut off his headed passes when Holliday's lack of accuracy left you guessing until the last minute where exactly they would land. That was a magic afternoon in a pathetic season. It was our second, and final, away win of the season. The excitement of watching a clumsy assortment of journeymen, strengthened by Andy Watson, Kelham O' Hanlon and the briefly on form John Holliday, had Jane out of her seat and may just have pumped a thimbleful of adrenalin through Thom's growing veins. His slowly forming ears may have heard the roar of the crowd, such as the 'crowd' was in our end.

Our little embryo grew up to love football, so maybe that day and that result did matter after all. It was, quite simply, a magical, lucky, exciting afternoon. We were obviously struggling to match Gillingham on skill. We matched them on running and outdid them on luck. The proof that something almost unfathomably strange was happening that day was on the scoresheet. We won 2-1. Our goals were scored by Holmes and Watson.

Great game, shame about the rest of that season.

In May, 1992, we finished bottom of the league because we were bottom of Division 4. The following year we still managed to make it to Division 3. It sounds miraculous. It wasn't. That year the Premiership was created and the three divisions beneath the top flight put a positive face on the fact that they appeared to have been cynically cut adrift. From now on there would be nothing below the Third Division.

In terms of league status it was around this time that serious suggestions were being made which could have changed the face of my team and their status for all time. These suggestions came from the perilous league position and desperate state of the playing squad. By this point we had Aiden McCaffery as manager. Another one taken from within the ranks of the playing squad. McCaffrey's first team appearances were limited to the season in which Newport did us all a favour and so he was under no illusions. In April, 1991, he inherited a team already doomed to finishing in the bottom block of the league, he managed them through the worst season in the history of the club, and was eventually booted out in September, '92, to make way for David McCreery. As the official history of the club so tersely puts it, 'His predicament was a difficult one, few managers would have stuck it out for so long.' McCaffrey had no money to spend and little in the way of real talent at his disposal.

Few sets of fans would have stuck it out so well either. By the end of the 1991/92 season there were intense discussions about the unthinkable. Part-time football was one possibility, it was well known that the club would accept any reasonable offer from anyone who wanted to buy it outright, and there was talk about the Scottish league. This last area has been the subject of rumour and speculation ever since, especially when United's league form has headed from bad to catastrophic. The rumours surrounding our possible admission to the Scottish league revolve around some standard arguments.

The longest round trips in the football league in any given season invariably pit Carlisle against the likes of Torquay, Exeter and Gillingham. Nowhere in Scotland is as far from Carlisle as these places.

Carlisle is so far from any English club - almost 60 miles from Newcastle - that we have no local competition. Queen of the South, in Dumfriesshire are a hell of a lot closer. Closer, in fact, than Workington.

Alongside these there are a few sound financial arguments. As I write this, Carlisle have a 16,000 capacity ground. This puts them on a par with credible Scots teams like Dundee, Kilmarnock and St Johnstone, all of whom have recently staged believable assaults on major silverware and the resulting qualification for Europe.

The more you think about it, the better it gets. I've held such arguments with uncomprehending work mates. Carlisle's support veers wildly in good and bad years. That bottom of the season run in 1992 saw pathetic crowds. Having said this, an assault on the Scottish Premiership would bring the crowds back and this is where my workmates get seriously worried about my sanity.

Apply a little crude maths and what I'm about to say looks saner than you think. There are teams in the Scottish Premiership sustaining successful seasons on an average gate of 8-10,000. Allow for the massive away support of Rangers and Celtic and you've got plenty of punters on some gates even if your entire home support takes the day off. Meaning, in real terms, that some games offer a genuine fan bonanza because the travelling support actually outnumber the regular home gate. Look at the middle of the Scottish First Division and you'll see gates and teams who couldn't survive against the likes of Lincoln City or Northampton. The gulf between first and 20th place in Scotland is absolutely immense. The team in which Mike Graham 'enjoyed' his final season at Carlisle would have been good enough for an untroubled season in Scottish League Division 1. Even Stranraer can get into that division!

Allow for the marketing potential of an undoubtedly Enlglish team in Scotland and you've got headlines every week and a pile of travelling support ready to watch their team give the English a beating, they think! The policing bill might go up, but so would the crowds. I love Carlisle United, but even I would admit they couldn't realistically oppose the likes of Celtic and Rangers, but there are few other teams north of the border who would pose an impossible task. Aberdeen, Hibs and Dundee United would certainly put more on the gate at Brunton Park than Torquay or Leyton Orient, and given the fact that these teams would all come twice a year (excluding any Cup games), you have the makings of a useful income and an attractive package. My workmates think I'm insane suggesting a club that has finished 91st on more than one occasion could survive so high up in Scotland.

I don't want anyone at Carlisle to seriously consider this at the moment because I live in Maidstone. Give me that dream job in Carlisle and I might well feel different. Which, in a round about way, says something else important about love, and football. Love has a selfish element. We tend only to love those people and things that can give us something meaningful in return. Carlisle United offer a few thousand diehards an emotional roller coaster with added twists, turns and stunning surprises. We throw our time, effort and money at the uncertainty, willingly giving in to hope at the start of every season. Deep down, I care so much that I want this team to do well and my head says they would do well in Scotland. My heart tells me I would struggle to survive without a fixture list to fill some Saturdays with long journeys to places I visit once a year. I would struggle to survive without a close up fix of my team.

In the summer of 1992, the hope, like the league position, was at rock bottom and any constructive suggestion was up for consideration. Part-time football was certainly on the agenda. Scotland was allegedly up for serious consideration. The rest - as they say - is history. Michael Knighton ended one lot of speculation by taking over the club.

In the end, he started an equal amount of speculation, but in those early days, we heard about his ten year plan for Premiership action, we marvelled at the fluid movement in the early season team, and felt more relief than we could usefully express that we had been spared the worse options on offer. The much maligned Aiden McCaffrey was on his way. David McCreery was in and a few new faces had joined him.

On August the 18th, 1992, I took the whole family along, Jane well pregnant by this point, as Burnley surrendered to a performance packed with movement. The skill was intermittent, but this looked like a new team. We were so good in that 4-1 Coca Cola Cup win that Ricardo Gabbiadini looked good. He even scored twice! The highspot of the night for me was the early back pass from Burnley in which they managed to forget the new back pass rule and give away an indirect free kick. Ricardo's first goal for Carlisle came from that move. Thom, still inside his mother, but considerably larger than he was at Gillingham the previous season, stirred as Ricardo drove home and the noise on that warm summer evening reached his growing ears.

We'd fought out a tough league opener, losing to the odd goal in seven, the previous Saturday. I hadn't managed to drag the family along to that, but in the circumstances, I'd got the right night for the mob outing. One great result was never going to make the season, but it did restore some faith. A few months after I'd seen the worst team ever to trade under the name of Carlisle United I was now watching an outfit that had some pretensions to class and a smattering of talent in every area of the pitch. Okay, Kelham and Andy Watson were still on board, but we also had two good young prospects from the youth team in Jeff Thorpe and Darren Edmonson, and a young midfielder signed from Swansea called Simon Davey. Darren and Jeff had been in the team I saw humiliated in Dartford, but the new set up appeared to benefit the younger players and allow them some space to play and develop their talent.

Normal service was resumed at Colchester, Barnet, Lincoln and Gillingham where narrow defeats on the back of fighting performances were the order of the day. I only saw Carlisle win during home trips that season, but I still came away encouraged. Like my job, I knew it was going to take a long haul. Some new ideas were working, some weren't. On the negative side we tried out the forward 'talents' of the woeful Jason Prins, who at least had the excuse that he was hardly out of nappies. Elsewhere we sank low enough to offer John Holliday another bite of the cherry in the hope that he could rekindle whatever it was he had kindled that afternoon in Gillingham. He didn't deliver. We delivered him to Mansfield Town but he was back in Cumbria, at Workington, pretty soon after.

In late October, Jane and I became parents to Thom. He arrived late, chunky and startled. Nothing before or since compares with seeing his entry into the world, holding our little bundle of life or looking into his eyes, as he tried to make sense of those first moments. Like all babies, he would disturb our sleep, rearrange our lives, and frustrate our efforts to comfort him. But I'd never known love like I felt then and Thom's first months were more contented and happy than I'd dared believe possible. By any standards he was a good baby and his sleep was usually so contented that his soft breathing was more musical, and more magical, than anything I'd ever heard.

Football was out there if I still wanted it. But, faced with a Gillingham strike in the second half of a tight game, I found myself still feeling good. We were both in the bottom bundle of clubs, although the monumentally crap Halifax Town were providing that all important 'we'll never be that bad' cushion of hope. In the circumstances, I could come away from the Gills defeat almost glad for Gillingham. Given their proximity to my home I wouldn't wish any ill on them. The only really bad news that season was the transfer of Andy Watson to Barnsley. But, our baby son was magic, and a Saturday afternoon that took in a trip to Pizza Express and a chance to feed him a bottle was preferable to a windswept terrace, a grey sky, and a point at best. I still stuck with the football, but there was a feeling that it was on hold until Thom could make more sense of the world for himself.

Michael Knighton duly obliged by saving the surge until that time. Thom was toddling, the winter of 1993/94 was rolling around to a half-cocked spring, and Jane and I were considering our first foreign holiday since our new arrival. Predictably, I scanned the league tables, doubtful about the wisdom of booking over the May bank holiday when Carlisle might just be at Wembley in the play-off finals. The day we booked Carlisle were 14th. A few months later, we made the play-offs and I lost sleep in agonies of split loyalties. I wanted promotion badly, but if we were going to win it, I would be thousands of miles away.

We didn't. In fact, history repeated itself in our last game capitulation. Over two legs we caved in to Wycmobe Wanderers. I faced the result with a mixture of disappointment, relief and guilt at feeling relieved. In the return leg at Wycombe we were workmanlike, but outplayed to the point of having no excuses when we left. In 180 minutes of play-off football, we found the net once, and that was from the penalty spot.

Wycombe won their way out of the bottom flight in their first season. We gave them a helping hand by scoring their first league goal on a hot August afternoon in Carlisle and then losing to them away in front of a creditable crowd for a freezing December afternoon. The presence of another bottom flight ground within striking distance of the M25 was a welcome addition to the itinerary. We travelled badly in the South East that season, but the quality of our football was improving and the addition of David Reeves was a clear signal of intent. We'd signed the lanky workhorse of a forward from Notts County for £121,000. The fee was a club record and an indication of the Knighton style in which stunts and gestures would feature prominently in Carlisle's story. Knighton had gone £1,000 higher than the fee we paid for Gordon Staniforth. He had apparently set out deliberately to give us our most expensive player at the cheapest possible price.

Our surge up the table in the last quarter of the season owed a lot to Reeves' 11 goals. The shape and confidence was there and Mick Wadsworth's management was gradually blending a shape and sense of style into this side. Even in defeat at Gillingham, we were a footballing side again. I'd forgotten what that was like.

Oddly, the most positive, stomach churning, emotional footballing experience I had that season came on April the 4th. We were up at home over Easter. Thom was old enough to recognise his grandad, and he, Jane and his grandad were enjoying some quality time in Workington! I'd gone to see the reds with Wayne, a lad who lived up the road from my Dad, and who ate and slept football. Carlisle United kicked off in Crewe that day, facing a home side who were well fancied for automatic promotion.

In the Workington team I saw were Jason Prins and John Holliday. In the blustering Solway wind, Workington struggled, squelched and surrendered space. Ace defender, Paddy Atkinson (late of Harlepool and eventually to join York City), was all that stood between the Red Army and a complete massacre. It was a measure of how far we'd come to see the performances of Prins and Holliday. The Carlisle fanzine, *So Jack Ashurst Where's My Shirt?* had it about right with Prins. They'd suggested the word 'Prins' meant running around with no particular purpose or aim. Jason was indeed prinsing about to little obvious effect. The main difference was that he could hang on to the ball a little longer at this level, before delivering a pass to be snaffled up by the mighty defenders of Great Harwood Town.

Holliday was hilarious. His aerial 'skills' were well employed on set pieces. Any dead ball situation to Workington's advantage within sight of the opposing goal led to a long wait as the massive, misfiring defensive enigma trotted slowly into the Great Harwood penalty box. The dead ball was lofted slowly into orbit where Holliday would use his massive frame to ensure first connection. The hilarity and high point of the game came with his 'header.' Big John's gangling innaccuracy meant the ball could land anywhere and the opposing defenders hadn't a fucking clue how to deal with him. They might as well have stood on the terraces, there was as much chance of the ball coming down on concrete as grass.

John's instructions appeared to be to knock the ball back where the beer bellied frames of the forward playing 'lads' were splashing in for a wild crack on goal. At their worst I've seen Carlisle play kick and rush football. This was an average season by Workington's Nineties standards and they were playing rush and try to kick football. Incidentally, they lost.

Two years before we were so desperate that Holliday and Prins had offered hope. Now we were so good that I couldn't wait to cross the road, get into Safeway's cafe, wait for the rest of the family and listen to the game I'd been thinking about all afternoon. The one in Crewe. We'd won a hard fought encounter 3-2, scrambling a late winner off a free kick. Wayne had a radio and we listened in close to the crackling report. Wayne's youthful enthusiasm was a tonic to a jaded fan. It took me back, listening to a report of a Carlisle team on the verge of something. A team that had fought to the wire and sneaked a result. A team that had taken on titans and humbled them. Okay, it was only fucking Crewe, but two years before we were barely fit to lace their boots.

Somewhere out across the windblown wastes of West Cumbria, Mike Graham, Derek Walsh and a handful of other Brunton Park old boys plied their non-league trade. Graham's chunky thighs might still have been pounding the soggy turf as I listened to that game report from Crewe. His frame hunched forward, spray flying from the sodden ground, an opposing striker blinking as the water hit him in the eye and marvelling at the sublime skills of the big defender who had invented a foolproof method of foiling the best attacks that could be mounted against Milnthorpe Corinthians. John Holliday was probably soaking his dodgy knees in the Borough Park bath as I surged into my coffee in the Safeway cafe. The flawed, blonde adonis of the Workington back-line could content himself with a role in the set pieces that would ensure his unmistakable mug shot was in the frame of the grainy black and white shots that appeared in the local press to celebrate Workington's scrambled strikes.

Graham and Holliday had found a theatre in which their shortcomings could pay off. Carlisle were better than these men. My working life was still an uphill struggle against reaching ever receding targets, but there were new media courses in my area and students were putting their names down in healthy numbers. My team and I were pulling ourselves up against heavy odds. They were well ahead of me and the end of that season offered real drama and set my pulse racing. Believing in my team like this, after years of little more than blind affection and hope, was life affirming.

How the hell could I have doubted them when they were 14th and booked a holiday in Menorca that coincided with the play-offs? Two days before this final I was telling the guy in the next apartment about my near miss of the play-offs. He shrugged, stared into space and struggled to put a sentence together as he confessed he was a Preston fan. He'd done the same thing and nowhere on that end of the island seemed able to put on a Sky broadcast of the Division Three final. In the end he downed beers like there was a hole in his stomach as he suffered ten minutes of highlights of a Wembley final in which Wycombe put his heroes to the test and beat them. I felt for that guy.

I also reflected long and hard on that season. Knighton offered us drama, promises, stunts, and an end of season cliffhanger. A formula that would repeat itself year on year from this point onwards. You want end of season drama? Get on board with Carlisle United.

Blue Nightmare #10

IT IS THE second of January, 1994, and with taunts of 'Knighton out' still ringing in his ears, Mr Knighton takes his family out to the pantomime. Fearing for his safety in the border city, canny Michael heads down the M6 and visits his old Mancunian haunts.

Troubled by calls for his head, wallet and other parts of his anatomy to be displayed in public view on the Brunton Park floodlights, Michael sinks into his theatre seat in surly discomfort, satisfied - at least - that the offspring will be occupied for the next two hours. One thing about getting out of Carlisle, he muses, is that the standard of entertainment improves.

Once the action starts Michael's mind heads briefly into overdrive. Classy Irish goalkeeper Kelham O' Hanlon was right to walk out after the regular drubbings of the previous season. The man had played international football after all, and despite his heroics over an entire season, as of May, 1993, he was employed as goalkeeper for the 88th best senior team in England. Preston North End might have been relegated into the bottom flight in the Summer of 1993, but they still represented a more fitting home for a seasoned stopper with enough class to last a few more seasons.

The lack of Kelham has told on Michael's team this year and the leaking of goals leads Knighton to speculate on new players. Perhaps former England goalie Chris Woods is looking for a player-coach position. 'Nah,' thinks Knighton, 'That's fairy tale stuff.' What United really need is a striker who can pull the crowds and hit the back of the net, and where does a struggling Third Division outfit find one of those in January?

Michael manages a smirk at the mention of Baron Hardup's impending appearance, but, in truth, the Carlisle supremo is weary, and the warmth of the theatre sends him into a dozy stupor. Knighton's eyes are just closing when the Fairy Godmother walks on.

And, with a chirpy 'I'm Free!' John Inman starts another turn.

'Free! The guy is free!' Michael repeats excitedly. 'Well, he will be when his panto contract expires later in the month.'

A fortnight later, Michael Knighton announces John Inman's arrival at Brunton Park.

'Inman has never played football in front of paying punters before. Are Carlisle United serious?' asks the man from *The Sun*.

Knighton points out that half of Carlisle first team haven't played football in front of paying punters over the last 12 months.

'Inman knows nothing about football,' says the serious looking type from *The Guardian*.

'Neither did Aiden McCaffery and he was manager here for over a year,' counters Knighton.

'Can he run?' ventures the guy from *Shoot.*

'Listen pal,' leers Knighton, clearly tiring of the negative line of questioning. 'Inman did two halves a night for over six weeks in pantomime. He covered more ground in a night than Eric Gates managed in a season, and most nights he did an encore too. Commenting that, at 57, Inman isn't much older than 'Pop' Robson when he played his final match for United, the chairman whisks the new signing into the deepest recesses of Brunton Park to await his moment of glory before the fans.

Call it curiosity, call it disbelief, but at 6am the following Saturday, the police are called to a disturbance in Warwick Road as punters queue for the footballing experience of a lifetime. By mid-morning the heaving crowd are being quizzed by tabloid reporters arriving early for the game. They can't properly explain why they are there or why they were fighting for the best places in the queue during the early hours, which is why the tabloids label it 'curiosity' and 'disbelief.'

That afternoon the gates are locked at half past one with the ground bursting to capacity. Scotch pies are dropped by helicopter onto the pitch when the caterers van turns back in the face of the huge throng locked out of the ground.

Visitors Bury have acquitted themselves well in the division during the first half of the season, but nothing has prepared them for this. True, John Inman doesn't look match fit, but once he is on the ball nobody is going to go near him. With the slowest 30 yard run in football history, Inman trundles to the edge of the box before a huge theatrical kick sees the ball leave his boot at an impossible angle and deflect off the meaty shanks of Ricardo Gabbiadini into the six yard area. As Inman starts a slow trot towards the ball, the defence split, and later the crowd will be split as to whether Inman actually touched the ball before it crossed the line.

The following morning *The Observer,* trying to be both patronising and witty, lists the opening strike as 'Own goal / surrender.' It doesn't matter, as United have run out 7-0 winners and the only complaints are from children angry that Inman didn't come out for the second half throwing sweets to the crowd.

Wigan tell the press and say they are considering not turning up at Brunton Park the following week for their traditional slaughter of the Cumbrians in the FA Cup. The back pages forget the big clubs and all the legalities of the impending Cup tie are aired. Eventually the word comes from FA Headquarters: mincing on the pitch is not an offence within the rules of the game and if Wigan Athletic want to treat a bloke on the verge of a bus pass as a threat to their masculinity that is their problem.

Keith Prowse is quoted in the press confirming that he has never handled tickets for a third division football club before and Inman raises more interest by handing over a £10,000 cheque to Carlisle's Football in the Community fund. He has raised the cash selling kisses to grannies on the library steps in The Lanes shopping development, and Football In The Community Officer John Halpin is so impressed he kisses Inman without paying. Inman receives the keys to a house in Carlisle the following day and the season's success is assured. And what a season it is . . .

Five down by the interval, Wigan fail to appear for the second half of the Cup tie citing 22 spontaneously clenched buttocks as the reason. In the league, the crowd get behind Inman as they have backed no other. Shouts of 'He's behind you' send opposing defenders into epileptic spins in search of the mincing menace and teams leaving Brunton Park complain that it is '15,000 against 11 out there.'

In this macho game nobody wants to turn their back on John Boy and the Blue Army learns a new chant. As teams back pedal like buggery, or at least with mind numbing thoughts of buggery in their heads, the Warwick Road end leads the chants of 'Mike Graham, Mike Graham!' Graham himself seeks a few quid from the affair by fronting a dance video in which chants of his name are inter-cut with footage of Graham's distinctive rearward running. The video finishes with ten minutes of the rabid attempts of Third Division defenders to master Graham's combination of extreme show of effort and complete lack of physical contact with the opposing player.

United's players don't have to worry about turning their backs on the new tactical spearhead, but they are not blameless as they show their own macho nature in a new formation which sees ten blue shirts marching up the pitch in line abreast at walking pace. A new dance video, *Wooly Woofter And The Walking Wall* replaces *Mike Graham's Manic Retreat* in the nation's hearts. Kelham O' Hanlon's stormy relationship with the United management is rekindled as Ireland's number one returns in the United goal and proceeds to top Eric Gates' efforts to gain the most money for the least ground covered in a season. To make his point Kelham signs up with the Open University and spends 90 minutes every Saturday sat on his line reading his course books. The Warwick respond with chants of 'Kelham, Kelham are you dead?' Kelham fights back by waving his arm in the air each time he turns a page.

The only barrier to the title are high flying Shrewsbury who continue to win by playing the passing game and the May the 3rd match at Brunton Park assumes the status of a Liverpool - Arsenal title deciding show-down. Re-scheduled for the end of the season, things are looking good until the FA complain that the game is too close to the Cup final. BSkyB and the BBC rip up their contracts on the spot and dial 01228 at the same time.

Anyone with an opinion is out for TV money before the game. Hughie McIlmoyle is almost speechless with anger as he discusses Inman's 45th goal of the season, breaking his own record by one. Paranormal investigators report live from the grave of free scoring pre-war United hero, Billy Ward, where underground disturbances have been reported. A bearded professor of something to do with soil calculates that the shock waves being picked up must be caused by something about six feet long turning over and over in a wooden box.

Medical experts continue to question Inman's fitness for the job, but an investigation watched by tabloid journalists reveals a surprisingly strong heartbeat for an ageing theatrical type. Inman later confesses that he can always manage a solid pulse when Darren Edmonson is in the same room receiving treatment for a groin strain. Asked by Jeremy Paxman whether United are planning their usual 'below the belt' tactics for the show-down, Inman pats his hair gently and says 'Ooh, I do hope so.'

The game, however, doesn't live up to expectations. How could it? Shrewsbury are in disarray going backwards. They haven't had to defend in depth since being dumped in the lower flight in 1992, and a serious lapse of concentration runs them foul of the back pass rule in the first minute. Conceding an indirect free kick eight yards out, Shrewsbury face United's trump card. Simon Davey lines up the kick as Inman lines up amongst the Shrewsbury defence on the goal line. In the confusion that follows nine players are shown the red card for leaving the pitch without permission and refusing to return. Only three of the players can actually be found and the entire Shrewsbury bench is cautioned for dissent. A full scale pitch invasion by the token group of away fans is only averted when Inman licks his lips and says 'Yes, please.'

Desperate mobile phone messages from television companies keen to deliver the scheduled adverts which have been sold for monumental sums force the continuation of the game which ends with Shrewsbury's two remaining players thumped 39-0. The last goal beggars belief as Inman theatrically chases what remains of Shropshire's finest round a corner flag as his team mates string together over 200 short passes before Kelham O' Hanlon walks 95 yards and heads home without taking his eyes from the book he is reading. 'I promised the people of Carlisle we would win the title by playing football,' says a deadpan Knighton.

Inman bursts into tears as he is handed the Third Division trophy. The tabloids read more than they should into his wave at John Halpin, and Michael Knighton is besieged by the press and fellow chairmen. It looks like the United supremo will be crushed under the weight of bodies pushing in on him. The crowd is too much, Knighton can feel the pressure right on top of him.

'Daddy, Daddy wake up!' they scream. 'It's the interval, Daddy, we want some popcorn.'

'Uh, what?' mumbles Knighton.

'Daddy, it's the interval, open your wallet, we want Butterkist.'

'Get lost,' grunts Knighton. 'Leave it till May, with any luck he'll have been released by then and I can sign him on a free . . . '

Chapter Ten - Kenny Lowe

MENTIONED FOR THE FIRST TIME IN THIS CHAPTER

Tony Caig - First choice United goalie for 94/95, product of youth policy. Great shot stopper, suspect on kicking during the early part of his career.

Dave Currie - Well travelled thirtysomething striker. On his way down the league. Miraculous first touch and deft striker of the ball. Faulted by some for lack of effort and by others for the kind of arguing that attracts yellow cards.

Rory Delap - Gawky prospect with speed and vision. A promising rumour at the start of the 94/95 season. Currently a Premiership regular.

Tony Gallimore - Classy left back, signed from Stoke. Found his feet at Carlisle and made a massive impact with 40 appearances in 94/95 season.

Joe Joyce - Experienced and intelligent defender. Signed in player/coaching role. Still cutting it on the pitch in 94/95 season.

Kenny Lowe - Much travelled, seldom established midfield / forward / waste of space, briefly on loan 94/95

Paul McGregor - Chunky forward with speed and skill, after a fashion, brought in as a stop gap from Nottingham Forest during 98/99 season.

Richard Prokas - Utility player, mainly midfield. Second to none in commitment and a worthy fan favourite. Progressed from youth team for start of 94/95 season.

Shane Reddish - Bargain basement relic of a bygone age, out of time by 1994 and outclassed by the rest of the squad.

Rod Thomas - Mentioned briefly before but this chapter is his era. Skilful, diminutive, dread-locked forward, England schoolboy, youth and under 21 international. Briefly revived stalled career at Carlisle.

Peter Valentine - Solid central defender, always willing to give it a go, short on style.

Dean 'Deano' Walling - Lanky and unflappable defender, former striker with non-league past. Found his niche at Carlisle with silky performances in defence supplemented with precise goal getting strikes, especially from set pieces.

WHEN THE DUST settled on the promotion campaign of 1994, I knew a satisfaction that stirred a strange mix of nostalgia and anticipation. At their best, Carlisle United had earned a reputation as an unwelcome nightmare on the Cup campaign of any fancied team and a tough run around in search of points, with some unwelcome Cumbrian weather thrown in, for any evenly matched team. But 'their best' meant the Seventies. That sprint up the league in 1994 reached parts of my mind that had been in cold storage for years. Over that summer my thoughts returned to the kind of incidents that had been a feature of my teenage years. Gathering around that radio in a Workington supermarket to hear about the stuffing of Crewe being one.

A minor incident but, the point was, it meant so much. I could picture the last few frantic minutes of that game. Time ticking away and Carlisle setting up a free kick. poised over the ball and a sense of purpose in the tension. An accurate strike, Rod Thomas darting in to cause confusion, Crewe's organisation surrendering to the pace and pressure before Rod with his close control and speed dived in behind to deliver the killer blow and take the points North. It was probably nothing like that, I wasn't there. I'd spent the afternoon watching Jason Prins and John Holliday safe in the knowledge that they weren't on the books at Brunton Park. What mattered was that, after a few false dawns and more turgid encounters than any loyal fan should ever have to endure, there was now an air of expectation about this outfit.

In the early years of following Carlisle, I'd hung on to every television, radio and newspaper report I'd heard. Short of a few games, these reports were all I had. With the optimism of my age I always believed these reports would deliver details of solid United pressure, classy teams left in a disorganised mess and stunning last minute winning goals. I wasn't there when we beat Sunderland in 1974, taking the points in a tough encounter that - in effect - set us up for promotion. Sunderland, it should be remembered, finished two points behind us and you only got two points for a win in 1974. But I remembered the report on Border Television that followed that game and the sense that United were achieving something special. It might have been young optimism, but it should be remembered that in those days Carlisle United could bloody deliver. They were a team to be reckoned with, and when it mattered, with the end of the season approaching and promotion rivals turning up at Brunton Park, we were good enough. Even when we were behind, you believed we could come back.

Two divisions lower and 20 years later we were doing the same thing. What mattered was that sense of real purpose, the knowledge that these players had the skills to do the job and Mick Wadsworth had the schemes and discipline to blend them into a winning team. Of course there were still the pretensions of Knighton's master plan. Wadsworth was 'Director Of Coaching,' that's a manager to you and me. Carlisle had a youth policy that had already put the likes of Jeff Thorpe and Tony Caig into the first team and several other fresh faces - Delap, Prokas, etc. - on the team photo and so arguably there was a top to bottom coaching scheme that demanded an overall director. But, in the end, having a 'Director Of Coaching' in the Third Division is like calling a dustman a refuge disposal engineer. It tells the world you've got ambition, but they'll only notice when you deliver something above the usual standard of service.

Whatever, as the days ticked away and the fixture list appeared, I started making plans. I reminded myself that if the previous season had started in January and finished in May we would have been champions. Of the Southern teams in the bottom flight from the previous season only Wycombe had managed to claw their way out. Fulham and Barnet, both fairly easy train rides to London, had fallen down and of the other teams close to hand none had finished close to us in the previous year. Of the marginal matches (those I'd go to if giving up a day looked worthwhile), Northampton was begging a visit. They had finished bottom of the league in 1994.

Wigan had finished in the bottom four the previous year and in the opening match of the year they scurried along to Brunton Park and scurried around with the shapelessness and nervous energy that characterises early season encounters. Wigan is far enough North and West to cop wet winters and generally shite weather. Maybe that explains why both teams played out an hour and a half of football with an odd combination of desperation and a sense that none of it mattered. Brunton Park, for me at least, can feel a bit unreal in Summer. Maybe because there is traditionally so little at stake for Carlisle at either end of a season. Perhaps because, as a Cumbrian, I don't expect decent weather this side of a charter flight and a gaping hole in my wallet, and so there is always that odd feeling that you've dreamed that first balmy game of the season.

The unreal collision of Wigan and Carlisle was settled 2-1 in our favour because the classy finishing of Reevesy and Dean 'Deano' Walling made the difference on the day. The air of unreality grew with the passing weeks as win piled upon win and a yawning gap began to open up between us and the chasing pack. The names of perennial plodding teams changed over the weeks. but we rattled in two and three in response to their ones and nils and triple point hauls were soon the expectation for the Blue Army. Within weeks I'd gone through shock, disorientation and what passes in the mind of an instinctive Cumbrian for deep thinking.

By October the 5th, as the Blue Army - with several away shirts in evidence - were piling into Loftus Road for a mid-week collision in the League Cup. I'd come to a realisation of sorts and I'd argue I was a slightly different supporter to the guy that had seen that opening encounter. That Coca Cola / League Cup clash in October brought an unfamiliar ground, some edible hot food and a fair bit of space showing in between the 6,5000 spectators. Carrying a one goal deficit from the Carlisle leg we weren't expected to go through, but the eventual 2-0 defeat on the night represented the first genuine loss of the year. 3-0 on aggregate. We'd avenged a first round defeat in the same competition at Rochdale by thrashing them in the second leg. By the standards I was used to, 6,500 was a reasonable turn out, but the sounds still echoed around Loftus Road with the home support seemingly there out of a sense of duty and many obviously bored with the whole thing. The Carlisle contingent, healthy in numbers, was mainly the London crowd. The unreality in my mind was compounded by the hassles of fighting my way to Loftus Road after a hard day's work, the half decent food on offer and the scale of the ground. It had been a season or two since I'd been anywhere that big. The serious work rate from the players and the sense that - even at 3-0 down on aggregate - it mattered to chase every ball, were a healthy sign. Still, the whole thing felt unreal to me. Partly, I'm sure, this was down to the situation. The usual will I won't I debate about going. The worry about missing a train by five minutes and getting home an hour later, leaving the jacket at work, being knackered the following morning. But there was more to it than that.

Football crowds change imperceptibly from match to match. Carlisle away in the South East pull an odd assortment of interested ex-pats, addicted types, Cumbrians with an unhealthy interest in bum aching coach journeys, over-priced motorway food and reading the tabloids down to the small print. Add the odd curiosity seeker - and I've met some really odd ones in Carlisle crowds - and allow for the small changes with each London borough, weekend / midweek games, the month, the weather, the seaside towns which host low grade football, and you've got the ever changing South East away crowd.

The mixing of the mystical formula on October the 5th, 1994, put a few professional types into the Loftus Road crowd and a number of interested bystanders there mainly to watch a good scrap on the pitch and carrying the vain hope that they would see an upset. You can get too analytical about this stuff, but the feeling of unreality hit me several times that season. Perhaps more that night than any other because those curiosity seekers were clearly in evidence. They'd come for an upset because - after an age in which it was unthinkable - Carlisle United were, by general agreement, good enough to punish anyone.

After some confusion at the start of the season, I got used to this new level of performance and got comfortable with the whole thing. By October the 5th, I'd turned a corner that would allow me to cope with the changes that season threw our way. So we were an odd assortment in the 'Carlisle' enclosure that October night, the oddest thing being the presence of people who couldn't tell you whether

Wetheral was a Cumbrian village or the latest designer coat in that pricey new outdoor range for men, but I could handle it. Within a couple of years I would find myself on a rain swept seaside football terrace standing next to a bunch of Americans who had targeted Carlisle and Bournemouth because they wanted something 'authentic'. They'd done the Cheddar Gorge and an English country pub, what else was there? With the oddly familiar shapes on the pitch - the fast running passes, skilful flicks and the certainty with which Dave Currie's first touch killed the ball - I was having an identity crisis along with the Blue Army. But I'd also begun to deal with it.

In the face of the consistent changes it makes sense every once in a while to consider your own reasons for being there. In the space of both legs of that Coca Cola Cup tie - September the 20th to October the 5th - I'd found myself thinking hard about the whole thing and why I was there. The surest sign that something was wrong was the inexplicable relief with which I greeted the news of a 1-0 defeat at Carlisle on September the 20th. Let's get this straight here. I want Carlisle to turn over fashionable teams, and London teams are a particular want in this department. Maybe I just didn't fancy the bleary train rides home on freezing Tuesday nights, the higher gate prices against the lower chance of a certain win, the stubborn refusal of my eyes to open the following morning, and the clock watching in the afternoon waiting to fight the rush hour on my way to some seldom visited ground with no fondly remembered burger cabin. If QPR had put four past us at the first attempt then a trip to the return leg at Loftus Road would have been easier to reject out of hand. Well those were the logical reasons for welcoming a defeat, but they'd never made me feel good when we took a stuffing before.

Frankly, by September, 1994, I was having an identity crisis as a supporter. I might have been coming up 35, but this was not a mid-life crisis. I'm hoping to avoid that one totally and the strategy for doing so is foolproof. I've spent my entire adult life so bloody confused about what it all means and wondering where the hell I fit in, that turning 40 made no difference and I doubt whether 45 or 50 will change that. So, in the way that I worry about these things, I worried seriously about why I was so relieved at that defeat. I had started to worry at it hard as I shuffled through Euston station at the end of September on my way to Northampton.

What I think it comes down to is this. We match ourselves with the people in life that reflect the way we see things. The weirdest crowd I've ever stood in had paid good money to see Neil Young thrashing out some furious electric rock. Young, old, male, female, punks, hippies, they'd all matched themselves to his famous creative and uncompromising streak. Each in their own way identified with a quality in his music. To some of the unrepentant hippies in the crowd, Neil Young is one of the few of their generation who never sold out. To some of the younger members of the crowd, he's the grizzled old bastard who can run from a guitar solo into howling feedback and back again and make the whole ear splitting mess sound glorious. The guy who inspired Kurt Cobain and ended up getting quoted in his suicide note. The reputation of one man drew that weird crowd together. They identified with the qualities they wanted for themselves, but they were a strange assortment. This side of a car accident, or other spontaneous disaster, you'd be unlikely to see a similarly mixed bunch standing around together.

On the face of it there is a difference between the way we support football teams and the way we pick our favourite rock stars. The unwritten rules of football give you a choice of glamour or local. I grew up with the belt and braces approach of provincial England which gives everyone a get out. You all support the local club and pick a glamour club that you follow on TV. Well, that was the theory for my generation and we've already established that 'local' to me meant a choice of Carlisle and Workington. In the context of the local rivalry of Carlisle and Workington, I'd - arguably - selected a local and a glamour club. At the start of the 94/95 season, it struck me for the first time that it isn't that simple for your whole life. Asked up to the end of the previous season, I could give a straight answer as to what a fixture list was doing on my computer diary at work, why I bothered to head off to Barnet on a wet Saturday, and all the rest. Depending on the person asking the question, my Cumbrian roots, our place as a little known outpost of England and the great Carlisle tradition of the hard working footballing side would feature.

The first leg of the Coca Cola Cup tie with QPR had taken place in Carlisle on September the 20th and, reading the report in the paper the following morning, I'd felt an odd mixture of emotion at the 1-0 defeat we'd taken. The fall out of the strange elation at the defeat by QPR, turning over in my mind for half a week, told me that these pat answers were bollocks.

I'd stuck with Carlisle for many reasons. But one that I'd missed was the way their progress and attitude had strangely mirrored my own over the best part of two and a half decades. This was something of a revelation and it struck me, in the manner of all great revelations, in the most unlikely place. I've had a few interesting experiences in train toilets over the years, but getting hit with a life defining revelation on an otherwise average Saturday morning ranks as one of the most memorable. What it comes down to is that, in an odd way - the part of me that waffles on about Media Studies would call it 'sub-text' - following a football team does match the personal qualities we see in rock stars, actors and others. Teams can have such a quality. Football lends itself to this more than you might think.

From one angle the whole beauty of football is the different meanings it can have for everyone. Mike Graham's furious back-pedalling stays with me as an image of panic and hopelessness from the darkest period of my existence as a United supporter. Then again, I was having a few dark moments of my own at the time. That pathetic crowd we fielded in the bottom of the league year matched my view of life at the time as well as any Smiths' album or gritty movie. The illusion - and it is an illusion - is that we have more choice over the records and movies which take our cash than we do about the football teams we support. In 1994, by contrast to the bottom of everything season, Carlisle and I were heading in different directions. I went through life at the time coming home knackered, struggling to fit more work into less time, and knowing that none of it was as important as grabbing what quality moments I could with Thom. Quality moments on the pitch had been at a similar premium for years, but now - even in the jaws of a home defeat by QPR - we were a quality outfit.

Carlisle United weren't matching my expectations of life, they were bloody well exceeding them. I couldn't read a grim Northern slant into their games because there was a confidence and quality about everything they were doing. The only thing that matched the way my life was going was that we'd got beaten, which was why I was oddly satisfied. Having understood all of this I stood there in that stinking train toilet, realised I was an enlightened man, pulled the chain and headed out to the rest of my life.

Don't get me wrong. It's not that I wanted the rotund back- peddling nightmare of Graham and his cronies to return and drag us down to the depths of Newport County. I just needed to adjust to the new situation. To make some sense of a confusing feeling that had dogged me for a few days. Whatever, I was a Cumbrian, they were my team and the reasons I'd loved them all along were still valid. The discomfort so far in the impressive season was like supporting your other half through a tough set of exams and then not being able to say you were jealous when they landed a better paid job than you. You might feel a bit odd, but you'd still sleep with them.

In the end, because it mattered enough, you'd work it out, and you'd both be better for it.. Hell, I still cared more than I could really say about Carlisle, and I was gonna work this one out. Maybe it was up to me to match United for once. I'd let life dictate to me a fair bit and all I had to show for it was a few more quid in the bank and a mountain of work on my desk. I sat down, got stuck into my copy of *The Sun* and looked forward with confidence to enjoying an away win.

We were going to win, of course. There we were three points clear of the pack. There they were keeping Wigan at bay by a mere point and almost propping up the football league. Not only that, but their nickname is the The Cobblers. Everywhere I looked the omens were really good. The train to Northampton went up beside the M1 where one of Eddie Stobart's trucks was trundling happily along. Yeah, this was gonna be a good un'.

Give me Workington over Northampton any day. Sprawling and without any soul. Northampton's home at the cricket ground was far enough from the station to leave an away fan equally confused every year. I never did memorise the route. The town centre was packed and I managed to get directions to the ground after a few unsuccessful attempts. To show you how much the people of the town cherished their football club, half of them didn't seem to know where the ground was and the Scotsman selling newspapers in the centre of town told me the game was in Carlisle.

There were crowds of people, a lot sporting football shirts, all heading away from the ground. Man Utd, Chelsea, Liverpool and fuckin' Arsenal all passed me in the other direction. I even spotted Jerry Garcia of the Grateful Dead coming away from the ground. A thought struck me. Could Northampton Town be so bloody awful that football fans and a rock star who had faced drug induced demons head on refused to watch them?

Northampton were stuffed and it was still twenty to three. On top of that I was making sense of life and prepared to go hell for leather for the positive view. Belatedly, my season was really underway. About 200 yards from the ground, I spotted the first Northampton scarf. I got into the queue with the other four people who seemed keen to watch the game and got one of the cherished seats. There only were 400 or so because the rest of the stand was condemned.

Shuffling to the stand meant wandering in front of the away team bench and I got in a cheery chat with Jeff Thorpe. Just before kick-off, the empty seat next to me was filled by a well groomed professional looking woman. Call it intuition, call it experience, but something in her quality clothes, the whiff of perfume and her confident strut told me she wasn't your average travelling member of the Blue Army. I said as much to her and she quietly confided she was 'with the referee'. He might not have parents, but this guy was a fully fledged heterosexual with something considerable in the way of pulling power. Having just got myself sorted out I started to get edgy. What do you do when your instincts demand you get up and scream for an offside and the wife of the guy who denied it is practically sitting in your lap?

Northampton played like a team second bottom of the whole lot should play - they were fucking angry. Not too skilful maybe, but they ran at the game like they wanted some result. The nerves were bloody transparent when chances and half chances were snatched by panicking forwards. They could string their passes together. But in front of goal they were somewhere near the accuracy of a blind school. Carlisle were penned back, but when they did break free they had time and skill to measure the attacks.

The first sign that something was seriously wrong came with Rodders first touch. A skilful shimmy turned into some inspired break-dancing as he lost control on the low grade Cobblers' pitch. 'He thought the pitch was a bit uneven,' said Mrs Ref. Uneven, it was obviously uneven. Rodney's flailing dreadlocks were just about visible from behind the nearest hillock! Let's add 'heavy' to the criticisms of the pitch and mention the wind that was blowing over the low wall behind the Blues end and right into Tony Caig's goalmouth.

With massive defensive clearances doing a swift 180 degree turn, United were up against it until half-time. Still with most of the first half gone I wasn't worried.

We were soaking up pressure, but that's why we bought Deano. Tony 'Gally' Gallimore and Joe Joyce were superb at the back. When Northampton scored I thought back to the revelation on the train and didn't even consider feeling good about it. We had skill, we had shape, we had pace and more points than this lot would see before March. A temporary set-back, nothing more. Half-time was approaching and with that wind being worth an extra man in midfield I was figuring two or three goals for us.

To be fair, the signs were already there that we needed the extra man. Kenny Lowe was definitely mentioned in the team check at the start, but he must have been off getting in the pies because I didn't notice him playing football during the first 45 minutes. Elsewhere the pace was lacking, probably on account of the miles run in pursuit of QPR a few days earlier, although Reevesy's aggression and the odd Rodders touch were still worrying Northampton.

We broke out a bit more in the second half, but from the restart I realised I'd been wrong about that wind. Where Northampton had really penned us in, we were holding them and getting caught on the break. The conditions demanded short passes, simple moves and several miles of running from every man. Give Northampton their due - they were doing all of that. The older heads in the away pyjama strip could be seen doing their best to calm things down and David Currie's gob was getting as much work as his legs in this department.

This was a job for a Director Of Coaching and Wadsworth duly responded. I finally spotted Kenny Lowe - he was the one heading for the touch-line. His number was up, thank fuck. So was Valentine's. Poor old Pedro looked knackered, but then he had spent 90 minutes marshalling a defence against the might of Les Ferdinand a few days before. As for Kenny Lowe, I'm glad he was a loan job. If we'd forked out as much as ten grand for the sod on that form I'd have been back down to the bench for a chat. Players have come and gone over the years, but Kenny Lowe - a short lived loan signing from Birmingham - continues to trouble me. I saw his only start in a Carlisle shirt. He made one more appearance as sub and was promptly despatched back to St Andrews. In my mind he is forever marooned in a fast moving midfield, lacking match fitness, chasing a pass that has already fled and battling a hard wind into the bargain.

At the end of the season, I voted for Kenny Lowe in a United fanzine poll as the biggest waste of space I'd seen that season in a Carlisle shirt. In fact, I saw him play for around an hour. The only other time I remember seeing him play I caught sight of his thin frame and thinning thatch as he made a workmanlike attempt on goal in a Birmingham City shirt the following season. My reaction to the chance encounter surprised me. 'Kenny-fucking-Lowe' I muttered as images of the Northampton game came flooding back. It's personal, or it feels it, and my hatred of Kenny Lowe is irrational and unjustified. I've followed his career down to Hartlepool and Darlington by means of checking out the *Who's Who* over the years and noted his handful of appearances for unfashionable outfits. I've ranted in half-time queues for pies about his lack of pace, wayward touch and feckless attempts to grasp a tactical structure, and none of this makes that much sense. I saw the poor sod play for around an hour, he played a minor role in an average performance by a side trying to shake off a gruelling mid-week Cup match and looked short of match fitness himself.

The truly amazing thing is that poor old Kenny scored impressively in the biggest waste of space category in the fanzine that year. He walked the award with more than double the votes of his closest competitor, Shane Reddish. There were good reasons for voting for Reddish too. He was a genuine throwback, signed at the end of a poor season, he'd clocked up over 30 appearances to the start of the 94/95 season, managing a goal, but he belonged in the aimless outfit he'd joined in 1993 and the better we got the more out of time he looked. We had more reason to hate Reddish - Lowe was simply on trail and we were glad to see the back of him. Reddish belonged to us and he'd made enough gaffs to be an unwelcome name on any team sheet.

So what was it about Kenny-fucking-Lowe? To be honest, you've got me, but every now and again I read something in a paper suggesting that an unusual Christian name gives you a better chance of a good exam grade, wearing green makes you successful in interviews on Monday and unsuccessful on Friday. Other people in the office mumble about the papers making up the news, researchers not knowing what they're on about, and the like, but now and again I remember Kenny-fucking-Lowe. A journeyman pro who turned out with an unfamiliar team twice in 1994 and is still discussed in nightmare terms to this day. My own irrational hatred I could put down to a strange period in my career as a supporter. But, despite K-F-L's appearance in front of a limited Blue Army that day and one other run out as sub, he was universally hated. I'll bet he's a decent guy. Maybe if he'd had a really unusual name he would have scraped a few more qualifications, he could have worn a green shirt to that all important interview and . . .

Kenny Lowe walked out of my life with half an hour of the Northampton game to go. With Prokas and Edmonson on we hit the heights. The first move of the new line up saw a quick cut through midfield, a tidy ball out to the left, some deft control, a pass and Reevesy was one goal nearer being the leading scorer in the Division.

Northampton, totally outclassed, and United discovering some shape for the first time in almost an hour, I started explaining the tactical switch and the subtleties of young Darren's home grown skills to Mrs Ref. I'd got as far as the location of Coniston - scenic Lakeland village and home to the young Darren Edmonson - when Northampton scored again. Simple passing, loads of running and a wicked ball across the area. Despite the public address system claiming the strike for one of their own, the Blues I met later on the train to London insisted Joe Joyce had been the last to touch it, hitting home with the same deadly accuracy that had humbled Huddersfield. I didn't have the angle in the cramped stand to know for sure. If it was Joe it was bloody cruel luck because his cool and vision had done a hell of a lot to hold back the scurrying maroon tide for most of the afternoon.

We chased the game, but didn't get back in. Our first league defeat of the season. Two games against Southern teams, two defeats in one week and I went home happy from the second one. Genuinely happy. Having figured out why I'd been quietly relieved the first time, seen myself for the quietly miserable sod I was becoming and deciding to get behind a winning team, they went and fucking lost on me. Lost to a team one point off the bottom of the whole league and I went home happy because I'd seen them chase, show skill and somewhere deep in the confused cesspit that you might just call my subconscious, I knew I'd seen a team fit for promotion. When they won or matched Premiership opposition I got nervous and confused. When they lost to a bunch of darting and desperate crapites I came away happy and confident of promotion. Funny old game innit?

By the start of October I knew I was on the right track with my revelation because I was cheered for all the right reasons at Loftus Road, not because we lost 2-0 but because we leaked the second goal precisely because we kept on chasing the game. And for periods in that game the massive gap in league positions was a complete nonsense. If we could hold our own against this standard of opposition we could storm the Third Division.

Apart from the stunning revelation that at least one ref out there had pulling power, the Northampton game was memorable for another reason. On the train home I ran into 'Foxy Ferret' Phil Lorimer. Phil was talking with another ex-pat, Sean, and if my memory is working properly I think Sean is from Workington. Sean lived in London at the time, like a lot of the 'travelling' United support, which gathers for Southern games. The memorable bit about Phil is that I would see him on and off for years at United games and he would be the most visible - and the most inexplicable - of the group of supporters to which I would gravitate at games.

I'd always gone to games on my own on an occasional basis. In some cases because I was on my way somewhere and would head South from Carlisle via Brunton Park. On other occasions because I couldn't persuade anyone else to come. However, this had been an isolated thing until the 94/95 season when the combination of a fair smattering of Southern games, more disposable cash than I'd enjoyed for years, and Owen getting old enough to want to hang out with his mates, left me making solo trips on a regular basis. It didn't bother me that much. I'd usually find myself talking to someone within a couple of minutes of finding a space on the terraces.

Phil was a regular presence that year and in future years when the numbers fell away along with our hopes of a steady climb to the top of the pyramid. With his flowing tresses, he looks memorable enough but he made a massive impression on

195

me simply because his reasons for membership of the Blue Army were unusual, to say the least. Phil is from the South coast. He makes his living transporting greyhounds and this takes him in and out of Cumbria on a regular basis. He has explained on at least three occasions how and why he came to adopt Carlisle and - in the manner of a great Frankie Howerd performance - it always makes sense when I hear it and disappears like morning mist when I try to run it through my mind at other times.

The amazing thing to me is that, being a Southerner and all, Phil clearly had a choice about his adoption of Carlisle. Looking at the whole thing logically I can't see why someone from Brighton would want to adopt them and why they would continue through the unmitigated shite of the season from hell in 1992 beats me. Then again, the guy that runs the publishing company that put this book in your hands lives in Lockerbie, speaks with a Scots accent and swears blind he supports Gillingham!

The point is that much of this behaviour and allegiance, the way the ramshackle army of travelling support gather together and unite (after a fashion) for a couple of hours on a Saturday defies logic. You could adopt a team because of their great footballing tradition, but put this logic to the test and its complete bollocks outside of the Premiership. You could argue that Carlisle are a footballing side with a pedigree worth defending. But, that argument was history by 1994 despite the flashes we'd seen on the pitch in recent games. The flashes that brought a rush of anticipation to a radio news report and a strange nostalgia to my heart may have been the start of something important, or a freak outcome of a surprisingly effective blend of youth and experience in the squad. Any casual fan or off-comer adopting United who was forced to defend their reputation in the decade to 1994 was seriously up against it.

CUFC supporter: 'Oh yeah, we're a footballing side, brought on some great ball players in our time, Beardsley, Stan Bowles, lads that know the value of the first touch. Dave Currie these days, he might have his best years behind him, but that first touch . . . magic'

Someone else: 'I saw you lot in 1992, they weren't a footballing side then, cloggers mostly, some fat git up front that played for England twice and this back-peddling nightmare in defence who couldn't play football cos he never made contact with anything.'

CUFC supporter: 'Telly was crap last night eh?'

No side that has sunk as low as we have over such a long period can seriously claim to maintain a great tradition. When you are reduced to journeymen pros, a youth policy and the kind of 'talent' that leaves you change from £50,000, the best you can realistically hope to start with is ambition, attitude and a few useful skills that might just blend themselves into something effective. Okay, we had a Director Of Coaching, but you could have called Mick Wadsworth the flamin' ring master for all the difference that made. And anyway, the man who takes on the development of hopeful talent in a lower league club is really part of the sales force.

Mick Wadsworth achieved a lot for Carlisle and one honest measure of that is the presence of his former players in higher placed teams than ours over future seasons. He found the best and brought it out. If Wadsworth achieves nothing of national notoriety in the game then let it be said here that the guy was a welcome break in a succession of managers who failed to turn it all round. Look, you could pack the entire fan base of Scarborough onto an Inter City train and leave a few empty seats, so how the fuck does a team with a start like that make the Third Division play-offs in 1998? Because Mick Wadsworth was their manager and he pulled more out of that team than anyone had a right to expect.

So, anyway, as of October 1994, we were a footballing side again. The shape and confidence in the side allowed us to hit passes with a reasonable degree of accuracy and the roles were cut out so well that our tactics were seen to work. I came to reflect on this as the train - packed with more bodies than Scarborough mustered that afternoon - sped back to London. I also came to reflect on how a Southerner who shipped greyhounds in his van knew so much about my team.

The conversation started with a competition to find the best insult we could throw at Kenny-fucking-Lowe, but quickly moved to the big picture. Phil was a revelation and I knew I'd found a kindred spirit of some sort when the conversation swung round to the nightmare season and our nightmare centre half, John Holliday. Phil had been at Gillingham the day we won away, one of only two such wins that season. He'd seen the miss-timed tackles, the clattering challenges and the desperate climbs above the oncoming attack that had made Holliday an oddly effective presence that day and he put Sean to rights when the Workingtonian suggested that Holliday was total crap. Within a few minutes we'd come to some sort of agreement. Holliday was total crap with the exception of the Gillingham game, which put him marginally ahead of Kenny Lowe.

To the outside we were just three supporters sitting on a train and running over the days events. When a crowd from Reading joined us later we set about discussing the England scene and struck up the kind of bond that unites loads of the ramshackle travelling crowd on cold train journeys into the early hours of a Saturday evening. The whole thing is so normal it tends to pass unnoticed and yet it is worth thinking about because when you ask some of the obvious questions it makes less sense than you think.

Phil Lorimer wouldn't come to my funeral for two good reasons. Firstly he's unlikely to be that bothered and secondly if I did beat him to that great windswept terrace in the sky he'd never bloody well find out. I wouldn't ask him to shift my greyhound because, quite frankly, I don't give a shit about greyhound racing. So why would I feel kinship with this bloke for more than a second? Not because we shared a schooling or even a county when we grew up, not because we were drawn to Carlisle by a rich and rewarding tradition of playing entertaining football, and not because the experience of watching a hard fought bottom flight tussle in a howling gale at a crumbling cricket ground several light years from the nearest station offered us that incomparable big match atmosphere. I reckon we belong together, for a short time at least, because our needs as people were met by Carlisle United more than we would ever want to admit.

It's worth a thought. The travelling Blue Army are the same odd assortment that any team shackled with descriptions like 'regional' and 'unfashionable' would expect to pull. When I've wandered out to the car park at Brunton Park in recent years I haven't as a rule been knocked out with the quality cars and dripping wealth mustered by the likes of Shrewsbury, Hull, Cardiff or Gillingham. All of these clubs have ambition and some argument to say they belong above the bottom flight. I've seen all of them play pathetic, plodding football and slog with little more than desperation in search of points. So why would any sane person give up a valuable Saturday and an appreciable amount of cash to check them out? We might say they are 'our' team, except that they aren't always our local team. We might link our support to some past good experience but that is - roughly speaking - the equivalent of trying to muscle your way into bed with someone else's wife on the grounds that the pair of you once went out together when you were both 15.

The more I think about this the more I realise we have a choice and we've had one all our adult lives. Whatever we say, we go because we want to and we want to because deep down our teams reflect our lives. Not totally, and not in some pretentious bullshit way that matches a few seconds of Rod Thomas' weaving his magic through a pedestrian defence with my own hopes of escaping a rigid working system to write dazzling novels. In fact, for the most part, it's so bloody simple it's frightening. Most of us 'rank and file' supporters follow ploddingly average teams with ambition before returning to our ploddingly average lives in which we set targets and work forward with ambition. Whatever we say about local teams, footballing traditions and the rest, we seldom spend time in the half-time queues admitting we have a choice about whether we are there. In fact, you are more likely to hear complaints from people who claim they have no choice.

The proof that we have a choice is in the absence of huge numbers of flash cars from the travelling fleet. Conspicuously successful people are more evident in the quality seating areas of Premiership high flyers than they will ever be at Brunton Park. Phil Lorimer and I support Carlisle because our allegiance has paid off in a manner of speaking. We've spent years watching teams that have matched our vision of life. Deep down, we've got to be optimists, but we've also got a realistic streak strengthened through years of slogging to make a living. We're both likely to seize opportunities and make the most of their possibilities. Which, in a manner of speaking, explains why we would seize on the clumsy efficiency of John Holliday and briefly see the potential for avoiding the shame of propping up the entire bloody league. It sounds grim although it isn't really all that bad.

The sense of companionship is real. All the more so because the bonds go deeper than the action on the park and deeper than the jobs we do. The real pessimists - the ones for whom life can be truly grim - gave up years ago and you might catch some of them dragging around with their wives on a Saturday afternoon debating the merits of buying a new towel rail. Ask 'em about football and they may say they packed in on it years ago because there was no point. They'd sooner get something done on a Saturday afternoon. I'll join them myself the second I get an adrenalin rush looking at a towel rail!

Taking this logic a little further, it is no wonder that the massively successful tend to avoid the lower division teams. There always were those with prodigious gifts far in excess of their classmates and the other kids in the street. Those for whom success and imagination came easily. For a while in the late years of junior school and the early years of the psychopathic comprehensive, there is the tempting illusion that none of us are that different. Everyone has their team and the ability to reel off the names of players. Okay, I'm talking about the lads here, as far as my generation goes, but you'd see the same pattern with both sexes. There are women who went on to be hugely successful who could stand shoulder to shoulder with their class mates and recite every line of a song by David Cassidy, Wham! or Take That.

Time tells a different story. The 'different' kids, often conspicuous by the fact that football matters less for them at ten years old than it does for most of us tend to be the first to depart the fold. If they ever went to games at all they are the first to disappear from the terraces, especially in the bargain basement. They are also the most likely to turn up unexpectedly on your screen as you channel hop. Their departure from the terraces probably has everything to do with the fact that lower division football - with its reflections of the grim struggles that will reflect grim moments in life for most of us - has nothing to do with their view of life.

The ones who really get on from your class in school usually are the different ones. The ones who don't sell out or allow the local headcases to beat the ambition out of them. These people are likely to find the kind of bullying meted out by lower division defenders to a fledgling talent like Matt Jansen or Peter Beardsley a little too close to home. If football offers these people anything it is the chance to belong with their age group at the time in their lives when they need to belong the most. Future years will offer them more opportunities to belong with an intellectual elite in college and a creative elite in a top flight advertising agency or wherever. If people in this company need football at all it is either as a fashion accessory, like designer stubble, or an opportunity to power lunch in an executive box. It has to be said, there are executive boxes in the lower divisions. But if anyone is power lunching in these the chances are that the discussions revolve around cleaning contracts for an office block or two.

Speaking of people who got on, the last time I spoke to Melvyn Bragg I stopped to chat with him on the road from High Ireby to Ireby. It was an August day before the 97/98 season and a friendly with Falkirk was due to kick-off that afternoon. The press had been speculating about the future of United and Melvyn's name had been linked with financing the club. The truth is he knew almost nothing about Carlisle, he didn't even know they were playing that afternoon. Sure, he'd taken an interest in Cup runs and seen us at Wembley, but the real interest he expressed was in Arsenal. The press speculation was - in all probability - a combination of wishful thinking, the need for a headline and the rounding up of the usual suspects. There aren't that many 'usual suspects' when this subject comes up. The book of great Cumbrian heroes is pretty thin. Once you've ruled out the dead ones, the list of high profile living Cumbrians - like Melvyn Bragg - is desperately thin. Melvyn Bragg, Eddie Stobart, Jack Scott, former BBC weather man . . . wait a minute, is Jack Scott still alive? Like I said, there aren't that many 'usual suspects'.

Melvyn's credentials as a genuine working class Cumbrian are better than mine will ever be. Statistically speaking he's a more likely football supporter than me, but I'm the one stuck in the traffic jam listening to *6.06* and wishing I wasn't on a rain sodden motorway returning from a pasting at Peterborough. We could both claim Carlisle as our local team, but I'm the one who made the choice because somewhere deep down it mattered enough. I don't share train journeys home from matches with the captains of industry or the conspicuously successful and I can't see the tabloid press reporting a helicopter crash that took the life of a prominent Carlisle supporter returning from a game. A freshly valeted car is hot stuff in our car park! Well that and Phil's greyhound taxi.

Somewhere along the line I got to thinking about why those of us who turn up on a regular basis actually bother, which, naturally enough, led me to figure out why I put all the effort in myself. The conclusion being that I belong with them. Because I can't identify myself with the world's high achievers but I'm not ready to throw in the towel yet.

I can't see me ever starting the week on Radio 4, fronting a show that Melvyn Bragg made his own, or sitting in the House of Lords alongside Lord Bragg. So, I'm not exactly a high achiever. Then again, the in-built defence mechanism which reduces me to a disfunctional zombie every time I find myself in the soul destroying confines of a major DIY chain is as strong as ever. I don't give a shit about towel rails. So, all told, I exist somewhere below Melvyn's level of conspicuous success based on massive intellectual gifts and somewhere above the hopeless level of desperation that sees my creative peak firmly rooted to the bathroom wall. If you consider my position as a lifestyle choice you start to see why some things that lack genuine high profile gloss achieve a level of success that stuns a certain section of the community. Who buys all those Bee Gees records, who bought all the Ford Escorts, and who goes to those lower division games that don't matter at the end of the season?

Well, it's me, or people like me, although I'd plead not guilty in the case of Ford Escorts and, out of choice, I'll go for rougher and louder music than The Bee Gees. But you get the point. There's quite a few of the ambitious but average brigade out there. Some of us work in colleges, some of us deliver greyhounds. There are quite a few ambitious and average teams out there for those of us who can rustle up an excuse to become involved with them. Shrewsbury, Gillingham, Bournemouth . . . and Carlisle.

Me and Carlisle United, we were made for each other.

Blue Nightmare #11

YOU'LL NEVER DENT Deano's cool.

The mid-Nineties was the heyday of cheap stunt television. *Beadle's About*, *You Bet* and *The Word* pushed back the TV boundaries. On *The Word* there were 'the young hopefuls' who would eat toe-nails, lie in a bath of slurry , or have their legs waxed in front of the cameras to get on telly. As *The Word* sought even more perverse thrills, they invented 'The Revengers', a cruel hit squad who would imitate the hopelessly incontinent and let leg bags burst on the unsuspecting in search of laughs.

This item, and the show, were put to sleep at the end of the series by which point *The Word* had few friends in the press, and the general consensus was that the era of plumbing the depths of taste in the form of stunts was over for the time being. Meanwhile, programme makers hit on the docu-soap, an area in which transexuals, the stylishly challenged, and the unashamedly feckless could be exploited under the blanket excuse that the producers of the programmes were representing reality and bringing life's rich tapestry to the nation's television audience.

This move ended the development of *The Word*'s most ambitious and outlandish item. As a follow up to 'The Revengers,' producer Paul Ross had developed an item called 'Dent Deano's Cool'.

In this extreme feature the general public were to be invited to push their imagination and body to the limit and devise a performance which could dent the cool of ace Carlisle United defender, Dean Walling. Anyone managing to get Dean excited could win ten grand on the spot. Anyone managing to get him really excited and could win £25,000.

It sounded easy, but in rehearsals several people tried and failed.

Goalkeeper, Tony Caig from Carlisle said: 'When Carlisle United were at Wembley I lost out to Kevin Francis in a challenge and the six foot seven Brummie forward sent the ball heading for a certain goal. Deano calmly collected it on the goal line and punted it upfield. Most defenders would have gone apeshit and started a right row. Deano shrugged his shoulders and said 'Hey, that was going in you know.'

Several dozen Third Division players tried to dent Deano's cool. One told us: 'We voted him into the Third Division team for the 94/95 season. There were a few useful defenders around that year so it was a bit of an honour. On the evidence of a camera cunningly hidden in his kitchen, Deano got the news in the post, looked up from his cornflakes, said, 'Mmmm decent,' and went on munching.

In one rehearsal an atomic bomb accidently went off. Most of the camera crew went wild with panic, but Deano grinned and said, 'That'll save on shaving my head for a week or two.'

Paul Ross confesses, 'We had a load of stunts lined up, ritual disembowelments, explosives experts who were willing to blow themselves up, and a game of Russian roulette to be screened live from a very dodgy South Asian bar. We could have put on the most amazing stunts in television history, but in the end it would have been pointless. We'd never have got a result because we'd already figured out, you just can't dent Deano's cool.'

Chapter 11 - Paul Conway

MENTIONED FOR THE FIRST TIME IN THIS CHAPTER

Paul Conway - Wandsworth born 'American' midfield ball winner. Son of former Fulham idol, Jimmy Conway, who moved to the USA, allowing his son to grow up Stateside. Generally impressive on positioning, distribution and work rate.

Tony Elliot - Well travelled reserve keeper. Agile, brave and maintaining the great Peter Shilton tradition of extending his goal area to the halfway line by means of loudly barking instructions at the defence. A favourite with me if not the managers charged with selecting him.

Peter Hampton - Long serving Physio, shortish dark-haired dead ringer for Mick Wadsworth, giving the physical and mental master planners behind United the bizarre appearance of twins

Steve Hayward - Attack minded midfielder with strength, accuracy and a level of nerve and commitment that was seldom found wanting.

Paul McGregor - He wore a blue shirt briefly, on loan in the 98/99 season. The word 'striker' appeared next to his name when his loan signing was announced. Maybe he was a 'striker' in the great British tradition of a bloke who refuses to do the job for which he is paid. Ten games, three goals.

Derek Mountfield - Seasoned campaigner, centre half with class, a level head and a knack for well timed - if occasional - forays up front.

Paul Murray - Home-grown talent. Unfussy midfielder with high work rate and a knack for ball winning followed by well placed lay off.

AS I WRITE this line my long term love with Carlisle is being tested again. We're stumbling around within sight of the bottom of the entire league, but deep down I know they'll deliver again. In such dark moments, like most loyal fans, I've got memories. If I want, I can remind myself about those seven months that shook the world, well they shook my world anyway. If I want to touch the feelings that remind me why it matters, why I'll stand in the freezing January rain with little more than hope and a bacon roll to sustain me, I can

**think back to a handful of matches that touched me more than a mere game
should. Experiences that strengthened my very hold on life.**

One that I will treasure for as long as there are two brain cells working with a
spark between them goes back to October the 22nd, 1994. This ranks as one of the
best afternoons I'm likely to have as a Blue. It looked a little unpromising. Held 0-0
by Colchester in the previous game, even if they were on a roll, our home form
should have been enough to leave the net bulging at least once. Getting to the
ground the programme showed Kenny Lowe at number 12. Oh hell, bring back
Ricardo Gabbiadini.

My Dad and 13 year old Owen were along for the ride. Dad hadn't been to a
football match since the grim Boxing Day encounter with Doncaster in the season
from Hell. By this point in his life Owen was looking for the things that made him
different and he'd started telling his mates at the grammar school that he supported
Carlisle. I pointed out the be-suited figures of the team as they arrived and gave
him potted details of Rodney's matchless ball skills. This explanation came in
response to us witnessing one fan throwing himself down in an 'I'm not worthy'
gesture as Rodney's Ford Escort trundled into the player's car park. In the hope that
he'd get serious about football I bought him a scarf in the club shop but the life of a
Kent grammar school hardly revolves around football, especially the unfashionable
Northern variety. I knew then it would be an uphill struggle.

We were an unlikely band. One terminal case bringing along his Dad who was
in it more for the bonding / quality time angle, and a teenager filling in his time as
he stayed with a grandparent and not yet old enough to head out into uncharted
territory on his own. But, this afternoon in October brought the three of us together
in shared awe at the breathtaking skill, vision, skill and more skill on offer. Barnet
did their bit too.

Second against fourth, a six pointer to be sure.

Things started off well when the team was announced with Jeff Thorpe at
number 12 and Kenny Lowe's name totally absent. Barnet's pathetic performance
in the previous season had been turned round suspiciously fast and a few minutes
into the game the reasons were obvious. Manager, Ray Clemence, hadn't much
more skill or class to call on than his team could muster 12 months before, but what
he did contribute was organisation and discipline. His Barnet side resembled
Carlisle's best under Clive Middlemas, the team I'd seen crumble at the boots of
Maidstone United the day Owen got his head jumped on. Barnet were journeymen
organised into an effective unit, but always suspect in the face of skill and vision.
No wonder we stuffed 'em.

The kick-off saw Reevesy out on the right and a clear plan to get round the back
with a quick move. It didn't come off, but from the start we were running at them,
round them and into them. When David Currie got close after six minutes they
were clearly rattled. With passes being hit accurately and moves starting from

anywhere a Blue found the ball, the Barnet system was under threat. Barnet played it straight and aimed to stand up and stop the opposition. Their strategy was down to holding their shape and giving every player a clear job to do. Drilled and disciplined, they were there for the taking as Carlisle ran off their men and Rodney and Reevesy sought new positions. The increasingly assured touches of Paul Conway took them on from midfield and Carlisle ran in at the defence, turning them and pulling them out of position. As the gaps opened up behind the full backs the chances started to come.

Reevesy got in a shot just after the quarter hour. Derek Mountfield got his head to Currie's free-kick soon after and Barnet's counters looked weak and desperate. When Simon Davey almost got on the score sheet in the 20th minute the whole stand was up with me. The probing and invention was coming so fast that I couldn't keep up the explanations to Owen. Not that I wanted to, there was some serious stuff out there to enjoy.

This was the only occasion on which I saw my Dad genuinely worked up about a football match. One of the odd things about my Dad was his fair-minded attitude in terms of most sports. His admiration for many stars was a lesson in fair play and enjoyment without cynicism. For all that, his attitude was a world away from the traditional British fair play for which this country is famed / a laughing stock. During the Seventies, the Welsh rugby team humbled the world with a brand of open, skilful and running rugby that is found in the video collection of any self-respecting rugby coach to this day. My Dad would celebrate these performances by leaving his chair and yelling 'Come on, run it, run it!' even if JPR Williams was busy cutting a swathe through the English team. To the best of my knowledge, there isn't a drop of Welsh blood in the family tree on Dad's side. There was skill, vision and a sense of rugby as an accomplished art in that Welsh team, I know that because my Dad would tell me such things. His other passions in sport revolved around athletics, and Steve Ovett, Sebastian Coe and Steve Cram in particular got the same vocal support that was lavished on the all time greats of Welsh rugby. My Dad was a fast running rugby player of some distinction and his middle distance running at school had its moments too so he knew these sports well enough to appreciate the skills he was applauding.

His football interest generally revolved around high profile games and supporting underdogs. He loved Sunderland's victory in the 1973 Cup Final for all the romantic reasons. But he briefly saw the shape, skill and vision he'd seen in rugby games on a football pitch that day in October 1994. In the first half hour Carlisle had set up a fast moving siege of the rigid Barnet defence and the move that got Reevesy onto the score sheet after the half hour would have done justice to Dad's beloved Welsh rugby union outfit. Dave Currie's pass inside the defence was inch perfect and Rodney ran to the by-line making space, turning in an instant and BANG!!!!!! - in stormed Reevesy with £121,000 of clinical finishing and Barnet knew they were gonna have to come out to save anything like a result. When they did come out we held them and the only other real chance of the half fell to Deano off a corner.

Sodding Manchester schoolkids, three million of them in the queue for pies at half-time, left me staggering into the stand just in time to see Barnet hit the bar in the second half. End to end stuff and no explanations needed as Dad and Owen were getting behind Carlisle too. Rodney's greed and a snatched shot knackered a seriously good move sometime after the hour and young Tony Elliot saved things at the other end off a decent Barnet shot. We needed something fast to make the clear superiority count and did we get it or what?

Paul Conway had been inspirational considering it was the first competitive game he'd started all season. I'd been singling him out for shouts of encouragement. Call it psychic phenomena, call it wishful thinking. The second he got the ball off that Barnet corner and started his run goalwards I knew it was in. Okay, there was the small matter of him being in our half when he started and a few defenders and goalkeeper being on hand to try and stop him. 'Goal' doesn't do justice to his defence defying run, perfect positioning and split second delivery of the killer shot - 'fucking awesome' comes somewhere close. I could spoil the whole thing by heading downstairs to watch it on the video now. If I did that I'd discover it was a well timed run and a well struck shot, but in my mind that goal has grown in its paranormal power because I could sense the thing as he started his run, and when it hit the back of the net I was yelling so loud it felt like an out of body experience.

Whatever, we had three points sorted. Barnet did manage one more shot but their system was in tatters and sharp moves and intelligent passes would haunt their dreams for the next few days. All credit to their goalie for the save with his feet that stopped Reevesy's shot near eighty minutes, but Barnet were there for the taking and two moves from the right got behind their defence. It struck me in a rare lucid moment during those ecstatic last few minutes that Barnet's Shaun Gale was a Mike Graham in the making.

 deservedly got on the score sheet with a crisp first-time drive. And Rodney's closing goal was a deserved reward for the usual skill, even if his back heel into a Barnet gut was out of order earlier on. When the final whistle blew I'd lost all track of time and Barnet had lost all semblance of being an organised football team. Classic!

A word about Paul Murray here. He was bloody brilliant and along with Conway put together the kind of flowing, skilful football that allowed the whole team to play to their greatest strengths. There were two rumours circulating about the absence of Tony 'Gally' Gallimore from the left back position - one linked it to the need to hide him from the prying eyes of Premier division scouts. Another linked it to ten pints too soon before the game. The hot rumour over the non-appearance of Kenny Lowe on the pitch suggested he was crap.

Let's get this defence shredding performance in perspective, it was brilliant. With Paul Murray and Darren Edmonson overlapping and getting in a shot each and the midfield exploring space in search of opportunities, the whole team were buzzing. Reevesy, Rodney and Dave Currie made space, squeezed the ball through angles and pulled off the defence in a way that suggested a tactical master plan even if there wasn't one. Being a Carlisle supporter for years I'd forgotten football could be like this. Even the team that won promotion to Division One didn't always do it so well. Given his dominance in midfield Paul Conway looked as assured as Ray Train and Les O Neil, men who had assumed legendary status in United folklore, and Reevesy's incisive strikes were as good as anything Brunton Park had seen in over a decade. All that and he looked more like an athlete than Joe Laidlaw ever managed.

Writing it up later for *So Jack Ashurst Where's My Shirt,* I thought long and hard about the words 'total football' because they sounded so bloody pretentious, especially in a fanzine, but the fluid overlaps, the covering for players out of position, the invention, the chances coming in from all angles . . . Okay, it's over the top to compare Wadsworth's generation of the Blue Army to Cruyff-era Holland, but Tommy Docherty vintage Man Utd are a good comparison. Alright, 'The Doc' had a class outfit with a host of current internationals, but he brought players up through the ranks and bought well, just like Mick Wadsworth. Stuart Pearson, Arthur Albiston and a few others found a role in a successful team which combined an understanding of each other with a love of playing that created openings out of nothing.

That afternoon was a watershed, a truly transforming experience. From the second - Barnet destroying - goal I'd witnessed the kind of performance I had never seen. Almost an entire half of total domination. Carlisle hadn't beaten Barnet, they'd dissected them, running through an organisation drilled to perfection on the training ground, but unable to withstand imagination and skill in the quantity we'd dished it out. Like Saddam's Republican Guard overrun with an airborne bombardment, they'd simply been no match for the firepower massed against them. If my mumblings about our certainty for the title as I considered what to write for the fanzine had a purpose, it was to ground me. Grim bottom flight reality headed off into the distance sometime after four that Saturday afternoon and remained a stranger for weeks. I hadn't been programmed for this!

The team comprehensively destroyed that afternoon had started the day in fourth place. Serious promotion or play-off contenders, and we'd spent most of the second half playing an exhibition as they watched. That alone is enough to give that afternoon a place of affection in my memory. Thinking back, it matters for more personal reasons. My Dad had understood, the way caring parents do, that football was in my life to stay, but until that afternoon he'd never really felt it. It wasn't ever likely to be *his* game, but he was on his feet as we surged forward again and again because the shape, invention and the passion to get the job done were infectious. As infectious, say, as a team of red shirted rugby legends running around the best the other home nations could manage in the Seventies.

We headed to the car park talking about the moves, the goals and the players who'd made it all possible. We met Jane and recounted it all in detail, happy that the three of us, all coming at the game with a different need, had shared something that made for a good afternoon. Even then, I knew it was a great performance that would live on in my mind. Driving home the most important things were the confidence I'd seen in that team and the points that were in the bag. Now, years later, the most important thing is that, just once, I shared an experience that special with my Dad.

'Toilet paper!!! Look, paper, fuckin' toilet paper!!!!!'

The accent was thick Cumbrian, which might explain the puzzled looks from a few Fulham fans in the same bogs, but to tell you the truth, I didn't get it myself at first. It was all a bit strange. A gents the size of an indoor gym and a floor that was almost clean. The screaming Blue in the cubicle had one up on me, he'd ventured in for a slash and discovered that there were clubs in the bottom flight who provided a few trappings that would pass for civilised, like toilet paper. He emerged, younger than I'd imagined and totally stunned by his encounter with the strange rolls on the khazi wall. It struck me then that this guy had probably never seen the inside of a decent football ground. Why should he? If he'd been supporting the team for five years he'd known nothing but the bargain basement with trips to the grassy banks, crumbling facades and fenced off cricket pitch that were Halifax Town, Rochdale and Northampton Town. A cavernous gents that would do credit to an un-fussy hotel was palatial by the usual standards at this level.

Owen's new found love of Carlisle didn't extend to drizzle ridden trips into London when he could hit the centre of Maidstone with his mates, and I made this journey on my own. This time around I settled into a seat surrounded by Barbour jackets, posh accents and discussions about Carlisle's chances that afternoon. The Barbour crowd in question continued the great tradition of odd people in the next seats to me at a football match. They knew their football, claimed some Cumbrian connections and knew precisely sod all about the Carlisle team other than their ability to lead Division Three. Football tourists, but then successful clubs - like Carlisle - attract these people. They saw some sights that afternoon. Elsewhere a kid from Carlisle marvelled at the surroundings and shouted 'Look!' as he pointed skywards. Figuring I'd have the chance to see a UFO at long last I looked up and saw a Jumbo jet. That lad didn't get to many away games.

Fulham had some guts and wanted the points badly enough which was just fine by me because when they ran at us the gaps at the back started appearing. In the

Fulham back four, Terry Angus had an attitude problem from the start, suggesting that he knew his fellow defenders were up against it and a mountain of blubber and surliness that answered to the name of Terry Hurlock shuffled around looking increasingly displeased as the Wadsworth Academy Of Total Football Excellence got the measure of the basic offside trap. The class difference told and once Reevesy had hammered us into an early lead I was back to the out of body job. Each move and skilful lay off further proof of our superiority. Fulham put in a couple of cheeky attacks which only served to give Tony Caig the opportunity to show his increasing class and confidence. And then . . . Derek Mountfield got himself on the score sheet.

Let's be straight here, Derek was a defender with a defender's instincts. Brought into the side in the twilight of his career, Mountfield had seen action at the very top, notably with an Everton side which had stormed to Championship and European glory. His steadying influence and unflappable class had allowed Carlisle to withstand desperate assaults and he ran the back line with confidence that afternoon. If he had the space and confidence to come forward, we had to be playing well.

The planes swept up into the sky at the rate of one a minute and the Carlisle kid out in the big town spotted Concorde. Soon he'd sussed that there seemed to be a fair few sightings of Jumbos and reasoned that it must be the same one going round in circles! These observations were interrupted by more probing attacks and some serious wing play as we turned the Fulham defence in circles.

Come the second half and Carlisle were attacking our end. We ran at them - big time. Rodney broke on one occasion looking like five foot one of class with the dreadlocks trying like hell to keep up with his flying feet. Hurlock's fitness was fast failing and with the balls from midfield measuring the offside trap to perfection we were running side by side with the defence in mad sprints on goal. Reevesy missed one that would have been easier to bag. Fast crosses were squandered and when captain Simon Davey got one with time to spare, he stopped, checked and convinced us all that he'd blown a good opportunity, but when his pass connected with a speeding Paul Conway it was YESSS!!!!!! FUCKING MAGIC - GOOOALLLL !!!!!!!

History, in the form of the *Playfair Football Who's Who* records a middling career for Paul Conway. The Wandsworth born 'American' midfielder who scored twice in that memorable week would stay with us for another two seasons, move to the dizzy heights of Northampton Town, struggle to establish himself and then re-unite with Mick Wadsworth at Scarborough, playing his part in their sprint for play-off glory in 1998. It is the lot of the regular fan to see the twists and turns that produce the cold statistics that - eventually - find their way into the black and white summaries in the books beloved by Statto clones the length and breadth of the football world. Conway's failure to appear more than 25 times a season owes something to injury, something to changes in management at Carlisle, and something to his own form. However, every journeyman has his moments and during that week in October, Paul Conway was magnificent. Two goals, a matchless touch in midfield and the anticipation that put him in the right position to create his own goal scoring opportunities. No set of statistics in any anorak book will begin to tell you just how good he was that week. You just had to be there and you had to be supporting Carlisle.

Most of us are journeymen. Our inspirations and great achievements delivered in journeyman careers, our wisdom imparted around average kitchen tables in unremarkable homes and carried on for future reference and uses we may never intend. In all probability we will spend more time wondering about whether we matter than we ever will making great decisions or achieving great things. The legacy of my journeyman teaching career, in part at least, is a handful of young people who could explain to you how it is possible to combine chart topping singles with empty bank accounts and how the ins and outs of cross-collateralisation and recoupment targets in record deals may reduce the best performers to cynical wrecks as their record companies continue to earn vast sums. It might matter to 30 students a year to know such things, but most of the world remains understandably indifferent. I'm good at what I do, even if my average gate is around 15. My Championship winning performances come in the shape of 'inventing' the Professional Writing course that leads a handful of students every year closer to a degree. It matters to them, and me. Outside the college, the world goes on. My Cup winning performances are the book deals or script contracts I've signed. So, from one journeyman to another, let me say that Paul Conway was superb that week in October, 1994, and that I've seen many great goals in a lifetime of going to football matches but very few that have lifted me in the way of that second strike against Barnet.

I can think of no better image to sum up our mastery during that wonderful season than Conway - one week after the Barnet game - running into a perfect position to take 's pass and finishing with accuracy and confidence to humble a fancied team with a stadium and tradition that suggested their rightful place was above ours. Ultimately it would fall to Conway to score our last league goal of the season and to perform conspicuously well in our highest profile appearance of the year, career highlights that should have taken him higher. As I write these words, Conway is 28 years old, his career amounts to a little over 100 first class appearances with a goal tally just under 25. Statistically unremarkable and, barring a miracle, doomed to remain so. A journeyman for sure. So let it be said that his moments have been inspirational. Inspirational to the point that I've rerun those two goals in conversations with people who barely understood the game, but wanted - just briefly - to know what might motivate someone to travel miles on a drizzling Saturday and spend the kind of sums that eat a hole in the average bank account with nothing more than the hope of a result. I'll tell you how good he was, I missed Fulham's late consolation goal because I was still re-running the Conway strike with the Blues in the seats around me.

Could it get better? Well yes, and no.

At the end of 1993 my Dad got involved in organising a charity auction to help finance a local centre set up in the old school at Fletchertown. One of the items pledged was a free seat, the chance to meet Carlisle United before a game, and a signed ball. The auction was unbelievably successful in gathering decent items to attract bids and the presence of several Premiership items reduced the bidding interest in Carlisle United. My Dad put in a bid for the Carlisle items, and in my early thirties I got the kind of Christmas present I dreamt about as a kid. I should have got the whole lot at one go at the Barnet game, but the organisation on the United pitch didn't translate into the back room staff. In the end, it fell to the one guy they could trust to get things done, Mick Wadsworth, to make good on the deal before we met Gillingham on New Year's Eve. When I was younger the thought of meeting the Brunton supermen would have terrified me. As 1994 drew to a close it was a curious experience.

When they tell you the truth about Santa Claus it's only the start. My Dad once cheerfully explained to me that one role pets serve is to teach us to cope with death. They live shorter lives than we do and our attachments, though deep, don't as a rule reach the levels of depth we get with the people we learn to love. The cheerful discourse from my Dad was heading in the direction of grim Cumbrian humour. The basic point being that we're all gonna die anyway and that little stiff upturned hamster is your starter for ten. Oh sure, it's tragic but it's also cuddly, cute, and seemingly peaceful. Your grandparents might pull off looking peaceful in the chapel of rest but cuddly, give me a break! It just gets worse, by way of a few relatives, at least one of whom will - statistically speaking - go before disease and decay get a chance, possibly as the result of getting on the wrong end of some unforgiving machinery that'll reduce the contents of the casket to something resembling a kebab with the tabasco seriously overdone.

The Grim Reaper just keeps lurking in the shadows. Those creeping dark thoughts that started with the speculation about how that beloved pet might really 'be' with the angels gradually turn round to you and the fact that your fading frame won't withstand the cells from within trying to kill it, the wearing out of the vital bits of machinery and the gradual drip drip effect of the abuse you hand out to your metabolism every time you open the biscuit tin. The longer you live the more you realise those grim reminders from the Grim one are there for you and you alone. That's age and experience for you and in the face of the grimly unavoidable the least you can do is get in the odd sick chuckle.

It's worth planning ahead, because there is an ahead for all of us. I'm waiting for the day when the cancerous lumps are pushing up against my skin to give it that unmistakable bag of spanners effect, my lungs are stubbornly refusing to push against the inside of my body and that worrying pain in my chest has reduced my arms to flapping and pathetic extensions of my useless body. Maybe then I'll admit I need a visit to the doctor.

DOC - Ermmm....Mr Nixon, what appears to be the problem.
NEIL - Well, you see, Doc, it started with my hamster.

Life's like that. There is a stubborn predictability to the way things carry on with absolute indifference to our own growth and death. Football for starters. There is a point to the fining of footballers for bringing the whole thing into disrepute, but oddly, it seems to me, those imposing the fines don't really get that point. They throw fines and bans at a bunch of men in the prime of their athletic lives and the highest profile penalties are reserved for the role models, those whose earning power and ability to pull crowds has already told them they are special. Let one of these players commit some atrocity of bad conduct and the authorities punish them with massive fines and bans that simply remind the world how gifted these people are. The petty machinations aimed by the football authorities at a few outspoken 'characters' don't belittle these mavericks and trouble-makers.

The game - most certainly - is bigger than anyone and the point of fining and suspending people for threatening the reputation of their sport is to remind us all that football is the constant and the people in the game are the short term means by which the game continues. If you really want to bring them down and make this point you would be better forcing an Eric Cantona or Stan Bowles to read dusty books of statistics and census data to trace the lives of past internationals. Let them marvel at the crowds in front of which the internationals of the Twenties and Thirties played. Let them consider what it meant in those days and then give them the task of convincing a bunch of present day Arsenal loving schoolkids that they should give a shit about the career of George Male. If they fail in this task, give them 100 hours community service emptying bed pans for a bunch of terminal confusion cases with their minds stuck hopelessly in the past. You know, people who can talk about nothing other than George Male.

CASE - David Beckham, never heard of him son. 'Ere, when you've done with the bedpan bring us me paper and then you can polish up me signed photo of George Male. Hell of a player, George Male.
FOOTBALLER IN TROUBLE - Er, yeah, right.

That'll hurt more than fining them a week's wages.
So, as I was saying, before we got into death and all that, I met the team on New Year's Eve. Carlisle United, give or take a few extreme seasons were the constant.

Meeting the players would have been a different experience for me 25 earlier. In the way that pets teach us about life, our heroes also instruct us more than we realise.

As a kid I would have been humbled in the presence of Alan Ross. By the time I came to write this book he was a housing officer in Carlisle. I'd be interested to know whether his agility, work rate and unflapping commitment deflected paper from his desk as efficiently as those outstretched arms once deflected goalbound shots. I spoke to people who knew him as I was working on this book. They reminisced about his goalkeeping skills but - in reality - they were happier to talk about the man they knew. A decent bloke.

One of the good guys. In the time between finishing this book and seeing it published, Alan Ross died. I'd love to have met him. I would have told him that I stood on the terraces and wanted to be like him then. Meeting him as an adult I'd have got those words out without the nerves that would have silenced me all those years before. I guess, in those circumstances, I'd have been more impressed with the qualities that his friends in 1999 were happier to mention. I'd have admired the decent bloke in his fifties. The one who cared about his family and worked hard for the council. A modest man who was a priceless ambassador for the club until the day he died. The Alan Ross who gladly suffered fools, like the endless stream of long-standing fans who'd seen him in his heyday and simply had to talk about it when they met him. You know, people like me.

There is a point to the hero worship of local footballers and fleeting pop stars. These people present a picture of life that appears simple. The message which appeals is that mastery of one set of skills will bring recognition and rewards. We need skills, but life will never be that simple and, around the time we discover this in life, our heroes are also vanishing, their skills unable to stand the ageing process or changes in fashion. This was brought home to me with stark reality. Around the time that I met the mighty league leading United squad, I also started work writing for *The Rough Guide To Rock*. My job here was straightforward enough. Writing potted histories of rock careers, several of which had touched my life to a significant degree. Some of the people concerned were genuinely role models to me, but I realised within a week of starting this work that once I'd got their phone numbers I could ring them at home in the afternoon and they were always in! I didn't spend long talking to agents or managers because the careers in question seldom warranted the devoted attention of such people. Oh sure, they might be on someone's books, but if I wanted information, a quote or simply a chat, I could deal with the 'star' himself. None of these things involved generating a percentage for anyone else, and so it wasn't worth the manager's time.

So, life had taught me a fair bit about heroes, the passing of time and the rest before I stepped into that crowded dressing room. It must have taught me well because I found what I expected to find. I'd pictured the United dressing room as something between total chaos and last orders time, and I wasn't far wrong. I'd love to bring you an in depth and insightful account of the thoughts of the Championship squad during the successful Christmas campaign, but to tell you the truth the United dressing room reminded me a lot of my time in fitting shop at British Sidac in Wigton.

At least I'd imagined things the way they would be and my own game plan went to perfection. Locate the mighty David Reeves and Rodney, get some pictures, exchange a few words and split. The conversation was all a bit ordinary as well. Rodney seemed pretty positive considering his absence through injury on the day. During his long dark winter in the wilderness at Watford, Rodney had briefly trodden the turf as a loan signing in a Gillingham shirt. As they beat us the previous season he'd faced chants of 'Rodney Rodney What's the score' from Gillingham's Rainham End. He told me he had heard the chants. He would have liked to be playing that day, but he said a couple of times that things were in 'capable hands' and he seemed confident enough.

For a flashy performer on the pitch, Rodders understated modest charm was a pleasant surprise and Reevesy was the business. Classic *Boys Own* centre forward stuff and I've never read *Boys Own* in my life. Straightforward, honest, eager to please, the man lives life the way he plays the game. When I got out the camera for a picture of me and Rodders, Reevesy confessed that he didn't know much about photography, but he got stuck in and I'll treasure the results for as long as I'll treasure anything. All being well, there is an original David Reeves photograph on the back of this book! The one real revelation of the dressing room was Dave Currie. For a guy whose gob and attitude got so much exercise on the pitch he was a surprising non-event in the dressing room. If he moved whilst I was in there, I didn't notice.

So much for my game plan - where the hell was United's? My mate Steve was in the Maidstone contingent that day. His occasional football trips take him to see Liverpool or Chelsea. I'd filled him in on United's stylish and inventive play. The most stylish and inventive move of the first half saw Richard Prokas heading off the line when Tony Elliot was beaten for the only time in the game. The gap between the two teams was 32 points. By two o clock it was 35 points. On the pitch it was bloody close and Gillingham just shaded it as the better team over 90 minutes. Somewhere in the second half a disgruntled Gill heading home addressed the Carlisle fans. He'd finally discovered the secret of Championship teams, they win even when they play badly. True enough I guess.

About 20 of us chipped in to tell him that things could be worse, after all Gillingham were playing badly and losing. Look, this game was a scrappy mess looking for some shape, not worth a description at this point in the book. A sore disappointment after our early season adventures, but - in terms of points - it was the equal of Barnet and Fulham. Deano was having a quiet game and when we got a corner in the 71st minute my mate Steve couldn't understand why the 'Deano'

215

chants were going up. Within seconds we were on our feet celebrating the classiest thing United did all afternoon. A clinical header that gave the goalie no chance. Let it also be known that Tony Elliot was superb and without him we would have gone home with less than three points.

When the departing Gills fan delivered his verbal broadside I was glad because that was more interesting than the game. A Gill hit the deck in our penalty area and the Rainham End went mad. None of us said a thing, it looked a clear penalty to me. The ref didn't give it, about 30 seconds later somebody behind me shouted, 'The referee is a Cumbrian!' I'm a Cumbrian and I'd probably have given that penalty. This ref was Michael Knighton's long lost brother more like.

Another three points in the bag and a 12 point lead. I headed home with a signed match ball, memories of meeting my heroes and Steve telling me we were the jammiest bastards alive. My new year's resolution revolved around longer train rides than I'd made in living memory and improbable 'romantic' hotel weekends in unfashionable toilets of towns that just happened to play host to bottom rung teams.

If I'd taken the whole squad out at the end of the season and stumped up for the bill as they filled me in on their performance, I'd probably have got off more lightly than I did forking out for all the games, but it was worth it.

The performances changed but they all bore the mark of a side whose time had come. Of the stuff that matters I think it worth recording one hard fought victory, one considered percentage game and the final chapter at Colchester. We completed the double over Barnet with a gritty performance in which we withstood their well disciplined moves on a sloping pitch, measured our assaults through their midfield and stung them with two clinical finishes from Dave Currie and Simon Davey. It mattered because we fought our way through 90 minutes and I stood on a roofless terrace chomping on rubber burgers handed out by the local YTS with coolie boxes slung over their shoulders. The tea tasted like dishwater and I had a headache from fighting the M25 traffic all the way from work and I still count it a privilege to have been there.

By Easter our lead had reduced football commentators to boredom and a greater interest in who would be Champions of the other divisions. It inspired me to pay good money for a reserve game. By this point we had clinched our first ever date at Wembley Stadium in the final of the Auto Windscreens Shield. I'd seen none of the games that got us there. The qualifying matches are played by region, North or South, and our opponents - representing the South - were Birmingham. Even by my standards, midweek slogs to Rochdale to take in a match were ambitious, but I got a Wembley ticket soon enough. Thoughts of the upcoming game were obvious in the first team, who were conspicuously keen on avoiding injuries. Still we kept on winning.

A game that stands out for me is Gillingham, at Carlisle on April the 8th. The Kent local papers had made much of the recent 'revival' at Gillingham and given the lack of any new talent in the side I'd been wondering how they'd done it. 15 minutes and several fouls in to the game it was obvious enough. What we got for our money was 90 minutes of Gills taking out any Blue with pace and a bit of vision. Hell, Revie's Leeds team were never this bad. In a word, cloggers. Not that it changed the outcome in terms of points.

The build up on Jeff Thorpe's opening goal was superb and the passing that got the ball to his feet was the kind of thing that was giving the Gills attitude problems. The idea of using Jeff Thorpe in a striker role and giving Reevesy space at the side to cut in and feed Thorpe didn't strike me as brilliant, but before he was clogged into submission and an early bath, Jeff was doing a superb job. The contrast with the away match against the Gills was clear. In that game Jeff had covered miles chasing Gillingham players in possession. Here he looked confident, sharp and dangerous.

Steve Hayward was also doing some serious stuff and his sheer work rate was impressive. His goal was a class piece of finishing that once more reminded the Gills that they were in the presence of greatness. Their response was predictable and directed with some force at Rodney's ankles. To be fair, Rodders had been having an off day by his own standards. That said, we still missed him when he limped off. The two goal half-time lead was well deserved and I'd support the second half tactics that involved shutting up shop and letting a team that was half full of reserves preserve the three points and as much of their bodies as they could.

The Gills supporter who had wandered away slagging off the lack of entertainment on New Year's Eve would've hated it. I marvelled at the virtually unbelievable sight of United playing the percentage game and toying with the opposition. In the almost unreal atmosphere of that season the sight made perfect sense.

Three days later I was one of 500 who turned up to the semi final of the Cumberland Cup. This annual knockout competition involves semi-pro sides from the county and beyond. Penrith, Gretna and other legendary homes of football. Traditionall,y Carlisle give the others a chance by entering the reserve side. I saw Gretna's men turn over a side made up mainly of youngsters and it was my first sighting in action of a certain Matt Jansen who had a good game, got hustled out of challenges by solid defenders twice his size, and managed to squander the best chance that fell to a blue shirt all night. Tony Elliot was bloody good and his double point blank stop in the second half was as good a reflex save as I saw all season.

Given the lack of atmosphere in the under-attended game, Elliot's shouts carried to the stand. The guy learned his tact and diplomacy from the great Shilton for sure and - as with Paul Conway - it pains me to record that his career carried on with a handful of appearances for us the following season before moving to Cardiff and that inevitable meeting with Wadsworth at Scarborough for the successful play-off push of 1998.

The twists and turns in our standards of performance delivered a consistent stream of points and the team that took the field at Wembley on April the 23rd were already promoted and - barring an inconceivable series of final results - guaranteed the Championship. Wembley was like nothing before in my history as a United supporter. Steve, who had come to Gillingham, came along, as did Owen whose inconsistent Carlisle support certainly extended to the big occasion.

The video of the game tells me that Birmingham City had most of the possession and that our hard fighting performance was undermined by some obvious nerves. The papers saw fit to highlight the incredible crowd and the atmosphere. Certainly with over 76,000 jammed into the stadium and Mexican waves rocking the ground in rapid succession, this was a good advert for the great things in football.

You could touch the wonder of it all in the Carlisle end. The special hats - including a stunner with a deck-chair sheep on top, placed a couple of rows in front of me - are sharp in my mind to this day, as are the odd scenes from that game. The nerves and the pumping adrenalin at the time have reduced the whole thing to a confusing jumble in terms of the order of things, and when I watch snatches of the game on video, I get the curious sensation that I'm watching a different game. The main difference is that the images that stand out for me include the chances that we could have put away in normal time.

From where I was sitting Rodders chance looked like a bad miss, my video blames the pass and shows the whole move to be working at the limits. Conway got close and Deano's chance off a set piece was a better opportunity than we knew - sitting at the far end of the ground. Tony Caig managed one superb save and the team made up for their nerves with a work rate that still stuns me to this day. The covering and commitment meant that the game never let up in pace. One image sums all of that up for me, with Caig soundly beaten for the only time in the 90 minutes, Deano followed a looping on target ball, positioned himself to perfection and with a combination of scoop and punt cleared it. The man's cool and unflappability were never more tested and I was truly proud of the team and Deano.

A measure of the pace is that the 90 minutes flew past in a blur and it occurred to me at the end of normal time that my throat was shredded and sore and that hardly any time appeared to have passed. The possibility of history being made before our eyes loomed. This game was the first senior final in the UK to hold the possibility of a 'golden goal' finish.

Peter Hampton was out there leading the efforts to revive exhausted legs. The fire in the minds of the team had barely dipped out of sight throughout the game. The reality of the game being decided in a moment added an unbearable tension to the restart and the tired legs on both sides were sending passes astray. Jeff Thorpe put in a run that gave us a move and the deck-chair army, waving sheep and all, were up as one and then sighing and deflated as they sank back down.

All around glances were exchanged as people in the Carlisle end shared the tension and experienced a dimension of fandom that was as new to the long-term crowd as the new recruits. Nothing in over a quarter of a century had prepared me for those minutes. My video tells me that the quality of the action went down and yet I can still touch that tension, the sheer unreality of it all and the realisation that the massive pitch and knife edge game was populated with faces I'd seen a few feet away at other times that season.

Whatever happened was going to make history for Carlisle, a golden goal would make football history. It fell to Paul Tait to bury the ball from a standard move. Great move, well taken goal, history made, and deck-chair shirts throwing themselves on the ground in despair. I've heard people who have been shot saying you don't feel it. In the heat of battle, with the adrenalin pumping to hand shaking levels, a bullet feels more like a punch. The pain dulling effects of your body's natural survival mechanism and the sheer lack of anything else with which to compare the experience render the injury momentarily unimportant. So it was with that goal.

Given the relentless pace and tension, my natural reaction was to will the fallen bodies to get back up and fight. It took hours, and the gradual appearance of familiar motorway sights, to bring about the realisation that we had lost. At that time, in that place it was a stunned silence that told me things had changed. The slow realisation that I hadn't much of a voice left and that the movement on the pitch had taken on an unfamiliar and distant appearance. Distant enough to locate most of the noise at the far end amongst the most dedicated of the Brummie hordes. Paul Tait's celebrations, which involved exposing a t-shirt with a message that didn't impress the more po faced of the Midlands own Blue Army, would take some of the headlines.

Following a standing ovation that came from the bottom of our very souls, the Cumbrian Blue Army trooped out of the stadium and headed home without much fuss. The papers would write up the game as a great advert for the lower leagues and a footnote in the history of the game in the UK.

We'd had our chances to win it and overall I had no complaints, apart from the final score. It would be unfair to blame anyone who missed a chance. Paul Conway, who'd promised so much that season may have missed one chance, but his work, spraying out passes and chasing anything with the remotest promise in midfield, was worthy of praise. Rod Thomas missed one, but tried to dribble his way through the entire Birmingham team. I heard murmurings then and later that he was doing his best to dazzle his way into a higher placed team, but he earned his rightful place amongst the United heroes that season and as the great team of 94/95 fades into legend, Rod's name is mentioned more than most as we hurl abuse at the more recent outfits. I've heard Paul McGregor and others roundly cursed for losing possession with comments to the effect that 'Rod Thomas would have pissed on this defence.'

The papers would rightfully herald the combination of a lowly final and massive crowd as a great advert for football. They claimed the golden goal as a successful innovation. On the day, maybe, but it strikes me that a golden goal finale to a bad tempered Leeds v Man Utd Cup tie, perhaps one that came in the form of a hotly disputed penalty, might give the game a disaster of historic proportions. I hope I'm wrong.

History records the visit to Colchester in April as coming six days after Wembley. My mind tells me it was several centuries later. At stake this time was the chance to take a Championship on the pitch. It was a sobering thought for me to realise that - in my entire history as a supporter - we'd never won a Championship. The only such achievement in living memory was 31 years before when United had taken the old Fourth Division Campionship with a team that had included a couple of my own heroes - Hughie McIlmoyle and Alan Ross.

I ended up escorting three youngsters into Colchester's far from impressive stadium to see a shapeless and nerve wracking struggle. We pitted our Championship dreams against a Colchester side with their own play-off ambitions and - arguably - more need of three points than we had. The Gillingham away game earlier in the season had been similar. To say either team deserved it would be to say that one of the teams had strung enough together by way of purposeful football to look like they knew what they were doing.

It was desperate and I was more nervous than I'd been at Wembley. We'd proven something simply striding out in the shadow of the twin towers six days earlier. On April the 29th, I knew I was seeing my last game of the season, I knew we were promoted and I knew we'd lost our last two league games. I wanted a win and the Championship that day as much as I'd wanted anything at a United game.

I wanted it so much that the game remains in my memory as a nervous 90 minutes punctuated by the brief joy of celebrating a Reevesy goal and the desperate willing of the ref's whistle. After several thousand hours of injury time and a series of Colchester attacks that took on a shape and appearance of a slow motion spaghetti western, three whistle blasts signalled an away win, three points and an unassailable lead at the head of the table. The game didn't deserve its place in our history, the pitch invasion and salute to the fans in return were a worthy finale. I knew as I clapped and cheered that team off the pitch that - come hell or Division Two - I'd love them and what they had given us that season forever.

When the dust settled on the season Carlisle United had managed to gain 91 points, losing only five times in the league all season - three of the defeats coming when promotion was secure and one of them in our last home game with a Championship in the bag and nothing to play for. Ironically we lost that last game in front of the biggest Division Three crowd any team saw that season. No team in England could match our record and David Reeves came close to leading the score sheet for the entire Division. A team that only three years before had plumbed the depths of despair now stood on the brink of a higher Division and basked in the praise of pundits the length and breadth of the country who predicted great things.

The team that had humbled the best the bottom flight could offer had been constructed in the best traditions of Carlisle's greatest years. The purchases had been well chosen - Rod Thomas poached from a becalmed career spell at Watford was every bit as astute a buy as Reevesy, our record signing, and cut price Deano who finished second highest scorer. All three figured in the PFA select side of the year. Most encouraging of all was the presence of so many from the youth team. Darren Edmonson, Jeff Thorpe and Tony Caig in particular had shown their worth. The first two had been there in the season from hell and, in their short careers, they had tasted both ends of the same Division and final Saturdays of complete contrast three years apart.

The Knighton era was upon us for sure, there was talk of great things and the days of the crumbling scratching shed were numbered as new plans for a state of the art stadium emerged. Die-hard Carlisle fans everywhere knew a hope they could barely control that summer, whilst others dredged up Cumbrian credentials, bought season tickets and shirts in impressive amounts and planned for the all out assault on a higher division.

Blue Nightmare #12

IT IS A little known fact that all the major trophies that really matter have come to Brunton Park. Forget the Auto Windscreens Beer Tray for a second. Forget also that semi-final run of 1970 in the old League Cup and think big, really big. FA Cup, Premiership trophy and, really, really big. The European Cup!

They've been to Brunton Park, and I'll tell you how it happened. But, first of all, we need to explore an incident shrouded in secrecy. Something that happened as the 98/99 season wound to a close and the rolling and relentless football machine at Manchester United strolled unstoppably on to a unique football treble. A treble that would conspire to lift all three of these trophies within a matter of weeks.

The early summer of 1999 was also a period of major press stings. High profile cocaine dealers, low profile sleazebags with incriminating pictures, and several embittered individuals with axes to grind, had been cultivated and paid off by the tabloids. The results included the England rugby captain arguing he was a liar, and not a cocaine snorting liar. The improbable spectacle of a well known DJ with his career in the balance because he'd been rumbled as a coke head. Improbable because the DJ in question had a show on Radio 2 where - judging by the popular image of the station - the drug of choice appeared to be industrial strength Prozac.

Looking for a football related sting and remembering fondly the furore that surround the entrapment of two hapless Magpie directors who had blagged about shirt profits, Alan Shearer's failure to score in a brothel, and their own inscrutable smartness, a tabloid editor despatched some serious bait in the hope of catching the biggest football prize of all. It was time to 'get' Alex Ferguson.

The 'reporters' in question were the sisters that Caprice and Claudia Schiffer wanted out of sight. You know, the sisters who were so beautiful their improbable good looks would end the modelling careers of their ugly siblings for life. The target in the first instance was the board of directors at Old Trafford and the mission was simply to loosen tongues, get dirt and then pass on the leads that mattered to the dirtiest newshounds in the business who would, without the slightest hesitation, run the story to ground. The prize for the tabloid in question was a scoop that would make careers, slash the circulation of other tabloids, and once more establish the news gathering mastery of the tabloid press in the face of its rivals in the other media.

The 'reporters' were groomed for their task and set about their work with admirable passion and a selection of Gucci clothing at their disposal. It was the obvious suggestion of passion - as in horizontal, 'bloody hell, the wife never did it like this' passion - that loosened the tongues of the United directors. Faced with the two female reporters, both posing as representatives of a major film studio, intent on sealing a deal for *Manchester United - The Movie,* the directors threw caution to the wind. The well groomed girls writhing on the sofa in an exclusive Northern hotel could never have guessed at the dirt they were about to gather. This was more than hiking the price of a shirt, more than the young women of Manchester being 'dogs.' This dirt was fucking surreal!

Several double measures of spirits into the conversation one director finally unburdened himself of the deepest secret in the boardroom. His face was red, his speech slurring at the edges, his gaze headed up the short Gucci skirt that faced him across the plush carpet. The director was making his pitch for a close encounter and he would say anything to impress. The secret revealed that night had been told to nobody outside the boardroom. And what a secret it was.

'Well,' dithered the director. 'Before the European Cup semi-final, we had a training session behind closed doors on the Old Trafford pitch. We don't use the pitch for much more than first team games. Even the reserves don't get a sniff. They play at Gigg Lane.'

'Gigg Lane?' put in a Gucci clad reporter.

'Yeah, Bury's ground.' He fumbled. 'Anyway, this training session was so secret there was no press, no ground staff and no back-room staff bar Alex and Steve McClaren. I was there, because I'd been in to do some work, I have an important role at the club you see, I . . . "

'The training session,' sighed the girl reporter deflecting the obvious 'I'm so important you'd better come to bed with me' pitch.

'Oh yeah,' he prattled. 'It was so secret some of the players left their cars at the training ground to act as a decoy for the press. The only problem was that we had so few people at Old Trafford that there was nobody to sort out the stuff after the training session. Turning on the bath, that kind of thing. Steve McClaren was working on a free kick move and so Alex Ferguson, I mean, the man himself walked down the players' tunnel, went into the dressing room and turned on the bath. Ten minutes later McLaren turns to him and says, did you leave the bath running?'

'Hmmmm,' sighed the reporter wondering where the hell this was leading.

'Listen up, luv. You won't believe the next bit. I was standing in the players tunnel, watching the session. Alex Ferguson comes past me and goes into the dressing room. I heard the bath stop and he comes back, totally dry except for a damp footprint he left on the floor of the tunnel.'

The air was silent. Finally the other reporter said, 'So what?'

'Oh, I'm forgetting myself,' rambled the director. 'The bath in the home dressing room has a tap against the far wall.'

'Yes, and?'

'It's against the far wall. We normally start the bath running at the final whistle. The players have to turn it off. The only way to get to the tap once the bath is filling is to be in the bath.'

'So you're saying?'

'I'm saying the bath was full. Alex himself turned it off and he came back dry. I saw nobody else because there was nobody else around. He left one damp footprint. I'm telling you - Alex Ferguson walked on water!'

This story matters in our tale of every day footballing folk at Brunton Park because to understand this final Blue Nightmare you need to take two important points from this tale:

i - That director did not lie.

ii - By the summer of 1999 it was almost impossible to measure the respect in which the directors at Manchester United held Alex Ferguson.

And so it was that Alex and his good lady wife decided to visit 'the family' in Scotland. After a hard season they filled the top of the range Jaguar with lavish presents for their relatives and took a few surprises to show. These 'surprises' were the most treasured possessions in the Old Trafford trophy room. These relics were allowed out of the trophy room with the full knowledge and approval of those charged with their safety, the board of directors of Manchester United. Alex was heading home to show off The FA Cup, The Premiership Trophy and....gasp!!!....The European Cup. The directors were no fools. They knew that it was a risky and foolish act to allow these trophies to travel to Scotland in this way. They agreed to the risk because the alternative - saying 'no' to Alex Ferguson - was totally unthinkable.

In Scotland the hospitality was lavish, the atmosphere was warm and a selection of relatives were almost too afraid to touch the prized silverware that was paraded in the modest living rooms of the Ferguson clan's Scottish homes. As Alex packed the trophies into a sturdy and unassuming box that took up most of the Jaguar's boot, his head was still spinning from the abundant flow of whisky. Mrs Ferguson took the keys, Alex slumped in the passenger seat and the mighty car sped South from Glasgow.

The great man fell into a contented snooze as his wife, a tough character in her own right, came into her element. She might appear as the perfect foil to a tough tactician, but put her in the driving seat and she could make that finely tuned engine purr to high-performance perfection. Motorway miles were eaten with incredible speed and when Alex finally awoke from his contented snoring Gretna was already flashing past in a rapid blur.

'Oh hell!,' he grumbled. 'Pull over, lass. I've got to pee.'

'Not on the hard shoulder!'

'Cathy, I'm busting here!'

A moment of indecision, a slowing of the engine and - luckily for the Fergusons - immaculate timing. As the mighty machine entered England the sporadically mighty motorway police of Cumbria took an interest.

There were two police, one Range Rover, and a long and lonely night shift watching the traffic.

'Will you look at that Jag?' said a policeman. 'That's worth £42,000 brand new.'

His companion started the Range Rover without a word and a random pursuit was underway.

'Who the hell drives cars like that round here?' asked the young rookie cop in the driving seat. 'Is it Eddie Stobart?'

'Nah, he's got a Ferrari, I'll run a check on our man and see who he is.'

And whilst the police are running a check we'll digress for a minute because I want to tell you a story about my Dad. My Dad had two Jags in his life. The second he bought from a scrap dealer and ran straight to his trusted mate, Stan Palmer, for an all over check, just in case the car had started life as two different cars. In general, he had nothing against scrap dealers, but my Dad felt affection for this car. There was a danger that his love of the car had over ruled his senses.

Stan gave it a clean bill of health. 'Father' Stan Palmer was to Cumbrian garages what Matt Busby was to football. Stan's word, like his work on cars, was always solid. The cheque duly cleared and my Dad owned a car that would eat miles and travel in style. To the best of my knowledge the car was still on the road in 1997. My Dad bought it in 1973. A Jag is a good car and a good Jag is a truly exquisite machine. In this car, my Dad was twice tailed and stopped by the police. Both of these incidents took place on the A66 as he sped past Keswick late at night. On both occasions the same thing happened. The police car in the rear view mirror flashed its blue light, flashed its headlights and obliged my Dad to pull over. When he did so a burly cop muscled his way into the passenger seat, looked my Dad straight in the eye and said, 'Talk to me Eric, I'm lonely.'

The burly cop in question was my Dad's mate Les. He knew the car, he was on a lonely night shift, and the passing of the distinctive jag was his best hope of breaking the monotony.

This information matters at this point in the Blue Nightmare because it helps us to understand the events that followed that vehicle check in 1999. The one run by the motorway police on that distinctive £42,000 Jaguar.

'Fuckin' hell, are you sure?' barked the policeman in the passenger seat.

'Mike two zero one from control, that is affirmative, over.'

The microphone was replaced by a shaking hand. 'It's only Alex Bloody Ferguson in that car. The greatest football manager alive. The man who brought a unique treble to . . . '

'I've heard of him too you bloody pillock!' grunted the rookie cop.

Meanwhile, in the Jaguar, the tension was also mounting.

'They're on our bloody tail, I can't just pull over and let you water the grass.'

'Arghhh, I'm dying here, speed up a bit, just do something.'

'We're bang on 70, I'm not getting booked just so you can have a pee. You should have gone before we left.'

'AWWW, shut up.'

Five minutes of tense silence were broken only by the grunts of the great man as he screwed up his face, contorted his legs into a tight knot, broke sweat, grabbed at his crotch and mumbled, 'Ooh hell.'

The Carlisle exit offered itself like a beckoning toilet to a tortured man. Mrs Ferguson indicated and slowed down.

'Follow him,' said the older cop in the passenger seat.

'Look, we're supposed to stay on the motorway and if we head into town . . . '

'Just do it, there's nowt doing on this night shift. Sometimes your only hope of breaking the monotony on a lonely night shift is to tail a distinctive Jag. We're carrying on a great Cumbria Police tradition, you know.'

The cop's decision did nothing to lower the tension in the swish Jag.

'The grass, pull over to the bloody grass.'

'Look, Alex, that bloody Range Rover is right on our tail. Oh, aye, I can see it now. They'll nab you for exposing yersell' before you've so much as started peeing. 'Fergie the Flasher,' aye, *The Sun* will have a field day with that for sure.'

'AWWWW, but I'm dying here.'

'Aye well, shut up a wee while, I can handle this baby, I get a fair bit of practice when you're away.'

And she was right. Bang on the speed limit, accelerating out of corners and never betraying the slightest suggestion of driving without due care and attention, a housewife in her mid-fifties drove a young tyke from the Cumbria Police into the distance. From the outside it looked flawless, inside the car the air was rent with screams.'

'Arghhh, I'm gonna pee myself if you corner like that again.'

'Shut it you,' I'm gonna lose them on this roundabout.

As the Jag left Hardwick Circus, the Range Rover entered the roundabout, skidded over two lanes and left its occupants white knuckled, sweating and breathless.'

'Leave it!!!,' screamed the older one. 'If we tip the car here we'll have some bloody explaining to do.'

'Fergie is one hell of a driver too,' sighed the rookie cop. He restarted his stalled car and drove slowly back round to Stanwix Bank, and the motorway.

The Jag hauled itself up from the roundabout in the other direction. Headed for the next motorway junction and was passing Carlisle College when Alex delivered an ultimatum.

'One more minute or I'll soak this bloody carpet in here, I can't hold it.'

'Okay,' she said, her chin firm, her gaze in the rear view mirror and the police car now definitely lost.

One minute later, having passed an alleyway that looked too thin for the mighty Jag, a wider opening appeared on the main road out of town. 'That'll do,' screamed Alex. And it did.

Around this time, something else was also occurring. A Cumbrian was walking across the massive car park that separates Stoney Holme golf course from Brunton Park. This man called himself a Cumbrian although he had lived far from his home for many years. In the early hours of a late June morning he was on a quest so strange that even he struggled to understand it. For the previous six months this Cumbrian had laboured. He had struggled to write a book that could state how this place, and the teams he had seen at this place, had woven their way in and out of his life. Now, in the early hours of the morning on which he would finally hand over the final pages of his work, he needed to be at Brunton Park.

His movements that night were slow, as if directed by a large and unseen hand. His quest vague, his hands shaking. Wandering past the main stand he felt an unstoppable wave of emotion, the tears welled into his eyes as he pictured a boy, a ten year old boy, in a drab gaberdine coat and a blue and white scarf lovingly knitted by his devoted grandmother. That boy was on his way to his first football match. He saw also a teenager, his unruly crop of blonde hair evoking the tragic styles of the Seventies, his platform soled boots a chunky and embarrassing fashion statement. The night air was thick with visions.

Heading now to the paddock entrances he saw a young man, hollow eyed, young and yet, in some way, traumatised, perhaps for the first time in his life. His thickening moustache offering a tentative hold on adulthood, his jeans and denim jacket screaming 'student' to the world. Looking round to the silent burger caravan the Cumbrian pictured another sight. A grown man in a replica deckchair shirt, no longer 'young' exactly, but still moving with a sense of purpose that suggested an athletic past, was stooping to talk to a little boy. The boy wore a Carlisle scarf, but he fingered the crude knot with embarrassment. The man mentioned crisps, Kit Kats and bacon rolls.

The boy took the suggestions eagerly but his gazes around showed something else. To his young eyes this place was no great wonder. It was the man who was attempting to bring wonder to the day. Any treat from the caravan, any vaguely wanted treasure from the club shop would be bought. The boy, though young, was wise to this. He was also wise to the many delights and wonders that offered themselves to him. This place was a novelty, it would take time to decide if it offered the excitement of a good computer game, an indoor adventure playground or the deep end of the pool at the health park.

The Cumbrian pictured these sights and ran his hand along the cold walls of the sleeping stadium. He had laboured so long to tell the world how this place had

227

shaped his thoughts, haunted his conversations and filled his weekends. The emotions, though ever present, had often eluded him, the words never adequate to focus an attachment so deep, so overwhelming and so much a part of his being. He pressed his face against the cold brickwork of the paddock wall and the tears began to flow. Alone in the night he ran his hands over the wall. With his book now written, he could give in totally to the feelings that overwhelmed him and so he . . .

The commotion in the alleyway startled the Cumbrian. The roar of a strong engine, the screech of tyres and the rapid extinguishing of headlights. Someone was around the far side of the ground. The Cumbrian felt a chill, his senses scrambled to get a hold on the situation. It must be the police. Someone had seen him creep in from the golf course and head for the ground. Now he faced questions, the kind he dreaded. How could he explain his presence in the early hours of the morning? He couldn't, in all honesty, really explain it to himself. A door had opened and slammed shut almost instantly as the car screeched to a halt.

The Cumbrian thought fast. He would jog, make out he was training. He couldn't sleep and he had decided to go running. A pathetic ruse, but you try explaining your presence at a Third Division football ground at two o' clock on a June morning. He had blinked the tears from his eyes and managed a steady shuffle when he rounded the corner and saw . . . a man peeing all over the entrance to the boys pen!

Stunned, angered and falling into incomprehension, the Cumbrian took in the sight. The man groaned in loud and obvious relief and appeared to be set for a long session of relieving himself on the very turnstile door that had first offered admission to Brunton Park for the Cumbrian.

'Hey!'

The Cumbrian didn't decide to shout. It simply happened. This sight, this incredible sight, had produced the reaction on its own. Never flinching, the man slowly turned. The sound of splashing water stayed strong and steady. Feeling the strength of character and a justification for being there that had deserted him less than a minute before, the Cumbrian approached the man.

'You, you're pissing on Carlisle United, you're . . . '

Slowly the Cumbrian made out the familiar features of the man.

' . . . You're Alex Ferguson.'

Incredulous, the Cumbrian could only repeat. 'You're pissing all over Carlisle, and Michael Knighton.'

'Aye,' said Alex Ferguson, 'That sounds about right to me.'

They stood without speaking as the endless stream of water finally faded into a trickle. Alex Ferguson shrugged, adjusted his clothing and turned to face the Jaguar. He looked back at the Cumbrian. 'Hey, c'mon,' he said, 'I wanna show you something.'

Alex stooped at the driver's window and entered into a brief conversation. There was obviously some disagreement, but as Alex directed a rapid whisper into the car the boot jumped open. Alex headed to the back of the car, the Cumbrian followed. There, as the orange glow of the Warwick Road street lights crawled up towards Brunton Park, Alex Ferguson opened the boot, and the large box inside. The unmistakable treasures in the box reflected the glow. 'Go on,' said Alex, 'Just touch them.'

The Cumbrian did.

'Not bad eh?' grinned the great man.

The Cumbrian nodded silently.

'You can tell yer friends that all the great trophies have been to Carlisle,' grinned Alex as he closed the box, and the boot.

So I have. Because, I was that Cumbrian.

Chapter 12 - Jimmy Glass

MENTIONED FOR THE FIRST TIME IN THIS CHAPTER

Graham Anthony - Midfielder, couldn't get established at Sheffield United, Scarborough, Swindon or Plymouth. We gave him a regular run.

Owen Archdeacon - Defensive stalwart from 1995. Classy, in an understated way.

Warren Aspinall - 'Sumo,' Chunky and committed striker who included Aston Villa and Everton on his pedigree. Loaned in 1995, signed the following season, carrying the weight of our forward playing hopes, along with his own considerable bulk, a season later.

Billy Barr - Proven defensive stalwart at Halifax and Crewe, signed to provide some stability in a back line always likely to leak in Division Two.

Jon Blott - Goalie who played two games in 1985. His is a one hell of a story, but it doesn't have much to do with Carlisle. We'll get to it at the end of the chapter.

David Brightwell - Experienced defender, with some practice in last ditch bottom of the league campaigns, therefore useful in 1999.

Andy Couzens - Struggled to break into the midfield at Leeds United, dropped down to our level and got a regular run out.

Mervyn Day - Goalie with impressive pedigree. Made his final league appearances and first steps in management at Carlisle.

Scott Dobie - Youth team forward, first team regular when just out of his teens.

Steve Finney - Another net busting super hero of the Knighton era who turned out to be a well travelled clubable sort who could score if the opposition were holding white sticks.
Jimmy Glass - On loan goalie at the end of 98/99 season who went on to history.

Matt Jansen - We've been here before. But his Carlisle career takes place in this chapter. Phenomenal prospect, slight, fast and flashy striker brought forward from youth team. Briefly rekindled memories of a young Beardsley.

Richard Knight - A goalie. Teenager dropped in over his head as a brief stop gap replacement for the departed Tony Caig in the grim end of season run in 1999. Within weeks we would famously tell the Football League we were 'without a goalie,' a statement that made perfect sense to some who saw Richard Knight play that season.

Lee Peacock - A forward. Scots born YTS trainee became established in mid-Nineties sides. Briefly played in goal, arguably a better keeper than Richard Knight.

Gareth McAlindon - Product of youth team, playing as a teenager by mid Nineties. Almost a regular by the time he was 20.

Ross Milligan - Young defender signed from Rangers for start of 97/98 season.

Tony Philliskirk - Much travelled striker who had partnered the mighty Reeves during a spell at Bolton. Loan signing to Carlisle in 1995 with a view to rekindling the old magic.

Stephane Pounewatchy - Classy French centre back, allegedly thought he was coming to a higher flying club in 1996.

Damon Searle - Cardiff, Stockport, Carlisle. A defender who was used to ugly sights, therefore unlikely to panic when the bottom of the league loomed large.

Allan Smart - Lanky Scots striker with clear promise. Young and inexperienced when signed in part-exchange for older and proven David Reeves. Came up with the goods when it really counted at Wembley, but he was playing for someone else then.

Ian Stevens - Well travelled striking machine, signed from Shrewsbury late on in 96/97 season.

Richard Tracey - Teenage prospect, thrown into the thick of it when serious trouble loomed, denied his place in history by the Brunton Park woodwork.

Will Varty - Central defender who stuck to his task, and his club, when many others deserted.

Ronnie Wallwork - Another bloody loan signing. Looked useful, went somewhere else.

David Wilkes - Defender who played a few games up to the shameful finish in 1992, from when he joined the coaching staff.

Nick Wright - Hadn't got a game at Derby in over three seasons. Got 25 for us up to the summer of '98. Went on to Watford.

IT WAS A measure of the optimism that the fanzines were openly speculating about another promotion in 1996. I'd started writing for the United fanzines by this point. I was sending material off to one in particular, *So Jack Ashurst, Where's My Shirt*. The zines were seeking predictions from the United faithful of our league position at the end of the season. I couldn't go with a second automatic promotion. I reckoned on a season of consolidation and a league position somewhere around mid-table in Division Two.

Turning up in the near certainty of seeing a win that season had been one of the better aspects of my life. By the summer of 1995, like Carlisle, I had moved into a higher division. The tide of change sweeping the public services under the Conservative government had, by 1995, extended to turning colleges into private operations which, amongst other things, could go bust. In the case of my employers the financial situation was more secure than that of many of our rivals, but slowly there were new contracts being introduced for staff and, with effect from September of 1995, a new and more substantial role of the middle managers was on offer. The alternative for those of us already in middle management jobs was to decline applying for the new positions and face a future on the old contracts without the prospect of any pay rise to cover the cost of living.

In terms of massive industrial shake ups this huge upheaval in Dartford registered somewhere around 0.00000000000001 on the Richter Scale. In most cases, the 'new' jobs bore a very close relationship to the responsibilities of the existing middle management staff. These new jobs were open to applications from others, but the 'others' in question would lack the experience of having done the job. In the end, many of the posts had only one applicant. I did face competition but - frankly - my own involvement in the whole reorganisation was so momentous that I can't remember who told me or where I was when I found out I'd been 'promoted' within the new structure. Then again, at least I can remember being interviewed.

A couple of years later the vice principal told me that he hadn't been at my interview. He was there and he was yawning right through the whole thing. I would have taken it personally, but he was yawning when I walked in so I figured it couldn't have been anything I'd said. They'd just turned a lot of people round in a whole series of interviews. If I'd asked the VP what day it was the chances are he would have replied, 'Milk and two sugars.'

Given the horror stories that came from industry at the time concerning the sacking of entire departments our situation didn't seem so bad. The massive holidays of old were the only real casualty. My new contract cut those in half and left me booking out my annual leave when and where I could. The biggest impact from my point of view was on my writing work. In the good old days where staff rooms had been home to small time spiv operators, marathon runners and people who would shuffle out and teach if they couldn't think of anything else to do, my writing work had fitted in well to the 'day' job. Writing items for sicko comics and magazines had meant I could stockpile the stuff over those weeks in the summer when I wasn't in college. Working that way was out of the question under the new pattern when I simply wasn't going to get long breaks anymore. Then again, I'd got a raise in money out of the new position which was, in effect, a promotion.

So, the new division was strange to me. I wasn't going to quit writing, but I needed to rethink. I didn't have the time to chase a pile of editors with ideas, but I could cut down the number of ideas and make them bigger. Pitching book ideas seemed an obvious solution. There were some things I knew about well enough to put together a mountain of words. The paranormal, rock music, football and Media Studies were the obvious areas. Well those and writing fiction. Up to this point my only book writing experience had been the 'novel' I'd started whilst I was working for comics. This 'book' dated back to 1990, a time in which I was so naive that I thought you had to write a complete book and then send it to publishers in the hope that they would be interested. The few people who had bothered to read it reckoned it was a wind up or simply too sick to sell. The book - which had received abuse and rejection under various titles, *Sex-Food-Violence* and *Taste The Paste* being particular favourites, was a non-starter at this point.

A few years previously, whilst I was writing for every sicko comic under the sun I'd headed off to a Media Studies conference. Climbing out of an underground station I ran into Brian Dutton. Brian worked across the road from Thurrock Technical College in Palmer's VIth Form College, he taught Media Studies and he'd written a couple of books on the subject. Both of his books were absolute winners and I'd been nicking ideas for classes from his writing the day before I met him at that underground station. We got talking about our side projects and I was appalled to discover how little he'd earned writing one of his books. To put this in perspective, he'd spent six months writing a book that had earned him the kind of money I could get for a month's worth of work on the comics. Bloody hell, there was no justice in the world.

That conversation came back to me in 1995 when I was thinking about trying to get a book deal. The beauty of writing books is that the deadlines are months away and you can fit the work around a demanding job. I knew Media Studies backwards, but I also fancied making some halfway decent money off a book. I made a submission to BPP Letts, a publisher who had no track record in Media

Studies and a vast tonnage of books in Smiths, Menzies and Waterstones. Nobody in their right mind was going to go looking for a book just because I'd written it. Then again, any GCSE student with ambition bought Letts study guides. Within a few weeks I had a deal and I spent my last long summer holiday knocking out a book that Letts would be able to sell on the back of their brand. It was the first serious book submission I'd written.

So, like Michael Knighton in the early summer of 1995, I stood on the threshold of a more demanding league. We'd both proven we could perform in the easier climes below. Both of us had shown some flair and we'd pushed our levels of performance to the limits offered at that level, such as they were. The question was whether or not we could deliver on the promises we'd made. He'd talked about ground improvements and a ten year plan for Premiership action. I'd told a publisher I could deliver them a book worthy of their jealously guarded reputation inside eight weeks.

By the time I delivered, Carlisle were stumbling out of the starting gate in Division Two. Oddly enough, that didn't bother me too much. Maybe I just had things a little too good all round. In July, I'd signed on for a writing job on *The Rough Guide To Rock*. In this one I got to write entries for a rock encyclopedia. This was a dream come true, I could share my love of some of the most transparent drug abusers, shameless eccentrics and unquestionable lunatics who had ever been allowed time at someone else's expense in a recording studio.

The Rough Guide To Rock and Carlisle United collided in October when, flushed with the income from some of the writing work, we added a new dimension to our family life. Since this time I've scanned each successive fixture list in search of the ideal venue for that all important 'romantic weekend'. Jane and I have had a few romantic weekends away in hotels over the years, but from October, 1995, some of these have taken place in hotels near to the football grounds of stalwarts of the lower divisions. To date, not one of these weekends has allowed me to see an away win.

The first such encounter took place in Bournemouth. Let's face it, Jane is an understanding wife. I'd be tempted to say she's one in a million, but on that first romantic weekend, I met another one. The hotel in Bournemouth was a bizarre affair. In fact the whole place was a little strange. The town is so full of the elderly that many shop windows are made with bi-focal glass and stooped bodies queue up to squint through the thick windows at a dazzling array of Glen Miller CDs and funky looking support bandages. Anyone with normal eyesight sees only a blurred series of colours as they look in the prescription windows. The lifestyle drug of choice in Bournemouth is a chocolate digestive biscuit. I'm tellin' ya, this town doesn't begin to kick ass. Mainly because half the residents can't lift their legs high enough to connect with someone else's rear end.

On that Saturday morning in Bournemouth, Jane, Thom and I found ourselves surrounded by a convention of Rotarians in the dining room. The totally surreal sight was completed when I spotted another resident arriving in a Division One Carlisle United shirt. Rob Lees - for it was he - was a regular contributor to *So Jack Ashurst, Where's My Shirt.* He was also married to another wife in a million, and Rob, his wife Sue, and I found ourselves standing in the teeth of an off the sea wind as Carlisle faced the kind of team we should easily have humbled if Knighton's plans were to mean anything.

Some frantic and even handed first half football ended with us 1-0 down. Worse was to follow. Tony Elliot had been sidelined the previous season as Tony Caig had established himself in the team. I was a real admirer of Tony Elliot's goalkeeping. The guy was a crowd pleaser with a spectacular line in last ditch thrashing convulsions at the feet of opposing forwards. His ability to get down quickly and move with lightning speed through a crowded area was exceeded only by the entertaining tongue lashings he could dish out to napping defenders. During the Championship run, Tony Caig with his exemplary shot-stopping was - arguably - the right choice, but with the defence under test from Division Two's more mobile striking forces, Elliot had come into his own again. Caig's shortcomings at this time included an ability to hit his own corner flags from goal kicks and land the team in trouble. During the previous season Caig had exited a game following a full-on assault on a Scarborough striker. Caig was forced into this action because his 'kick' from goal had stalled in the stiff breeze and landed at the striker's feet, offering him a free one on one.

Elliot gave too much in the way of bravery at Bournemouth and ended up badly injured. So badly that they called for his parents on the tannoy and he left the game to put Lee Peacock in goal. Peacock gets a check as a 'forward' in the *Playfair Football Who's Who*, but given his passable performance in that second half he might usefully be described as a 'utility' player. Hell, he wasn't that bad in goal. I've seen worse displays from genuine goalies. We ran at Bournemouth, into them, round them and finally over them. For 80 yards we were deadly, but we ground to a halt in the opposing box and got caught with a late break. From 2-0 down, there would be no way back that afternoon. After the game, with Carlisle sitting second bottom of the Division and having nothing to show for so much effort, it dawned on me we were in the shit.

At the higher level we were struggling and Michael Knighton was finally taking some serious stick from the support. There were building works underway at Brunton Park, but not much on the pitch. Reevesy needed a partner up front and one brain-wave was in evidence on the pitch at Bournemouth. Reevesy and Tony Philliskirk had formed a formidable partnership at Bolton. Their vague physical similarity and strong double act had seen the locals name them 'Bros'. The first album Owen ever owned was *Push* by Bros. He once made the telling observation that Bros made the right noises, but didn't sing that many songs. Roughly speaking, it was at this level that football's Bros picked up their partnership.

The idea was there but Philliskirk and Reeves couldn't rekindle the old magic. Three games, one goal, no magic on offer and Philliskirk was on his way to Cardiff. We'd signed him on loan from Burnley, making it bloody obvious that he was simply trying to 'bag' a few weeks at any club and he hadn't got past 'C' in the *Groundhopper's Manual*. If he stays true to form he'll finish his career at York on his 40th birthday in a stunning finale which will see him, Paddy Atkinson and nine unemployed waitresses turn in another Bootham Crescent bonanza of stylish football. Don't knock it, you'll probably be in for more entertainment than I got from my team in the season after we won the Third Division Championship.

Somewhere between Bournemouth and Peterborough I found my voice again. Having been there to cheer and admire the previous season, Carlisle had taught me about being positive. As my first book came out, and the offers to write more came in, my team and I had gone in opposite directions. I'd moved up a gear and coped. They'd moved up a Division and run into a brick wall.

Peterborough was the pits. A 6-1 defeat that left me shuffling in the pie queue at half-time, sullen and speechless. We were four down by then and six down by the time we finally remembered which direction we were heading in. The scattered remnants of the Blue Army who'd made the trip gave it everything. 'You only sing when you're winning!' came out a few times and once we'd found the back of the net we chanted, 'We've got a goal!' over and over again.

It wasn't good. There were things to cheer, but mainly it was commitment in the face of overwhelming odds. Reevesy sealed it for me at that point. In the face of a massacre at London Road, he was back in defence, running in midfield and trying to make something happen up front. Captain Marvel, except that the only thing to marvel at was his positive attitude against an opposing team who were faster and more inventive than the players with whom he would share the coach home. In all my years of following Carlisle, I've seen nobody who could replace Alan Ross as a hero and example. Given that Ross got to me when I was impressionable enough to be need a hero, his place in my affections has to be secure. There was no other player to whom I would have considered dedicating this book.

By 1995, I was - supposedly - older and wiser than all that. However, somewhere in the teeth of that humiliation in Peterborough, David Reeves proved for all time that he too was a worthy hero. He still tried with the surging runs, only by this time they were starting well into our own half. He yelled encouragement to the team and, when we were 6-0 down and nothing mattered, it was Reeves who got on the end of a rebound as the Posh goalie parried Prokas' shot. 6-1, that goal could have made all the difference at the end of the season. In the end it didn't, but it could have.

Reevesy left us the following season and one article in a fanzine blasted him as a clumsy forward who would never qualify as a natural goal getter. Bloody harsh in my opinion. When Reevesy left, I did, as I often do, conjure up an image of the departing player in my mind. When you lose someone quickly you often focus on one moment, one image. Strangely, the image that came to mind was Reeves in the away shirt at Peterborough, his sleeves rolled up, running and encouraging the team when everything was well and truly lost. This is where I can't get on too well with anyone who would slag him. Reeves, quite simply, represented the spirit of that side.

Lacking much in the way of strengthening signings over the summer, this Second Division team was little more than the team that had humbled the Third Division, with a few new faces from the youth team. A level higher than the previous year, they were struggling to find their feet. Some players had a nightmare that day in Peterborough. Tony Gallimore mistimed, misjudged and missed the ball completely. Tony Caig's positioning was desperate and his handling showed his shattered confidence. If these players were going to take time to adjust, then at least we had Reeves with his fearless and unfailing assaults on opposition turf.

Driving home from that pasting was like returning from the drubbing from hell that night in Dartford. Except, there was no way I would even consider walking away from this side. During the previous season, they'd shown me more domination and flair than I'd seen from any Carlisle team. Okay, they dominated the lowest professional flight, but this team had pumped hope and affection into every Cumbrian with eyes to see. In the kind of decision that started deep down and crawled up to club my senses into submission, my reaction to the stuffing was to check out any trip within three hours of Maidstone so I could get along. They needed support, how could I refuse?

The results of the previous season had still left us wondering when exactly Knighton's dreams would connect with reality. By February, 1996, reality was there in spades. There were other games to see that season, including home wins. But, for me, there are three defining moments. The first was that hard fought loss at Bournemouth which convinced me beyond doubt that we were going to have to fight for anything. The second was that 6-0 drubbing that showed which players had the fight and which needed to work. The third defining moment was the predictable sinking feeling I got driving out of a car park in Dartford after the season had all but finished.

This feeling came courtesy of Radio 5 who relayed the news we were all expecting. York had won away in Brighton to secure their own Division Two status. This game was played long after the rest of the season had finished because the original match had been invaded and called off as a result of a mass demonstration from the totally pissed off fans of Brighton. Those Brighton fans had a point, with a chairman who seemed hell bent on running the team into oblivion.

The guy needed police protection in and out of the ground. We might have been doubtful about Knighton's claims, but his physical well being wasn't in much danger from us in those days. Maybe from the vast tonnage of pies he appeared to be shifting, but not from the fans.

Knighton made noises about legal action given the position we were in. That replayed game at Brighton was - near enough - a formality. Brighton were hopelessly relegated and had nothing to play for. York were in the highest relegation spot and had escape within their hands. They might have been a bunch of press ganged waitresses, but by this point in their careers they preferred win bonuses to the vagaries of customer tips, and they had a few ringers in the ranks. I can picture the scene in the York dressing room before the match. Paddy Atkinson adjusts his stocking tops as the manager wades in.

'Listen Paddy,' he grunts, 'If you let any opposing striker past you then, so help me, I'll have you on the next train back to Workington.'

Less than two hours later the relieved York team are rubbing their sore shins and savouring the thought of Second Division football with the odd crowd over 10,000. One of the girls suddenly pipes up, 'Where's Paddy Atkinson?'

At the same time a steward barges into the York dressing room. 'There's this mental bastard out there in a red shirt and he's just floored the fucking groundsman.'

'Why?' asks the manager.

'Cos the groundsman wanted to get into the goal mouth. This mental git says, "You get in there and they'll send me back to Workington," and then WHAM!, he floors him.'

If that sounds like a pantomime, so it should. The end of that season, with relegation, the threat of legal action that was never a starter, and the gradual dismantling of the team that had humbled an entire division twelve months before, showed us what we had for sure. It may well have been that our new level, with the finances available then, was somewhere between the two divisions. We certainly weren't good enough to survive by right in the Second. The Knighton tradition of major excitement at the end of the season was well established. We'd had the play-offs, a Championship and relegation in successive years.

The whole pantomime of threatening to sue the League made the national press where Knighton's unsuccessful bid to take over at Old Trafford was - once again - trotted out. At the same time the country was stumbling from crisis to crisis, economically speaking. There was debate and disagreement over which financial division was the nation's correct home. *Newsnight*, the quality press and the long-winded early morning discussions on Radio 4, the ones which appear designed to make sane people want to get to work on time, were all speculating on whether we'd ever escape the boom and bust cycles. Strangely, none of these discussions ever extended to a consideration of boom and bust football. A style which appeared to fit the climate of the times and a style that appeared to be establishing itself at Brunton Park.

Okay, we've had a few flippant digs throughout the book, but let's get into really strange territory by football standards. Let's talk long-dead Japanese literary talent and Zen Buddhism. Just stick with me on this one, okay, we'll emerge on the other side into an understanding of what it is that makes football our national pastime.

If I ever get offered a gig on *Desert Island Discs* I'm gonna cheat at the end. That is the bit when they ask you which book you would take. The book I want isn't written. But, after I've subjected the Radio 4 audience to Neil Young, Captain Beefheart, Napalm Death, The Aphex Twin, The Smiths, and some reggae and psychedelia that are totally out of their respective trees, I'll clear off to the sun, sand and surf to read *The Complete Basho*.

If this book did exist it would compile every known word written by Matsuo Basho alongside the best critiques of his work. Basho was born Matsuo Kinsaku in 1644 and died, near enough, 50 years later. He is remembered as the first great haiku poet. His life's work was travel, poetry and Zen Buddhism. The greatest expressions of his art were a series of 17 syllable haiku poems which continue to spread their stark beauty today, over three centuries after his death. Basho's greatest work supported his own belief that such writing should contain *muga*. To have *muga* a work needs to have so close an identification with the things featured in the writing that the poet loses touch with his own self. In Basho's case this contact with everything and the loss of his own selfish identity reflected his own belief in the way of Zen which, to Basho, offered both enlightenment and life beyond the physical. His best poetry reflects this. One of the very best is, also, indisputably, his last. On his deathbed he was approached by disciples begging one last haiku, he gave them:

> Sick on a journey -
> over parched fields
> dreams wander on

Haiku in Basho's tradition combined an observation with a wider - spiritual reference. Basho's parting shot pits the image of the dying poet with the wider belief in eternity. His sick body, and the dry country is nothing compared to the bigger picture in which his dreams wander on into eternity. This looks dangerously like Glen Hoddle and 'My body is just an overcoat' territory. But it has its merits. Whatever your view on the whole thing, it offers us life after death and suggests that, at some level, everything we see is connected. This thought isn't as woolly as it looks.

I'd argue that football is connected to the very core of our own identity and passions. The images of football, the pictures we pore over in magazines, the sights we recall from games we've seen, are connected to the wider world. These are images that tell us something about our own emotions and identity. It was no accident that my instant image of David Reeves on the day he signed for Preston North End was of him sweaty, passionate and going for goal when we were already six behind. That, in the end, was Reeves. Strong, surging, determined and a true captain by example. I think that image came into my mind because I know my team are not natural winners. Their achievements have always been hard fought. The picture of a surging and determined David Reeves matters to me because it connects to the best qualities of the best sides I've seen. On a wider scale, I also know that anything I've achieved in life has been worked for. I want the qualities David Reeves brought to Carlisle for myself.

On merit, you would be pushed to argue Reeves into an all time Carlisle United 11. By the time you'd got in the unquestionable choices, Peter Beardsley, Ivor Broadis and Stan Bowles, you'd need a particular kind of striker to fit in to their skilful and space creating play. Bob Hatton's strength and ability to hold the ball would - arguably - be the sensible choice. But Reeves simply lived football in front of us. It might have been Third Division but I'd paid my money, I wanted a team that cared as much as I did, and Reeves delivered the goods most of the time. When he didn't deliver, I saw him try. If you picked an all time Carlisle 11 with your heart, there would have to be a place for David Reeves. Reeves represented a spirit in the early Knighton era team. A spirit that had been missing for so damn long we'd brought up a generation of fans who knew nothing about it.

Pit the image of Reeves against the things we really want from our teams and you're getting close to the point at which this meditation about all things spiritual came in. Assuming a team can win, then the next thing that matters is how they win. The greatest teams contain a spirit and vision. Manchester United 1999 had it in abundance. The spewmongous and obligatory Cup final single might have talked about belief but, on the pitch, that really was the difference. It's no wonder Bayern Munich looked disbelieving at the end of the European Cup final. The German team had done a professional job and had a right to think that injury time would offer them the chance to play the percentages and see that job out. They were stung by two flashy late winners.

Those goals represented the life force itself hitting Bayern Munich. I don't care how much Manchester United were paid, or how big the squad was, that team in that season, played football as if it was the be all and end all of life. They went on the pitch to live for their achievements. If Manchester United took the field with that attitude and their opponents went onto the same pitch thinking they were simply professional footballers, it really was no contest most of the time.

Money, sponsors, agents and the rest can corrupt football. If that 1999 Manchester United team have to squeeze in and watch their successors battle for a European Cup in 30 years time, it'll be interesting to see how Beckham and his pals look so far down the line, and which of them have starred in the tabloids, drug dependency clinics and divorce courts. In the meantime they are magnificent because, for most of that historic season, they played football as if it was more than a game.

For my generation that picture of Geoff Hurst, airborne, puffing his cheeks and blasting the shot that would seal his place in history, was a powerful and telling image. So were the newspaper pictures of George Best, improbably thin, phenomenally talented and the first person who make us understand that there were people in this world who could elevate a job of work to an art form. These were people who taught us about football, but also about possibilities. About conquering the world and being all you could be. Today ten year olds line up corners and free kicks dreaming of the accuracy that let Beckham find Sheringham's head deep into injury time in Barcelona. Those kids simply crave the skill and the life enhancing feelings that come with the skill. If they get corrupted or disillusioned along the way, they still had dreams. And to have dreams is to have a hold on life itself.

Football throws up images all the time. Images of players, images of incidents and images from off the pitch. The images that football throws up are about more than a game. Basho had it right when he connected simple things he saw with the wider thoughts on what life is about. In fact, most of us do this all the time. We certainly do this with football.

I care about football, and my guess is, you care because you've invested part of your being in the game and the way it leads you through uncertainty into new realisations every season. Take an image from a game you paid to watch or a line overheard in the crowd and look at it in a wider way. There is more at stake than just one result over 90 minutes. I don't honestly think football is more important to most individuals than life or death. But I do think it is a hell of a lot more important than a simple game and I think it tells us a hell of a lot about who we are and what is going on in the world.

I'm going to focus on an image. That chilling night in February, 1992, when Mike Graham forever walked into the deepest corners of my subconscious from where his porky outline may forever return to haunt my most vulnerable moments. It's more than a game alright. Let's give Graham and that nightmare season the Basho treatment. In the great Blue Peter haiku tradition, here's one I prepared earlier. A haiku that 'celebrates' that season and drifts to a wider picture.

> The feet of fat Mike
> pound holes in the turf
> Economy in free fall.

So, Mike Graham's furious back-pedalling stands as an image of a time when boom and bust economics saddled us all with uncertainty and left the work force of the whole nation flailing, thumping and achieving less than we had before. The economic uncertainties in the country gave us Black Wednesday. The same economic climate helped to put Carlisle United in a position where they were considering part-time football and employing the likes of Mike Graham, pounding feet and all, as a professional footballer. It ain't exactly spiritually uplifting, but I'd argue it's bloody true.

In fact, I'd argue more than that. I'd argue that no team has provided more fitting images to show the most significant changes in the British game and beyond in the last decade than Carlisle United. Gather these images together and we need more than three lines of haiku, there's an epic saga to be written here.

Central to Buddhist belief is the law of karma. The notion that all things are in balance and the acts we commit come back to us in kind. Maybe - if we follow the logic of this law - I face a future in another reality in which I pit my fading athletic talents against rapidly moving opposing strikers as a terrace packed with massed ranks of Mike Grahams loudly questions my parentage.

We'll all find out what - if anything - awaits us when we finally go to that great terrace in the hereafter. For now, let's stick to what we already know. Let's discover just how Carlisle United set out on their quest to show the nation what was right, and wrong, with the game of football.

The tale of Carlisle United to the end of the twentieth century is one that tells us a lot about the state of the British game at the grass roots. There are images to conjure with. Images that would make a good opening for a haiku because they are linked to big truths. Truths that touch all of us who care about the game.

We started the 96/97 season back in Division Three. The smart money that year was on a rapid return to the Second Division. All of the bookies had us down amongst the promotion favourites. We started the campaign with some strength, but less flair than we'd displayed two seasons previously. We also started it without some of the players who had made the previous promotion run a complete celebration of talent. Tony Gallimore had already completed a season at Grimsby by May, 1996. By the start of the 96/97 season we'd lost others. Tony Elliot went to join Tony Philliskirk at Cardiff, Derek Mountfield was at Walsall, and then eight games into his season we sold David Reeves to Preston where he could link up with Simon Davey who had been at Deepdale from the promotion season. Mick Wadsworth was also gone, leaving Mervyn Day in charge.

We got replacements, notably the young Allan Smart up front in exchange for Reeves, but this new team had a bargain basement look compared to their predecessors. For all that, the campaign in the South East took in one defeat, at Fulham in late August. I missed this to go to my mate Bif's wedding and so I never saw Carlisle lose away from home that season. If one game stands out in my mind as defining of that season it is the last ever visit to the Goldstone Ground. Brighton's plight was hopeless and they looked certain to leave the League that year before a last ditch draw with Hereford saved them. The same game condemned Hereford, a rural outpost and home of the SAS, to Conference football.

We beat Brighton 3-1. It wasn't pretty, it was hard working. We went 1-0 down in an opening spell that saw The Seagulls running like headless chickens and suffering panic attacks when they got possession. Given its unpredictability, this was an oddly effective tactic that penned us in for the first quarter of an hour. Put simply, we had ideas, but we didn't have the authority to break out from the manic onslaught being staged by the worst team in the country. The people who could have offered us that authority - Davey, Reeves, Mountfield - were playing elsewhere that afternoon.

The goal scorers that day summed up the best of what was on offer. After Paul Conway had blasted a few seagulls out of the sky with a sitter of a chance, it was the bulky frame of Stephane Pounewatchy who headed the first goal. What Pounewatchy was doing at Carlisle was a debatable point. French born and black, he wasn't exactly in the great Bill Green / Don O' Riordan / Derek Mountfield tradition of no nonsense defensive generals who'd cut their teeth across the length and breadth of the no nonsense British game. Pounewatchy was ludicrously good for the level at which we blooded him.

The second goal that day came from Warren Aspinall, thinning on top, grey haired and gap toothed, Warren looked like your dodgy old uncle who'd come round for a summer barbie and spend the whole afternoon feasting his eyes on your little sister's chest. His physique didn't exactly scream 'athlete' to the world, but that afternoon he fought and bundled a run through the Brighton defence that turned the game. The best goal from a Carlisle player I saw all season. Well into the second half, Allan Smart managed a gangling storm on the opposing goal that raised his aspiring Reevesy credentials. This team had a bizarre mismatch of skill and sweat with hot spots of each.

An image to sum up the whole situation was the plight of Rod Thomas. Marooned in no man's land for long periods, he would still dazzle with runs only to find nobody had read his move. Injury prone and often making appearances off the bench, Rod played - off and on - all season and didn't score once. In his first two seasons at Carlisle he'd hit the back of the net 15 times.

We were like a misfiring racing car, storming when we were on form but fragile enough to fall apart when challenged, and forever capable of veering out of control. We never looked like the side of two years before and still we managed to crawl into the top three. By the time I'd seen enough of the Third Division to know that the widespread desperation at other clubs was our greatest asset, I'd got another problem to contend with.

My Dad was ill with what - at first - appeared to be a kidney problem. He'd had diagnosis of possible cancer before Christmas and had a kidney removed the day after New Year. His 'recovery' was slow and beset by problems, by which point it

243

was obvious that he wasn't really getting better. By this time my work and family took up, near enough, every waking hour. It was hard to get anything like the time I'd had during my mother's illness, but I was at my Dad's one Friday in March when it appeared that his one remaining kidney had given up. We went to hospital where he headed off for tests and I got a taste of the lonely desperation it is possible to feel when you leave someone so close at the mercy of doctors and find yourself faced with the cold comforts of a hospital canteen. My Dad had been through the same desperation over ten years before when he'd had to leave my Mum in the care of doctors.

As the sky darkened outside, Lesley and Rich arrived. My stint up North was supposed to give them a weekend off, but we were all gathered to hear the doctor tell us that the one remaining kidney had also been stopped from functioning by a tumour. The options - major invasive surgery or something less than three days to live - had been given to my Dad. He didn't have to tell me. I knew right off that he'd opted to die sooner without the grief and indignity.

I drove him home where he was magnificent. Reading the directions on a bottle of pills he informed us they weren't to be taken with alcohol before washing them down with a wonderful red wine uncorked to celebrate the occasion. At best, we had days to say anything that really mattered. I was able to say everything that I wanted and share the time with my Dad. Two days later, with Jane having come up from Maidstone, the remaining kidney was working again and something had obviously gone wrong with the imminent certainty of death. My Dad, like Basho, had made an art of the supposed final days. He wasn't going to die right away, but he was obviously ill. The things we'd 'known' only days before were replaced with uncertainty. This was a mixed blessing. Deep down - I think - he knew he wasn't going to get better.

He told me a story once, when I was young enough to believe in the truth of everything he said. A story about a Chinese family. He told the story a few times as I got older. By which time I knew it was a wind up. I also realised that he liked this story a lot.

A little Chinese boy is coming home from school and as he passes through the crowded streets he sees a man pushing a wheelbarrow. There is an old man sitting in the barrow. As he gets closer he realises that the man pushing the barrow is his dad and the man in the barrow is his grandad.

'Where are you taking Grandad?' asks the boy when he gets closer.

'He's too old to work anymore,' says the dad, 'And he is starting to get sick. I'm taking him down to the bridge. I'm going to tip him in the river.'

'I love grandad,' protests the boy. 'He's funny and he tells me stories.'

'But we can't afford to keep him,' says the dad, 'And grandad can't work to keep himself anymore.'

244

Eventually, against the boy's protests, the two men head off to the river. The boy thinks about losing his grandad as he walks away home. A few paces later, something occurs to him and he turns round to shout. 'Hey, Dad, bring the barrow back, I'll need it to tip you in the river one day.'

My Dad had a sense of humour that took in the grim aspects of life. During that weekend when we thought we were going to lose him at any point he made a performance and celebration of his imminent death. Like Basho, he had a sense of artistry with it, and although he was ill, he still wasn't an old man. He was 70, but his mind was much younger than that. He was still the same person who had told me the grimly funny story about the Chinese boy all those years before. All my Dad got from a mix up that had briefly fooled the doctors into thinking his kidney was surrounded by cancer was a few more weeks of life. They turned out to be a mixed blessing. He got more ill, less capable and less like himself. In those weeks his life lacked the quality he'd known before. It took a few weeks for us to know for sure that he was dying. I felt that I'd known it all along.

We got more time and, although fitting it in next to holding down a job was demanding, there were treasured moments in those days. There were also strange moments. One of the strangest came the day Carlisle went to Wembley for the second time. Two years after our first appearance we were back in the Auto-Windscreens Shield final and this time the opposition were Colchester United. Both finalists were from Division Three and with our league position bobbing around the automatic promotion zone we were favourites. Colchester were eyeing the final play-off place and in the end they missed out on this by a single point. Then again, they did record a 7-1 win against Lincoln that season.

For me, the Wembley trip was a strange day. I'd talked my mate Steve into coming along. Steve had been to the same Final two years before when we lost. In 1997, I also talked my mate Michael along. Michael had been working with me for two years by this point. In 1995 the Auto-Windscreens Shield final had filled Wembley Stadium. In 1997 there were less than 50,000 there to see the game, including, apparently, many more Cumbrians than people from Colchester. It's always difficult to tell. On one side of me I had South Eastern born and bred Steve. On the other I had Mike, more 'English' in his tastes and outlook than I could ever hope to be, and also the son of Jamaican immigrants and - therefore - never very likely to pass for a Cumbrian. However we mustered this crowd, our end was as packed and noisy as it had been two years before.

Only five of the team that had played two years before were back for a second attempt at the prize. Caig, Hayward, Conway, Walling and Rod Thomas. Rod only got into the action off the bench. Five of the 1995 side had been sold. We had Rory Delap, a young defender / midfield player who had established himself in the side that season and who provided the most entertaining moment of the first half when he demolished a corner flag and put the game into five minutes of inactivity before a Wembley official ran the touch-line to massive cheers with a replacement. It was a non-event of a game. Our great scoring idea, the pace and power of Allan Smart, had limped out just after 20 minutes to be replaced by the pace, lack of height and injury prone body of Rod Thomas.

Rod faced the man-mountain of bad attitude and blubber that was Peter Cawley. The shaven headed executioner at the heart of the Colchester defence kept us out for most of the game although neither side looked like scoring. When Rodney fell foul of the repeated attempts at execution, Matt Jansen's jinking runs were thrown into the fray in the first period of extra time. Jansen was a phenomenal prospect, but - like Delap - still learning the game at this point. It was a strange experience all round for me. These were days in limbo, knowing my Dad was so ill and struggling to see anything else as important. To make matters worse that day at Wembley it was obvious that this team were not the equals of the line-up two years before, neither was the 120 minutes of football that preceded the shoot out.

Up front we had ideas, but little else. Dave Currie's first touch ball killings were now finding an easier life in Scarborough, whilst Reeves' commitment was clattering through defenders in a Preston shirt that weekend. Lee Peacock hadn't the pace, penetration or vision to trouble Colchester too badly. At the end of the season we would sell him to the matchless footballing machine at Mansfield where his sublime scoring talents would net five goals in his first season.

A whelter of conflicting emotions ran through me in the first 120 minutes. I'd got the adrenalin pumping hard enough as the seconds ticked down to the shoot out. And it got even more tense, because even in the shoot out it went down to the wire.

Colchester shot first and scored. Up stepped Paul Conway and equalised. Colchester scored again. Owen Archdeacon missed. 2-1 to them and us one shot behind. They scored again. 3-1. Deano's cool was not dented and he slotted an easy strike into the back of the net for 3-2. 19 year old Karl Duguid stepped up for Colchester, and Caigy saved his middling attempt. Duguid wandered off and burst into tears. 'Sumo' Aspinall buried the ball with the strength of ten men. 3-3 and everything on the last kicks. Peter Cawley, bald blubber-monster, bad attitude on legs and scourge of the Carlisle crowd all afternoon, choked on his shot and Caigy got in a stop, 3-3. One kick left and it was Steve Hayward stepping up. I saw the clean strike, saw the net bulge, heard the roar, registered that one of those screams was mine, and briefly forget every concern in that troubled period of my life.

In that moment, none of the previous 120 minutes of average football mattered, never before had Carlisle United won a final of this magnitude. 45,000 people, Wembley Stadium and a sea of bobbing sheep in the crowd. Inflatable sheep, woolly sheep placed on top of pork pie hats and customized t-shirts with Sean The Sheep pledging an allegiance that his Welsh creator would be unlikely to support. There was a lap of honour to parade the prized beer tray and a deafening exchange of mutual appreciation with the team. For those moments the scale of the achievement didn't matter. We came, we saw, we conquered and we did it against a Southern team on Southern turf. A Cumbrian dream that had been a long time coming.

On our way home through Victoria Station Steve headed off to get some food in. I went to ring my Dad. It all poured out of me, the shoot out, the demolished flag, the sea of green, blue and sheep. He kept asking me to describe different things. What Wembley looked like inside, that roar when Captain Marvel Hayward had buried the decisive goal.

When I was a kid I remember my Dad going places and coming back to tell me what it had been like. Parties I wasn't allowed to, events he'd organised, things he'd seen. I'd picture the scenes in the way that impressionable children do. Years later, when Thom was old enough to imagine the same things I'd tell him stories. One night he wouldn't go to sleep and I lay on his bedroom floor and told him about my train home from London being diverted to make way for a Eurostar. He didn't even know what a Eurostar was. He just knew fast trains and slow trains. Still, he drifted off to sleep mumbling, 'A fast train was coming, and daddy's train had to go on another track,' over and over again. To him, and me as a boy, the big world was made up only of things we could imagine. Now, in April, 1997, I was describing one of those great scenes to my Dad and he wanted the whole story. Happy, I think, that the moment had meant so much to me and - just possibly - glad that he'd lived long enough to see my undying love for this team allow me one such moment in my life. It was strange and poignant, describing things like this to my Dad, almost as if he was the child. Strange that he, like his own son and his own grandson, was asking for more details, wanting to live the scene in his mind, and share in the magic.

It was an odd reversal, like a scene from a movie. As if to underline this point, the strangeness of the moment took an unpredictable turn. Glancing around for Steve and some welcome food, I looked right into the eyes of a flustered Charlotte Rampling. Quite obviously late for something important, she glanced around and strode over to platform one where, presumably, a train was waiting for Paris.

My Dad didn't make it to 71. He died as a warm summer took hold of Cumbria and a few days later we walked down the road behind his coffin to the church we'd always been able to see from the house. In his final hours, he slept peacefully away as a sliver of moon climbed up over the fields outside. The last time I spoke to him we'd talked about the Conservative humiliation in the elections, an event he had enjoyed to the maximum. That was one long night when the constant dull pain and his prolonged wakefulness had been a positive blessing. He stayed awake to see it all, Portillo's hopes of leadership wrecked with his lost seat. Martin Bell taking Tatton with an anti-sleaze landslide and the sheer mind numbing magnitude of the massacre gradually making itself evident.

From that first weekend of impending death in March he lived with most of the loose ends tied up. We talked and said the things that mattered. He was happy with many things. He'd seen his children married and settled with partners who had become close to him. He'd seen another generation of the family born. He knew that we would be secure into our futures.

He had many more things to live for and, until that final illness, my Dad was not in any typical way, an old man. He'd take pleasure in winding up a policeman keeping a watchful eye on hunt demonstrators, he'd enjoy the wild inventiveness of an Ash b-side I taped for him and he'd take sides with Owen against Jane and I. In the final weeks of his life, he would take pleasure in those victories which got him away from his failing health. Like an election massacre or my descriptions of Carlisle's first ever Wembley victory. My Dad lived just long enough to be dependent on others and that was never his wish. The one person on whom he might just have been happy to be dependent had died over ten years before, and he never really came to terms with losing her.

We all took some time to put our lives together, but by this time they were busy and demanding lives. The kind where legislating for a death in the family equates to a set amount of leave in the corporate rule book. I took time when I could to get up home.

The signs of some healing were there when I managed to get interested in the following season. After Wembley, whilst my Dad went downhill, Carlisle had earned third place, and automatic promotion from the lower flight for the second time in three years. The pre-season friendlies blooded some new talent and showed the extent of the underlying desperation in the state of the clearout. Steve Hayward, who had brought composure and some direction to the Wembley team, was now at Fulham. The most exciting face of the new intake was an inexperienced defender called Ross Milligan. Well, he looked great in the pre-season run out.

A few games into the real campaign and none of the new faces - signed or brought forward from the youth ranks - were looking that impressive. Up front Gareth McAlindon and Scott Dobie both got a serious run out that season. Youth team forwards, they managed three senior goals between them, all by Gareth. The fall off in class between the Championship team who had lost at Wembley and the third placed team who had won the same competition suggested that this new adventure in Division Two could be more traumatic than the previous campaign. The fact that we were prepared to sell the un-dentable composure of Dean Walling to Lincoln City added to the feeling. Deano still played well and the dispute that led to his departure was, apparently, about the length of any new contract he might be offered. In other words, there was no doubt he was still good enough for us. I don't know what was said, because I wasn't there. But, the departure of so much talent - Reevesy, Hayward and Deano, stalwarts the lot of them - suggested that the tight financial ship was scuppering any prospects of advancement on the pitch.

I took Thom along to his first game in August as we started the season against Southend with a 1-1 draw. Thom was four and ten months, much younger than I was at my first game, and he was frightened by the wall of noise echoing from the low roof at Roots Hall. By the second half, when we scored, and Thom was chasing a little girl round an empty row of seats and having a thoroughly enjoyable day out in the hot sunshine. Allan Smart scrambled the goal that gave us a point and put us in 11th place in the totally meaningless league table that followed the first Saturday. League wise, that was as good as it ever got.

A few weeks later I heard Michael Knighton implicitly blaming everyone from his players to the departed Mervyn Day for the previous season's performance. 'We limped across the line,' he said before going on to share his vision of a team that were so clearly better than anything in Division Three that they should have bettered their 1995 performance. I didn't recognise the team on the pitch from Knighton's description. On the pitch we were replacing lucrative sales with untried new talent or proven old salts who had seldom seen the higher reaches of the footballing pyramid.

We were signing players like Billy Barr. I've got nothing against Billy Barr personally, but his track record was a solid performance at Halifax and a couple of seasons with Crewe. A couple of seasons before Barr's arrival, the well travelled professionals in the ranks had included the likes of Reeves and Currie who had seen higher levels and performed credibly in these climes. Billy Barr's dizzy heights were in Crewe, a little club, performing miracles at the time under the management of Dario Gradi. Their 6,000 capacity ground hosted First Division football, and when they got relegated to Division Two, they fought right back into the play-offs. In his best days, Barr was a player for such a club. David Currie's best days were at Nottingham Forest where a crowd equalling Crewe's average gate would have been a cause for panic. Like Billy Barr, ace goal getter, Ian Stevens, had briefly dropped to non-league football during his career. Already past 30 when we signed him, he had spent most of the season to May, 1997, netting 17 goals at Shrewsbury.

The turnover of players and the frequency of loan signings appearing in the team was one sign of the creeping problems. The other was the results. Mervyn Day eventually gave in to the inevitable and we began a period in which the media and fans would tell everyone that Michael Knighton was managing the team whilst he would insist that John Halpin and David Wilkes were responsible.

Given what we know now it seems fair to see the Second Division season from August, 1997, to the end of the nail-biting season that followed as one long campaign. A campaign distinguished by the selling of the best players, the frequent appearance of loan signings and unproven reserves, and the certain knowledge that the real talent would depart sooner rather than later.

This sounds cynical, bitter even, and I've described worse teams than the those who ran out in the last two full seasons of the century. The tragedy of these sides wasn't the lack of class, it was the nagging uncertainty and the sense of powerlessness on the terraces. The satisfaction I got in those seasons owed a lot to Thom and his growing love of the matches and the atmosphere. Knighton's blue and white army did me a perverse favour as they spiralled to the bottom of the Second Division. In the way of kids who push a situation onto their own ground just to wind up their parents, Thom would find his own voice on the terraces, with five year old cries of 'Come on Dad, they're useless.' I'd feign wild anger and then buy him some chocolate at half-time.

In this way we built a bond that made football a thing to be shared. When the weather cooled, Thom wrapped up and came along to Gillingham and Fulham. By which time he'd seen us draw once, lose twice and concede eight goals. Fulham had come up from the Third Division in May, 1997, one place above us. The following year they made the play-offs and we went back down. A result that helped seal both of those achievements was fought out at Craven Cottage near the end of the season. Thom had never seen five goals in a game before, he got the football bug that day. That game was fast, open exciting and packed with incident. For my part I'd never seen us suffer a 5-0 defeat before, so it was a first for us both. Peter Beardsley played brilliantly in a white shirt, seemingly unaffected by long-term bullshit talk about him coming to Carlisle.

He may still come, who knows, all I can tell you is that he played brilliantly for Fulham that day and brilliantly for Hartlepool when he was 38 the following season. On both occasions we had cause to regret his skills. We didn't get Beardo, but we acquired Nick Wright from Derby, Andy Couzens from Leeds and the on-loan Ronnie Wallwork from Manchester United. These players had ability. Wright was blinding against Northampton in another losing encounter at the Sixfields Stadium. But, time and again, the uncertainty undermined whatever there was to cheer.

In a full-on 90 minute encounter the team I saw lose to Northampton would probably wipe the floor with most of the line-ups we scrambled in the final season of Mike Graham's professional career. We fought hard and the young players we'd drafted in knew the value of a first team place. But always, behind it all, was the unknown. Matt Jansen was absent at Northampton because he was 'training' with Manchester United. Given his skill and our League position we had to be resigned to losing him, and Delap, in the near future. Like Stanley Bowles before them, they shone given half a chance. Unlike the Carlisle teams of old we couldn't keep talent like this until the end of the season because the gap between ourselves and the others was now a great yawning chasm.

When Matt Jansen finally left he signed for Crystal Palace, he was 20 years old. In his short career he had turned down the chance to join Manchester United twice. Both times in favour of more lowly clubs who could offer him first team football. For all that, he stepped up a degree in class when he left Carlisle. This was brought home to him when - on arrival at Selhurst Park - he got half an hour of Steve Coppell's undivided attention. 'Good to have you here, Matt,' Steve began. 'I've got plans for you and they start on Saturday. By First Division standards it should be an easy match so I want you to get out there in the first half, express yourself, show the crowd what you've got and we'll have you pulled off at half-time.'

'Pulled off!,' yelled Jansen. 'Pulled off! Fucking hell, that's a result. All I got at Carlisle was an orange.'

Like I said, it was a step up in class to go to Crystal Palace. Our class was suffering for the loss of players like Jansen. Watching Carlisle free-fall from the Second to the Third Division and stumble along the bottom for a whole season brought back the dark days of 1992, the team in which Mike Graham and John Holliday had clattered, huffed and surrendered possession. There were moments to cheer, but these were straws to be snatched at. In the Second Division we had a great 45 minutes at White Hart Lane and actually managed a 2-1 lead over Spurs in the Coca Cola Cup. The whole team played brilliantly, Jansen was superb. We lost the game and the return at Carlisle, but we lost well.

Thom finally saw Carlisle win against Brighton in the Third Division with a second half display that turned a 1-0 deficit right around. The 3-1 win included a storming Steve Finney strike and a Damon Searle free kick that shook the goalposts to their foundations. We'd taken some other friends to that game, a habit I'd begun to develop.

The day job was grabbing hours like never before and writing on the side was satisfying, but pressured. In January, 1999, I got a phone call I found hard to believe at first. Steven Wells, a bloke whose copy I'd been reading for over a decade in the *NME* was ringing on behalf of a publisher. He'd discovered my ancient demented rant of a novel in a pile of rubbish in the corner of an office. The 'rubbish' in question amounted to books they had on hold, but were never likely to use. The book had been through several titles and now - as *Raiders Of The Low Forehead* - it was finally to be unleashed on the public. It was almost ten years since it had first left my desk in search of a commissioning editor with a sick sense of humour. Steven wanted to meet up as soon as possible. I mentioned that my next trip to London involved passing through on my way to a Carlisle game and the pair of us met at Liverpool Street station, talked business to and from Prittlewell, and saw Carlisle scramble a hard fought win in a game that could have gone either way. It was the best day's work I'd had in months.

On the pitch the 'stars' of this team were striker Steve Finney, who'd been in and out of teams at Preston and Swindon, and David Brightwell, playing out his career after years on the books at Maine Road. We'd signed Brightwell from Northampton so it might be fair to say he was easing his way down the League. And, of course, we still had Tony Caig. With all due respects to the others, who tried hard every time I saw them in that desperate season, it was Caig I pointed out to my new publisher as the only real class left in the team. With weeks left to the end of the season, Caig went to Blackpool for £5,000. He was out of contract at the end of the season and certainly a better goalie than our position - one off the bottom of the whole Football League - would indicate. The justification offered was that we would have got nothing for him had we allowed him to go when his contract expired. So we needed the money then? A couple of weeks later Carlisle United reported profits, on a losing season, of £1.4 million.

Caig's replacement was Richard Knight, listed in football reference books as a goalie. Knight was 19 years old, overawed by the task that confronted him and painful to watch. He may have a great future in the game, but we needed someone with the potential to have a great present day spell in goal. In a move that would later tax the understanding and charity of other teams - especially Scarborough - we invoked a clause in the League legislation and signed another on-loan goalie after the transfer deadline. We signed Jimmy Glass. The rest may be history, well known history to most of you who've read this far. We'll get there in a minute, but first I want to gather some of the strands of this chapter together.

We have - I hope - established that I'm a terminal case. I'll carry my support of this team to the grave. Wherever they may be in the League, I'll be there and I'll will them on. I came away from Roots Hall, Southend, with a sore throat in 1999, having just seen an undeserved but hard fought away win. Less than a quarter of a century before I'd come away from top flight games with the same hot feeling in my throat. Top or bottom of the League, it doesn't matter. When the referee blows to start the game all that matters to me is the next 90 minutes and the fact that one of the teams is Carlisle United.

We've been all over the place in this chapter. From a Wembley win to the bottom of the entire League, and from Haiku poetry to the £5,000 sale of our 'class' goalie. For me, these things are linked because they are all part of my life. But there is more to this than mere co-incidence. Add these things together and you begin to see how, on the morning of May the 8th, 1999, Carlisle United stood 90 minutes away from exclusion from the Football League. A win, and only a win, could save us. Even then, we were at the mercy of another result. A win for Scarborough would condemn us regardless of our own performance.

This was not the team I had started to support as a boy. In those days the only team I knew in this predicament was Workington. Their tiny ground and reputation for taking our cast off players, in my young boy's mind, put them hopelessly in that place. Now, as my own young boy became familiar with the sights and sounds of football, he was watching a team fighting for its very League survival. He took an interest and pretty soon he knew more than anyone else in his class about the GM Vauxhall Conference. Enough said.

Given the sales of key players, the makeshift look of the side and the number of loan signings, a diehard supporter might just have been tempted to take Carlisle

United to court under the Trades Descriptions Act. Legally speaking this would have involved trying to prove that Carlisle were no longer a football club. I heard similar points argued on the terraces a few times that season. Maybe, the legal action would have uncovered some uncomfortable truths. Imagine getting the papers at Companies House and discovering that we had changed our listed business to 'impersonators of headless chickens,' or 'providers of military re-enactments, large scale retreats a speciality.' Frankly, nothing that season would have surprised me.

The 1997 Wembley win and the 1999 result or relegation encounter at Brunton Park featured the same club, but hardly the same team. We could have done with that Wembley winning team to fight us out of the mess. They were not the greatest team I ever saw, but they would - in all probability - have beaten Plymouth Argyle in May, 1999. The truth is that of the 13 men who had played at Wembley in any part of that game little more than two years before, only one, central defender, Will Varty, could possibly have played for Carlisle on May the 8th, 1999. The other 12 had gone.

Varty, to give him his due, was one of our better players in that desperate season. Predictably, we rewarded his abilities by loaning him to Rotherham, a team for whom he played on the afternoon that we fought for our very survival. The following year, as we fought again for survival, Varty was a fully fledged member of a Rotherham squad fighting out a promotion campaign.

So, to the game that brought us - briefly - back to national prominence. We were not great. Not even passionate, given the circumstances, and we rode our luck. As one paper would later put it, it was 'mediocre stuff . . . played by men of poor touch and indifferent fitness.' Out on the Yorkshire coast Scarborough missed a penalty that could have saved their league status. They didn't think it mattered. We were one goal behind before David Brightwell equalised with a 30 yarder that actually did justice to the seriousness of the situation.

With the time running out and no real prospect of a goal, many eyes were on Knighton in the director's box and the 'Greedy fat bastard' chants were ringing round the ground. Four minutes into injury time, I mean, four minutes in!, we got a corner. Everyone went up, including Jimmy Glass, the loan signing goalie from Swindon. Graham Anthony flighted an accurate ball over the penalty box, Scott Dobie's header was pushed out by Plymouth goalie, Jim Dungey, and Jimmy Glass got his boot on the rebound. He buried it, walloped the bloody thing like it was a goal kick and the net bulged.

The place went mental that moment, that perfect moment had cleared the troubles for the time being. Like Hayward's penalty strike which had taken away a burden for me two years before, that Jimmy Glass goal, briefly took over 7,000 Cumbrians into ecstasy. Glass was mobbed, the pitch was covered and, eventually, Plymouth kicked off. Ten seconds later, the ref blew for time.

253

The press made a meal of the whole thing, Carlisle were national news for one day. The hero - without question - was Jimmy Glass. The club shop started a lucrative run on red goalie shirts, the press quoted Glass's few words on the subject with reverence, and there was serious debate about whether he would sign in the longer term. Glass, a man who had started his career at Crystal Palace and been denied any first team appearances in almost four seasons was, briefly, one of the most famous goalkeepers in the country.

Jimmy Glass's moment of fame was a media dream. 'It fell to me, wallop, goal, thank you very much,' he said. Asked if he was planning to stay at Carlisle he wouldn't commit. 'I'll tell you this,' he said, 'Some very funny things happen in football.'

Too bloody right they do. For starters, Jimmy Glass gets to be a national hero for a day. I found a newspaper picture of Jimmy Glass, arms outstretched, being chased by an invading army of support, stuck across my computer screen when I returned to work the Monday after that nerve wracking weekend. Like so many others before, it just seemed to be his moment. Fame like this, would appear to be chance and yet, in reality, there is often more to it.

There were some strange coincidences that weekend. Graham Anthony, who took the all important corner, had signed for Carlisle from Plymouth Argyle, the team we were playing that day. He had also played for Swindon, the previous home of our 'hot' striker of 1999, Steve Finney. Swindon were also the team who - technically speaking - employed Jimmy Glass on the day he scored that goal. Spooky co-incidence? Well, not really, more a statement of where we were. By the summer of 1999, Carlisle United offered a hopeful career break for those players stuck in the reserves of middling First Division clubs. Clubs placed somewhere around 30th in our League structure. This book opened with Carlisle United performing well, placed around 30th in the League structure as it was then. So, by 1999 we were reduced to fielding the quality of players who would have been our reserves in the late Sixties.

In another twist of football fate the last competitive game of the English season took place on May the 31st, 1999. Bolton Wanderers played Watford for a place in the Premiership. Watford were a team who had done the double over us in the Second Division during the previous season. The game at Vicarage Road was one of our better displays that year. Jeff Thorpe's performance pegging the fast moving Watford attack had its merits, and up front, Allan Smart and Nicky Wright had linked to good effect. Ian Stevens scoring form had been solid at the time and he'd got our only goal in a 2-1 defeat. At the end of the season, I'd been miffed at Watford's promotion. It is the lot of the expatriate fan to feel this way. What I really want for Watford is for them to be in the same Division as Carlisle. My affection for Watford rests mainly on the standard of facilities at their ground, the fact the ground has its own railway station and that this makes it easy to get to games at Vicarage Road without having to drive round the M25.

Financially prudent and under the direction of Graham Taylor, a proven motivator of journeymen and a blender of disparate talents, Watford signed only two promising players at the end of the 97/98 season. When Watford won their second promotion in a row with that memorable 2-1 play off victory these two players were the scorers. Both those players were signed from Carlisle United. Their names were Allan Smart and Nicky Wright. Graham Taylor had seen them play against Watford the previous season. His achievement in spending so little and achieving so much was a triumph of Stokeoesque proportions. Alan Ashman couldn't have done it better. Watford would argue they are a bigger club than Carlisle. I would argue their achievements are built on the same approach that was the hallmark of the Carlisle sides who taught me to love football as a boy.

These connections are not spooky, or coincidental. They tell us a lot about where the team I have loved for years found themselves in May, 1999. It is not a comforting truth. The things that were possible when I was a boy are still possible. Little teams, well managed, supported by people who can see these limitations but feel a sense of belonging to their club, can still be successful. Some of these teams, like Watford and Bradford City, can make the top flight. Other teams can fight, achieve and win. They can win promotion, creditable places in Cups, and the respect and fear of their fellow professionals. In my mind Carlisle could also be such a team. In my mind their rightful place is amongst these teams. They were there when I found them. They were well managed, their players were known and respected.

These days the stakes are higher. More money moves around the game and the differences between rich and poor are a gulf of unimaginable proportions. This, in all probability, is a backward step for most professional teams. It is, however, not an excuse for teams to give up. Football belongs across the length and breadth of the country, it belongs throughout the world. It belongs in communities and it belongs in the hearts and minds of those who support it. Without the passion and the contact between teams and their public the game is nothing. To reduce it to an exercise in good money management is to forget why the game came into existence in the first place.

It is the people's game, at heart a simple struggle between two teams, with rules most can understand and passions that can be seen by supporters from a few yards away. Football makes money because people care enough to pay. These people do not pay out of admiration for the club's annual statement of accounts. They want the club to be solvent and well managed, but they also want to feel a trust with their club.

One year before we stared the abyss full in the face we were relegated from Division Two. In that year Carlisle United made £1.4 million in profit. Our income

255

from transfers, including the sales of Matt Jansen and Rory Delap, was £2.12 million. Our response to this income included spending £100,000 on new players. These figures and the income of the directors, including our chairman, were published in the press in May, 1999. They were well known to the crowd at that stomach churning game. For substantial chunks of the game the chants of 'One greedy fat bastard!' were all that could be heard at Brunton Park. The target of the abuse was, of course, our Chairman, Michael Knighton. What I would have made of those chants as a ten year old at my first game, I don't know. I'm glad I didn't take Thom to Brunton Park that day, glad I didn't have to explain why those people thought the man with the moustache was taking all the money. What does an image like that do to a child's wish to support a football team?

All things are connected. The sale of Tony Caig and arrival of Jimmy Glass didn't happen in isolation. There were reasons, some of them way outside the club. In the way of Basho's Buddhist haiku, look at the picture and know everything that is linked to the picture. There may be amazing results in football. Games written up as incredible achievements. There were a few of these the year we snatched victory from outright disaster with ten seconds to spare. Watford's well managed and craftsman like display in winning a Premiership place was one.

Look deeper into Watford's win and in those images of Allan Smart's telling strike or the incredible bicycle kick of Nicky Wright to score the first goal, you see players with passion. Players who want it badly enough, players who know their team mates are running in support and pulling together. In those moves you see also the resilience of Graham Taylor, the manager who - by common consent of the press - wasn't good enough for England. Branded by *The Sun* as no more intelligent than a vegetable and ridiculed with a picture of his own face on a turnip. In May, 1999, Taylor was the turnip who turned. He achieved a minor miracle at Vicarage Road for the second time in his career. The result might be amazing, but those images of his players scoring the all important goals, with the addition of some thought, show us how it was done. This was a team willed on by fans with a belief in itself. A team that knew, on the day, they could do it.

David Beckham told the press that he saw the European Cup on its way down the steps, already draped with the ribbons of Bayern Munich. Still he kept his composure to deliver that final corner right onto the head of Teddy Sheringham. In that measured performance which finally prevailed in injury time you see the confidence of the Manchester United squad. A team who knew they were blessed, and lucky. A team with so much skill and a team that still wanted to play for the right reasons. It is easy to be cynical, but why else would those two goal scorers stay? They were good enough for first team football in almost any other Premiership outfit. Skolskjaer and Sheringham knew their day could come, knew what was at stake and what that club could achieve. Even in the reserves, they could belong, and they could believe in what they and their club might achieve together. It sounds almost corny, but the truth about Watford and Manchester United is that they had dreams and belief. At the same stage of our season, we had desperation and luck. Without dreams there isn't much reason to support a football club. Without dreams, turning out in the colours of a club is a paid chore for spectators and players alike.

If you compare last ditch winners from a corner, we just about matched Manchester United that season. If you look at the things that put the respective teams in that position you could, just about, say Alex Ferguson was pissing on Carlisle United, and Michael Knighton.

Any image of achievement that season, Manchester United, Watford or Carlisle, bears thinking about. The image that will go into history for Carlisle fans is Jimmy Glass, arms out, eyes wide, about to be buried under a pile of bodies as he celebrates the amazing turn of his career.

This book started with a goalie and - had it come out in schedule in August, 1999 - it would have finished with one. Alan Ross played more games than any other player for my team and he played them over 15 years. He belonged to the club, we knew that and admired him all the more for it. Like Ross, Jimmy Glass will go down in Carlisle legend, and he deserves to. But think further and you realise that any Carlisle hero that day would have been an unlikely hero. Richard Tracey, a teenager blooded in the heat of the Carlisle free fall, hit the woodwork in search of the goal that would give us salvation. He too, would have been newsworthy, and he too would have been an unlikely hero. Ask the crowd that day about their football heroes and they would - in all probability - have mentioned the men who have run through these chapters scoring goals, stopping the opposition in their tracks and pleasing crowds into the bargain. I'm sure that many in the crowd at 3.00pm would have told you there were no heroes in the team they were about to cheer on.

Jimmy Glass earned his place, but it was close. He nearly passed up the chance to shoot himself into history. He saw us lose 3-0 to Scarborough a few weeks before his moment of glory and almost headed back to Swindon. A loan signing, a man whose right to a place on that pitch was so marginal it drew complaints from other teams, a man who would only have been there in a team where the balance sheet was the complete king. Did we - with our considerable profits on the previous year - need £5,000 for the only 'class' player on the books that badly?

The last time a Carlisle goalie with so few games to his credit made the national news it was for the wrong reasons. Jon Blott played twice for Carlisle in 1985, I saw him at Craven Cottage, a game we lost 2-0. A reasonable goalie. He went on to join the police after his football career was ended. When he was rumbled for living with the unlikely combination of a police career and a sideline in serious sex crimes, the national press got interested. Carlisle United made the news pages that day as well! Blott's was an unlikely story, the kind that makes a blaze of news for a day. A freakish story. As freakish perhaps as the on-loan goalie who wanders up the field with nothing to lose, gets himself on the end of a loose ball and creates history in a split second.

Glass said it all himself. 'Wallop, goal, thank you very much!' Think about those words, they tell you it was chance, and nothing more. A chance goal from a player who was there, almost, by chance. If you'd wandered into a bookies at the start of the season with the *Playfair Football Who's Who*, opened the book to the page with Jimmy Glass's entry and put a tenner on him scoring a goal that kept Carlisle United in the league you would have been able to retire on the winnings.

A couple of weeks after Jimmy Glass shot himself into legend we had a party at our house. A handful of the people about whom we cared the most. Amongst those gathered together that day were a loss adjuster, a social worker, my psychotherapist wife and me with my writing and teaching careers competing for space in my life. We all knew each other well enough to share the things that would bother us in other circumstances. Different jobs but similar worries. Work places run by systems, new targets heaped on desks every week and the general awareness that we were all less productive and less satisfied than we had been a few years before. Every age has its follies and we kid ourselves sometimes that we are smarter than previous generations. There was once a general belief that science and reason would tame every test that nature could provide. This translated into a safety policy at sea in which the biggest ships, with many watertight compartments, would act as their own lifeboats. The scientific and reasoned thinking was logical enough, there could be nowhere safer at sea than aboard a massive ocean going liner. Some of the best brains of that age built the biggest ships they could for the sake of safety, crammed them with people, and promptly killed them on a scale previously unimagined when the Titanic sank in 1912.

Today we've created more artificial intelligence, more movement of information and more ways of doing one single job than ever before. We use this technology to work people into the ground in search of profit and the achievement of targets. We often ignore emotional intelligence because it complicates the issue. It strikes me that future generations will look back on the present times and wonder about the human cost of our decisions. The push for profit above everything, the identification of targets at every opportunity and the reduction of many of the most skilled in the work force to another resource to be relocated and fired on the strength of a balance sheet.

Since we married, my wife has trained as a psychotherapist. She pieces together shattered lives, helps people understand the causes of their problems and works to help people who can't function to make sense of their troubles and heal themselves. She is good at her work, very good. She has never once had to advertise for clients. As a country, we have, apparently, never had more wealth, more choice and more information at our disposal. As a country, we have also never been more miserable and more in need of emotional help. The evidence for the last bit is the our ever increasing willingness to seek the help of therapists.

This has more to do with football than many of us realise.

Our national game has always reflected the age in which it was played. The subservience of the working classes which did much to convince wave after wave of men to charge the machine guns which would mow them down in World War One didn't end in 1918. It could also be seen in the first Wembley Cup Final in 1923. A crowd, way over capacity for the new stadium, spilled onto the pitch and were methodically cleared. The old newsreels show an image of a policeman on a white horse. There is more to this picture. That crowd were cleared, partly, because there were many in that era who still had a blind respect for authority. People who - to coin a phrase - 'knew their place'. Football has produced more recent images that say everything about their times.

George Best, obscenely talented, clear enough about the fact he had problems and strangely incoherent about what these problems were. A media star who couldn't put into words the fact that the media had made him, but also changed him. He knew how to have fun, but it's doubtful how well he knew himself sometimes.

George Best made us aware of how much ruthless intrusion could wreck lives and talents. Given the financial interests in football, casualties like George Best were expensive. In the corporate Eighties, an era of grabbing economic policies, football once again produced an image that defined the age. Diego Maradona, a footballer of ferocious skill and pace, scored a crucial goal in the greatest tournament we had, with his hand. His whole 'hand of God' spiel afterwards was an exercise in spin that said - in effect - 'All that matters is achievement, the only crime is getting caught.'

In 1999, an era when people's lives and careers changed more rapidly than at any time in history our national game once again gave us an image. Jimmy Glass and his moment of glory. And it was a moment. On loan at the very end of the season. Our second stop-gap goalie after the transfer deadline. Snatching a goal with ten seconds to go. This was, in every sense, a moment. If you want a picture to symbolise the state of the game and the state of the age that supported it in the last season of the twentieth century, look at Jimmy Glass, sprinting from his goal after they had played out those final ten seconds. The wild relief on the faces of the supporters chasing him up the pitch. Remember then that this was a team more profitable in the previous season, a season in which it had been relegated, than most in the Premiership.

If ever a team represented the follies of this era, when lives are changed to fit corporate plans, reshuffle follows reshuffle and the only thing that matters is the bottom line on a balance sheet, that team was Carlisle United. A team of youngsters, journeymen and loan signings with the financial performance of a Premiership outfit.

The haiku poem I quoted earlier, Basho's last, puts together two images and a thought. On the surface they don't appear to have much to do with each other. The sick poet and the dry fields against the poet's hopeful dreams. You could write a hell of a haiku putting together two other unlikely things, like the Third Division league table at the end of 1999 and the balance sheet showing the profits of Carlisle United! On the surface you'd wonder how they could be linked. A club so profitable and so close to disaster. In an era where we think more in terms of systems and profits than of people and their emotions, those two do belong together.

My psychotherapist wife has taught me quite a lot about sanity and hope. In the main, people get depressed because they feel powerless or they lack the chance or the confidence to express their anger. I've shared many emotions with Carlisle fans over the years. In that last season of the century I saw depression, and felt it, supporting my team. A lot of that came from the thought that our own hopes were being ignored.

I'd argue I'm realistic in my hopes. I don't seriously expect Premiership football at Carlisle this side of a major financial change in the game as a whole. I don't mean any disrespect to the other teams facing oblivion that season, but none of them were like us. None of them featured on *Grandstand* on the day of the final game with colour footage of a team less than 25 years before which had settled on the very top of the Football League.

Some of the relegation candidates that season were the usual suspects. Hartlepool, Torquay and poor little Scarborough. Coastal towns who could draw a ten mile radius around their ground in search of support and catch nothing more than fish in half of the circle. On May the 8th, 1999, none of their grounds would legally have held the crowd we scrambled at Brunton Park. None of those clubs had turned round a massive profit on the back of a footballing disaster the previous season. I feel for those clubs, especially Scarborough, because I know the despair of paying money to watch a team which will - in all probability - be humiliated in front of your eyes. I know the gnawing worry that comes with contemplating the uncertainties of non-league football.

For all that, some of these lowly teams mustered more honest hope in that season than we ever could. Their hopes and ambitions might never take them to the highest achievements in football, but if they felt an empathy with their directors and saw a squad of players who showed some continuity, the supporters at Scarborough and Hartlepool probably felt more hope over that season than their cousins in Carlisle.

I love that last haiku of Basho, the one which contrasts his expiring body with his dreams wandering on. I love it because it is so hopeful. On his deathbed, a place where he had nothing to gain from telling a lie, Basho still saw the hope in what he was doing. For my part, I hope he was right. He died still believing in his dreams.

If you take away the dreams and hopes of people you take away their reason for being at all. If you take them away from football fans, you are left with nothing but 22 blokes chasing a lump of leather whilst somewhere out of sight, someone is counting the cash. When you reduce it to that, you've got a pointless exercise. One that says nothing to us about who we are or why we should be there. You've got the very thing that those outside the game, the ones who could never understand why the rest of us bother to go, always told us it was.

If you've read this far you'll know I'm a hopeless case. Yes, I'd have followed them into the Conference. I'd have sought out romantic weekend breaks in Stevenage and I'd have screamed and cheered as the skilfully challenged crew fought it out in the January mud, the sounds of the squelching pitch drowning out the meagre rumble of the crowd. I love my team, my history with them means too much to me to even think about walking out and I'll be there until I'm physically incapable. I hope I am there until the day I die. If my man Matsuo Basho was right about what comes next, I'll probably be going after that.

I started writing this book about my life long support for a football team. Whilst I was writing this book my team staged one of the most improbable escapes from total disaster ever seen in British football. They were within ten seconds of the biggest Blue Nightmare of all time. During the period I was writing this book the fans of Carlisle United chanted ever more loudly for change. Their argument was that the club wasn't channelling enough money into the team. A common argument from fans, but these fans had a point. There was - apparently - enough money to have made a difference. The argument from the club stated that it was important to establish a sound financial footing off the pitch before committing money into building a team, once more a common argument from directors and a credible one in many circumstances.

For all these arguments, my team took both sides of its operation to extremes. On the pitch we could hardly have come closer to complete disaster. In the boardroom we were up with some of the very best in the land. On the terraces we touched two completely different levels of insanity in the last few minutes of the season. My own feeling - for what its worth - is that somewhere in this unholy mix of emotions we have almost lost sight of what it is really about. Supporters, teams and everyone else, pulling together. All of us with dreams and a sense that we are willing these dreams to happen.

My team have produced this combination over the years, you've read about it in this book. When they haven't delivered the magic they've delivered other things, characters, laughs, and honest effort. They've tested me, never more so than in the last full season of the century. But I'm still there.

Like Basho said, 'Dreams wander on.' But, as we've seen in this book. Some dreams are Blue Nightmares. In June, 1999, I didn't know which dreams were coming next.

Blue Nightmare #13

'GEORGE, IT'S NEIL, how are things?'

'Aye, not bad.'

'Have we got a date yet?'

'Well, the web site is a bit behind schedule.'

'What you mean the one at www.terracebanter.com/'

'Aye.'

'We'll have the Carlisle book out for Christmas, won't we?'

'Maybe, but I've got to get the Millwall book sorted. The advance orders on that look good and they'll help us get some distribution organised with a few shops.'

'You mean Colin Johnson's *We Fear No Foe?*'

'Aye, it's a good book. Everyone that's seen it really rates it and I've got another one that looks promising coming along.'

Is that *St George In My Heart* by Colin Johnson, the same guy who wrote the classic *We Fear No Foe?*

'Aye, *St George In My Heart* is about his following England. He's not exactly a member of the official travel club and there are some cracking stories in the book.'

'But we missed the start of the season, we'll have the Carlisle book sorted for Christmas won't we?'

'Well, you see, the other stuff is keeping me busy. We haven't even mentioned *And Up Steps Michael Gray - The Secret Diary Of A Sunderland Fan* or *Bring Out Your Riot Gear Hearts Are Here!* A pair of brilliant books those. Then I'm busy with the fiction. Our anthologies of the classic Richard Allen novels still do well, not many people realise that we've got 18 books, bound three books at a time into half a dozen anthologies. The first one has the all time classic *Skinhead* and a couple of other Joe Hawkins novels. I'm trying to make the world understand that they can get a full catalogue of this stuff by logging onto the web site.'

'What the one at www.terracebanter.com/'

'Aye that's it, www.terracebanter.com/'

'Hey George, is my Carlisle book coming out in 1999?'

'Maybe, I can't promise.'

Chapter 13 - Andy Dibble, Michael Ingham, Peter Keen, Barry Thompson, Peter Van Der Kwaak, Luke Weaver

MENTIONED FOR THE FIRST TIME IN THIS CHAPTER

Paul Baker - He'd played for us once before, in a team that suffered consecutive relegations in the Eighties. It was news to me that he was still alive, still playing and still willing to commit his time and effort to Carlisle.

Peter Beardsley - Okay, we've mentioned him before. Not the manager.

Johnny Blom - A classic striker in the great Carlisle tradition. You know, Eric Gates, Gary MacDonald, Tony Fyfe . . . Christopher Dias.

Peter Clarke - In the great Stephane Pounewatchy tradition, a classy defender who gave up the higher aspirations (in his case at Highbury) to showcase his skills in front of 2,000 on a freezing January night in Carlisle.

Nigel Clough - Not the manager.

Neil Cooper - Coach who took on the challenging task of making good things happen on the pitch at the turn of the century

Andy Dibble - A goalie used in the 99/00 season.

John Durnin - Veteran forward who - like Steve Soley - moved to Brunton Park from local rivals, Portsmouth.

Steve Halliday - Bargain basement goal machine, a welcome sight as the dark clouds gathered in late season 99/00.

Paul Heritage - A goalie not used in the 99/00 season.

Tony Hopper - In and out of form and in and out of favour, central defender who lasted several seasons and found himself on the books at the turn of the century, whilst most of those blooded with him were plying their trade higher up the League.

Michael Ingham - A goalie used in the 99/00 season.

Peter Keen - A goalie used in the 99/00 season.

Peter Van Der Kwaak - A goalie used in the 99/00 season.

Rob McKinnon - The physique of a late period Joe Laidlaw, the skills of a late period Eric Gates. In a word, desperate. He played for Scotland you know.

Brian McClair - Not the manager.

Keith Mincher - The manager, briefly. Rumoured not to exist.

Nigel Pearson - He managed us to league survival, 98-99.

Matthew Pitts - Signed from Sunderland, 1999. Useful striker of the ball with a work-rate that suggested he cared and a first touch that suggested his only hope of seeing Premiership action was to take a referee training course.

Gavin Skelton - Looked like a head on collision between a baby and journeyman boxer. Moved from the youth ranks to show a passion for the game that warmed the crowd, starting in 1999.

Steve Soley - Free-running, free scoring attacking midfield playmaking genius. Also spent a lot of time being crap.

Shaun Teale - Experienced defender. Decisive, effective and - generally - the equal of Third Division strikers.

Barry Thompson - A goalie used in the 99/00 season.

Luke Weaver - A goalie used in the 99/00 season, easily the best news of the season on the pitch.

Stuart Whitehead - Defender who made his debut for Carlisle in the 'Jimmy Glass' season. Better than some in the team. Then again, 'some' included Rob McKinnon.

Martin Wilkinson - Go easy on the man, he's managed Carlisle United.

Graham 'Tot' Winstanly - Mentioned in chapter one. Classy defender from classy teams of the past.

ON JUNE THE 4th, 1999, I delivered the manuscript for *Singin' The Blues*. In the following months I wrote two novels. The second of which - *Tokyo Bloodbath 2002!* - concerns a team from Workington, even worse than Workington Reds, who go on to represent England in the 2002 World Cup. Well, as a man used to the ins and outs of Knighton era Carlisle, I had no problem imagining that football and the totally improbable went hand in hand.

A week after finishing that book I was back writing *Singin' The Blues*. Having missed the August, November and December dates for publication, the only option was to bite the bullet, fit in another season and pitch the book into the market for the first complete season of the new millenium.

There were sound business reasons for the cancelled plans and chaotic re-organising that dropped the final chapter into an increasingly cramped writing schedule. I could console myself with several thoughts. The bigger selling books from the publisher would help the distribution of this one, the new website would promote it, and my increasing contacts with the Carlisle websites would help even more. On top of this, the tragic league position we 'enjoyed' as the millenium turned was marginally less desperate than the previous season. I had a hunch about the 99/00 season, like 87/88 and 91/92, that the real good news was away from our pitch, in the blood-red bank accounts and pointless huffing runs that were the lot of other bottom of the pile teams like Exeter City, Chester City and Shrewsbury Town.

A cold comfort for sure, but one the Blue Army had come to understand all too well by this point. We hadn't the security of watching Aldershot fold in mid-season or Newport County running off the pitch at half-time into the waiting arms of their concerned mothers who'd supply them with a loving Wet Wipe and a change of trainer pants. But - from our side - there was a touch more skill, enough aggression to leave Adolf Hitler incontinent with fear, and a seemingly endless procession of new faces. Andy Dibble, Michael Ingham, Peter Van Der Kwaak, Barry Thompson and Luke Weaver to name a mere half dozen. Now we've named those six, we've dealt with the new 'goalie.' For the sake of thoroughness we should mention Paul Heritage, another goalie on the books that season who played a starring role on the treatment table.

Such endless parades - of course - can go in two directions. Out the other end with little ceremony went Nigel Pearson, a manager who - with little to work with on the pitch and precious little time to achieve anything - had achieved the considerable feat of securing our League survival. Back down the M6 after 270 solid minutes and one totally sublime moment went Jimmy Glass. The journeyman who shot us to League survival with ten seconds to spare. His career would take further turns, in and out of favour at struggling Swindon, Glass would turn down a move to Chester City on the transfer deadline, citing his affinity with Carlisle. The man wanted a future in football, but as he struggled for a regular run-out he refused to go to the bottom club, and put himself in the position of endangering Carlisle's chances of league survival. In the end Brentford got lucky and secured Glass's services. It figured. Stan Webb went to Brentford years before. That unfashionable London outpost had clearly cornered the market on players with a certain unique quality about them.

In Jimmy Glass, we have a legend for all time. If he can't appear for Carlisle he can still be sure of an appreciative crowd wherever the team's supporters gather. In fact, all told, it's doubtful if he got a better reception that season than the one he received from the London branch of Carlisle's support.

The bitterness and cynicism that spread around the terraces in the wake of the high profile departures was damped down a little when we discovered that Luke Weaver's skills in goal were the equal of anything we'd seen in ages. As good as Caig before he left, as old as Caig when he started. Hell, Weaver won us three away points at Brisbane Road in December. He turned on this matchless display against his old club, Orient. The extent of his dominance that day is best gauged by the newspaper report I read in Walthamstow.

My writing career at this stage included working for and hanging backstage with Sooty and his puppet pals. In a stinking flea-pit of a theatre at the end of a national tour, the cast, crew, hopeful writer and the boy on the front of this book were reduced to scratching up tepid cups of tea and bought in sandwiches. In an atmosphere soaked with disappointment and deflation, I had more reason to be cheerful than the others as the local paper, soaked through with a tea stain, offered a back page that discussed that game in terms that suggested only one man had been playing. Fair enough, Weaver was brilliant that day. The only thing he didn't do was score the solitary goal - that fell to Matthew Pitts.

Pitts had come from Sunderland, he - along with the half dozen new goalies - found himself in a squad that with three exceptions dated back no further than 1997. Forgetting for a second, Jeff Thorpe, Richard Prokas and Tony Hopper, this was a team built on loans, trials, youngsters who'd failed their first auditions higher up the league, and some dependable older heads on the way down.

One of these old heads was the biggest shock of all to me. On the phone in the autumn of 1999 to one of the dedicated few who were prepared to run Carlisle United websites, I was informed of the hot news that would temporarily solve our striking crisis.

'Paul Baker, is he still alive?'

I knew damn well he was, he'd been at Hartlepool the previous season. He turned in a fair enough performance the first time I saw him after his return, at the Sixfields Stadium, Northampton. Baker was no stranger to struggling Carlisle. His sweaty and combative performances had been consistent through two free-falling seasons of successive relegation in the Eighties. All told, he was qualified for what he found at Carlisle. His role took in coaching, which was just as well, given the attrition rate of anyone charged with decision making.

Neil Cooper's coaching career at Carlisle followed in the great 'blink and you've missed it' tradition of Martin Harvey. However, this was as nothing compared to the legendary Keith Mincher who came and went in the Summer of 1999. Anything you read about the man is likely to be pure speculation. Officially he left owing to unavoidable commitments abroad. Unofficially, his reason for departure appears in the one place Carlisle United truly dazzled in the millenium spanning season, the rumours pages on the internet! There - you may discover - some people doubt that he ever existed.

Given the seething frustrations on the terraces, the endless parade of 11 guys who'd made the mistake of walking too slowly past the ground on a Saturday afternoon before being press-ganged into 90 minutes in a blue shirt, and the steady stream of claim and counter claim that did the rounds to explain it all, this was a team that belonged in cyberspace. Safe from prosecution and fired by frustrations, the internet was buzzing with Blue Nightmare rumours. Some of the entertainment was simply standard imagination-firing stuff. Like the fearsome skills of Swedish striker, Johnny Blom, that would soon sort out the problems up front! Hell, the press releases and internet stuff made Blom sound great. We'd been here before, notably when Eric Gates' matchless experience, international pedigree and quality skills were mooted as the solution to the early Nineties goal famine.

Elsewhere it had become really exciting. Mincher's management career was one orgasmic aspect, though on second thoughts I've had orgasms that lasted longer than his stint in charge, and - sexually speaking - I'd count myself pretty normal. None of this five hours, out of body stuff beloved of pretentious rock stars for me. Hell the chance of five hours uninterrupted and unknackered from work to attempt a tantric bonk would be very welcome!

Mincher's management career was celebrated on the rumours page. It was eclipsed for entertainment value by the management careers of the guys who were gonna come and sort us out. In cyberspace, you couldn't move for Carlisle United's new managers. Like King Arthur and his army waiting, asleep under the ground, until the moment when disaster threatened to overwhelm us all, Peter Beardsley, Nigel Clough and Brian McClair were - apparently - ready to pit their tactical skills against the grim realities of another struggle for League survival.

Someone else - allegedly - on the way to sort things out was 20 stone, no-nonsense 'die of shame you scum-bag' telly star, Roger Cooke. Before the muck-raking end of the tabloid press suggested that the 'truth' wasn't all it appeared to be in Cooke's programmes, there were regular stories suggesting that Cooke's encounter with Michael Knighton might be screened at any time. Cooke had taken on the most feared enemies of all. This was the man who once claimed on television that Martin McGuinness was the IRA's chief of staff and, near enough, challenged the man and the organisation to call him a liar. On this evidence, the man's bravery and suicidal tendencies knew no limits. I'd often found myself watching Cooke with admiration, such a reaction tended to be followed - on my part - by thoughts of how I'd like to live a long and healthy life and would therefore not fancy his job, even if it went with a salary of Knightonesque proportions. If Cooke was regularly to go where others feared to tread - ran the logic - then surely, this tendency would, eventually, put him face to face with Carlisle United's larger than life chairman. Well, all we can do is . . . wait.

As this book goes to press - again! - rumour central on the internet continues to push any and every story about Carlisle United. Some of the milder ones are simply old favourites, the move into the Scottish League, the imminent bull-dozing of Brunton Park to create a supermarket. Some other bizarre 'rumours' have been backed up by observation. Like the one about Martin Wilkinson watching games from behind glass in the East Stand, relaying instructions by phone to the director's box and driving halfway round the ground at half-time to give his team talk. Whatever the truth of this arrangement, there was busy late-season traffic between the director's box and the forlorn figure of Paul Baker urging his men on from the touch-line.

And the 'men' in question! The stars of the new crop had come from the usual routes. Steve Soley and John Durnin were out of favour at First Division Portsmouth. A club that could claim some affinity with us, blue strip, lonely geographical location, glory days a fading memory, you know the kind of thing. We took the pair of them and watched them struggle to put shape into an outfit who were chasing clear air half the time and struggling for a telling first touch on a skidding ball all season. Peter Clarke, a defender who'd moved from Arsenal, got plenty of appearances in the first team and impressed on several occasions, sometimes for entire games at a stretch.

The youth angle was best demonstrated by Gavin Skelton. A lad with heart in the admirable mould of the great Richard Prokas himself, he threw himself at everything and won the crowd over, even when he failed to make a telling touch on the ball. Skelton's shaved head reminded me - strangely - of Baby Crockett, an overgrown toddler who starred in late Sixties kids' comics. Skelton had potential, that much was obvious when I first saw him in a boring 0-0 draw with Grimsby in the Coca Cola Cup in August, 1999.

The fact that we went away to Grimsby and lost the return leg 6-0 tells you something about the way we could be found wanting in the face of organisation and commitment. We took some stuffings away from home. Add a rail fare that offered a few pence change from 50 quid, a train fire that caused serious delays on the line and the small matter of a 5-0 stuffing at Sincil Bank, Lincoln, and you've got the makings of a trauma that could lead a man to abandon football following in favour of dragging round DIY stores on a Saturday. A lesser man than me, that is. Hell, I'd grown hard to it by this point.

That Lincoln game wasn't even the worst performance I saw that year. That honour has to be disputed between the final match of the campaign and the 80 minutes of complete and unadulterated shapeless shuffling shite that provided the 'entertainment' for a fraction over 3,000 supporters as Carlisle went down 1-0 at Brunton Park to Macclesfield. The Macclesfield performance was all the worse because we started that game as if we meant it. The first ten minutes were okay. But, the writing was on the wall when Pitts squandered a begging chance in the opening skirmishes. Macclesfield - it must be said - were friggin' abysmal.

I'd returned to the paddock by this time, mainly because the loneliness in every other part of the ground was crushing. When I first went to Brunton Park there was a standard chant of 'You'll never take the Warwick.' Looking at the bare expanses of concrete visible at that end of the ground as the century turned, the Warwick could have been taken by any well organised group of people who shared a fondness for wide open spaces. The fact was, few people could be arsed to take a position on the Warwick and the whole ground echoed in a sad, empty, mockery of better days. With crowds sometimes plunging to within sight of a paltry 2,000, the reminders of the darkest days of past nightmares were all too close.

They were all to close on April the 15th, 2000, as Macclesfield rattled in the only goal of desperate game. Our stars: Pitts, Soley, Halliday and Durnin were squandering possession, running about in disorganised impersonations of a tactical master plan, and clattering the odd challenge into the opposition when it all got too much. On this final score at least, we were matchless. By Easter we were out there on our own as undisputed caution and dismissal champions of a skilfully challenged lower flight.

And still the improbability of it all pushed the envelope. A winning streak as the winter finally lost its grip had seen promotion chasing teams humbled. The best travelling performance within striking distance of my patch had seen Peterborough take a manful stuffing at London Road on a Tuesday night in March, and, all told, we were worth that win. A more typical performance in this era was the manner of the victory in a tense encounter at Chester City's compact and bijou residence, the Deva 'Stadium'. Outplayed for skill, we retaliated with 'commitment' enough to see two men marching for the early bath. Steve Halliday and Stuart Whitehead were both ordered out of the action in the final ten minutes. Naturally enough, down to nine men, totally outplayed, short of anything approaching a winning idea in the opposition half and running well into injury time, we broke away and scored a spectacular winning goal, our first shot on target all afternoon and it came from Scott Dobie's boot 20 yards out.

Knighton's press conference patter was a stream of sublime copy, tailor made by a master of the media art.

- 'The fans love matches like this. They pretend they don't, but they do.'
- 'I thought we played better after the sendings off so maybe we'll start with nine men in our next match.'
- 'This club is the epitome of the rollercoaster ride that football is all about.'
- 'There's never a boring season at Carlisle.'

Those of us faithful enough to keep on paying the admission prices had opinions too. Not necessarily the same as those outlined by our Chairman after the Chester game. By this point, it has to be said, two things were evident. First off, the desperate balance sheets and pointless, panic driven football on the pitch at Chester and Shrewsbury were slowly turning the tide. Staring into the abyss, these teams were giving it everything. Our security after the win at Chester was ill-deserved and pretty thin. We could still be caught. The fans watching this stuff knew how bad it had become. Sure, this wasn't the worst team I'd ever seen, but this was a team struggling against the rest of the Division. The year Mike Graham had back-peddled his way into my nightmares himself we weren't threatened at all. Hell, we could have done with another Aldershot style mid-season collapse of a rival team in 2000.

A measure of the distance between Knighton's stream of sound-bite gems and the gut feelings on the terraces was there for a few dozen of us to hear in the Paddock as the last game before Easter played itself out. As Carlisle made their first two substitutions and left Rob Fuckin' McKinnon on the pitch against Macclesfield, a guy in front of me in the Paddock screamed out loud. Maybe, taking Knighton's comments after the Chester game, you could claim the screamer was pretending not to love such a match, epitomising the glorious rollercoaster ride that is football and reminding everyone that our season was anything but boring. You could claim that. Then again, you could say that after the best part of a season's torture, the most consistent spell of desperation in the club's history and the lack of anything resembling salvation on the pitch that afternoon, the screaming Blue had simply had enough.

My early season optimism - I didn't think we'd win anything, 'optimism' meant believing in League survival - was now under serious test. As I had eight years before, I picked on the most athletically challenged member of the first team and noticed his blunders. As the season wound to a close I could see Rob McKinnon and in my mind his porky frame was symptomatic of everything that was so wrong with the team I couldn't help but love.

McKinnon took some fine abuse that afternoon against Macclesfield, as he did on the odd occasion he managed to last a complete match. 'Experienced' to the point that his contract negotiations probably revolved around his assurance that he could 'do a job' for the remainder of the season, McKinnon had grafted his glory years out at Hartlepool and Motherwell, throwing in a totally incomprehensible loan

270

to Manchester United in which he had failed to make a first team appearance. By the end of the 99/00 season, chunky Rob was showing that same love of pointless running, passes into nowhere and yard-short chases of opposing players that had characterised the final months of Mike Graham's career. Say what you want, McKinnon wasn't boring. His frequent slips could reduce a supporter on the edge of sanity to that ear splitting, 'ARGHHH!!!!!' we have all heard from time to time. That's what the guy in the Paddock sounded like, before launching another tirade at Paul Baker as our player-coach tried again to instil some shape into his men.

In an odd way, I envied the screamer that afternoon. At least he could muster the pumped up fury to scream. Since the demolition afternoon at Sincil Bank, I'd been reduced to burying my head in my hands and groaning on a regular basis. My other odd habits - like two Scotch pies a game, as many Kit Kats as I could handle and spontaneous and totally unnecessary forays into record shops on my way to away games, were another clear cry for comfort. If I could have screamed, I'd have saved myself a few quid that season.

I guess I should count myself lucky. My Dad had to venture into Asian undergrowth and see men hit by bullets to share in the screaming depths of life's rollercoaster. All I had to do to see men reduced to terrified screaming wrecks was to pay £8. I got this experience with the added bonus of leaning against a crush barrier and munching my way through a Brunton Park Scotch pie. Great pies, at least something is as good as it used to be at Brunton Park.

By this time, Knighton's talk for the press concerned two great escapes in successive seasons. His reasoning clearly revolved around the white knuckle ride that came with a desperate struggle for points, possession and telling passes. It should be said that teams behaving in this way tend to adopt a different approach to their 'season.' In the mould of a Wimbledon, Southampton or Coventry, we had now reduced our active participation in the matters of football life and death to a rabid sprint for points which reduced everything to the final few games and provided those interested with a ready reckoner as the papers continually printed lists of remaining games, current positions and speculation on the outcome.

Given the importance of the final run in, we were better placed than most. We still had eight games remaining when some of the others had only six. Our final games included two six pointers, the massive result and desperate display against Chester City being the first of these. This final run in also included more home than away games and some encounters against teams who - in all probability - would find themselves mired in mid-table mediocrity with nothing to play for by the time we lined up against them. Teams like Macclesfield and Brighton. The fixtures list promised a comforting finale to the season for Carlisle. Two of the late season strugglers, Exeter City and Shrewsbury Town, were due on the same pitch at 3.00pm on the final Saturday. All we had to do was ensure a two point cushion over the pair of them by May the 6th, and we couldn't drop.

So, there was hope. And - like the sight of Richard Prokas finally replacing McKinnon in the Macclesfield game - we could relate to this and feel positive, now and again. Then again, 'hope' in this context related more to the desperate depths to which we had sunk the year before. The turn of the millenium side were fractionally better on skill than their predecessors and they showed their commitment in that collection of cautions. Not exactly entertaining and barely qualifying as football some of the time, this was still a campaign that dragged my emotions in with that same mixture of salivation and horror that sees alcoholics, wired up to panels in bare rooms and sipping pints in snatched nanoseconds, knowing for certain that another electric shock will surely follow.

By this point, my team and I were heading in different directions in terms of performance. After a year in which I'd hardly got a moment to myself it was time to do something about the situation. 1999 had opened impressively for me, the writing had thrown a few opportunities my way. This book and the chance to see *Raiders Of the Low Forehead* rescued from a pile of 200 pieces of 'crap' in a publishers office were only the start. By the time the new football season kicked off Stanley Manly - the nutter who wrote *Raiders* and bore a striking resemblance to me, complete with cloth cap and ever present smouldering fag - was planning a live appearance, considering further novels and branching out into journalism. Under my own name I was working on a range of other stuff from treatments for TV shows to some more music journalism. The day job had finally seen the start of a pet project I'd been working on for years, our Professional Writing course had taken in its first group. This work was great, but it was also a problem. The sheer scale of the whole thing was impossible, and getting worse.

I'd tried a few things, but getting other day jobs with the same flexibility wasn't easy and full-time writing jobs were out there offering exciting six month contracts with the vague possibility that there might be more work. In the end I figured what I wanted in terms of cutting down the day job I had and went into work on the first week of 2000 prepared to negotiate. It didn't come to that, I asked for what I wanted, and got it.

By this time Stanley had done his first gig, a London launch party for the media. Not the greatest performance of my life, but another dimension to my writing and access to a few phone numbers I'd have struggled to attract otherwise. If this was a mid-life crisis I could handle it! Too friggin' busy to worry about getting older and - from September, 2000 - working a four day week in the 'day' job and allowing myself the rest of the time to write up the mountain of ideas that were scribbled into notebooks and logged on the computer in the hope of convincing someone out there they were worth time and money. It was up to me now, more than ever before. But, having brought up a family and supported Jane through her training, it was my turn!

272

By Easter, 2000, I'd come through some dark days of exhaustion and found something to aim for. Carlisle, by comparison were crawling along the bottom for one more year. Win lose or draw - and I'd seen them do all that season - they were a team desperate for shape and confidence. The regular news updates I downloaded every night talked about reserves wanting to get into the side, plans for the future and what could be achieved. The action on the pitch talked about struggle and desperation, with a few skills and some solid tackling.

The Peterborough game was - probably - as good as it got in the South East. 2-0 winners over promotion contenders, we were worth the points even if we hardly dominated. John Durnin's goals were clinical, inspired and special and, on the night, that was about the difference. Elsewhere in the South East, notably at Barnet and Lincoln, we managed some shape on the odd occasions we found ourselves in possession. The Peterborough win was part of a sequence that saw us climb from the bottom to a lofty 22nd place. Our points and the desperate state of things at Gay Meadow, Shrewsbury, gave us a chance or survival.

But whenever things began to look hopeful we managed to squander these chances. On Easter Monday we needed a point's gap to take the pressure off the end of season run in. Away at Southend, a team mathematically safe but hardly a 'class' side, we had a perfect opportunity to take a result home. We deserved the 2-0 humbling we got and Peter Keen - in goal for the injured Luke Weaver - was the only thing that kept the scoreline respectable. The signs by this time were so ominous even an optimist on my level could see this was a desperate position, even if the team were not quite as bad as those who'd hit rock bottom in previous years.

Our captain, David Brightwell, had made just over 40 appearances in eight and a half seasons on the books at Maine Road, Manchester. He followed this with a slide down the Divisions and a smattering of loan spells before finding his level at beleaguered - Nigel Pearson managed - Carlisle. His moment of glory, like almost everything else he'd achieved - had been overshadowed. The one true moment of sublime footballing skill the day we beat Plymouth to stay alive in the League was not Jimmy Glass' short-range burying of the ball, it was the long range strike from Brightwell that equalised Plymouth's lead.

That - it would appear - is the story of Brightwell's career. One of a pair of famous brothers at Maine Road he was overshadowed by his brother Ian, used less and sold earlier. In the Carlisle defence, a year later than his fleeting second of Blues glory, Brightwell was outmanoeuvred by Shaun Teale, another old head on his way down. Teale had turned out regularly for Aston Villa and still had the touches, positional sense and clinical efficiency to show the level of skill he'd once commanded at will. In the Carlisle defence his skills had to blend with a level of panic and disorganisation that left everyone in danger of punting the ball into space.

At Roots Hall, Southend, Brightwell and Teale marshalled the back line as best they could. Their respective performances said everything about the state of our plight. Teale, by and large, cut out passes, foiled runs on goal and punted loose balls into the path of our breaking midfield. Brightwell sliced passes, looked ineffective and had me and the Blue I chatted to throughout the game tearing out what was left of our hair. During what passed for a promising move, our thwarted attack watched the ball as it was booted back to Brightwell. With a similar position and situation to that massive strike against Plymouth he sliced it clean into the crowd as we groaned in desperation behind the goal. I groaned again when I realised the refreshment room was closed and I couldn't console myself with a pie. Shaun Teale did his bit to hold the score to 0-0, but it was his slip that let Southend in for their first goal that killed off the game.

The following morning I was checking out the League tables, looking at the promotion and relegation issues that would have a bearing on my trips to away grounds and I found myself saddened at the drop zone positions of Welling and Sutton United in the Conference. I'd taken up research against the day I might need to navigate the lower reaches on a regular basis. Where exactly was Forest Green Rovers anyway?

At the very time my life was looking up, I had a hefty dose of reality to keep things in perspective. Reality is the promise of journeys to grounds where they'd laugh if you rang up and asked about the car park, reality is the crumbling concrete and threadbare crowds in some of football's less fashionable outposts, and reality is the knowledge that - with one promotion place on offer - getting out of the Conference is a scary prospect for former League teams.

I was thinking these thoughts with two games left. One against promotion chasing Darlington and one against mid-table Brighton, out of the serious competition but awesome in the current form league. Suddenly our run-in to the end didn't look so good.

I didn't go to Carlisle for the Darlington game. My prior commitments included covering the Fortean Times Unconvention as a journalist. Unlike the previous two years, I wasn't on stage at the annual festival of the strange, but I had my moments that weekend. The best of all being the hour I spent chatting to Paul Harrison, Loch Ness monster expert, author of a best selling Nessie encyclopedia and the man who wrote *The Lads in Blue*, the definitive history of Carlisle United to 1995. We didn't plan to talk for an hour, we simply couldn't shut up. Two 40 year olds, old enough to know better, sharing a love for their club and some honest feelings of panic.

350 miles to the North, Carlisle lost to Darlington.

On the day of the Macclesfield game I'd gone to a reunion of my old year at school. In the Bowling Club at Wigton I'd shared stories, and caught up on decades worth of news. There was plenty of both. One guy we'd thought dead turned up alive! Another guy I'd wanted to see badly was my old mate, Anton. He stood head and shoulders above the others in the 1974 picture of the rugby team which had featured in the local paper alongside the story about our re-union. Anton wanted to make it as a pro-footballer. He tried hard, really hard. At the re-union he wasn't as mobile as the guy I remembered and his name was on the waiting list for a cartilage operation. Let's face it, time had caught up with a few of us by this point. Some of the others, looked almost the same as I remembered them.

I spent most of the night talking to people I'd hardly known at school. Almost a quarter of a century down the road from the last time we'd all been together, we had more in common. Kids, mortgages, druggy pasts, more kids, criminal pasts, jobs we hadn't expected, jobs we had expected, more kids, a smattering of divorces, the odd boat, the odd second home and a few more kids we didn't talk about until we'd really sunk some pints. Having all taken our chances in life and found ourselves together in the Bowling Club that night we had something to share. Hell, I'd grown up with some good people and some real characters. It was privilege to meet them again. Some of them - in all honesty - I was getting to know for the first time. I bought pints for people I'd barely spoken to as a teenager, snapped enough pictures to remember the faces for the next reunion and stayed until they chucked us out. One hell of a night.

The following afternoon, I thought - in the way I always think on long journeys away from Cumbria - about life, the universe and leaving Cumbria. It seemed to me that I'd come a long way from the mouthy posh git who squandered most of his education. And yet, oddly, there were some parts of that person still there. One part of me, almost untouched by time, was the love of my team. I had a few conversations that reunion night that followed the same pattern. The one that started with the comment that I'd moved away.

'Just up for the weekend then?'
'Yeah.'
'Been up to owt?'
'I'm staying with my sister. I took in the match this afternoon.'
'Fuckin" hell, are you still going to watch them?!'

The truth was, I'd come further than anyone else in the Bowling Club that night. And I was one of the few still making a habit of watching my 'local' team. One or two others hadn't been since the second time at Wembley and most didn't go at all. So part of me had moved on a long way from the cross between Hair Bear and Art Garfunkel who'd taken his O-levels alongside these people. Another part of me had moved less than anyone at that reunion.

Two weeks later, at the Fortean Times Unconvention, Paul Harrison and I sat surrounded by a bunch of free-thinkers prepared to push the limits on having an open mind. Rabid conspiracy theorists, UFO abductees, raving sceptics fit to challenge any claim, and a bunch of curiosity seekers out to expand their mind with anything on offer over the weekend. Faced with the option of attending talks on such subjects, Paul and I talked about Paul Bannon, Michael Knighton, Alan Ross and Eric Welsh. For that hour none of the other things going on that weekend - including the people paying me to cover the whole thing for a magazine - mattered at all. So, I could kid myself that I'd come a long way. But I sat there and talked about Alan Ross in the way that I'd done for decades. And, I could still see his stringy frame, lightning fast dives and the gloveless hands with which he'd played the first time I ever watched my team.

As Carlisle struggled that season, Alan Ross and Chris Balderstone both died. I wondered, darkly, in the week after the Unconvention, if there was any kind of omen in that. The draw at home to Darlington left us needing a win away at Brighton to be sure of survival. Anything less would leave us at the mercy of the other results involving Shrewsbury and Chester.

In the company of the Unconvention, I'm sceptical about many paranormal claims. Faced with the dark uncertainties of another relegation battle, I'm not so sure. Incidentally, Carlisle have been labelled by some as a 'spooky' team. Especially so in the light of Michael Knighton's claims about a UFO sighting and contact with alien intelligence. The truly odd thing about this - from my perspective as a bloke surrounded by UFO books as I write these words, is that in his UFO claims Knighton is surprisingly ordinary. UFO events change lives and come in all manner of spectacular guises. Seeing an airborne light from the M62 and hearing a message in your head is pretty tame in this company.

If you want to talk about extraordinary events, consider that, on May the 6th, 2000, for the second time in as many seasons, Carlisle United kicked off on a Saturday afternoon knowing that a win, and only a win, could put their League survival in their own hands. I'd spent time the previous week reviewing the work I'd put into this book. Two uncomfortable things had struck me.

Firstly, given the new deadline I had to plan two possible endings for the story, one of which took into account the grim realities of trips to Rushden, Dover and Forest Green. Secondly, as I re-read the opening of the book, it occurred to me that in the time I'd been supporting Carlisle United they had almost turned into Workington! With a defensive formation that saw no shame in adopting a 5-4-1 line- up to hold on to 0-0 score-line and pump long balls into the path of Steve Halliday, Carlisle had never looked more like our skilfully challenged West Cumbrian cousins who had fought for League survival throughout the early and mid Seventies.

Jane and I had booked the 'romantic' weekend away in Brighton months before. I'd hoped the game would count for nothing. I took Thom, and found myself apologising to him. It was one of those 'If you could have seen what I saw at your age, son' kind of conversations. And as a rule I'm not that kind of Dad. Then again, the picture of Tot Winstanly in the programme didn't help.

They put donkeys in with race horses sometimes. The idea is that the simple and unconcerned demeanour of the donkey will keep the highly strung creature calm in the face of the hormone pumping terrors to come. In truth, I needed Thom with me that afternoon in Brighton. Choosing to be responsible for him was, in the circumstances, both a selfish and sensible act. The brain-blunting 'what if they lose' thoughts were running riot by one o' clock that afternoon and the gut churning nerves had taken hold before I even saw the Withdean Stadium. It was an athletic stadium with the kind of temporary / permanent makeover that suggests a band with pretensions to monumental gigs are about to arrive. It was hot, really bloody hot. The whole thing was challenging a seasoned football fan's grip on reality before the kick-off.

I knew we were crap. The more the pressure screw had turned since that lucky win over Chester, the worse we had crumbled. For the second time in as many seasons, a Carlisle team playing for their very survival squandered possession, struggled to find a shape let alone a tactical idea worthy of the name and tested the nerve of people who'd paid to see them because they still cared. I was so nervous I held on to the conversations with Thom. He was the one familiar, trustable thing in that unreal place. The concerned parent in me could think some strange thoughts. Having taken him to that desperate display I could only feel protective. I hoped at that moment that he'd never understand, at any point in his life, how much it helped me to have him there. In the puzzling logic of being a parent, that is an honest enough thought.

In other areas that afternoon, frankly, I'd lost the plot. The week before I'd suggested to some of the students at work that we'd pull it off on goal difference. I'd even told them Shrewsbury would win and we would lose, but not badly enough to take the dive. That afternoon, at Brighton, I couldn't think clearly enough to work out the possibilities. I'd convinced myself, the way a man dying of starvation convinces himself he can taste things, that we had a point lead over Chester. That morning, showing Thom the league table, I'd known well enough that we only led them on goal difference.

The whole game passed in a blur of moment to moment despair. Our passing was hopeless, the attacks for the most part desperate runs against a well marshalled defence. Peter Keen was easily the best player we could muster. He pulled off one spectacular save. I groaned, held my head in my hands, stood and held on to little more than hope. When we heard that Shrewsbury were winning, the enormity of the situation was crushing.

We were going down. We didn't look like scoring and we needed a miracle. We got it in the shape of the Peterborough goal that condemned Chester City to non-league football. A year before Peterborough had scored against Scarborough, a goal that allowed Jimmy Glass to shoot himself into history. Now they beat Chester City, and shot us into marginal survival. The margin, a better goal

277

difference. You could say our salvation on the strength of a Peterborough goal for the second season running confirmed our 'spooky' team status. In reality it was coincidence, nothing more. You could say my prediction of staying up on goal difference was a full-blown premonition. It wasn't. I knew (whilst my mind was still working with a slight degree of calm in the middle of the week) that hoping for a more secure survival was really pushing our luck.

In the end it came down to our minus 33 against their minus 35 goal difference. You could say that a 600 strong Blue Army celebrated the achievement. It was relief, nothing more. Hell, I felt for Chester City that day. They had seen certain relegation at the midway point that season and then staged a revival that put hope of survival in their hearts. They came close to scoring in their final match - something we didn't manage. Above all, those Chester fans went to their game able to believe that their team could do it. Something that was, frankly, in short supply in for us at Brighton.

I got one magic moment for the collection, but I had to wait until that night when the paralysing fear had loosened and the reality of survival had sunk in. With Thom and Jane in tow I was wandering past a bar on the seafront when I saw the baseball cap that read 'Knighton is a cunt.' There is a stall on the Palace Pier at Brighton that allows you to pay for the motto of your own choice on a baseball cap. The Blue sporting that corker had been in front of me during the game and we'd exchanged opinions on the horror show that went on in front of our eyes. That night, he and some like-minded people, had put their money where their mouths were. His mate, who'd had the nearest tranny to us in the crowd, had shelled out for a sister motto 'Knighton is a twat' Grim humour, the Cumbrian way, forever.

The spirit of Carlisle United. Sometimes down, never counted out.

Epilogue - Why Not Arsenal?

A FEW MONTHS before I was asked to write this book. Jane, rang her Mum. In the usual conversation about the things going on in the rest of the family she got some news about my brother-in-law, John. 'He's started supporting Leeds now,' said Jane's Mum.

John, born and raised in Sheffield, was now going along to Elland Road. On the one occasion he and I went to a game together, he was a season ticket holder at Bramhall Lane, and I got in with him to see a fast and furious 1-1 draw on Boxing Day.

Jane's reaction to the news was automatic. 'Neil wouldn't do that,' she said. And she was right.

To be fair to my brother-in-law, he now lives and works much nearer to Elland Road than Bramhall Lane. In the same circumstances I would certainly be tempted along for some quality Premiership action and the chance to marvel at the talents of Beckham, Giggs and the expensive foreign contingent of the Premiership. Hell, I've been in stranger places watching football. Some of these have delivered breathtaking surprises. I've never seen a more dramatic setting for football than Fort William's pitch in the shadow of angry cliffs. I've never seen greater passions in the face of mediocre levels of skill than I did one March day watching Omovia, the Communist titans of Cypriot football. I've been all over the place to enjoy this great game, but the only team I've watched on a regular basis is Carlisle. My guess is John still feels most for Sheffield United, but you'd have to ask him about that.

Sometimes, people change. They change their priorities and outlook and the things that were once unthinkable become commonplace. A few years before he died my Dad rang me up to talk about his new car. 'It suddenly struck me when I was driving along the road to Carlisle,' he said. 'I thought, bloody hell, I'm driving a Japanese car!'

The point being, of course, that the dads of the people who built that Japanese car may have spent a few hours in their younger days trying to kill my Dad. 45 years later, the same people, more or less, sell him a car. He loved that Honda. He loved it so much that when an oncoming out or control car hit him on the edge of Uldale Common he wanted another car, just like the written off wreck.

Like I said, things change. So what exactly is it about me and my team that won't let me change? Because, quite frankly, I'm not big on change. Ask my wife. We've had our moments.

JANE - You just won't change will you. You're so stubborn and predictable. What is it with you?

279

NEIL - What can I say, I'm proud to be a Cumbrian.

Living over 350 miles from the ground isn't exactly a practical way to go about supporting your team. But it hasn't stopped me. I haven't even considered stopping. Mike Graham couldn't stop me, Michael Knighton couldn't stop me and the GM Vauxhall Conference wouldn't have stopped me. Practically speaking, I'd be better off switching to Arsenal. Thom reckons he is an Arsenal supporter, he owns a complete Arsenal kit, I couldn't talk him into the same rig for Carlisle United. If he continues with this passion it is highly possible that within the next few years I'll be planning trips around Arsenal games. Fast moving Premiership affairs with dazzling first touch ball control and ambitious set pieces planned to precision to crack an efficient defence. I would love this, to take him to such a place whilst he is still young enough to see the magic, find heroes who will live in his mind for all time and develop a love for the game that will hold an affection throughout his life. Of course, I'd love it beyond words if he could find that in Carlisle United. But his life and decisions are already his own, as mine was at the start of this book. And, more than anything, I want him to have his life, his way. It isn't always easy to make this happen. I did talk him into my shirt and onto the cover of this book! I know what I want for him, but sometimes it is hard to be impartial.

We make our own decisions. We know the choices on offer and they speak to our needs. For me, Alan Ross, Brunton Park, and the passion in my team that could humble the best was the only start I needed. Years later, the legend of Jimmy Glass, away grounds and a passion that can just about hold it's own against Southend United and I'm still there, still dreaming and still totally involved whoever the opposition might me.

Practically speaking, it would have been more useful to call myself a football fan, sit on a couch with my Sky subscription safely in a drawer, and 'support' Arsenal. Thom would have thought it wonderful to see his Dad in an identical shirt to his own. I could have talked on equal terms with the students at college, especially Arsenal mad Darren Giddings. Darren and I have talked football for years. His joy at their 1998 double, frustration at Manchester United's domination of everything a year later, and his hopes for new signings. A 'new signing' for Arsenal at the moment would, in all probability, be worth more in transfer fees than the 11 players who will take the field in Carlisle United shirts at their next game. Tony Adam's weekly wage packet amounts to more than the transfer value of some of my present 'heroes.' He seems a reasonable bloke, Tony Adams. Just as well, if he turned really nasty he could stay in for a week and put the money saved to good use. He could buy any one of the Carlisle first team and parade him to cheers from the North Bank the following Saturday. What would those Arsenal fans do if Adams, a man who is to their team what Alan Ross is to mine, turned to the Carlisle player he had bought as a toy and said, 'Oi you, you scabby apology, come here and mop my brow.' Well, that's the gulf between my team and one of the best in the land at the moment.

Arsenal are an easy commute from my home and, piling onto stinking trains on a Saturday morning I see Arsenal, Chelsea and Spurs shirts. I'm on nodding acquaintance with some of them. This started when they looked and looked at my deckchair shirt with the 'Stobart' logo. They had to ask me which team I supported. Carlisle United aren't exactly massive in Maidstone.

It would be easier if I could stop, but that is unthinkable. Faced with growing family commitments my solutions to the problems of time management have involved weekends away in hotels, strategically close to lowly football grounds. Faced with increasing pressures on my working time, I have brilliantly suggested holding a business meeting with regard to a book deal on a train to Prittlewell. It's all credit to the publishing company in question that they agreed. I don't think I'd have got a many commissioning editors to that game. Then again, I couldn't have torn myself away from it.

My work mates know more about Cumbrian geography than they could ever usefully hope to know. Mike, who by his own admission represents middle England and still has family ties in Jamaica, came to see Carlisle United at Wembley. Steve - Southern born and bred - went there too. He also came to Barnet, Gillingham and . . . well, the people I've burdened with Carlisle United and the places I've taken them just go on and on. I'm on a mission here.

Carlisle United isn't my whole life. Had it been that bad, I'd never have left Cumbria. But, I've never stopped going and I've been there when they needed me. It is matters of life and death, and only matters of life and death, that have come between me and this team. Along the way there have been distractions. Sex, drugs, rock 'n' roll and then the really good stuff, falling in love, getting married and having a family. Druggies man, bloody cop outs the lot of them. They only get into that stuff because they can't take the real life changing, emotion churning, adrenalin surging addiction that comes with the really hard stuff in life, like having a family. Or supporting a football team.

We should get one thing straight here. Any mention of drugs or immorality on my part in this book is a lie. I made it up to prove I was as clever as Lawrence Dallaglio, the England rugby hero who confessed to making up tales of his drug abuse. But really, I never did any of that stuff. Why should I when I've got football?

The truth is that I was around drugs once, I had this mate who was on some student exchange from America and he rolled me a couple of serious joints. I was going to get a blast, really inhale, but he wouldn't pass the stuff round. I've never seen anyone inhale smoke like that. He sucked it right down and his eyes went wide, watered and rolled back into his head. Hell, the stuff that guy used to come out with when he was smoking the gear. He'd ramble on about anything. One day, he fixed me with this big stoned grin and he just went for it.

'You know,' he said, "It's all about choices in this life. You can be what you wanna be, don't let people put you down none, if they try to drag you down just stick with what you want. Go for the things that matter. Don't let nobody tell you different. It's your life, your choice.'

He made like he was going to hand me the joint, then he snatched it back. I guess he'd just 'chosen' to inhale the rest. Decent bloke for all that, his name was Billy Clinton, Big Bill from Little Rock. I never did find out what happened to him.

But he was right. It is about choices. All along the line, I've chosen to stay. It was my choice in the first place. It wasn't anything we did as a family. When every temptation offered itself in later years I still made space for my team. When nobody at college was interested, I still went back to the comfort and familiarity of my team and when I was at that age where being different to everyone else was simply an obligation I made a hero of the enigmatic Paul Bannon. I've survived for most of my adult life hundreds of miles away from Carlisle. I've endured a free fall down the pits of the League three times in little more than a decade. Shit pies, shit weather, shit grounds and shit results have not stopped me.

They will never stop me because I've grown with this team, they are part of my life. The pretentious angle would be to say they speak to me about my heritage and my history. This may be true, but at twenty past three on a Saturday afternoon at Leyton Orient, it is complete bollocks. I'm there because the next free kick or the next fingertip save will still get my adrenalin pumping. The reaction I have won't require me to think about what the whole spectacle says to me about my life. I'm there because I still love it.

Somewhere along the line this whole spectacle hooked me and at every turn of my life it has offered me something more. I've worked to fit it into my life but every new twist has been worth it and if I've come this far, you won't stop me now. This much is obviously true. As I write these words the most recent game I have seen was that complete cringing surrender against Brighton in a game that could have marked our exit from the professional ranks. How many sensible people would have stopped before it got that bad?

This is love. Not the greatest love affair of my life and not the thing I'd think about if I was drowning, but love for all that. This team are part of me and I will change that for nobody. I'll forgive, forget, try and understand and share every good thing they bring to me. Because being together and making it work is what matters most. When it works there is nothing much in this world to compare to it. I don't know what you'd call that. I think it's love.

This team are part of me, and we'll go out on the oldest cliche in the world. You might take the boy from Carlisle, but you'll never take Carlisle from the boy.

Mike Graham, Mike Graham, Mike Graham.............arghhhhhhhhhhhh, fuckin' hell,
never again!!!!!!!!!!!!!!!!!!!!!!!!

By Colin Johnson, the author of We Fear No Foe!

St George In My Heart

confessions of an England fan

"It heats the blood whether you're with him or running in the opposite direction."
Sport First, April 2nd, 2000

Title: St George In My Heart - Confessions Of An England Fan

When he's not on domestic duty with Millwall, Colin Johnson spends his time and money following his beloved England over land and sea. And not as part of the official travel club either. Here's his account of trips to Scotland, Italy, Ireland, Wales, Poland, Czechoslovakia, Sweden, Spain, Holland, and of course Wembley before it became populated by happy smiley people chanting "Football's coming home".

available from all good bookshops
or for £8.99 (post free) from:

STP Mail Order

P.O. Box 12, Lockerbie. DG11 3BW.
Please make cheques, postal orders payable to STP Mail Order.
www.terracebanter.com

We Fear No Foe

A Decade Of Following Millwall

by Colin Johnson

" . . . By now, it was already three o'clock and so we resigned ourselves to missing most of the first half. By the time we got to Fratton, Millwall were 2-0 down and it seemed pointless paying to watch the game. Unfortunately, we chose to pay up anyway, and entered the turnstiles just as Portsmouth scored their third.

I went for a piss and made a bit of a mess of myself. Another few minutes were spent cleaning myself up and by the time I left the toilets for the terraces, Millwall were 4-0 down. The away end was roaring with the chant "Rioch out!", while the Portsmouth fans next to the away end were constantly taking the piss out of us, and I soon found myself involved in an incoherent slanging match with one of their fans. A policewoman threatened to arrest me for being drunk and disorderly, and so this was the signal to leave the ground voluntarily, find a local pub, and drink more Stella.

About ten of us left at the same time and headed towards the Milton Arms. I knew this was a pub frequently used by the 6:57 crew, and the possibility of trouble soon sobered me up. I was surprised to see the pub was empty, but the reason why soon became obvious. The game was still in the first half. We carried on drinking, playing pool and keeping an eye on the scores on the TV. None of us was surprised to see Portsmouth win the game by six goals to one. The Portsmouth fans slowly started returning to the pub after the final whistle and they were not too happy so see a mob of Millwall drinking in their pub. Most of the Portsmouth fans left after seeing our little mob in there. I fully expected them to firm up in another pub and come back to have a go at us, but fortunately nothing materialised. We stayed in the pub for another hour or so and eventually left and found another pub, nearer to the station.

After a few more pints in that pub, we boarded a train and returned home. We had a few more pints in one of the pubs in the town before going for a chicken vindaloo at closing time. Whilst waiting for our dinner to arrive, my friend went to the toilet to be sick and I fell asleep at the table. After finally eating our dinner, we took a cab home and sat talking absolute bollocks to the driver.

The football had been terrible, although in truth I had not seen any of it as I was just too pissed all day to take any notice. For that reason, it had been a great day incorporating all things that are good in life; beer, football and curry . . . "

coming soon . . .

Invasion And Deportation
A Diary of Euro 2000
by Jamie Mash and Matthew Bazell

Darlo fan, Jamie Mash, and his Arsenal following cousin, Matthew Bazell, have been documenting the trials and tribulations of following England during their Euro 2000 campaign. This book is their diary of two England fans from the first qualifying game in Sweden right through to the Euro 2000 finals. It began as an extended beano to foreign lands to support England. It ends with all England fans being branded thugs and hundreds deported, whether guilty or not of footballhooliganism. Meanwhile, Turkish fans riot and it's dismissed as "celebrations".

Forget the tabloid headlines. Read the truth about being English at Euro 2000.

Expected publication date: September, 2000

available from all good bookshops
or for £9.99 (post free) from:
STP Mail Order
P.O. Box 12, Lockerbie. DG11 3BW.
Please make cheques, postal orders payable to STP Mail Order.
www.terracebanter.com